The RHP Companion
to
Youth Justice

Edited by
Tim Bateman
and
John Pitts

Russell House Publishing

First published in 2005 by:
Russell House Publishing Ltd.
4 St. George's House
Uplyme Road
Lyme Regis
Dorset DT7 3LS
Tel: 01297-443948
Fax: 01297-442722
e-mail: help@russellhouse.co.uk
www.russellhouse.co.uk

British Library Cataloguing-in-publication Data:

A catalogue record for this book is available from the British Library.

ISBN: 1-903855-49-7

Typeset by TW Typesetting, Plymouth, Devon
Printed by Antony Rowe, Chippenham

About Russell House Publishing

RHP is a group of social work, probation, education and youth and community work practitioners and academics working in collaboration with a professional publishing team.

Our aim is to work closely with the field to produce innovative and valuable materials to help managers, trainers, practitioners and students.

We are keen to receive feedback on publications and new ideas for future projects.

For details of our other publications please visit our website or ask us for a catalogue. Contact details are on this page.

Contents

Foreword

The reformed youth justice system in England and Wales established by the Crime and Disorder Act 1998 is coming of age. The infrastructure of the Youth Justice Board at the centre and the devolved, local authority-based, multi-disciplinary Youth Offending Teams (YOTs) has bedded in. New programmes and sentencing options for young offenders have been developed and are beginning to be evaluated. Inspection reports, government agency reviews and critical monographs, are beginning to appear.

Meanwhile the arrangements for youth justice in Scotland and Northern Ireland are very different and the landscape within which the new framework in England and Wales operates is shortly to change fundamentally, yet again. As this text goes to press the Childrens' Bill is completing its passage through Parliament, local Childrens' Trusts are about to be established and the Probation and Prison Services are to have aspects of their organisation and functions drawn more closely together under what is as yet the embryonic framework of a new National Offender Management Service. The Welsh Assembly is beginning to find its feet which may mean that youth justice in Wales, with its different constitutional relationships with contiguous services of housing, drugs, employment advice, etc., may begin to take a subtly different shape and direction to that in England.

All of which makes this collection of essays timely. According to different commentators, the reformed youth justice system in England and Wales is either New Labour's greatest 'modernising government' success story or one of its most dismal policy failures. These contrasting views are represented and reflected in the essays that follow. The structure – the purchaser/provider split, the relatively light touch central policy, commissioning and monitoring approach and the devolved delivery system – works in the sense that the processual cogs positively mesh. But the number of children in custody remains stubbornly high and many children who should almost certainly not be criminalised continue to be so. Minority ethnic young people are still greatly over-represented within the punitive depths of the system. The multi-disciplinary YOTs work well together, but their capacity to access for their charges the mainstream services that have typically failed them – in particular education, housing and health – continues to be substantially less than adequate. Much hope is invested in the Childrens' Trusts, but it remains to be seen whether those formations will fundamentally improve the life chances of some of our most damaged and troublesome children who so often become persistent young offenders with long adult criminal careers ahead of them.

We have not yet learned to treat our children with the respect they deserve. We continue, depressingly, to demonise some of them. The discourse of control rather than care too often predominates in discussions about young people and their occasionally disturbing behaviour. This text should assist the education of a more professional, practitioner workforce and promote a more balanced public debate about youth justice. If it does so it will have served a noble purpose.

Rod Morgan, Chairman, Youth Justice Board, November 2004

About the Authors

The Editors

Tim Bateman has been a senior policy development officer for Nacro's youth crime section since 1998, having previously been employed as a youth justice social worker for more than 13 years. He has also worked as a lecturer in sociology and general studies and a residential social worker. Tim has written widely on youth justice practice and has a particular interest in the use of custody for children and how it can be reduced. His recent publications include *Patterns of Sentencing* (2002) for the Youth Justice Board and a series of reports for Nacro's committee on children and crime on the theme of *Reducing Child Imprisonment* (Nacro, 2003a and 2003e). Tim sits on the editorial board of *Youth Justice*, the management committee of *Safer Society* and is secretary of the London Association for Youth Justice.

John Pitts is Vauxhall professor of socio-legal studies at the University of Luton. He has worked as a 'special needs' teacher, a street and club-based youth worker, a youth justice development officer, a residential social worker and a group worker in a young offender institution. He has been a consultant to youth justice and legal professionals and the police in the UK, mainland Europe, the Caribbean, the Russian Federation and the People's Republic of China. His publications include *The Politics of Juvenile Crime* (1988), *Developing Services for Young People in Crisis* (1991), *Preventing School Bullying* (1995), *Working With Young Offenders* (1990 and 1999), *Planning Safer Communities* (1998), *Positive Residential Practice: Learning the Lessons of the 1990s* (2001) and *The New Politics of Youth Crime: Discipline or Solidarity* (2003c). He is a member of the editorial and advisory boards of *Youth Justice*, *The Community Safety Journal*, *Social Work in Europe* and the UNESCO journal *Juvenile Justice Worldwide*. He is also Associate Editor of *Youth & Policy*.

The Contributors

Rob Allen is director of Rethinking Crime and Punishment, an initiative set up by the Esmée Fairbairn Foundation to change public attitudes to prison and alternatives. Rob was previously director of research and development at the crime reduction charity Nacro. He has been a member of the Youth Justice Board for England and Wales since 1998 and has undertaken a number of consultancy assignments overseas. He is the author of *Children and Crime: Taking Responsibility* (1996) and many articles on youth crime and criminal justice.

Jill Annison is a senior lecturer at the University of Plymouth. She worked as a probation officer and specialist social worker in the 1970s and 1980s. After obtaining her undergraduate degree with the Open University she undertook postgraduate research, being awarded a PhD in 1998 for her thesis on gender and organisational change in the probation service. Since 1998 she has worked as Academic Programme Co-ordinator for the Community Justice (Probation Studies) programme covering the SW of England. Her research interests centre on developments in probation policy and practice, gender and crime and criminal justice agencies, and risk in relation to crime and the criminal justice system.

Sue Bandalli is a lecturer at the Law School, University of Birmingham, solicitor and magistrate. Sue is primarily interested in criminal and family law and teaches courses on Women and the Criminal Justice System, Juvenile Justice and Children in Family Law. She has been involved with European organisations concerned with the rights of the child. Recent publications include *Children, Responsibility and the New Youth Justice* (2000) in B. Goldson (ed.) *The New Youth Justice* and *Droits de l'enfant et responsabilité pénale: vers une citoyenneté Européenne? En Angleterre at au Pays de Galles* (2003) in DERPAD, *Protection de L'Enfance et Diversités Européennes.*

Susan Batchelor is currently researching her PhD in the Department of Sociology, Anthropology and Applied Social Sciences at Glasgow University. Funded by the ESRC, her research topic is violent young women in prison in Scotland. As a researcher, she has worked on a range of projects relating to young people and crime, including girls' views and experiences of violence and violent behaviour, young women and recreational drug use, Safeguarders in the Children's Hearing System and Fast-Track Hearings Pilots. Susan has also been a befriender for Barnados and is a Children's Panel Member for Glasgow East.

Charlie Beaumont qualified as a probation officer in 1978 and worked in Kent. In 1988 he was seconded to the newly established multi-agency juvenile justice teams and in 1990 joined Kent Social Services with a policy lead for both juvenile (subsequently youth) justice and leaving care services. In 1994 he returned to practice before joining the Youth Justice Board as a policy adviser in 1999 where his portfolio included management information and information sharing in addition to supporting the development of Youth Offending Teams. In 2002, he returned to Kent where his responsibilities included ISSPs, referral orders and service development. At the end of 2003, he rejoined the Youth Justice Board.

Ros Burnett (DPhil) is a Research Fellow at the Centre for Criminological Research, University of Oxford, and Deputy Head of its Probation Studies Unit. Much of her research has centred on desistance from crime and the role of criminal justice agencies in assisting desistance. She is currently investigating (with Shadd Maruna, Cambridge) a 'strength-based' approach to prisoner reintegration. She has published in the areas of interpersonal relationships, probation practice, recidivism and desistance, and has recently co-authored (with Catherine Appleton) *Joined-up Youth Justice: Tackling Youth Crime in Partnership* (2004b).

Spike Cadman is a senior policy development officer with Nacro's youth crime section. Since starting in residential work with children some 30 years ago, he has run a family support team and moved into youth justice work during the late 1980s. After some 14 years as a youth justice practitioner, Spike joined Nacro in 2001. Spike is an experienced trainer in social work and youth justice law and practice and he has contributed a range of articles to periodicals on youth justice matters. He has recently been involved in Nacro's work for the Department for Education and Skills to assist local authorities to reduce offending by 'looked after' children who offend.

Rob Canton worked for the probation service for over 20 years and is now principal lecturer at De Montfort University, Leicester, where he is programme leader of the BA in Community and Criminal Justice/Diploma in Probation Studies Programme. His interest in compliance and enforcement originates from attempts to practise rigorously and fairly as a probation officer. He has written on this subject with Tina Eadie in *Youth Justice* and, together with Hazel Kemshall and other colleagues, undertook research in 2002 for the National Probation Directorate on the related issue of drop-out from accredited programmes.

Tim Chapman's practical experience of group work with young people who offend is based upon over 25 years in the Probation Service in Northern Ireland. For the past five years he has worked as an independent youth justice consultant and trainer in Ireland, Scotland and England. He has published *Time to Grow* (Russell House, 2000) which links research, theory and practice in working with young people who offend. Several youth justice agencies have adopted this model of practice.

John Coleman is the Director of the Trust for the Study of Adolescence. He is a clinical psychologist, who has specialised in work with children and young people. For 14 years he was a senior lecturer in the University of London. He has written widely about adolescence, his best known book being *The Nature of Adolescence* (1999), now in its third edition, co-authored with Leo Hendry and published by Routledge. From 1984-2000 he was editor of the *Journal of Adolescence*. He has served on a variety of government committees, and has been an advisor to the Youth Justice Board.

Sarah Curtis began her career on *The Times Educational Supplement* and *The Times*. When editor of *Adoption & Fostering*, the BAAF journal for professionals in child care, she became a juvenile court magistrate and served in juvenile, youth and family courts in inner London from 1978 to 2001. She has also been a member of the Lord Chancellor's Committee for the appointment of justices of the peace in London. Her two books on youth offending, *Youth Offending: Prevention through Intermediate Treatment* (1989) and *Children Who Break the Law* (1999) highlight the development of community programmes for young offenders and those at risk. She reviews books regularly for *The Times Literary Supplement.*

Tina Eadie is a senior lecturer in Community and Criminal Justice at De Montfort University, Leicester working primarily with students undertaking their BA (Hons) degree as part of the Diploma in Probation Studies. Drawing on a background of practice and management experience in the Probation Service, she has been involved in the training of probation officers since 1991. Her interest in issues of enforcement began when the first National Standards for Community Service were introduced while she was working as a Community Service Officer in the mid-1980s. She has published on the subject in *Criminal Law Review* and *Youth Justice*.

Rod Earle is a lecturer in criminology at Surrey University. He has worked as a printer and as a social worker, spending many happy years in a south London youth justice service. Since 1999 he has worked in criminal justice research and helped to conduct the national evaluation of referral orders. Rod has held research positions at The Public Policy Research Unit, Goldsmiths College, and the Mannheim Centre for Criminology and Criminal Justice at the London School of Economics. His published work includes articles in *Youth Justice, Criminal Justice Matters* and *Anarchist Studies*.

Tamara Flanagan is the Director of European and Statutory Affairs at CSV – a national voluntary organisation working in the fields of volunteer action and training. Prior to that she was Assistant Director at The Rainer Foundation. After entering teaching in 1975 she worked in the Free School movement and with young people who offend for 18 years before specialising in European funding. She is chair of the Third Sector European Network, the voice of the voluntary sector in respect of Objective 3 funds in the UK. She has also written extensively on work with the disadvantaged, equal opportunities and the role of social action in combating exclusion and is author of *Talking Changes (1995) –A Handbook for Young People and Teachers on Distress in Adolescence*.

Ena Fry is development worker with the Fostering Network, taking the lead on issues relating to remand fostering. This work has included promoting the use of remand foster care through consultancy, training and providing information. She co-wrote the Nacro publication *Remand is More Than an Address: A Guide for Remand Foster Carers* (2001). Currently, Ena is undertaking a feasibility study on behalf of the Home Office and Youth Justice Board on the development of intensive fostering for young people who offend. Previously she worked for 20 years as a local authority child care practitioner.

Loraine Gelsthorpe is senior lecturer and Director of the M.Phil. Programme at the Institute of Criminology, and a Fellow of Pembroke College, University of Cambridge. She has broad ranging research interests in criminal justice policy and community penalties, and has published extensively in the areas of youth justice and gender. Recent publications include: 'Recent changes in Youth Justice Policy in England and Wales' (2002) in I. Weijers and A. Duff (Eds.) *Punishing Juveniles: Principle and Critique*, and 'Restorative Justice: The Last Vestiges of Welfare?' (2002), with Allison Morris, in J. Muncie, G. Hughes and E. McLaughlin (Eds.) *Youth Justice: Critical Readings*.

Peter Gill has worked for Nacro for eight years and is currently a divisional manager providing a senior management function for a range of projects including ISSPs and YIPs. Peter is currently chair of the National Youth Justice and Family Group Conference Forum. Relevant publications include: good practice guides on *Remand Fostering* (2001) and *Quality Protects; Reducing the Rate of Offending by Looked After Children* (2002); and various youth crime section briefing papers. Before joining Nacro, Peter worked as a practitioner for 12 years in a number of posts including a probation officer and social worker in youth justice and children and families teams. Peter has a BA Applied Social Studies and CQSW.

Barry Goldson is a senior lecturer at the Department of Sociology, Social Policy and Social Work Studies, the University of Liverpool. His teaching and research interests include the sociology of childhood and youth, state policy and welfare settlements, and youth crime and youth justice. He has researched and published widely in each of these areas and he is the editor of *Youth Justice*, the leading learned journal in the field in the UK. His two most recent books are *Vulnerable Inside: Children in Secure and Penal Settings* (2002d) and *Children, Crime and the State* (2002a).

Dr Patricia Gray is a principal lecturer in Criminal Justice Studies at the University of Plymouth. Her research and publications are mainly in the areas of youth justice, the politics of risk and penality, restorative justice and social exclusion, and gender and criminal justice issues. She has recently completed research on behalf of the Youth Justice Board as part of the national evaluation of restorative justice, mentoring and bail support programmes for young people who offend.

Dr Ann Hagell is research development adviser at the Nuffield Foundation charitable trust. Previously she was Co-director at the Policy Research Bureau, which she co-founded in 1998. She is a chartered psychologist specialising in social policy research on high-risk young people, editor of the *Journal of Adolescence* and author/co-author of approximately 40 articles, reports and books on at-risk young people. She has worked in the US at the University of North Carolina, and is a visiting Research Fellow at the University of East London. She is a trustee of the Prison Reform Trust, a professional adviser to the Research in Practice Management Board, and member of the Executive Advisory Board for Elsevier's *Encyclopedia of Adolescence*. She is currently writing a book on children in custody.

Denis W. Jones was a youth justice practitioner from 1975 to 1998, and is now a training and development consultant with East Sussex Social Services Department. He is an Honorary Visiting Research Fellow at the University of Sussex, and currently doing a PhD on youth justice history at the London School of Economics. He is the author of two influential recent critiques of the Crime and Disorder Act 1998 in the *British Journal of Criminology* (2001b) and *Youth Justice* (2002), and is on the editorial board and book review editor of *Youth Justice*.

Anita Kalunta-Crumpton is a lecturer in Criminology at the School of Business, Social Sciences and Computing, University of Surrey, Roehampton. She has published widely in the field of race and criminal justice. She is the author of *Race and Drug Trials* (1999) and co-editor of *Pan-African Issues in Crime and Justice* (2004, forthcoming).

Sarah Lindfield is the project leader of Parenting and Youth Justice at the Trust for the Study of Adolescence, with responsibility for managing two projects: development support and parenting, and involving young people in parenting programmes. Sarah's background is in youth work, social work and youth justice. She is a trained social worker and family mediator and has a special interest in positive conflict resolution and restorative justice. Sarah's MPhil thesis (Sheffield University) was based on research into Community Justice Forums in Canada.

Alan Marlow is Visiting Professor in Criminology, University of Luton. Alan joined the University in 1994 upon retirement from Bedfordshire Police, where he held the rank of Chief Superintendent and commanded the Luton Division. His publications include the books *Planning Safer Communities* (with John Pitts) Russell House 1998, *Young People, Drugs and Community Safety* with Geoffrey Pearson, Russell House 1999 and *After Macpherson: Policing after the Stephen Lawrence Inquiry*, with Barry Loveday (2000). He has also conducted research for police service clients and the Home Office. He edits *The Community Safety Journal* published by Pavilion.

Guy Masters is currently Youth Crime Prevention Co-ordinator with Wandsworth Youth Offending Team, having been Referral Order Co-ordinator at the YOT for 18 months. Prior to that he was Project Development Officer for Essex Family Group Conferencing Service. He has been involved in the restorative justice field since 1993 as a practitioner, researcher and consultant and has written widely on practice. His key area of interest is the mainstreaming of effective restorative practice.

Fergus McNeill has been lecturer in Social Work at the University of Glasgow since 1998. Before assuming this post, he worked as a criminal justice social worker in the East End of Glasgow for five years. His previous research and publications have addressed a variety of issues in probation and youth justice. His current projects include an exploration of front line probation ideologies, an ESRC funded study of social enquiry and sentencing in the Scottish Sheriff Courts and the evaluation of the Pathfinder Provider Initiative in Scotland for the Scottish Executive.

Geoff Monaghan has been a senior policy development officer with Nacro's Youth Crime Section since 1998. Prior to that he worked as social worker for a local authority for 23 years, qualifying in 1983, at first in residential child care and subsequently as a specialist in youth justice. Geoff is also chair of the National Association for Youth Justice. He has maintained a strong commitment to children's human rights and has written widely in the area of youth justice and is co author of *Children in Trouble: Time for Change* (2003).

Carole Pickburn is a Principal Co-ordinator for the Trust for the Study of Adolescence (TSA) – Parenting and Youth Justice. She has been a social work practitioner with children, young people and their families for over 20 years in a variety of settings. Carole was the Development Officer for the Kirklees Parenting Adolescents Project, developing support strategies for parents in the youth justice context. She is the author of the *ESCAPE* and *Parallel Lines* (2003) parent and young people's programme published by TSA.

David Porteous is a senior lecturer in criminology at Middlesex University. He has researched and written about mentoring, exclusion from school, drugs prevention and violence in schools and is co-editor, with Brigitte Volonde, of *Working with Young People in Europe* (2002), also published by Russell House.

Sandy Pragnell's involvement in the Juvenile Criminal Justice System spans 25 years. During that time she has worked within residential, custodial and community settings. She is a qualified teacher and youth worker and has a Masters Degree in Public Sector Management. Since 1984 she has been manager of multi-disciplinary teams working with young people and adults in the criminal justice system. Currently she manages the Northamptonshire Youth Offending Service. Prior to this she was manager of the Northampton Juvenile Liaison Bureau and Diversion Unit.

Chris Stanley has been a magistrate for over 30 years, serving in both youth (formerly juvenile) and adult jurisdictions. He currently heads Nacro's Youth Crime Section having worked for the organisation for 14 years. Before that he managed a number of alternative to custody schemes. Recent projects include managing Nacro's staff responsible for producing the Youth Justice Board's *Factors Associated with Differential Rates of Custodial Sentencing* and the subsequent report *Patterns of Sentencing* (2002b). He is a former Chair of Children Law UK and Vice Chair of the Family Courts Consortium. He was a member of the Audit Commission's Youth Justice Study Advisory Group which produced *Youth Justice 2004, A Review of the Reformed Youth Justice System*.

Sue Thomas has worked as a senior policy development officer with Nacro's youth crime section since 1995. In this capacity she provides training and consultancy services to YOTs. She has produced a range of published work including briefing papers, reports and articles in journals. For the last five years, Sue has specialised in remand management issues. During this time she acted as the national supporter and evaluator to Youth Justice Board funded bail supervision and support schemes. She co-produced the Board's effective practice guidance and the source document for remand management. She is also author of the *Reader (Remand Management)* for the professional certificate in effective practice and the INSET training materials for this area.

Roy Tomlinson qualified as a social worker in 1977 working at a practice level primarily with children and young people until 1984. Since moving on from this practice base, subsequent jobs have all involved policy and service development in child care work with particular focus on youth justice. Roy's current role is as Policy Officer for Devon

County Council with county lead for community safety. He has served on the ADSS/LGA Youth Crime Group since 1996 and on the National Committee of the National Association for Youth Justice for four years.

Ann Wheal is a Senior Research Fellow in the Social Work Division at the University of Southampton. Ann has a broad experience of obtaining the views of young people, carers, families and professionals regarding services within the caring and youth offending fields including meeting young people who offend in Wiltshire to find out why they offended and what could be done to prevent them re-offending. Other work includes carrying out a feasibility study for four London boroughs into the introduction of remand fostering and research into the sexual health needs of young people leaving care and those who offend on the Isle of Wight. Ann was also a volunteer independent visitor in a secure unit for several years.

Dick Whitfield is an Independent Member of the Parole Board for England and Wales. Much of his working life was spent in the Probation Service, finishing as Chief Probation Officer for Kent. He has a long standing interest in electronic monitoring and co-organised three European Workshops for CEP, between 1998 and 2003, with the aim of developing best practice. He is the author of *Tackling the Tag* and *The Magic Bracelet* (both Waterside Press, 2001) as well as works on other aspects of criminal justice.

Bill Whyte is a senior lecturer in social work at the University of Edinburgh. He is Director of the Criminal Justice Social Work Development Centre for Scotland at the Universities of Edinburgh and Stirling, funded by the Scottish government to promote research based practice in criminal and youth justice social work. Prior to his university appointment, he was a social worker and a social work manager in the Lothians. His teaching, research and publications have focused on youth justice in Scotland, the children's hearing system, and social work in the criminal justice system.

Brian Williams is Professor of Community Justice and Victimology in the Community and Criminal Justice Division at De Montfort University. His main teaching interests are in the values and ethics of probation work and in working with victims of crime. His research in recent years has concentrated upon professional services for victims of crime, restorative justice, staff training and professional ethics. His most recent book was an edited collection on *Reparation and Victim-Focused Social Work* (Jessica Kingsley, 2002) and he is working on another about the role of victims in social policy in the UK and elsewhere. He is co-editor (with Paul Senior) of the *British Journal of Community Justice*.

Dr Howard Williamson works in the School of Social Sciences, Cardiff University. He is also a practising youth worker, Vice-Chair of the Wales Youth Agency and a member of the Youth Justice Board. He has been closely involved in research, policy and practice on 'youth issues' for the past 30 years, in Wales, the United Kingdom and within the European Union and the Council of Europe. His most recent research has been a life course follow-up study of 30 men he first studied when they were young offenders during the 1970s (to be published as *The Milltown Boys Revisited*, Berg, 2004).

Introduction

Tim Bateman and John Pitts

Youth justice is not what it was and this is a cause for both celebration and concern. Celebration, because the Crime and Disorder Act 1998 (CDA) introduced many of the reforms for which progressives in youth justice had been campaigning for many years. These were the introduction of fully funded multi-agency groupings dedicated to work with young people who offend, the youth offending teams (YOTs); and the creation of a centralised, governmental body, the Youth Justice Board for England and Wales, charged with the realisation of an accountable, youth justice system and with the power and reach to deal with the problem of justice by geography, address the inequitable distribution of resources, and to effect a thoroughgoing reform of custodial institutions for children and young people.

The concern stems from the ambiguities and contradictions in New Labour's approach to youth justice. When the new administration came to power in 1997, it had a clear agenda to reform the arrangements for dealing with children and young people in trouble. Jack Straw, then Home Secretary, declared in the introduction to *No More Excuses*, the White Paper which led in short order to the CDA, that the government's intention was to *'draw a line under the past'* (Home Office, 1997b). The message was not hard to discern: central to the criticism of the existing system was the contention that those working within it had, in their practice, excused the criminal behaviour of young people who came to the attention of the police and the courts. Henceforth these young people would be made to face up to the consequences of their actions for themselves, their victims and the communities in which they lived.

One of the five pledges on which New Labour based its election campaign was to halve the time it took to process 'persistent young offenders'. The pledge symbolised the importance the incoming administration attached to the issue of youth crime and of its determination to respond robustly to the sharp criticisms levelled at the youth justice system in the previous year by the Audit Commission in *Misspent Youth* (Audit Commission, 1996). The message, implicit in this pledge was that 'persistent young offenders' would be punished more rapidly, more harshly and, where necessary, removed from the community for much longer. In many instances, that is precisely what has happened (Nacro, 2003a).

The tension, between the obviously sensible objective of speeding up the justice process, for example, and the government's apparent determination to appease punitive public attitudes, characterises the youth justice reforms as a whole. Multi-agency YOTs, able to draw on a broad range of resources, are no doubt better equipped to deal with youngsters in trouble than the social services youth justice teams which they replaced. But the creation of these new bodies went hand in hand with an unreflective repudiation of the history of 'old youth justice' (Pitts, 2003a) which had, on the basis of evidence of the deleterious effects of early induction into the criminal justice system, striven to divert many children into non-stigmatising mainstream youth provision. Instead, YOTs were to respond vigorously to the earliest indication of 'anti-social' behaviour in order to 'nip offending in the bud'. The effect has been to spread the net of the youth justice system far wider; involving a clamp down on low-level 'anti-social behaviour' which is not in itself criminal and drawing in children, some below the age of criminal responsibility, whose offending would not previously have warranted a criminal justice response (Pitts, 2003a). YOTs do not simply provide a high quality service to 'adjudicated offenders'; they are pre-emptive, weapons in the armoury of the 'fight against crime'. As a result, although resources ploughed into youth justice have expanded enormously since 1998, the amount of face-to-face contact between youth justice workers and young people on higher tariff community penalties has barely changed (Audit Commission, 2004).

It is of course early days, and the pace of change can hardly be said to have slackened. The CDA was followed in short order by the Youth Justice and Criminal Evidence Act 1999, the Criminal Justice and Court Services Act 2000, the Criminal Justice and Police Act 2001, the Anti-Social Behaviour Act 2003, and a big new Criminal Justice Act followed in the same year. Moreover, the government has recently announced its intention to introduce yet more youth justice legislation in the near future (Home Office, 2003i).

Nonetheless, the six years which have elapsed since the establishment of the Youth Justice Board, with responsibility to provide a national oversight of the reformed system, allow for a provisional assessment of how the tensions inherent in the reforms have worked themselves out in practice. *The RHP Companion to Youth Justice* provides an opportunity for such reflection. It offers a comprehensive, and accessible, overview of the youth justice system in its current configuration with some account of how each aspect of that system is working. The contributors are deliberately drawn from a wide range of backgrounds, and include senior practitioners and practice managers, policy makers, penal reformers, members of the Youth Justice Board and well known academics and researchers. This diversity allows the reforms to be viewed from a variety of perspectives and at a number of different levels. It is hoped that in so doing, it will provide a valuable resource for an equally broad readership and form a useful starting point for further debate about the best way to realise a youth justice system which deals effectively and humanely with children and young people who offend.

Tim Bateman and John Pitts, South London, May 2004

Part 1   Youth Crime and the Youth Justice Apparatus

1 The Recent History of Youth Justice in England and Wales

John Pitts

Key points

1. The recent history of youth justice is one of discontinuity, in which policy has been developed largely on the basis of current political, social and intellectual orthodoxies rather than scientific evidence.

2. From the 1930s to the 1960s, a child-centred approach, sometimes known as 'welfarism', which focused upon the needs rather than the deeds of young people who offended, gradually supplanted earlier retributive responses.

3. However, the 'welfarist' policies of the 1960s were never fully implemented and an expanded, 'hybrid', system emerged in the 1970s which drew far larger numbers of children and young people into the purview of the criminal justice system while apparently doing little to curb their offending.

4. The backlash against this carceral bonanza took the form of a 'back to justice movement' and a 'nothing works' orthodoxy which led to calls for minimal intervention in young people's lives and spawned the 'delinquency management' policies of the Conservatives in the 1980s. These policies were concerned primarily with the cost-effectiveness of the youth justice system. However, by 1991, the tide had turned and a governmental strategy of 'penal populism' led to a rapid rises in the use of security and custody for juveniles.

5. The recent reform of the youth justice system is rooted in a repudiation of both welfarism and delinquency management, seeking to draw more, and younger children, into the criminal justice system in order to confront their offending and deter them from a deeper involvement in crime. It is not clear however that this is the effect it is having.

Justice for juveniles

In 1908, juvenile courts were established in England and Wales to deal with both children in need and children in trouble. A separate juvenile court was deemed necessary because the government of the day had been persuaded by penal reformers and scientific experts that, by dint of their relative immaturity, children in trouble with the law were less able to control their impulses, less able to understand the seriousness of their offences and less able to foresee the consequences of their actions. However, while the juvenile court recognised that children and young people might be less culpable than adults, it was still, first and foremost, a criminal court which, like the adult criminal courts, was concerned with the misdeeds of the children and young people who appeared before it and the need to impose an appropriate penalty upon them.

A child-centred justice

As the century progressed, however, the emphasis upon justice was tempered by an increased emphasis upon the juvenile. For the architects of the Children and Young Persons Act 1933, it was not just that a child's immaturity mitigated the seriousness of their offending, but that the offences committed by the child were of far less significance than the underlying social and emotional disorders of which the offences were a symptom. The 1933 Act was imbued with ideas, derived from Kleinian child development theory, which pointed to the primacy of the mother-child relationship in the development of a healthy, pro-social, ego. This type of thinking is epitomised in the work of John Bowlby (1953) who argued that early separation of the child from its mother produced 'affectionless characters', a disorder which was, he believed, at the root of juvenile crime. Thus the Act attempted to usher in a 'child-centred justice', establishing the principle that young people who offended should be dealt with in ways which promoted their 'welfare' and that any necessary 'treatment' for psychological disorders should be available to them (see Chapter 8).

Penal modernism

Arguably, what David Garland (1985) has called 'penal modernism' found its fullest expression in the UK in the 'child-centred' youth justice policies that emerged in the 1930s. Tim Newburn (1995) points to a 'sea-change' in penal affairs in the UK in the 1930s in which prison populations were substantially reduced and new forms of child-centred youth justice were constructed on the foundations laid by the reforms of 1908. Although responsibility for the youth justice system in England and Wales had previously been shared between the Home Office and the Ministry of Health, between 1933 and 1969, the Ministry of Health came to play a major role in the development of policy.

'Welfare' versus 'justice'

Perhaps inevitably, this changed emphasis upon the 'needs' rather than the 'deeds' of young people who offended, created a widening rift between traditional Conservative politicians, senior police officers, magistrates and judges, who wished to retain an element of retribution in the youth justice system, and those like academic social scientists and health and welfare professionals, who believed that, because the 'welfare' of young offenders should be the paramount consideration, they should wherever possible be dealt with by experts in the care and protection of children and young people. This argument trundled on into the post-war period but, in the 1960s, the claims of 'welfarism' were given greater impetus by research which showed that the children who passed through the juvenile courts were overwhelmingly, poor, badly educated and, in many cases, victims of violence or abuse (Titmus, 1963). With the election, in 1964, of a Labour government whose members included, and whose policies were crafted by, leading UK social scientists, it appeared that the 'welfarist' argument would prevail (Pitts, 1988).

Welfarism ascendent

The 1964 White Paper, *The Child the Family and the Young Offender*, proceeded from very similar assumptions to those which had informed the 1933 Act, but placed far greater emphasis upon the idea that poverty and social inequality, because they undermined healthy child development, could propel a child into a life of crime. It also took the idea of a 'child-centred justice' to its logical conclusion by proposing the replacement of the juvenile court with a family council, composed in part of health and welfare professionals. The White Paper drew heavily upon *Crime a Challenge to Us All*, a Fabian Society pamphlet produced by Lord Longford (1964), in which he observed that:

> No understanding parent can contemplate without repugnance the branding of a child in early adolescence as a criminal, whatever offence he may have committed. If it is a trivial case, such a procedure is indefensible, if a more serious charge is involved this is, in itself, evidence of the child's need for skilled help and guidance. The parent who can get such help for his child on his own initiative can almost invariably keep the child from court. It is only the children of those not so fortunate who appear in the criminal statistics.

The Child the Family and the Young Offender proposed a radical shift of power, from the police, magistrates, lawyers and judges to psychologists, psychiatrists and social workers. Once again, the Conservative opposition, the police, magistrates, judges and the probation service vociferously opposed these proposals. As a result, a significantly modified reform package, which retained the juvenile court but restricted the magistrate's power to sentence, was presented to parliament in the *Children and Young Person Act* 1969. A key innovation introduced by the Act was Intermediate Treatment (IT), the forbear of the present youth offending team (YOT). IT allowed local authority social services departments to make special provision for children and young people in trouble. This took many forms, including evening clubs, literacy classes, outdoor activities and voluntary work. Although the Act allowed for the insertion, by a juvenile court, of an IT requirement in a supervision order, most IT was undertaken informally with children and young people thought to be 'at risk' in some way. The radical edge of the initiative lay in the stated intention of government to phase out the detention centre and the attendance centre as IT proved its worth.

The 1969 Act marked the high water mark of the 36-year struggle to construct a child-centred youth justice system, in which a concern for the 'welfare' of the child, their needs rather than their deeds, was paramount. The Act was a testimony to the powerful influence exerted by the social work profession and the social sciences upon Labour Party policy in the 1960s. Ten years on from the 1969 Act, however, social work and the social sciences were in retreat before a hostile government and a prime minister who claimed not to believe in a thing called 'society'.

A hybrid system

1970 saw the election of a Conservative government which, although unwilling to limit the powers of juvenile court magistrates, implemented many of the new provisions introduced by the 1969 Act. Thus, care orders, supervision orders and IT were introduced alongside the fines, discharges, probation orders, attendance centres, detention centres and Borstals of the existing system. This expanded, hybrid, sentencing framework gave juvenile court magistrates and social workers more options than ever before for dealing with young people who broke the law. By 1977, an estimated 12,000 children and young people were involved in IT, of which only about 1,500 were adjudicated offenders (Pitts, 1988). At the same time the police had established specialist Juvenile Bureaux to deal more cost-effectively with young people apprehended for committing petty offences. Between 1965 and 1977 the numbers of 10–17 year olds cautioned by the police rose from 3,062 to 111,922 (Pitts, 1988). The numbers subject to informal intervention by the police were higher still. However, according to some commentators (Thorpe et al., 1980) early informal intervention had a tendency to draw youngsters further into the system, as the discovery of new needs and new problems appeared to necessitate the formalisation of these interventions (Pitts, 1988).

In consequence, ever-larger numbers of children began to appear in the juvenile courts and, as the 1970s progressed, an increasing proportion of these were receiving custodial senten-

ces. Whereas in 1965, 21% of young people convicted in criminal courts were sentenced to detention centres and Borstals, by 1977 this proportion had risen to 38% (Pitts, 1988).

The rise of 'progressive minimalism'

As a result, by the late 1970s, not only were residential and custodial institutions for juveniles chronically overcrowded, thereby placing additional strains on an equally overcrowded adult penal system, they were also costing a great deal of money (Pitts, 1988). Margaret Thatcher's Conservative government was elected in 1979, on a pledge to crack-down on youth crime. However the youth justice system, was one of several areas of government spending perceived to be spiralling out of control and this was acutely embarrassing for an administration elected on a promise of low taxes, 'small government' and 'good housekeeping' (Scull, 1977). Thus, Mrs Thatcher's blood-curdling, pre-election, 'law and order' rhetoric notwithstanding, the 1980s saw a sustained attempt to rationalise the youth justice system. Successive Conservative Home Secretaries therefore paid more attention to the advice of their civil servants and researchers, than to the tabloid press or the 'law and order' rhetoric of their leader. As a result, Conservative responses to youth crime in the 1980s were shaped in significant ways by contemporary research and scholarship which, at the time, appeared to be suggesting that not only did punitive or rehabilitative programmes make little impact upon re-offending (Martinson, 1974; Wilson, 1975), they also had the potential to worsen the very problems to which they were the intended solution, through a process of 'labelling' (Becker, 1963; Lemert, 1970).

'Progressive minimalism', a term invented by the American criminologist Elliott Currie (1985), combined two highly influential intellectual currents; 'radical non-intervention' and the 'back to justice' movement. Radical non-intervention had its roots in the disillusionment of Anglo-American political activists of the left, right and centre, scholars and welfare professionals, with state intervention in private lives which, they maintained, must necessarily boomerang, yielding outcomes at stark variance with policy intentions (Gouldner, 1971; Pearson, 1975). In evidence, they pointed to the ways in which behaviour, perfectly acceptable in its own social milieu, was transformed into pathology by the heavy-handed interventions of agents of the state (Becker, 1963; Matza, 1969). They counselled that the best that governments could hope for was to do 'less harm' rather than 'more good'. So, in its dealings with young people who offend, the state should when-ever and wherever possible, simply 'leave the kids alone' (Schur, 1973).

For its part, the 'back to justice' movement, appeared to be ready to abandon the ethos which had underpinned the juvenile court for best part of a century, that by dint of their relative immaturity, children are less able to control their impulses, less able to understand the seriousness of their offences and less able to foresee the consequences of their actions. The movement was vehemently opposed to the type of welfarist approaches to youth justice developed in the UK between 1933 and 1969. Its supporters argued that a child or young person would only receive justice (as distinct from care, protection or welfare) in a youth justice system which recognised the child's right to the protections afforded by 'due process of law'. This right was eventually secured in the USA as a result of an obscure court ruling in Arizona. On the 15th June 1964, 15 year old Gerald Gault was committed to a State Industrial School for boys until his 21st birthday because he was found guilty of making obscene telephone calls to his teacher, and his parents appeared unwilling or unable to exert adequate control over him. The American Council for Civil Liberties appealed the Gault case all the way to the Supreme Court, which ruled that in adjudication hearings that might result in a young person being sent to an institution, they had the right to the protections of due process of law. The implication of this ruling was that a juvenile could not be subjected to longer periods of deprivation of liberty, in any type of institution, than an adult who had committed the same offence on the basis of their 'welfare' needs. The ruling was to have immense repercussions in youth justice systems in the USA and Europe.

And so, by the early 1980s, in the UK, the 'progressive minimalist' message was being articu-lated by an increasingly influential youth justice lobby, comprising youth justice professionals, penal reform groups, progressive Home Office and Department of Health civil servants and academic criminologists. They were pressing for the replacement of a 'welfare'-oriented system by a 'justice'-oriented system which accorded with the principles of due process of law and mini-mised intervention in the lives of young people who offend.

Progressive minimalism in the UK – the Intermediate Treatment Initiative

In an attempt to reduce the numbers of juveniles held in custody, in 1983 the Department of Health launched the Intermediate Treatment Initiative. The initiative transformed early IT which, having failed to supersede attendance centres and deten-tion centres, as the 1969 Act had intended, had slipped into the doldrums. It established IT as a 'direct alternative to custody' for 'heavy end' young offenders, granting £15,000,000 over three years to the voluntary sector to develop 4,500 'alternatives to custody' which would divert young people who committed serious or persistent of-fences back into community-based provision, in collaboration with the police and juvenile court magistrates. Apparently it worked. Between 1981 and 1989, the numbers of juveniles imprisoned in custodial establishments fell from 7,700 to 1,900 per annum.

Corporatism: a third model of youth justice?

However, these radical reductions in custodial sentencing were not solely attributable to changes in the attitudes of sentencers and their greater willingness to use alternatives to custody, although this clearly played a part. A major factor was a huge reduction in the numbers of children and young people entering juvenile courts. Whereas in 1980, 71,000 boys and girls aged 14 to 16 were sentenced by the juvenile courts in England and Wales, by 1987 this figure had dropped to 37,300, a reduction of over 52% .

This was made possible by the development of local multi-agency diversion panels, composed of representatives from the police, social services, education, the youth service and the voluntary sector (see Chapter 10). Multi-agency diversion panels, being imbued with the minimalist ethos, developed a range of educational, recreational and therapeutic 'alternatives to prosecution' to which children and young people in trouble could be diverted as a condition of their police caution. Many panels offered robust informal intervention in the spheres of education, family relationships, use of leisure, vocational training and drug abuse. The apparent effectiveness of many of these schemes led to a practice, known as 'cautioning plus' in which a youngster might be cautioned on several different occasions if they and their parents agreed to participate in particular programmes or activities. Between 1980 and 1987, the cautioning rate for girls aged 14 to 16 rose from 58% to 82%. For boys the figures were 34% and 58% respectively (Pitts, 1988). Although this approach was subsequently scrapped in favour of a less flexible system of final warnings and reprimands (see Chapter 12) recent research has demonstrated that cautioning plus, when backed by a range of robust diversionary programmes, was remarkably effective in diverting youngsters from court and reducing their offending (Kemp et al., 2002).

John Pratt (1989) argues that the advent of the multi-agency diversion panel ushered in a new model of youth justice, 'corporatism', which supplanted both the 'welfare' and 'justice' models. In the corporatist model, all the relevant agencies and organisations spontaneously enter a (bottom-up) partnership to deal effectively and efficiently with young people who offend. Corporatism is, however, an organisational 'model' and Pratt is concerned with the changing organisational structures of youth justice rather than theories, ideologies or professional practices. Thus it is not the case that corporatism simply supplants welfarist or minimalist models of youth justice since it is quite possible to conceive of a corporatist organisational structure with a welfarist or minimalist orientation. Indeed, as I argue below, the 'new youth justice' introduced by the Crime and Disorder Act 1998, marks the advent of what we might call 'top-down corporate correctionalism'.

A very peculiar practice – the rise of the justice model

The forms of face-to-face practice developed in the 1983 IT Initiative came to be described as the 'justice model'. The justice model doffed its cap to the 'back to justice' lobby by developing interventions for adjudicated offenders only, which focused solely upon their offending. The influence of the minimalists could be divined in the duration of the orders imposed upon these adjudicated offenders, which were determined by the length of the prison sentence to which they were an alternative. The influence of both was evident in the practices of the more radical youth justice sections, which outlawed any consideration of the welfare needs of their clients. If a child was obviously suffering from neglect, abuse or a psychological disorder of some kind, they would simply be referred to an agency outside the youth justice system.

Delinquency management

Multi-agency working, based on the 'justice model', was sometimes described as 'delinquency management' because, in the 1980s, the focus of youth justice had effectively shifted from the rehabilitation or punishment of individuals to the cost-effective management of entire cohorts or categories of young people who offend. Writing of analogous developments in the USA, Feely and Simon (1992) describe the emergence of a *new penology*; a politically ambiguous development representing the convergence of two ostensibly antagonistic intellectual and political currents; progressive minimalism, and an emergent neo-conservative criminology, which held that 'evil people exist' and that the best we can do is to incapacitate the most serious offenders with exemplary jail sentences and subject lesser criminals, and those on the edge of crime, to cost-effective management and surveillance.

Clearly, the Thatcher government's 'delinquency management' strategy had effected a marked reduction in the numbers of young people being incarcerated. However, this was a government that had been elected in 1979 on a pledge to 'restore the rule of law'. It was therefore necessary to cloak governmental pragmatism with the trappings of toughness, not least because by the mid-1980s, a rising crime rate and growing media and parliamentary concern about violent youth crime was placing the government under growing pressure. And so, just as the Children and Young Persons Act 1969 had marked the high water mark of 'welfarism', so the introduction of the Criminal Justice Act 1991, which aimed to enshrine the successes of the IT initiative in statute, paralleled the demise of 'progressive minimalism'.

Penal populism and the renaissance of youth imprisonment

Record rises in the crime rate at the end of the 1980s and youth riots on out-of-town housing estates in 1991 and 1992 were to force the government to defend its minimalist policies on youth crime. But it was the murder in 1993 of two year old James Bulger by two truanting ten year olds which put youth crime unequivocally back on the 'front page'. As a result, the key reforms embodied in the Criminal Justice Act 1991 were abandoned. In March 1993, only five months after the newly implemented Act had abolished custody for children under 15, Kenneth Clarke, the Conservative Home Secretary, promised to create 200 places for 12 to 14 year old 'persistent offenders' in new 'secure training centres'. This *volte face* signalled a new era in which crime in general, and youth crime in particular, was to be moved back to the centre of the political stage.

The defining characteristic of penal populism is that both policy ends and policy means should accord with the dictates of an invariably retributive, 'common sense' rather than the imperatives of 'experts' and criminal justice professionals. New policy initiatives are no longer justified by reference to the criteria of these 'experts'. Now the experts are called upon to advise on the means whereby populist policy goals may be realised, rather than the ends to which policy should strive. Whereas, in an earlier period, growing penal populations were represented as a shameful error on the part of the authorities, under the sway of penal populism they may be celebrated as a political achievement (Currie, 1985; Simon, 2000).

In 1994 a new Home Secretary, Michael Howard, set about toughening the probation service by allowing direct recruitment of junior officers from the armed forces and ex-police officers. In October 1994 he told the government's annual conference that:

> *Prison works, it ensures that we are protected from murderers, muggers and rapists – and it makes many who are tempted to commit crime think twice.*

Michael Howard's period in office marked a key moment of transition in the English justice system in general and youth justice in particular from 'penal modernism' to 'penal populism'. In this period, the issue of crime was moved out of the de-politicised space it occupied in the mid- to late 1980s to become a 'hot' political issue. In the process policies forged by political and professional elites gave way to those which resonated with 'popular' retributive sentiments. The 'victim', not the perpetrator, now emerged as the central object of penal policy and, increasingly, being 'for' the victim meant being 'against' the offender. In this changed ideological climate, prison became a tool of incapacitation rather than rehabilitation, while community supervision became, first and foremost, 'risk management'.

Garland (2001) has argued that during this period we witness a move away from a modernist vision of the perfectibility of man to a darker, neo-classical, vision of self-seeking man contained by a strong family, a strong community and a strong state, and constrained by fear of the penalty. Clearly the courts were now being sent a very different message by the government and, between 1993 and 1998, the number of young people under sentence in penal establishments, rose by nearly 85%, from 3,900 to 7,200.

Hard Labour

New Labour which, like the US Democrats, had spent best part of the previous 20 years in a political cul-de-sac, reckoned that if it was to revive its electoral fortunes it must bury its image as the natural party of penal reform and seize the mantle of law and order from the Conservatives. In the wake of the Bulger case, Labour mounted a full-scale attack on the Tory 'law and order' record, orchestrated and led by their new shadow Home Secretary, Tony Blair. New Labour, Blair maintained, would be 'tough on crime and tough on the causes of crime' and, in the ensuing debate, the Labour Party deployed the entire lexicon of 'get tough' sound-bites in an attempt to wrest the political initiative on 'law and order' from the Conservative's grasp (Chapman and Savage, 1999). New Labour's legislative intentions, embodied in the portentously titled *No More Excuses* White Paper (1997b), were translated into statute in record time; attesting to the political centrality of youth crime and youth justice policy.

The Crime and Disorder Act 1998

According to then Home Secretary, Jack Straw, the Crime and Disorder Act 1998 (CDA) represented 'the most radical shake-up of youth justice in 30 years'. The Act epitomised the New Labour project, embodying ideas from across the political spectrum and attesting to New Labour's new-found 'toughness'. The criminal justice provisions promised the victims of crime a voice in the outcome of criminal cases, while the new civil measures offered to 'empower' 'middle England' by handing it the legal and administrative means to re-establish order and civility in its 'communities'. The entire system was to be robustly managed at a local level, to ensure that it all 'joined up' and offered 'best value' to the public.

The structure of the 'new youth justice' (Goldson, 2000a) was derived in large part from the recommendations of the Audit Commission (1996) report on the youth justice system. *Misspent Youth* was primarily concerned with whether, or not, the youth justice system of England and Wales offered 'value for money'. Its authors brought extensive experience and expertise in economics and social policy to their task and, in consultation with psychologically-oriented criminologists in Britain and the USA, they deliberated upon the origins of youth crime and the likely impact of a range of interventions upon young people in conflict with the law. They concluded that:

> *The current system for dealing with youth crime is inefficient and expensive, while little is being done to deal effectively with juvenile nuisance. The present arrangements are failing the young people – who are not being guided away from offending towards constructive activities. They are also failing victims – those who suffer from young people's inconsiderate behaviour, and from vandalism and loss of property from thefts and burglaries. And they lead to waste in a variety of forms, including lost time, as public servants process the same young offenders through the courts time and again, lost rents, as people refuse to live in high crime areas; lost business, as people steer clear of troubled areas; and waste of young people's potential.*
>
> (p.96)

The central messages from *Misspent Youth* were that we should be intervening earlier, before the actual commission of offences if necessary, that we should be intervening more robustly at an earlier stage in a young person's criminal career and that we should be targeting their offending

behaviour. However, *Misspent Youth* was no mere blueprint for the CDA, as is sometimes argued. In fact, it has a strong diversionary theme running through it. While it emphasised the importance of multi-agency strategic planning, it also encouraged greater use of diversion from court. Indeed, in its 1998 update, which followed the publication of the CDA, the Audit Commission (1998) makes reference to the need to divert children, then receiving supervision orders, out of the system. Unlike the Act, the report argues that preventive services should, where possible, be located outside the youth justice system in order that responses to youngsters at risk might be 'normalised'. Indeed, it makes considerable play of the need for the 'normalisation' of preventive work through the provision of better nurseries, schools, leisure activities, careers services and drug treatment facilities. As we note below, while these kinds of preventive measures have subsequently been introduced by the government they have also, in varying degrees, been incorporated into the youth justice system and, to that extent, their 'normalising' potential has been compromised.

The 1998 Act marks a reaction against both 1960s welfarism and 1980s progressive minimalism. The measures it introduced focus upon the criminal deeds of young people who offend rather than their social or psychological needs. The idea that youth crime is a product of poverty, social inequality or psychological disadvantage is supplanted by an emphasis upon moral choice and responsibility. Whereas the minimalist strategies of the 1980s and 1990s aimed to minimise stigma by diverting youngsters in trouble out of the system, the 1998 Act aims to bring both first-time offenders and troublesome youngsters below the age of criminal responsibility into the ambit of the criminal justice system. The local child curfew, introduced in the CDA hands new powers for local authorities and the police to set up area curfews which prohibit children under ten from being in specified public places at specified times unless supervised by a responsible adult. Although this provision has never been used, in 2001 it was extended to 16 year olds and in early 2004 was supplemented by powers to take unaccompanied children back to their homes as part of new police powers to disperse groups (Nacro, 2004a).

In April 2003, the Youth Justice Board set up 14 pilot *Youth Inclusion and Support Panels* (YISPs), to target 8–13 year olds deemed to be at risk of offending. It is intended that, following the pilot studies, a national network of YISPs will be established. The panels are made up of representatives from a range of agencies including the YOT the police, schools and health and social services:

> *The local agencies identify young people who are behaving in ways that put them at risk of offending – be it drug misuse, mental health problems, family problems or anti-social behaviour – and refer them to the panel. The panel considers the case and recommends a programme of support for the young person and their family from mainstream services or provides key workers to offer dedicated help to those who need it most.*
>
> (Youth Justice Board, 2003n)

Leaving to one side the very considerable problems involved in predicting future offending from the present behaviour of 8–13 year olds (Pawson and Tilley, 1997), there remains the question about the likely impact of such an early induction into the criminal justice system on the self-perceptions, and subsequent conduct, of the children identified.

Systemic nemesis – top-down corporate correctionalism, and its discontents

The CDA provided both a stage upon which New Labour could demonstrate its political grit and an opportunity to remedy the administrative and judicial shortcomings of the existing system. However, the reworking of priorities, the creation of the multi-agency YOTs, the proliferation of new laws and the adoption of 'remoralising' rehabilitative techniques (Muncie, 2002) to produce what we can characterise as 'top-down corporate correctionalism', paid scant attention to the fact that a new *system* which, like all bureaucratic systems had a logic of its own, was being brought into being.

For example, it seemed to have occurred to nobody in government that if the YOTs, which were modelled on the multi-agency youth diversion panels of the 1980s, were inserted into a system which aimed to draw far greater numbers in, rather than to divert them out, it could be overwhelmed by the new influx. Nor did anybody

appear to have considered that early induction into the system might, through a combination of stigmatisation, 'deviancy amplification' (Wilkins, 1964) and administrative drift, accelerate young people's progress through it.

The 1998 Act is rooted in the belief that early exposure to the youth justice system, if linked with evidence-based programmes of intervention, will have long-term deterrent and rehabilitative effects. One of the consequences of this ideological shift was to place strict limits upon police discretion and require them instead to issue only one formal *reprimand* for a first offence and a *final warning* for a second. This had the effect of formally inducting larger numbers of relatively unproblematic children, and their parents, into the youth justice system, where YOTs were required to provide relevant 'offence-focussed' programmes for the children and to supervise the parenting orders imposed upon their mothers and fathers.

Whether early formal intervention with young people committing petty offences and the 'evidence based' programmes developed within the YOTs are effective is the subject of continuing debate (see Chapters 32 and 37). What is clear however is that the rapid increase in the numbers entering the system, together with the sheer speed of change, has posed formidable problems for the newly formed YOTs. Many found it difficult to square the new governmental time and throughput targets and statutory deadlines, with the demands of the courts and the needs and problems of their young clientele. However, because such failure threatened to place future funding in jeopardy, very soon the YOTs confronted the all too familiar public sector dilemma of whether to maintain the quality of the service or to tailor the service to the achievement of the prescribed targets.

In line with its robust interventionist ethos, the CDA extended the powers of youth courts to remand children and young people into secure and penal establishments. It also repealed the *Certified Specified Activity Requirement* that required magistrates to demonstrate that an alternative to a custodial sentence would not offer sufficient control and containment and a greater prospect of rehabilitation than a custodial sentence. Meanwhile, the 'fast-tracking' of persistent and/or serious young offenders, coupled with the tendency of the system to accelerate the progress of their less serious counterparts through it, already discussed, was creating a custodial bonanza. Between 1992 and 2002 the numbers of children and young people aged 10–17 sentenced to security or custody in England and Wales rose by almost 90%. Moreover, in the decade 1992–2001, the numbers of under-15s held in security or custody increased by, a remarkable, 800% (Nacro, 2003a). However, during this time, crimes recorded as having been committed by children and young people fell by 20% (Nacro, 2003a).

An expanding system

The youth justice system is expanding as a result of the growing numbers held in security and custody and subject to supervision by the YOTs. However, it is also expanding in two other directions. It is expanding by targeting those previously beyond the purview of the youth justice system, like the badly behaved 8–13 year olds involved with the YISPs discussed above, and it is expanding through the closer integration of agencies which previously had no criminal justice remit. Since 1997, along with concerns about their educational attainment and employability, the likelihood of lower class children and young people drifting into crime and disorder has been a major area of governmental concern, and these concerns have spawned a plethora of new initiatives. A study undertaken in 2002/3 (Crimmens et al., 2004), found that street-based youth work had expanded significantly since the election of New Labour in 1997, as a direct result of these new initiatives; indeed, over 50% of projects surveyed were less than three years old. However, whereas in the past, street-based youth work had tended to offer a broad-based 'social education' to the generality of young people in disadvantaged neighborhoods, the projects surveyed in 2002/3 were far more likely to be targeting young people involved in crime and disorder, drug use, truancy and excluded from school. Whereas in 1999, only 20% of projects targeted these problematic groups, by 2002 this had risen to almost 60% and over 50% of projects were involved in formal partnerships with community safety or criminal justice agencies. While many youth workers welcomed the increased resources made available by these developments, they also expressed concern about the creeping 'criminalisation' of street work.

Conclusion

Crime is mentioned only once, in a footnote, in the Beveridge Report, the document which brought the British welfare state into being in the immediate aftermath of World War II. Today, by contrast, we appear to be living in an era of 'government through crime' (Hughes and Muncie, 2002) in which every government department and government initiative is required to demonstrate how it is contributing to crime reduction and community safety. Commentators speak about the 'criminalisation of social policy' (Crawford, 2001) but a concern with crime infuses policy in the areas of health, housing, education, economic regeneration, and beyond.

Ulrich Beck has argued that, in the West, with the rolling back of the welfare state, the decline of deference and growing individualism, 'class society' has given way to the 'risk society', concerned less with the distribution of 'goods' than the distribution of 'bads'. In this risk society, the predominant logic is the avoidance of risk and this, he argues, gives rise to a 'negative solidarity of fear'. It is in these circumstances that government through crime comes to the fore.

The tendency of the youth justice system to annex other child and youth serving agencies has been evident since the 1980s (Pitts, 1988). However, from the late 1990s, as a result of the articulation of a far broader range of agencies and services, driven by changed funding regimes and facilitated by multi-agency working and the legal and scientific capacity to identify not only 'offending' populations but those young people who are 'anti-social', 'pre-delinquent' or 'at risk', the youth justice system in the 21st century has become a qualitatively different entity. Just as the boundaries between children and young people who are 'offending', 'anti-social', 'pre-delinquent' and 'at risk' are being progressively blurred in policy and law, so the boundaries of youth justice, community safety, education, drug services, social welfare, education and crime control are becoming ever more fluid; and ever more opaque.

Further reading

Goldson, B. (2000a) *The New Youth Justice.* Lyme Regis: Russell House Publishing

Muncie, J., Hughes, G. and McLaughlin, E. (2002) *Youth Justice: Critical Readings.* London: Sage

Matthews, J. and Young, J. (2003) *The New Politics of Criminal Justice.* Cullompton: Willan Publishing

Pitts, J. (1999) *Working with Young Offenders.* Basingstoke: BASW/Macmillan

Pitts, J. (2003b) The *New Politics of Youth Crime: Discipline or Solidarity.* 2nd edn. Lyme Regis: Russell House Publishing

2 Youth Crime in England and Wales

John Pitts and Tim Bateman

Key points

1. The involvement of children and young people in crime is commonplace but their involvement is usually short-lived.

2. Theft is the crime most commonly committed by juveniles, with violent offences making up just 15% of the total crimes committed by 10–18 year olds.

3. Recorded crime figures, victimisation surveys and self-report studies suggest that youth offending has been falling for the past decade.

4. The children and young people most commonly apprehended for crime are boys from poor families who live in multiply disadvantaged, high crime, neighbourhoods.

5. Black and black British young people are significantly over-represented among those apprehended for offending. Girls, by contrast, are under-represented.

Introduction

Youth offending continues to attract a great deal of media and political attention. One of the consequences of this focus is that controlling youth crime and the reform of the youth justice system have been priorities for the New Labour government. The Crime and Disorder Act 1998 (CDA), and a swathe of subsequent criminal justice legislation, is heavily weighted towards tackling the crimes and controlling the disorder generated by children and young people. Indeed, these reforms have been credited with creating a 'new youth justice' (Goldson, 2000a).

Yet, in spite of the high profile given to youth crime and disorder, and governmental attempts to combat it, we know a lot less about it than is usually supposed. Moreover, what is known does not support the popular perception of an eternally-rising tide of serious youth crime.

The definition of youth crime

What actually constitutes youth crime and disorder, and the seriousness with which particular behaviours are regarded, may vary over time and from place to place. In England and Wales, for example, the age of criminal responsibility is 10, whereas in Scandinavian countries it is 15 (Nacro,

2002b). One of the reasons these countries have less juvenile crime is that 10–15 year old Scandinavians, like under-10s in England and Wales, are deemed incapable of committing a criminal offence.

The volume of youth crime will also be affected by changes in the law. Since the 1990s, we have seen a veritable blizzard of legislation which has not only increased penalties for a broad range of offences but has also conflated 'crime' and 'disorder'. As a result, behaviours previously regarded as no more than a nuisance, like being in a public place after 9 p.m. or congregating with other young people on a street corner and being rude to passing adults, now fall within the ambit of the youth justice system. But whatever kinds of behaviour are designated 'youth crime and disorder', there remains the problem of discovering how much of it there actually is.

The incidence and nature of youth crime

There are three main sources of data about the incidence and nature of youth crime in England and Wales: the official Home Office statistics compiled from police and court records, victimisation surveys and self-report studies. However, each of these poses its own difficulties and none is able to provide a complete picture of criminal activity committed by children and young people.

Criminal statistics

These are compiled from offences known to, and recorded by, the police. However, they do not give a full picture because there is a large 'dark figure' of crime which is never reported to, or recorded by, the police. People fail to report criminal incidents for a variety of reasons. They may not be aware that a particular action, like 'threatening behaviour', is an offence. They may be unaware that a crime has been committed; if, for example, their wallet goes missing when they are drunk. Some victims may fear reprisals from the perpetrator, while others may not report a crime because they have little confidence that it will be solved by the police. Thus many minor offences go unreported because they are considered insufficiently serious to bring to police attention or there was no loss involved (Salisbury, 2003).

Similarly, the police may not record an incident if the information they receive is too sketchy or they are unable find either the victim or the perpetrator, as is often the case in late-night fights outside pubs and clubs. Moreover, police recording practice varies over time. Much of the recent increase in recorded crime is attributable to the new counting rules, introduced in 1999, and the more recent adoption, by the police, of a National Crime Recording Standard which encourages formal recording of more of the incidents reported to them by the public (Salisbury, 2003).

Furthermore, even where an offence is recorded, it is not possible to ascertain whether it was committed by a child or young person unless somebody is apprehended for it. 'Clear-up rates' – cases solved by the police – vary from offence to offence and from one police service area to another. Whereas 86% of reported murders are cleared up, the rate for robbery, at 18%, theft and handling stolen goods, at 16%, and burglary, at 12%, is far lower (Mayhew, 2003). It is estimated that in England and Wales in 2002/2003, for every 100 offences committed, 44 were reported to the police, 30.8 were recorded by the police, 7.2 were cleared-up by the police and 3 resulted in a caution or conviction (Salisbury, 2003; Mayhew, 2003). As a consequence, it is difficult to assess how many, and what types of crime, are committed by children and young people.

The picture is further complicated by the fact that fluctuations in recorded crime rates may be unrelated to the behaviour of young people but derive instead from changes in legislation, government policy and police priorities. For instance, statutory measures, such as the final warning scheme introduced by the CDA, may lead the police to deal formally with incidents which would previously have been dealt with informally. As a result, recorded petty crime committed by younger children is likely to rise, and the proportion of young people who are charged for relatively minor offences will also increase (see Chapter 12). Shifts in policing priorities involving the redeployment of officers can lead to higher detection rates for some types of offences but lower detection rates for other, lower priority, offences. The Street Crime Initiative, for instance, instigated by the government in April 2002, led to the deployment of more police officers in street crime 'hot spots' thereby increasing the amount of recorded street crime. However, because many of these officers were from the traffic division, convictions for road traffic offences fell. The fact that, in the face of changing policies, a finite budget and limited personnel, police priorities must inevitably shape crime data does not mean that the extent and nature of youth crime is unknowable. However, it does mean that it would be unwise to generalise about the characteristics of those who commit youth crime from what we know about the relatively small numbers of apprehended offenders who enter the youth justice system (Muncie, 1999).

Victimisation surveys

Recognition of the limitations of the criminal statistics has led to the development of victimisation surveys. The best known and most comprehensive of these in England and Wales is the British Crime Survey (BCS). Based on interviews with randomly selected heads of households, the BCS gives a more accurate picture of the nature and extent of crime than criminal statistics because it is able to capture information about the 'dark figure' of unreported and unrecorded crime (albeit for a limited number of offences). One of the more significant findings from such studies is that victimisation is distributed unequally, with the poorest people in the poorest neighbourhoods being most vulnerable (Aitchison and Hodgkinson, 2003). It has also revealed that risk is crucially shaped by race, gender and age (see Chapter 38).

Crime surveys have been adopted widely by crime and disorder reduction partnerships to enable them to target their crime reduction strategies. However, while respondents may know that a crime has been perpetrated against them; in many cases they will be unaware of the age, gender and race of the perpetrator. So, while victimisation surveys give us a fuller picture of the nature and distribution of criminal victimisation, they must necessarily give us an incomplete account of the involvement of children and young people in offending. A further limitation of victimisation surveys is that, until recently, they only gathered information from heads of households, usually a mother or a father, and this has tended to understate the nature and extent of the criminal victimisation of children and young people (see Chapter 38).

Self-report studies

Because of low levels of reporting and recording of crime, and relatively low police 'clear-up rates', any analysis of offending based upon the criminal statistics will show us to be a remarkably law-abiding society. For example, a Home Office study recently revealed that 67% of males and 91% of females born in England and Wales in 1953 had no convictions for standard list offences by the age of 46 (Prime et al., 2001). Yet, it seems clear that most young people commit an offence at some time in their lives.

Self-report studies are based upon interviews and, more commonly, questionnaires completed by adults, children or young people, in which they are asked to reveal offences they have committed. Such studies have the major advantage over the criminal statistics and victimisation surveys of giving us information on the prevalence of offending (how many people are doing it), the incidence of offending (how frequently they are doing it) and the seriousness of their offending. Belson's classic study (1977) of 1,400 London schoolboys produced a rate of stealing by finding of 98% and stealing from shops of 70%. Similarly, Rutter and Giller's 1983 summary of youth self-report delinquency studies produced a rate of 70% for theft from shops. Two thirds of 1,150, 11–15

year olds surveyed by Anderson et al. (1994) in Edinburgh admitted committing a criminal offence in the preceding nine months. Graham and Bowling (1995) reported similar rates of offending but, like these other self-report studies, showed that involvement in crime is usually episodic, short-lived and trivial and that only a small minority of young people went on to become serious, chronic or persistent offenders.

Like the other forms of data gathering discussed here however, self-report studies also have their limitations. They are reliant on the willingness of respondents to admit their involvement in crime and some people may be unwilling to do this. Conversely, some young people may be prone to exaggerating their involvement in offending. Moreover, questionnaires frequently have a low return rate.

A discernible trend

Although measuring the extent and nature of youth crime is problematic, data gathered from the police, courts and youth offending teams (YOTs) suggests some significant trends. Since the early 1990s, these data have revealed sharp falls in the numbers of children and young people processed by the youth justice system. Between 1992 and 2002, the number of 10–17 year olds convicted, cautioned, (reprimanded or warned from 1998) for indictable offences, fell from 143,600 to 105,700: a drop of almost 26%. This decline is not simply a result of demographic change: the fall in youth crime appears sharper still when expressed as a proportion of the youth population (Nacro, 2004c). Victimisation surveys have also indicated that crime has been falling from at least the mid-1990s. While these data give a picture of overall offending, rather than the crimes committed by children and young people, the pattern is certainly consistent with the data for recorded youth crime and might therefore be thought to add weight to the suggestion that the decline indicated by *Criminal Statistics* represents a real fall.

This 'reality' does not appear to accord with popular perceptions however. Most opinion polls reveal that the public believes that youth crime is spiralling upwards, and becoming more serious as it does so. Respondents also, typically, overestimate the risks of victimisation and overstate the amount of offending for which young people are

Table 2.1: Indictable offences committed by young people aged 10–17 years (inclusive) in England and Wales – 2002

Offence	Boys 12–14	Boys 15–17	Girls 12–14	Girls 15–17
Theft and handling	12,000 (47%)	19,300 (34%)	7,100 (72%)	8,100 (60%)
Burglary	4,000 (16%)	6,100 (11%)	400 (4%)	500 (4%)
Violence against person	3,800 (15%)	8,900 (16%)	1,400 (14%)	2,100 (16%)
Drugs offences	1,500 (6%)	11,700 (21%)	200 (2%)	1,000 (7%)
Criminal damage	1,800 (7%)	2,300 (4%)	300 (3%)	300 (2%)
Robbery	800 (3%)	2,000 (3%)	100 (1%)	300 (2%)
Fraud and forgery	200 (1%)	1,200 (2%)	100 (1%)	500 (4%)
Sexual offences	400 (2%)	600 (1%)	0	0
Motoring offences	100 (0.5%)	700 (1%)	0	0
Others	800 (3%)	4,100 (7%)	200 (2%)	600 (5%)
Total	25,400	56,900	9,800	13,400

Source: Derived from *Criminal Statistics for England and Wales 2002*, Home Office, 2003.

responsible (Nacro, 2001c). Yet, in 2002, almost 90% of detected crime was committed by adults (Nacro, 2004c).

For obvious reasons, public concern tends to be focused on crimes against the person, which inevitably attract the lion's share of media attention. It is therefore important to be clear that youth crime consists primarily of offences against property. As Table 2.1 above indicates, in 2002, theft and handling stolen goods accounted for 44% of all indictable offences. Violence against the person by contrast constituted just 15% of recorded crime with the absolute numbers of such offences having remained stable from the early 1990s. Moreover, in 2002, 58% of violent offences were dealt with by way of a reprimand or final warning, suggesting that they were not regarded by the police as particularly serious incidents. Street robbery is one of the crimes most feared by the public and it has risen in recent years. However, it is still relatively rare and accounts for

only around 3% of all youth offending. Finally, sexual offences constitute just over 1% of crimes committed by children and young people and such offences appear to have fallen recently: both in terms of absolute numbers and as a proportion of all indictable offences (Nacro, 2004c).

Who done it?

One of the most important self-report studies undertaken in recent years in the UK was that commissioned by the Home Office in the mid-1990s (Graham and Bowling, 1995). It found that amongst the 1,721 young people aged 14–25 interviewed, two thirds admitted committing a crime in the previous nine months, while 6.25% of the young men and 1.25% of the young women had committed five or more offences. Whereas the male-female ratio of self-reported offending for those in their early teens was roughly one-to-one, this rose to four-to-one for older teenagers.

Gender

Yet, as the table above indicates, around two and a half times more boys than girls in the 10–14 age group are processed by the youth justice system. The question of the apparent over-representation of boys, vis-à-vis their reported involvement in offending, is complicated by the fact that recorded offending by girls is considerably less serious. Nonetheless, boys might, on the face of it, appear to be getting a 'raw deal'. However, as Loraine Gelsthorpe argues (see Chapter 35) this is changing and the proportion of girls processed for indictable offences and dealt with by the courts, rather than by a caution, reprimand or final warning, rose from 12.5% in 1992 to 28% in 2002. Whereas custodial sentences for all juvenile defendants rose by almost 90% over this period, the increase for girls, albeit from a much lower baseline, was almost 600% (Nacro, 2004c). These patterns may be, in part at least, a product of a succession of, largely baseless, media scares about girl gangs and female violence through the 1990s (Nacro, 2001b).

Age and desistance

In Graham and Bowling's study (1995), the peak age of offending was 21 for boys and 16 for girls compared with equivalent ages of 19 and 15 derived from the criminal statistics (Home Office, 2003b). One possible reason for the difference as far as males are concerned, may be that the older offenders are less likely to be apprehended. From this peak onwards, involvement in crime appears to decline rapidly; a process sometimes referred to as 'growing out of crime' (Flood-Page et al., 2000; Rutherford, 1986). When young women desist from crime they tend to do so abruptly, leaving school, leaving home, setting-up an independent household with a partner and sometimes having a child as well. For young men, these landmarks have less apparent significance. In fact, major factors in desistance amongst young men appear to be associated with not leaving home and continuing to live with parents which, in turn, allowed them to avoid the worst excesses of drink and drug abuse and too close an association with offending peers. Their ability to do this depends in part, however, on the quality of the relationship they had with their parents. Graham and Bowling found that young men and women who offended persistently tended to come from poor families, headed by a single parent or step-parent. They usually had a poor relationship with parents, truanted from, and achieved little at, school, had 'delinquent siblings' and associated with 'delinquent peers'. More recent surveys conducted for the Youth Justice Board, confirm that offending by children who are excluded from school is significantly higher than that among those who are in mainstream education (Youth Justice Board, 2003p). For those over school age, persistent offending correlates with high levels of unemployment, with one survey showing that only one in ten 16–17 year olds who offend persistently had a steady job (Graham and Bowling, 1995).

Race

Levels of self-reported offending amongst white and African-Caribbean young people were broadly similar in the study by Graham and Bowling (1995). Yet those classified as 'black' and 'black British', although they constitute only 2.7% of the 10–17 population, represent 5.7% of adjudicated young offenders, almost 15% of those remanded to custody or secure accommodation, 11.3% of all those sentenced to custody and over 20% of the young people consigned to long-term detention (Youth Justice Board, 2003o). The recent Audit Commission report on the operation of the youth justice system (2004) suggests that variation in outcomes by race has widened since the implementation of the youth justice reforms associated with the CDA.

It is sometimes argued that part of this over-representation may be explicable in terms of differences in the types of offences committed by black and white young people, and wide publicity has been given to the involvement of black adolescents in street crime in general, and mobile phone theft in particular. However, much less attention has been given to the fact that black young people are significantly less likely than their white counterparts to commit domestic burglary or to steal cars (Youth Justice Board, 2003o). Research suggests that at least some of the over-representation of black young people in the youth justice statistics may be attributable to an 'amplification effect' of compounded disadvantage at a broader social level combined with differential treatment once they enter the system.

Social class and poverty

The youth justice system deals almost exclusively with socially disadvantaged children and young people. Most of the youngsters referred to YOTs suffer from the combined effects of poor housing, low income, family difficulties, poor educational attainment, school exclusion and truancy, mental ill health and alcohol and drug abuse (Youth Justice Board, 2001b). The association between poverty, social exclusion and youth crime is at one level unsurprising. However, offending is not simply the preserve of the poor. The yield from tax evasion and corporate crime, almost always perpetrated by well-educated, 'well-heeled', adults, dwarfs the proceeds of youth crime and victimises far more people, albeit indirectly. Yet relatively few resources are dedicated to the control of these forms of wrongdoing (Tombs, 2002).

In the 1990s a great deal of attention has been paid by scholars and policy makers to the individual and family risk factors associated with youth crime. The risk factor paradigm, based on a longitudinal study of 400 or so young people in south London in the 1970s and 1980s, provides an extensive list of the personal and familial factors associated with youth offending, although it does not tell us which of these factors is a 'cause' and which an 'effect', nor how they might interact to produce an offence (Farrington and West, 1993). More significantly, this concentration on individuals and families has diverted attention from the role of neighbourhood of residence in the aetiology of youth crime (Muncie, 1999).

The neighbourhood effect

As Malcolm Gladwell (2000) has observed, a child is probably better off in a good neighbourhood with a troubled family than in a troubled neighbourhood with a good family. A growing body of US research suggests that neighbourhood of residence may well have as significant an impact upon serious youth offending as the quality of parenting. A study of 15,000 young people in Philadelphia (Jones et al., 2000) found that individual and familial 'risk factors' will operate quite differently in different neighbourhoods:

The results showed clearly that significant variations exist among neighbourhoods throughout the city in terms of the propensity of high-risk early delinquents to actually become chronic offenders.

(p.8)

One of Jones' major findings was that in certain well-resourced, higher socio-economic status neighbourhoods, all predictions of future chronic delinquency based on a risk factor assessment failed to materialise. Wikstrom and Loeber (1997) in their huge Pittsburgh Youth Study, utilising a database of 18,000 young people, found a clear neighbourhood effect upon youth crime, with serious offending by children and young people with the lowest individual risk factors occurring significantly more frequently in the lowest socio-economic status neighbourhoods.

As a result of the seismic social, economic and political shifts of the 1980s and 1990s in the UK, crime in general, and youth crime in particular, came to be concentrated in areas of acute social deprivation. Thus the risk of being a victim of vehicle theft, burglary and crimes of violence in areas classified as 'thriving' is around half that in areas designated as 'striving' (Aitchison and Hodgkinson, 2003). Youth crime in these neighbourhoods is implosive in that it is usually committed by, and against, local residents in general and against local young people in particular. Indeed, in these neighbourhoods there is a strong correlation between being both a victim and perpetrator of youth offending (see Chapter 38). This pattern of intra-neighbourhood offending is a distinguishing characteristic of high-crime localities in Britain (Forrester et al., 1990; Hope, 1995). Its other distinguishing feature is that the young people involved are afforded fewer opportunities to grow out of it. So, as Graham and Bowling (1995) suggest, they may continue to perpetrate 'youth crime' into their twenties and beyond.

Thus, as we note at the beginning of this chapter, while recorded youth crime in general appears to be falling, in the poorest neighbourhoods, amongst the most disadvantaged social groups, it remains a serious problem. As social and economic polarisation worsens, so the potential for youth crime to become more violent increases. This phenomenon may go some way to explain the persistence of a widespread perception that youth offending is rising in the face of the recorded drop in the crime rate.

Further reading

Goldson, B. (Ed.) (2000a) *The New Youth Justice.* Lyme Regis: Russell House Publishing

Muncie, J. (1999) *Youth and Crime: A Critical Introduction.* London: Sage

Nacro (2004c) *Some Facts About Young People Who Offend: 2002.* Youth Crime Briefing. London: Nacro

Newburn, T. (1997) Youth, Crime and Justice. In Maguire, M., Morgan, R. and Riener, R. (Eds.) *Oxford Handbook of Criminology.* 2nd edn. Oxford: Clarendon Press

Pitts, J. (2003b) *The New Politics of Youth Crime: Discipline Or Solidarity.* Lyme Regis: Russell House Publishing

3 Youth Justice in Other UK Jurisdictions: Scotland and Northern Ireland

Bill Whyte

Key points

1. Children's hearings in Scotland deal both with children and young people in need of care and protection, and young people who offend, as 'children in need', within an integrated, non-adversarial, system.

2. The Scottish system separates adjudication of legal facts, which is the responsibility of the court, from disposals, which are the responsibility of children's hearings.

3. Integrated local authority social work departments supervise both juvenile and adult offenders.

4. Youth courts in Northern Ireland are adversarial criminal courts but recent reforms have aimed to put restorative justice at the heart of the process and promote diversion.

5. The Northern Ireland Youth Justice Agency is responsible for the supervision of juvenile offenders.

Introduction

The three United Kingdom youth justice systems, in England and Wales, Scotland and Northern Ireland, share common goals but pursue them in distinctive ways. Since the Act of Union 1701 which created the United Kingdom, Scotland has retained a separate legal system. The partitioning of Ireland in 1921 created a separate system of government and a parliament for the six counties of Northern Ireland which developed its own laws and policies. However, the suspension of the Northern Ireland parliament in 1972 and the imposition of 'direct rule' from Westminster curtailed developments for many years.

The re-establishment of a parliament in Scotland in 1998 and of Northern Ireland's Assembly in 1999 are likely to have a significant impact on youth justice in these jurisdictions in the coming years. Paradoxically, one immediate effect of political devolution has been a greater politicisation of youth justice which seems to be eroding the differences between England and Wales and other UK jurisdictions. In all three, we have seen a greater emphasis on due process, just deserts and a retreat from welfare.

The Social Work (Scotland) Act 1968, implemented in 1971, introduced a distinctive approach to youth justice in Scotland which has pertained for over 30 years. Scottish youth courts and the Scottish probation service were disbanded and replaced by 'children's hearings', which deal both with children in need and children who offend. The assumption underlying the system is that acting in the best interest of the young person and reducing offending will, in the long run, be in the interest of victims and the public at large. Supervision of young people who offend is undertaken by all-purpose local authority social work departments (Lockyer and Stone, 1998).

The Children (Scotland) Act 1995 provided a new statutory framework for the system and young people subject to compulsory measures because of offending are designated 'looked after children' and 'children in need'. It did not however fundamentally change its principles or institutions (Norrie, 1997; Moore and Whyte, 1998; Kearney, 2000). At the time of writing, a review of the hearings system is underway and recent developments have marked a shift away from the traditional child-centred approach associated with children's hearings. During 2002–4, the Scottish government expanded the powers of the children's hearings and established a pilot youth court to deal with young people aged 16 and 17 who offend as well as 15 year olds in exceptional cases.

Northern Ireland's youth justice system is based on a more traditional adversarial process. Decision making lies with a youth court consisting of a professional, legally trained, magistrate accompanied by two lay panel members. Recent measures contained in the Justice (NI) Act 2002 provide a new statutory framework for services provision. The introduction of 'youth conferences' in particular, seems set to bring about a significant shift towards a more restorative model of justice. The Northern Ireland Youth Justice Agency, established on 1st April 2003, has assumed executive responsibility for service provision with the aim of achieving better integration of services across the province.

Youth justice in Scotland

A distinctive philosophy

Scotland's system for dealing with young people who offend is based on the philosophy of justice advocated by the Report of the Kilbrandon Committee (SOHD, 1964). The Committee recommended an extra-judicial system of children's hearings and the re-organisation of social work services under the umbrella of all purpose local authority social work departments, which included work previously undertaken by the probation service.

Children's hearings provide a unified system for dealing with young people above the age of criminal responsibility (8 years) alleged to have committed criminal offences, those deemed to be in need of care and protection, and children under 8 years of age who commit what would be regarded as an offence if they were above the age of criminal responsibility.

The Kilbrandon Committee contended that the 'similarities in the underlying situation' of children who offend and children in need of care and protection 'far outweigh the differences' (para 15). Difficulties were considered to arise from a failure in upbringing in the family, the social environment and the school. Children's hearings were intended to deal with youth offending in a setting which, by its informality and allocation of time, would ensure, as far as practically possible, effective participation by the young person and adults in resolving problems and deciding on future action (Lockyer and Stone, 1998).

The Kilbrandon Committee viewed the criminal justice process as having two fundamental functions: the adjudication of the legal facts, whether or not an offence had been established

beyond reasonable doubt, and decisions concerning disposal once the facts had been established. The report contended that the two functions required 'quite different skills and qualities' and that attempting to combine them was a source of 'dissatisfaction' (para 71).

Accordingly, the Scottish system separates adjudication and disposal. A children's hearing has no power to determine questions of innocence or guilt, which remains the responsibility of the criminal court. Access to representation and legal aid is available to all young people and parents, who dispute the facts of the case, deny the offence, are unable to understand the evidence against them or wish to appeal against the outcome. This is intended to safeguard legal rights and provide a check against over-enthusiastic intervention. In practice the vast majority of children and young people brought before hearings in Scotland accept the facts and are therefore dealt with in this non-criminal setting.

A different practice

The children's hearing is a tribunal consisting of three lay panel members (at least one man and one woman), one of whom acts as chairperson. Meetings are usually held close to the young person's home area with the intention that decisions are taken by members who have 'personal knowledge of the community to which the child belongs' (SED, 1966). The whole procedure, including the decision making, is conducted in front of all the participants, usually in a round-table discussion. A majority decision is sufficient and the chairperson is required by law to share the substance and reasons for all decisions directly with the family and in writing.

Panel members are ordinary members of the community recruited by open advertisement in newspapers, through TV campaigns or the internet. Appointments are made by the First Minister, initially for up to five years. The age range for panel members is between 18 and 60 but in practice most are aged between 20 and 50 and, as a result, are often closer to the age and background of the young people and their parents than decision-makers in the courts. Panel members are specially trained and a government financed, national training curriculum is provided through four of Scotland's Universities.

The Children's Reporter is a key figure. It is only when the Reporter considers there to be a prima facie case, or that the young person may be in need of 'compulsory measures', that they can refer them to a children's hearing. The existence of an offence does not in itself indicate that a young person may be in need of 'compulsory measures' and the most common outcome of a referral to the Reporter is 'no formal action'. In making his decision, the Reporter may meet the young person and their parents in an informal setting and information may be sought from the social work authority or any other appropriate sources. The Reporter may decide to refer the young person to the local authority for 'advice, guidance and assistance' which can include a programme of assistance under a 'voluntary agreement'. Various arrangements can be made with the agreement of parents and the young person. These might include, for example, the confiscation of weapons, a letter of apology to the victim, or for making restitution with the assistance of a voluntary agency. Other restorative measures, including conferencing and victim awareness programmes are now available to Reporters in most local authority areas. From April 2004, all police warnings in Scotland adopted a restorative approach, which involves providing victims with information on decision-making and outcomes. By diverting cases from the children's hearings, the Reporter has a crucial role in minimising the risk of 'net-widening' which is sometimes associated with welfare-oriented systems (see Chapter 8).

Where a referral is made to the children's hearing, the Reporter attends and provides expert legal advice but does not take part in the official deliberations in respect of disposal. All Reporters are legally-trained but are drawn from a range of professional backgrounds including law, education and social work, on the assumption that they need an amalgam of skills to make decisions in the best interest of young people. From April 1st, 1996 a national, non-departmental, government service, the Scottish Children's Reporters Administration (SCRA), was created under a Principal Reporter whose duties are prescribed in law.

Normally, the young person must attend and the attendance of parents is also compulsory. A local authority social worker will usually be present to provide a professional assessment, to advise the tribunal and to support the young person and their family. Others, who may attend, with the permission of the chairperson and the agreement of the family, include school teachers or residential social workers, if the child is 'accommodated' by the local authority. Social work and school reports are often available three days in advance, to allow the panel time to examine the circumstances of the young person and consider any proposals for action. Additional professional reports – medical, psychological or psychiatric – can be requested and the young person is often encouraged to put their views in writing.

Representation at a hearing is encouraged but this need not be legal representation, since the role is a non-adversarial one aimed at assisting the young person to understand and participate in the process. Legal aid is available to young people and their parents to assist in preparation for a hearing but is available at the hearing itself only under special circumstances. Hearings also have the power to appoint a 'safeguarder' to protect the interests of the young person. However, these do not act as independent advocates for the young person, and are not frequently used in cases of young people who offend.

A hearing does not have the power to imprison, fine, order compensation or impose a community sentence. However, the disposals which are available to it include powers of compulsory supervision, with the power to attach a wide range of conditions, including reparation and mediation, or attendance at offence-focused or educational programmes. Residential conditions can also be inserted and may include confinement in secure accommodation. Given its extensive powers, the children's hearing must review all supervision orders within a year, or they automatically lapse. These powers notwithstanding, the stated aim of the hearing remains that of involving parents in a non-coercive way in order to 'strengthen, support and supplement . . . the natural beneficial influences of the home and family' (para 35). Unlike England and Wales, children's hearings cannot impose orders on parents (see Chapter 31).

Local authorities are responsible for young people 'looked after' because of offending. Each local authority has a multi-disciplinary strategic group responsible for planning services for young people who offend, within an integrated framework of children's services. A Youth Justice co-ordinator and specialist youth justice teams, generally located within 'children and family services' divisions are responsible for day-to-day service provision.

The age of criminal responsibility in Scotland is 8 years; extraordinarily low by European standards. The Kilbrandon Committee concluded that chronological age as such had no direct bearing on 'the capacity to form a criminal intent and to commit a crime' (para 64). Consequently it made no change to the existing age on the basis that few young people under 16 would be brought before a criminal court. In practice this has the advantage that any young person aged eight or over coming to the attention of the non-criminal hearing system because of offending can have the legal facts established or challenged before a professional judge in a criminal court, with the same representation rights and legal aid as any other citizen. The weakness of such a low age of criminal responsibility becomes apparent if and when the system brings young people before criminal courts.

The Lord Advocate retains powers to prosecute all young people above the age of eight years and under 16 in the criminal courts, and has issued instructions on which categories of offences are to be considered for prosecution. Generally this relates to the gravity of the offence (cases of murder, rape and armed robbery) some offences under road traffic legislation for those over age 14, which can result in disqualification; and offences committed with an adult. In 2001, 80 young people (5 girls and 75 boys) under the age of 16 were found guilty in a Scottish criminal court. Most were over the age of 14 (Statistical Bulletin, 2003: table 12).

The upper age for referral to a child's hearing is usually 16 years with young people above that age being subject to adult proceedings. However, those subject to supervision at 'school leaving age' can continue up to the age of 18 and the Criminal Procedures (Scotland) Act (1995) allows summary courts to refer young people under 17 years six months, back to a hearing for advice or disposal. In practice, this power is used rarely and those aged 16 to 18 are normally processed by the adult courts.

Youth justice in Northern Ireland

A restorative approach

Youth Justice in Northern Ireland has been significantly influenced by developments in England and Wales. Nonetheless the social and political climate has given it a distinctive character. In the context of political, para-military and sectarian conflict, criminal justice processes have not always carried universal support or the community collaboration necessary for credibility and effectiveness. Lindsay and Chapman (2001:52) noted that 'many of the most bitter and violent struggles have centred on the institutions of criminal justice . . . the police, courts and prisons'. One unintended consequence of these tensions is that voluntary sector agencies have played a particularly significant role in the development of youth justice provision in Northern Ireland. Moreover the province has one of the lowest victimisation rates in the western world. In 1999, 15% of the population had been victims of crime in Northern Ireland, compared with 26% in England and Wales and 23% for Scotland (United Nations, 2000).

As in other UK jurisdictions, youth justice has been a major focus of policy development in recent years. The Northern Ireland Criminal Justice Review reported in 2000 and in November 2001 a Criminal Justice Review Implementation Plan was published. It set a radical agenda for change including the creation of a National Youth Justice Agency and a range of diversionary measures of which the most important was youth conferencing. That agenda underpinned the Justice (Northern Ireland) Act 2002 which provides the new legal framework for youth justice developments with a strong emphasis on human rights and restorative justice.

The newly established Youth Justice Agency has a multidisciplinary workforce including social workers and community workers who are responsible for statutory supervision and the co-ordination of youth conferencing. In addition the Agency provides a range of community-based services and supports, in partnership with other statutory and voluntary agencies. These include providing counselling and support, cognitive skills training, and family work.

The statutory aim of the youth justice system in Northern Ireland is similar to that in England and Wales, 'to protect the public by preventing offending by children' (s.53(1)), by encouraging children and young people to recognise the effects of crime and to take responsibility for their actions. The distinctive characteristic of the legislation is the explicit requirement to have regard to the welfare of children within the system with a view to 'furthering their personal, social and educational development'.

Prosecution of children and young people is the responsibility of the Public Prosecution Service for Northern Ireland. The age of criminal responsibility is 10 as in England and Wales. Young people up to the age of 17 are normally dealt with by youth courts unless charged with an adult or, in the case of serious offences, when they may be dealt with by crown courts.

A youth court is a tribunal, normally consisting of a resident magistrate accompanied by two lay panellists from the Divisional Juvenile Court Panel. The youth court is relatively informal, the public is excluded, no wigs or gowns are worn and most participants sit on the same level, although the bench is normally raised above floor level. Legal representation, supported by legal aid, is available. The range of disposals available to the court include traditional penal measures such as an absolute or conditional discharge; a monetary penalty such as a fine, recognisance or compensation order; a community order, such as probation, community service (only available for those 16 years or over) or an attendance centre order (not available in every area), and two custodial orders: a 'juvenile justice centre order' (up to age 17) or a 'detention order'. Children and young people may also be consigned to secure accommodation.

Responsibility for the provision of custodial facilities for juvenile offenders is shared between the Youth Justice Agency, responsible for juvenile justice centres (JJC), and the Northern Ireland Prison Service. Northern Ireland's only secure JJC is in the process of being closed, to be replaced by a new purpose-built centre in Bangor by 2006. A JJC deals with young people sentenced to periods of between six months and two years.

These more traditional disposals are supplemented by the range of new diversionary measures referred to above, including youth conferencing, reparation and community responsibility orders. Community responsibility orders (s.55) require young people to attend at a specified place for between 20 and 40 hours within a six month period. The order is intended to involve young people in purposeful activity of a restorative nature, aimed at enhancing positive citizenship and emphasising the responsibilities which the young person owes to the community, promote victim awareness and address factors linked to offending. Unlike similar provisions in England and Wales, an order cannot be made without the young person's consent. Following a report from a relevant social worker, courts can also make a reparation order (s.54) requiring the young person to make reparation, excluding financial compensation, for up to 24 hours within a six month period.

Youth conferencing

Perhaps the centrepiece of the reformed youth justice system in Northern Ireland is youth conferencing. The intention behind this major new development is to bring together the parties most affected by the offence with the police and other professionals to develop a 'youth conference plan' tailored to the individual circumstances of the offence, meeting the needs of the young person and the victim. The Youth Conference Service (YCS) began to pilot conferencing in Belfast from December 2003 before rolling out the provision across the province.

A youth conference is defined by legislation as a meeting, or series of meetings, for considering how a young person ought to be dealt with for an offence (s.57–3A). The law requires that, normally, a youth conference co-ordinator, the young person, the police and an appropriate adult will be present during the conference. The victim of the offence or, if the victim is not an individual, an individual representing the victim, a legal representative, and, where relevant, a supervising officer are also entitled to be present. The youth conference co-ordinator may also allow others to attend if their participation is considered to be of value. Nothing that is said or done in connection with a youth conference is admissible in any subsequent criminal proceedings as evidence that the young person committed the offence. Legal aid is available.

A youth conference plan (s.57–3C) can outline one or more actions required of the young person, including making an apology to the victim or anyone else affected; making reparation to the victim or to the community at large; making a payment to the victim (not exceeding the cost of replacing or repairing any property taken); being subject to supervision by an adult; performing unpaid work or service in or for the community (only if over 16); participating in activities design-ed to address offending behaviour, including education or training; being subject to restrictions related to conduct or whereabouts. The duration of the plan may not be more than one year.

The Act makes provision for two types of conferences, diversionary (s.58) and court man-dated (s.59), for all young people involved in offending, except in the most serious offences. Where the young person admits an offence, the Director of the Youth Justice Agency has discre-tion to refer to a diversionary youth conference. This can recommend that no further action be taken, that proceedings be continued or instituted, or, where the young person consents to partici-pate, they become subject to a youth conference plan. If the Director accepts the recommendation for conferencing, proceedings against the young person in respect of the offence will be discon-tinued unless they fail to comply with the require-ments of the plan.

Where a young person is convicted of an offence in court proceedings, subject to certain restrictions (e.g. the penalty for the offence is fixed in law), the court must refer the case to a youth conference co-ordinator (s.57–33A) and cannot deal with the young person until it has received a conference report with recommenda-tions. The report may propose a youth conference order (s.60), requiring the young person to comply with the requirements specified in the youth conference plan. Alternatively, the conference may recommend that the court exercise its normal sentencing powers, including the power to impose custody. If a young person withdraws consent, the conference is terminated. It can also be terminated on the application of a youth conference co-ordinator, if the court is satisfied it would serve no useful purpose.

Effectiveness

Limited research has been undertaken on the youth justice systems of Scotland and Northern Ireland. Scottish research has highlighted that the Scottish system has been very successful at taking most young people under the age of 16 out of the mainstream criminal justice system with no appar-ent adverse effects on levels of youth crime, which are proportionately lower than in England and Wales. It has found too that while participation of

young people and their families is often brief, participants consider the non-adversarial system fair and feel their views are listened to by Reporters and panel members. Despite feeling nervous, families spoke positively of the informal-ity and relative ease of communication in hearings (Hallett et al., 1998; Waterhouse et al., 2000). The same research found inconsistencies in Reporter decision-making however and that most young people aged between 16 and 18 were being dealt with by adult criminal courts. Audit Scotland's review (2002) confirmed a lack of investment in provision and specialist staffing, with over two thirds of resources being taken up by process costs rather than service provision for young people.

It is too early, at the time of writing, to comment on the impact of reforms of the Northern Ireland system being implemented from 2003. Northern Ireland has a tradition of relatively high levels of diversion and relatively low use of custody for young people compared with England and Wales. This, combined with promising re-search on restorative approaches from other jurisdictions (see Chapters 16 and 28), could give grounds for optimism of improved outcomes for young people in the future.

Conclusion

All UK youth justice systems are committed, in principle, to the prevention of youth crime. For most young people under 16 in Scotland there is a clear commitment to the best interests of the child as the paramount consideration, whereas in Northern Ireland, like England and Wales, this is only one consideration in decision-making. In this sense, the Scottish system can claim to be welfare-oriented in a way that the others are not. The Scottish system is also distinctive by dint of its separation of the court functions (adjudication and due process) from welfare disposals (hear-ings). Northern Ireland, like England and Wales, operates a modified criminal justice system in which welfare consideration moderate the rela-tionship between crime and punishment.

Scotland's attempt to maintain an integrated approach for young people who offend and those in need of care and protection is equally distinc-tive and attempts to reflect the body of evidence that young people who offend often suffer from multiple difficulties in the areas of parenting and schooling and experience other social disadvantages, and that such young people are very often victims of crime as well as offenders. In principle, the Scottish system operates on the basis of shared responsibility while youth courts operate, primarily, on the basis of individual and, to some extent, family responsibility.

Political rhetoric in Scotland has recently become more punitive than in the past 30 years. For the first time, questions about personal responsibility, family responsibility and the hearing's inability to punish children and young people who offend have become a political issue, particularly in relation to persistent offending and anti-social behaviour. The Scottish Parliament is currently considering proposals to introduce anti-social behaviour orders, parenting orders, community reparation orders and electronic tagging for under 16s which, in the future, may change the characteristics of the Scottish system and result in a greater convergence within UK jurisdictions.

Recent developments across all UK jurisdictions suggest a certain convergence of responses to youth crime, although each retains its distinctive characteristics. Each jurisdiction now has a youth court, although its role in Scotland is still being piloted and it is not yet central to dealing with young people who offend. Restorative methods are now commonplace, promoting a problem-solving approach as, to varying degrees, is an emphasis on victims. Referral orders in England and Wales utilise a panel system with many features similar to those of the children's hearings in Scotland (see Chapter 16). Unlike

hearings, however referral orders are still firmly rooted in the criminal justice process and the thrust of the youth justice reforms in England and Wales has been to expand the remit of the youth justice system rather than seeking to divert young people from it (see Chapter 1).

Restorative justice is now the legal centrepiece in the youth justice process in Northern Ireland which, at the same time, aims to give weight to welfare considerations. Restorative conferencing has great diversionary potential, with its stress on voluntary participation. However, restorative approaches within welfare provision are still relatively underdeveloped.

Further reading

Kearney, B. (2000) *Children's Hearings and the Sheriff Court.* 2nd edn. Edinburgh: Butterworth

Lindsay, T. and Chapman, T. (2001) Youth Justice in Northern Ireland. in Roche, J. and Vernon, S. *Youth Justice: Topic 10 K201 Working with Young People.* Milton Keynes: The Open University

Northern Ireland Office (2000) *Review of the Criminal Justice System in Northern Ireland.* Belfast: Northern Ireland Office

Lockyer, A. and Stone, F. (1998) *Juvenile Justice in Scotland: Twenty Five Years of the Welfare Approach.* Edinburgh: T&T Clark

Moore, G. and Whyte, B. (1998) *Social Work and Criminal Law in Scotland.* Edinburgh: Mercat Press

Whyte, B. (2003) Young and Persistent: Recent Developments in Youth Justice Policy and Practice in Scotland. *Youth Justice.* 3: 2, 74–85

4 The Role of Central Government and the Youth Justice Board

Rob Allen

Key points

1. The Home Office has lead responsibility for youth justice and sponsors the Youth Justice Board (YJB). The DfES Children's Ministry and a variety of other departments also have important responsibilities in this area.

2. The YJB has been set up to provide focus and leadership, to monitor the youth justice system and to raise standards. It has established a performance monitoring network and provides a variety of tools for practitioners.

3. The YJB also purchases and commissions places in the secure estate for under 18s who are detained on remand or under sentence.

4. The Home Office responsibility reflects the principal statutory aim of preventing offending.

5. The political nature of youth crime means the very highest levels of government can be involved in particular issues. Prime Ministerial interest in street crime in 2002, for example, led to substantial pressure to deliver results. Not all of these were consistent with the longer term policy direction set by government.

Introduction

Youth justice is the responsibility of a wide variety of government departments. Since 1997 the Home Office has been in the lead, with the Youth Justice Board for England and Wales (YJB) providing focus, leadership and a bridge with the field. Government is responsible to parliament for legislation and resourcing the system while the YJB's role is to monitor and raise standards of practice. It has introduced a framework for performance management, developed practice tools such as the assessment profile ASSET and published a series of guides to effective practice. As well as setting targets for youth offending teams (YOTs) and the secure estate, the YJB has introduced a programme of quality assurance for those working within the system. In addition to the practical tasks of administering the youth justice system, government and the YJB are responsible for establishing the philosophical and policy direction and handling day to day media and political pressures in what is perceived as an increasingly significant area for the electorate.

Departmental responsibilities

When the Prime Minister embarked on a national initiative to tackle street crime in the spring of 2002, relevant government ministers and heads of agencies were summoned to monthly meetings in the Downing Street briefing room normally used for planning responses to national emergencies. The result was that nine members of the Cabinet found themselves discussing what should be done about teenage (and adult) street robbers. The reason is that preventing youth crime and dealing with young offenders through the youth justice system in England and Wales involves the work of a whole host of agencies and organisations whose work is the responsibility of almost half the departments of state.

While youth justice stands at the interface of the systems of criminal justice and child welfare, it is the Home Office which currently takes the policy lead in government. Since July 2003, the new Children's Minister Margaret Hodge, in the Department for Education and Skills (DfES), has been responsible for oversight of all children's and young people's policy across government in England. In an important change to the machinery of government, DfES has inherited a range of responsibilities previously held by the Department of Health (DoH). While it is too early to tell how the relationship between the two departments will work, some commentators fear that the reorganisation has the potential for a return to the confusion and lack of clarity which characterised youth justice prior to 1997. Perhaps significantly, proposals for further reform to youth justice were not contained in the Children's Green Paper *Every Child Matters* (DfES, 2003b). They appeared instead in a separate Home Office document *Youth Justice – the Next Steps*, suggesting that the Home Office may be unwilling to relinquish its lead role for the time being (Home Office, 2003i).

The operation of youth justice locally involves agencies and institutions that are the responsibility of several other departments. The Department for Constitutional Affairs (DCA) (which incorporated most of the responsibilities of the former Lord Chancellor's Department in July 2003), administers the justice system in England and Wales. While the decision-making of youth courts and crown courts are independent of the executive, the running of the court system, and the provision of legal aid fall to the DCA. So too does the appointment of judges and magistrates, although there are proposals for an independent judicial appointments commission. The crown prosecution service (CPS) is the responsibility of the Attorney General.

As for the agencies which make up youth offending teams (YOTs), the police and probation service are the responsibility of the Home Office (although a different minister is responsible for each). Local authority social services now fall under the Children's Minister in the DfES which, as we have noted, has assumed the responsibilities previously held by the DH in this area. The latter department continues to be responsible for the health representation in YOTs, as DfES is for education.

As for the facilities in which young people who offend can be locked up, the prison service is, at the time of writing, an executive agency whose Chief Executive is directly accountable to the Home Secretary. Following a review of the correctional services, it is planned that the prison service along with the probation service should, in due course, form a new National Offender Management Service (NOMS). Secure training centres are also a Home Office responsibility. Local authority secure children's homes, prior to July 2003 a matter for DH, are now the responsibility of the Children's Minister in DfES. DH remains responsible for the small number of secure places in the NHS and private sector hospitals.

The broader elements of youth crime prevention and rehabilitation bring in the Department for Work and Pensions, responsible for employment; and the Office of the Deputy Prime Minister which takes the lead on homelessness. Both jobs and housing are key to the prospects of young people leaving custody or under supervision in the community. Even the Department for Culture, Media and Sport (DCMS) with its responsibility for arts, sports and recreation has an important role in ensuring young people most at risk have access to the kind of constructive leisure pursuits which can help to keep them out of trouble.

To complete, and further complicate, the picture, while the justice system, police and prisons in Wales remain the responsibility of Westminster, culture, education, housing, local government, social services, sport and leisure are all devolved to the Welsh Assembly Government.

It is possible that youth justice may be further devolved in the future. The Welsh Affairs Committee of the House of Commons recommended in January 2004 that oversight of community-based measures for young people who offend be undertaken in Wales. At the time of writing the government has not responded. The report of the Richards Commission on the powers of the Welsh Assembly recommended, in March 2004, that legislative powers be given to the assembly. While it made no specific suggestions about transferring policy areas, there is likely to be debate about whether responsibility for criminal justice in general, and youth justice in particular, should be devolved or whether a consistent approach across England and Wales should be retained.

What does government do?

As the government department with lead responsibility for policy matters, the Home Office is accountable to parliament for most aspects of youth justice, proposing, drafting and processing new legislation through the House of Commons and the Lords, implementing new measures and negotiating with the Treasury – in the three yearly spending reviews – for the resources necessary to put them into practice. In recent years, to ensure 'value for money', government departments have been set aims or targets by the Treasury. These are linked to Public Service Agreements which specify what should be achieved over a set timescale.

Ensuring accountability

Like the Treasury, the Audit Commission and the National Audit Office, the government's spending watchdogs, also periodically review the youth justice system to ensure that it represents value for money. Independent oversight and accountability for the youth justice system are the responsibility of independent inspectorates for the police, CPS, social services and probation and prison services. There is a system of lay visitors to police stations. These are members of local communities who make unannounced visits to monitor the treatment of suspects held in detention. Every prison has an Independent Monitoring Board (formerly a Board of Visitors), comprising magistrates and local people who have unrestricted access to the establishment. There is also a prison and probation Ombudsman who deals with complaints from those directly affected by the work of those agencies.

The YJB, established by the Crime and Disorder Act 1998 (CDA), is a non departmental public body sponsored by the Home Office to monitor youth justice provision, providing a central oversight of local services.

The aims of the youth justice system

For youth justice, the key Home Office aims are:

- To reduce crime and the fear of crime, tackle youth crime and violent, sexual and drug related crime, anti-social behaviour and disorder, increasing safety in the home and public spaces.
- To ensure the effective delivery of justice, avoiding unnecessary delay.
- To deliver effective custodial and community sentences, to reduce re-offending and protect the public.

Ensuring that effective action is taken to meet these aims is now the job of the YJB.

The role of the Youth Justice Board

Established by the Labour government in 1998, the YJB has given a national focus to the youth justice system in Whitehall that was largely absent prior to 1997. The Board's functions, as defined in section 41 of the CDA, are:

- To monitor the operation of the youth justice system and the provision of youth justice services.
- To advise the Home Secretary on the operation of the system and the provision of services, how the principal aim of the system – preventing offending among children and young people – should be pursued and on the content of national standards.
- To monitor the extent to which the aim of preventing offending is being achieved and standards met.
- To obtain and publish information about the youth justice system.
- To identify and promote good practice.
- To make grants to local authorities.
- To commission research.

In addition, since 2000, the YJB has been responsible for the commissioning and purchasing of secure places for children under the age of 18, a function which consumes the lion's share of the Board's budget. Annual targets are set by Home Office ministers and the Board is required to report each year to parliament.

The YJB comprises a Chair and up to 12 members with extensive, recent, experience of the youth justice system. Members are appointed by the Home Secretary for up to five years. Although one step removed from government, in carrying out its functions, the Board must comply with directions and guidance from the Home Secretary. In 2003, it had a staff of about 150 and a budget of £380 million. It meets ten times a year and has established a number of committees which oversee the main areas of its work; service delivery, practice and performance, prevention, communications and human resources.

Since 1998, the YJB has produced several tools for use by practitioners in the field. The most important of these is ASSET, an assessment profile for measuring the needs of young people who offend and the risks they pose (see Chapter 19). More recently, it has started to publish guides to effective practice covering the most important areas of work and, from 2003, has published an annual statistical bulletin on the operation of the youth justice system.

The review of the correctional services undertaken by businessman Patrick Carter, which recommended far reaching changes to arrangements for adult offenders concluded that the 'success of the Youth Justice Board means that it should remain an independent body with responsibility to advise the Home Secretary' (Carter, 2003).

Key issues
Philosophy and policy

The fact that the Home Office exercises lead responsibility for youth justice reflects the prevailing philosophical approach towards young people who offend. During the 1960s and 1970s, the dominant view was that juvenile delinquency was best treated by meeting the welfare needs of children and their families. With the enactment of the welfare oriented Children and Young Persons Act 1969, lead responsibility moved from the Home Office, which had contained a Children's Department, to the Department of Health and Social Security (DHSS) (see Chapter 1). The Act provided for an effective raising of the age of criminal responsibility and the use of care rather than criminal proceedings for serious and persistent offenders. The Conservative government which came to power in 1970 chose not to implement the more radical aspects of the legislation however. During the 1970s and 1980s, the DHSS (and after its division into two departments, in 1988, the DH) shared responsibility with the Home Office for policy development.

For the most part, the departments worked closely together and differences in emphasis did not come to the fore. During the 1980s both departments favoured a policy of diversion from crime, prosecution and custody. The marked reductions in the use of custodial sentences that characterised this period, had their genesis both in the Home Office – which introduced important legislative changes and encouraged diversion in a series of circulars to police on cautioning – and in the DHSS which established a £15 million initiative to stimulate intensive programmes of 'intermediate treatment'.

However, in the early 1990s, the tensions between this child-centred philosophy and the 'tougher' policies emerging from government in the wake of the murder of James Bulger, began to show. The Criminal Justice Act 1991, built upon the diversionary developments of the 1980s but the tide quickly turned. Within six months of the abolition of detention centre orders for 14 year old boys, Conservative Home Secretary, Kenneth Clarke, announced a new custodial sentence (the secure training order) for children as young as 12. There was disagreement in Whitehall about whether secure training centres should fall under the aegis of the Home Office or become part of local authority secure provision, overseen by the DH. In the event, the Home Office view prevailed in the face of considerable resistance, including from the Labour opposition.

But the struggle between the DH's welfarist approach and the justice model – favoured by the Home Office – rumbled on, causing the authors of the Audit Commission report on youth justice, *Misspent Youth* (1996) to observe that 'these different approaches need to be reconciled if agencies are to work together and fulfil their different responsibilities'.

The incoming Labour government of 1997 attempted to resolve the justice/welfare dispute pragmatically by creating a statutory principal aim for the youth justice system of the prevention of offending by young people. To this end, Jack Straw, the first post-1997 Labour Home Secretary and his special adviser Norman (later Lord) Warner, first chair of the YJB, strove to improve both the infrastructure and the efficiency of the relevant services (Warner, 2003). The government had pledged to halve the time from arrest to sentence for 'persistent young offenders'. The Home Office, and subsequently the YJB, took the lead in ensuring that this pledge was met, but the efforts involved not only officials in the other relevant criminal justice departments but ministers themselves. This is symptomatic of the fact that performance management has become a key government function in recent years.

Monitoring and performance management

The emphasis across government on the effective delivery of public services means that one of the key roles for the YJB is the monitoring of both processes and outcomes in youth justice. The Board inherited what its first chair was fond of calling a 'data free zone'. One of the immediate tasks has been to establish systems for routine collection of information about the performance of the youth justice system, which enables judgments to be made about current effectiveness and future target setting.

The YJB has set a total of 21 targets for YOTs and secure establishments for 2004–5. They comprise two high-level targets and 19 which are more specific. The former are to achieve a reduction in re-offending rates of 5% in 2005 and to increase the proportion of children in secure establishments who feel safe by 5%. The specific targets for YOTs are to:

- Ensure that all areas have effective arrangements for targeting children most at risk of offending.
- Ensure that 80% of final warnings are supported by interventions.
- Reduce the use of detention for remands to 30% of remand episodes and for sentences to 6% of all sentencing outcomes.
- Offer 75% of victims referred to YOTs a restorative process and ensure that 75% of those participating are satisfied.
- Ensure the parents of 10% of young people with a community-based sentence receive a parenting intervention and 75% of participating parents are satisfied.
- Ensure that the ASSET assessment tool is used for all young people subject to community and custodial disposals.
- Ensure that 90% of pre-sentence reports for courts are submitted within timescales required by national standards.
- Ensure that all initial training plans for young people subject to detention and training orders are drawn up within timescales required by national standards.
- Ensure that 90% of young people supervised by YOTs are in suitable full-time education, training or employment.
- Ensure that all young people subject to community interventions or released from detention have satisfactory accommodation to go to.
- Ensure all young people with acute mental health difficulties are referred for specialist psychiatric assessment within five working days.
- Ensure all young people are screened for substance misuse and referred onwards as appropriate.

The specific secure estate targets concern time spent out of room, improvements in literacy and numeracy, reception assessment, the transfer of information from YOTs, the development of training plans and access to an independent advocacy service.

Data collection is not regarded as a paper exercise but as a precursor to taking action where performance is failing. The YJB employs a monitor in each of the government regions in England and in Wales and each Board member has responsibility for a particular area. The Board has also made much use of management consultancy to assist local agencies to improve performance. Where poor performance is not improved through such assistance, an escalating range of sanctions can be imposed. These include the abatement of grant to underperforming YOTs and ultimately the imposition of special measures, in which managers from the YJB take over certain responsibilities until problems are resolved.

The YJB is responsible for contract monitoring; assessing the extent to which contracted-out parts of the youth justice system are complying with contractual requirements. This is particularly important in respect of the commissioning and purchasing places for under 18s who are locked-up in prison department establishments or other forms of secure accommodation. The full time monitor in each of the establishments, oversees service level agreements with the prison service which provides the bulk of such places and pays particular attention to whether private sector detention facilities (of which there are currently four in England and Wales) are complying with the terms of their contracts.

Politics

Despite a pragmatic philosophy and a framework of performance management, government has had to cope with the fact that youth crime is a political 'hot potato'. Although there is a good deal of cross-party political support for the direction of the youth justice reforms, in an era of media-sensitive politics, pressures from the media outlets can cause difficulty for government. One example is the 'street-crime initiative' of 2002, set up to address 'what the media was portraying as a situation out of control' (HMIC et al., 2003). The details of the measures which were taken are beyond the scope of this chapter but two points are relevant to the role of central government.

First, in the words of the inspectorates who assessed the impact of the initiative:

> . . . *the personal leadership of the Prime Minister in strong support of the Home Secretary gave the initiative a momentum that was at times breathtaking and placed a huge burden of expectation onto those responsible for delivery* . . .
>
> (HMIC et al., 2003)

Since crime is currently a high-profile political issue, it receives a lot of high-level political interest, usually pursued via the various strategy and delivery units which make up the PM's office.

Second, there is a need to be seen to respond immediately to issues and events can impact on the overall direction of youth justice policy. The street crime initiative led the Home Secretary to implement legislative changes toughening up the remand arrangements for young people much earlier than planned. And the overall thrust of the initiative – cracking down on street robbery – with the consequent and predictable impact on court decision making, clashed with the targets set by the Board to reduce the use of custody at the remand and sentencing stages.

More recently, a similar tension has arisen in respect of government policy on anti social behaviour. The *Together* strategy launched in October 2003 urges the police and local authorities to make greater use of the range of powers available for cracking down on young people and adults who cause problems in local communities. As well as creating expectations that are hard to fulfil, 'the risk in using *Together* tactics to mobilise 'us' against 'them' is that enforcement is prioritised at the expense of prevention' (Hough and Jacobson, 2004) while prevention remains the statutory principal aim of the youth justice system.

Conclusion

The reports published by the Audit Commission and the National Audit Office in January 2004 found considerable improvements in youth justice and concluded that the YJB had succeeded in providing a clear national framework for the operation of the system. The review of correctional services undertaken during 2003 by Patrick Carter recommended that the existing arrangements remain in place. The audit reports do however contain a large number of detailed recommendations, some of which are directed at central government and the YJB. They express particular concern about the shortcomings of the education system in dealing with young people who offend at different stages of the criminal justice process.

The creation of the children's minister in the DfES could lead to an increased priority being attached to meeting the educational needs of delinquent young people. Whatever the shape of local services, and whether or not YOTs become incorporated into the new Children's Trusts, central government responsibility is likely to remain in the Home Office. While there may be ideological arguments for a more child focused system of youth justice, the pragmatic approach adopted since 1997 has led to progress in the prevention of youth crime and improvements both in the operation of the youth justice and the community-based supervision of young people who offend. The Home Office and Youth Justice Board have succeeded in attracting Treasury resources into a previously neglected area, and on the whole have sought to deploy these not in expensive and ineffective custodial places but in strengthening the infrastructure of community-based services. Whether or not this trend will continue depends in large part on the politics of youth crime and the ability of future governments to withstand periodic demands to take a tougher line.

Further reading

Audit Commission (2004) *Youth Justice 2004: A Review of the Reformed Youth Justice System*. London: Audit Commission

Home Office (1997a) *New National and Local Focus on Youth Crime*. London: Home Office

Youth Justice Board (1999–2003) *Annual Reports*. London: Youth Justice Board

5 Youth Justice at the Local Level

Roy Tomlinson

Key points

1. Youth offending teams (YOTs) are multi-agency bodies, brought into being by the Crime and Disorder Act 1998, with the primary aim of preventing offending by children and young people.

2. Crime and Disorder Reduction Partnerships (CDRPs) have been established in each area of the country to develop local community safety strategies.

3. The development of YOTs and CDRPs marks a recognition by government that 'tackling youth crime' could not be left to the police alone, and should become 'everyone's business'.

4. The long-standing debate within youth justice between the 'justice' and 'welfare' models remains a central problem, with recent government policy adopting a punitive, interventionist, approach which has to some extent sidelined the principle that the welfare of the child should be the paramount consideration.

5. While the YOTs are intended to exercise a brokerage function, coordinating services of a range of agencies for young people who offend, in practice their location as a specialist criminal justice provision, largely divorced from wider services for children, suggests that they have a limited potential for integrating excluded young people back into mainstream services.

Introduction

The Crime and Disorder Act 1998 (CDA) placed new duties upon local authorities to provide youth justice services and, in particular, to establish youth offending teams (YOTs). Police authorities, probation areas, and health services were required to co-operate in the staffing and resourcing of these services. The Act established, for the first time, that the principle aim of the youth justice system would be to 'prevent offending by children and young people'. In fulfilling this duty the partner agencies have to produce an annual plan setting out how youth justice services will be delivered and how YOTs will operate. The functions to be discharged by the YOTs are:

- The provision of an appropriate adult service (see Chapter 11).
- Assessment and the provision of intervention 'packages' linked to final warnings (see Chapter 12).
- Support for bail and remand including the provision of residential remand services (see Chapter 14).

- The provision of pre-sentence and other reports to criminal courts (see Chapter 18).
- The provision of responsible officers to supervise court orders imposed on young people who offend (see Chapter 21).
- The post release supervision of custodial orders (see Chapter 25).
- To discharge these responsibilities each YOT must have within it at least one, social worker, probation officer, police officer, person nominated by a health authority and person nominated by the local authority's chief education officer.

The 1998 Act also places a statutory requirement upon 'responsible authorities', local authorities and the police, to establish Crime and Disorder Reduction Partnerships (CRDPs). These partnerships are charged with producing three-year plans to reduce crime and disorder in their areas (the area being defined as that covered by a Unitary or District Council in two tier local authorities). The strategy has to be based on an analysis of the levels and patterns of crime and disorder, and the views of local communities on the issues which concern them.

The intellectual rationale of the new youth justice

The creation of YOTs was generally welcomed by those working within the youth justice system because prior to the CDA, there was little national coherence in the way young people who offend were dealt with by statutory agencies. In November 1997, the New Labour government articulated its critique of the existing system in the white paper *No More Excuses: A New Approach to Tackling Youth Crime in England and Wales* (Home Office, 1997b). The white paper drew extensively upon the findings of the Audit Commission report *Misspent Youth,* (1996) published a year earlier. The report identified the main areas of concern as:

- The crime committed by young people and its impact upon the quality of life in high crime neighbourhoods. 40% of youth crime was committed in 10% of areas.
- The youth justice system was costing £1 billion per year, or £2,500 for each young person sentenced, most of which was spent on processing repeat offenders through the system, leaving little for interventions once a young person was convicted or for preventive work with those on the threshold of crime.
- Delay and inefficiency were rife. On average, it was taking four months from arrest to sentencing and half the proceedings against young people were discontinued, dismissed or ended in a discharge.
- For many young people who offended, community supervision was minimal and there was no agreement about the form such supervision should take.
- Responses to young people who offend were fragmented and there was a need for all agencies to work together and for all services concerned with children and young people to share information and target neighbourhoods at greatest risk.

The authors opined that 'prevention was better than cure' and that offending by young people at greatest risk could be reduced if resources were targeted on offence-focused programmes, intervention with parents, early intervention in educa-

tion, support for teachers dealing with difficult pupils and the development of positive leisure activities. They suggested that local authorities should be given lead responsibility in developing multi-agency work, with central government support, and that resources freed from court processes could fund local services and that local agencies should contribute to the monitoring and evaluation of these developments.

No More Excuses heralded a major policy shift in youth justice by creating a coherent multi-agency strategy for dealing with youth crime. To oversee these developments, central government established the Youth Justice Board for England and Wales (YJB), a 'non-governmental body' with advisory functions to the Secretary of State (see Chapter 4). The YJB distributed funding, specified national standards and administrative procedures for youth justice and developed a national framework for monitoring and evaluating outcomes.

Establishing the YOTs

The Home Office, the Department for Education and Employment, the Department of Health and the Welsh Office (1998) issued joint guidance on the establishment of YOTs in December 1998, which identified a number of key issues which would need to be addressed.

The establishment of steering groups

Locating leadership of steering groups with chief executives of local authorities underscored the fact that the new youth justice service was a multi-agency responsibility. Prior to the CDA, responsibility for young people who offend had been split between social services and probation for the older age range, in many areas 16 plus. There were some ad hoc joint social services and probation teams but the field was characterised by separation of services. The joint guidance required the agencies that were to second staff to YOTs to be represented on the steering group, thus emphasising the multi-agency responsibility government saw as essential to deliver its commitment to reduce youth crime.

The role and status of YOT managers

Each YOT was required to appoint a manager of the new service who would be accountable to the multi-agency steering group for the creation of the youth justice plan and the subsequent delivery of effective youth justice services. The ways in which YOT managers were themselves to be managed and supported were not specified, but there were clear indications that chief executives should ensure this function was effectively carried out.

The size of YOTs

The geographical extent of the YOT was largely determined by the fact that local authorities with social services and education functions were required to provide them. But the guidance also indicated the need to take account of local demography and proposed that an optimum population size for YOT areas would be 200,000 – 300,000. However, this created a difficulty for many new unitary authorities, which served considerably smaller populations. Local authorities in this situation were encouraged to merge to achieve a sufficient size. In fact, few have taken this option which is probably attributable to a reluctance on the part of senior local government officers and elected members to enter such shared arrangements.

The funding of YOTs

The guidance suggested that the local youth justice plan should describe the volume and nature of the demand for youth justice services at a local level, and that the constituent members of the steering group should agree the resources necessary to respond to this demand. However, there was little clarity about how partners should share the overall costs of resourcing the service, nor what level of staffing would be required. In reality, most YOTs were established by the secondment of existing staff from social services and probation and, in many cases, police were introduced to the teams by the secondment of officers previously engaged in schools liaison or youth affairs. Education and health services have found it much harder to identify the relevant professional personnel and, in practice, a range of professionals drawn from education welfare, educational psychology, teaching, health visiting, community psychiatric nursing have been seconded into the YOTS (Pitcher et al., 2004).

Establishing crime and disorder reduction partnerships

At the same time that the government issued the joint guidance on YOTs, it also issued guidance on Statutory Crime and Disorder Partnerships (CDRPs) (Home Office, 1998c). The guidance once again gave lead responsibility to local authority chief executives and also emphasised the need for multi-agency initiatives which involved the local community in its development. The guidance did not specify a particular organisational structure or a set of procedures; this was left to local discretion. However, it did indicate that effective management of CDRPs required:

- The development of a shared strategy, based upon an assessment of local crime patterns and the crime and disorder-related concerns of local people, which drew upon the expertise and knowledge of all local government departments, local agencies and organisations.
- The specification of a manageable geographic focus for the operationalisation of the strategy, to ensure local and regional impact.
- The involvement of senior personnel from each of the participating agencies and organisations, with the power to make decisions and commit resources, as well as systematic engagement with members of local communities, including 'hard to reach', victimisation-prone, groups.
- The establishment of effective decision making and forms of accountability.

Youth crime, drugs and drug related crime were identified as major issues to be tackled by CDRPs. While YOTs were to play an important role in community safety, the effective processing of adjudicated offenders was identified as only one aspect of the work of addressing youth and drug related crime. Equal stress was placed on the need to deal with the underlying causes of youth crime and drug misuse, and to develop opportunities for young people to divert them from involvement in offending. There was also an emphasis on the need to engage young people in crime reduction strategies since, not only are they members of the community whose voice is all too often unheard, they are also a group which is particularly vulnerable to criminal victimisation (see Chapter 38).

In brief, this twin track approach to crime and disorder reduction at a local level, involves on the one hand the YOTs, charged with developing efficient and effective methods for dealing with adjudicated young offenders and CDRPs, on the other, charged with the prevention of crime and disorder by widening opportunities for young people to resist crime and reducing the risk factors associated with it.

Balancing the act

The range of tasks assigned to the YOTs and the strategic planning required of the CDRPs created new opportunities, but also placed significant demands upon local authorities and the multi-agency structures brought into being in the wake of the CDA. Five years on, we are witnessing both positive and negative outcomes. On the plus side, recorded youth crime is showing a sustained downward trajectory. However, this trend origin pre-dated the youth justice reforms and the extent to which the new arrangements have contributed to its continuation is unclear (see Chapter 2). There is too, undeniable evidence of the relevant agencies sharing responsibility for dealing with youth crime, outside the traditional boundaries.

However, certain tensions, inherent in the legislation and in the establishment of a discrete youth justice service, have been exacerbated by the subsequent development of YOTs and CDRPs. These tensions concern whether:

- We should be responding to children and young people who break the law as 'children in need' first and foremost or 'young offenders'.
- We should be dealing with these young people in specialist, and therefore potentially stigmatising, services for 'young offenders' or integrating them into mainstream provision.
- Services should be developed in accordance with national prescription or local discretion.

Children and young people who break the law or 'young offenders'

The long-standing debate in youth justice concerning whether we should be responsive to the 'needs' or the 'deeds' of young people who offend, the 'welfare versus justice debate' has not been resolved by the twin track approach of the CDA.

The legislation emphasised a 'justice' approach founded in a confrontation with offending behav-

iour and reparation to victims, robust, targeted, early intervention, increased levels of supervision and surveillance with a resulting increased use of security and custody. In this approach it is the offending behaviour rather than the needs of the young person which constitutes the primary focus for intervention.

Welfarist approaches, by contrast, emphasise the social, cultural, intellectual and psychological needs underlying offending by children and young people and suggest that if their welfare needs are met, subsequent offending and other forms of reactive behaviour will be minimised. Intervention focuses upon individual, group and family treatment and the achievement of better life chances by addressing poverty and social deprivation. This is the approach taken in many subsequent government initiatives such as Sure Start, The Children's Fund, Connexions and Neighbourhood Renewal, each of which is explicitly concerned with reducing youth crime.

Thus government offers us two contrasting images of young people who break the law and two quite distinct sets of responses to them. The creation of area-based Criminal Justice Boards has added fuel to this fire as they assume responsibility for monitoring and evaluating youth justice services and all other local initiatives designed to reduce youth crime. Alongside this, the creation of Children and Young People's Strategic Partnerships and Children's Trusts – also informed by an essentially 'welfarist' ethos – increases the potential for confusion about how we might best prevent offending by, and promote the welfare of, the socially disadvantaged children and young people who constitute the lion's share of the youngsters who become involved in the youth justice system.

Mainstream or specialist provision for young people who offend

Evidence from YOT evaluations and the workings of steering groups indicates that the aim of opening up mainstream services to children and young people in trouble in order to address the risk factors associated with youth offending more effectively, and in a less stigmatising way, is still a long way from being achieved (Audit Commission, 2004). The rise in school exclusions, continued delays in accessing Child and Adolescent

Mental Health services and drug treatment, and the apparently intractable problems of poor residential provision for young people unable to live with their families, are all undermining the goal of a 'joined-up' youth justice service.

Indeed the establishment of YOTs as 'offending specialists' located outside of mainstream services may have the unintended consequence of making it more difficult to reintegrate socially excluded young people back into mainstream provision.

Despite a range of mainstream services being represented on YOT steering groups, the teams' impact upon those partner agencies remains patchy. Each is still driven by targets and performance indicators which have the effect of sidelining the needs and problems of young people in trouble. Educational and health targets in particular, because they are geared primarily to improved academic attainment and reduced waiting times, tend to be unresponsive to the needs of young people who offend and other marginalised groups.

Attempts to overcome this disjunction are resulting in a move by an increasing number of YOT management groups to encompass youth justice services within strategic plans for all children and young people's services. The innovation of children and young people's strategic partnerships, children's trusts and joint age-focused chief officer groups, exemplify this attempt to re-integrate youth justice into the planning of mainstream services. The required development of Information Sharing and Assessment (ISA) systems which are intended to cover all children and young people at risk offers further opportunity for re-integration of young people who offend into the mainstream.

National prescription and local discretion

The advent of the CDA created tensions between central and local government. While, on the one hand, it appeared to encourage local autonomy, in the cases of YOTs and CDRPs, it also subjected local authorities to an unprecedented level of central government control.

As we have noted, the YJB was established to provide national direction and monitoring of YOTs and in so doing has created a new quasi-governmental bureaucracy. Its influence

flows not only from its role in setting national standards and auditing the delivery of services, but also from the fact that it provides up to 25% of a YOT's budget (Youth Justice Board, 2003o). This funding arrangement provides a platform from which the Board can influence and direct the focus of YOT activity. CDRPs have been similarly, if somewhat less directly, subjected to central government control via the establishment of regionally-based crime reduction directors and their teams. These new entities not only provide the major source of funding for CDRPs, they are also assuming increasing responsibility for monitoring and evaluating their functioning.

These tensions are more complex within areas of the country where two-tier local government still exists. In such areas three, and sometimes four, levels of strategic planning have developed:

- National targets (best value performance).
- Regional direction of national objectives (control over large elements of funding).
- County level strategies and planning for core services (education, social services).
- Local district identification and response to community need.

This complexity in the planning process is generating tensions and schisms between the different layers. Partners at the local level are often profoundly confused about where ultimate responsibility lies; in particular whether they are responsible to national prescription or local community need.

Conclusion

The CDA reflected the New Labour government's commitment to increased partnership working in the delivery of public services. Although this has been welcomed by most commentators and many practitioners, it has also generated complex working arrangements, characterised by fragmented funding regimes, lack of clarity over responsibility for delivery and competition between targets.

The tensions within planning for youth offending services are similar to those which were evident before the implementation of the Act. To some extent these have become heightened and new tensions, particularly over the central versus local interface, have been heightened. Whilst headline youth crime figures have shown steady reductions since the Act was introduced, the underlying causes of crime remain largely untouched.

Further reading

Audit Commission (1996) *Misspent Youth: Young People and Crime*. London: Audit Commission

Audit Commission (2004) *Youth Justice 2004: A Review of the Reformed Youth Justice System*. London: Audit Commission

Home Office (1997b) *No More Excuses: A New Approach to Tackling Youth Crime in England and Wales*. Cm 3809. London: Home Office

Home Office (1998c) *Guidance on Statutory Crime and Disorder Partnerships: Crime and Disorder Act 1998*. London: Home Office

Home Office, DfEE, DoH and Welsh Office (1998) *Inter-Departmental Circular on Establishing a Youth Offending Team*. London: Home Office

6 The Legal Framework for Youth Justice and its Administration

Sue Bandalli

Key points

1. A new system for the administration of youth justice was established in the Crime and Disorder Act 1998.

2. Local authorities now have a duty to provide youth justice services, including the establishment of a multi-agency youth offending team.

3. The new statutory aim of the youth justice system is to prevent offending by children and young people.

4. The substantive criminal law applies to children over 10 years old in the same way as to adults.

5. The welfare of the child or young person is just one issue amongst many taken into account in decision making in the youth justice system. The United Nations Committee on the Rights of the Child noted with serious concern that the situation of children in conflict with the law in England and Wales has worsened since 1994.

Introduction

All European countries have similar problems concerning 'troubled and troublesome' children: the way each country perceives and responds to the problem depends on its own political, social and legal circumstances. In England and Wales the response has been to reorganise and expand the jurisdiction of the youth justice system. The situation is becoming increasingly complex in legal terms as the numerous statutes of the 1990s push towards further criminalisation amid concerns about the effect of this on the concept of childhood (Fionda, 2001) and international criticism from the United Nations Committee on the Rights of the Child (UN, 2002; see Chapter 7).

A new system

The administration of criminal justice has always been a hot political issue, and particularly so with regard to young people in the last decade. The idea that most young people grow out of offending behaviour and should be kept away from the negative effects of the criminal justice system has been supplanted by a governmental rhetoric and a strategy which aims to 'nip offending in the bud' and direct intervention into the child's life at the earliest possible stage. The combined effect of the Crime and Disorder Act 1998 (CDA) and the

Youth Justice and Criminal Evidence Act 1999 – with some of the provisions now consolidated in the Powers of Criminal Courts (Sentencing) Act 2000 – has been to create a new structure and a new ethos for youth justice in England and Wales.

The administration of youth justice was changed fundamentally by the CDA, a statute designed to address problems identified in a number of Labour Party and government reviews between 1996 and 1998. The reform strategy outlined in *No More Excuses – A New Approach to Tackling Youth Crime in England and Wales* (Home Office, 1997b), and the youth justice system introduced in response to it in the CDA, aims to provide:

- A clear strategy to prevent offending and re-offending (see Box below).
- That young people who offend, and their parents, face up to their offending behaviour and take responsibility for it.
- Earlier, more effective, intervention when young people first offend.
- Faster, more efficient, procedures from arrest to sentence.
- A partnership between all youth justice agencies to deliver a better, faster system.

Under the CDA each local authority has a duty to:

- Develop youth justice plans for the area.

- Provide and coordinate youth justice services.
- Create crime and disorder reduction strategies in conjunction with the police.
- Establish a youth offending team (YOT).

The Youth Justice Board was established to provide overall direction, support, monitoring and advice to YOTs to manage funds and to advise and report to the government (see Chapter 4).

A statutory aim

The Crime and Disorder Act 1998, section 37, establishes for the first time that the principal aim of the youth justice system is to prevent offending by children and young persons and states that it is the duty of all those working within it to have regard to that aim.

The delivery of youth justice services

The local authority in co-operation with the police, probation and the health authority are legally charged with providing youth justice services which are delivered locally by the YOT (see Chapter 5). Each team has to include a police officer, a social worker, a probation officer, and a representative from the health authority and the education department. The duty of the YOT is to carry out the functions assigned to it under the youth justice plan formulated by each local authority and to coordinate the provision of youth justice services in the area (see Chapter 17).

Those services are defined in section 38(4), and include the provision for children and young people of:

- Appropriate adults to safeguard their interests when detained and questioned by the police (see Chapter 11).
- Assessment and rehabilitation programmes for those referred after being warned by the police (see Chapter 12).
- Support for those remanded in custody or bailed pending trial or sentence (see Chapter 14).
- Placement in local authority accommodation when remanded or committed to the care of the local authority.

- Court reports in criminal proceedings (see Chapter 18).
- Responsible officers for the supervision of court orders, such as parenting orders and child safety orders.
- Supervision of those sentenced to supervision/ community punishment/community rehabilitation orders (see Chapter 21).
- Supervision of those sentenced to detention and training orders including post-release supervision (see Chapter 25).

Youth justice services are the organised state response to offending behaviour by children and young persons and, as such, are dependent on the workings of the criminal law and the criminal justice system by which children and young people are charged, prosecuted, convicted and sentenced. In criminal law terms, this is fundamentally the same as for adults but there are some significant procedural and organisational differences aimed at the protection of the young, particularly with regard to disposals.

Some key terms
Youth, children and young persons

The renaming of juvenile courts as youth courts and the inclusion of 17 year olds within their jurisdiction, in the Criminal Justice Act 1991, led to the use of the word 'youth' to denote anybody aged between 10 and 17 years involved with the criminal justice system. The use of the word 'youth' also directs attention to the upper end of this age range, in acknowledgement of the fact that the peak age of offending is 19 for boys and 15 for girls (Home Office, 2003a). Much of the focus of the new youth justice system however seems to have shifted to the lower age range and, in practice, few people, in ordinary discourse, would describe 10 to 13 year olds as 'youths'.

The criminal justice system has previously defined 'children' as those under the age of 14 and 'young persons' as those aged 14 but below 18 (Children and Young Persons Acts 1933, 1963 and 1969). Moreover, in the Children Act 1989 and the United Nations Convention on the Rights of the Child (1989), a child is defined as a person under 18.

Criminal responsibility

The youth justice system is premised on the criminal law and, hence, on the idea of criminal responsibility. The criminal law applies in the same way to children over 10 years of age, the age of criminal responsibility, as it does to adults. To be convicted of a crime three conditions must apply. There must be an actus reus (a prohibited act or omission), mens rea (the intention to commit the offence with which one is charged), and the absence of a defence. Since section 34 of the CDA abolished the presumption of doli incapax (which placed the burden on the prosecution to prove, in cases of children aged between 10 and 14 years, that they knew what they were doing was seriously wrong as distinct from merely naughty (C (A Minor) v DPP [1996] 1 AC 1; Stokes, 2000)), there is no longer a special status afforded to childhood.

Criminal responsibility

Children over 10 years old are criminally responsible in the same way as adults.

Civil or criminal proceedings

After the establishment of the juvenile court by the Children Act 1908, children accused of criminal offences were dealt with in the same court as children in need of care and protection and sometimes received the same disposals, particularly those which became known as Care Orders. Since the Children Act 1989, the unified judicial system for dealing with children and young people has been divided into civil and criminal jurisdictions. Family matters and proceedings concerning the protection of children are heard in the family proceedings court, a court of civil jurisdiction, whereas children and young people charged with criminal offences are dealt with separately in the youth court or the adult crown court, and the disposals available in civil and criminal jurisdictions are now completely different.

The role of the family proceedings court is inquisitorial and proceedings take the form of an enquiry rather than a trial. The rules of evidence in the family proceedings court arc looser and allow hearsay evidence which is the reporting of what a witness was told, as distinct from what they actually witnessed. Unlike criminal proceedings where the court may only convict if the case is 'proved beyond reasonable doubt', in the family proceedings court outcomes are decided on 'the balance of probabilities'. Whereas in criminal proceedings the object is to establish guilt or innocence, in the family proceedings court the object is to identify a course of action which will be in the best interests of the child since, under the Children Act 1989, the child's welfare is the court's paramount consideration.

In criminal proceedings, the process is adversarial which means that the prosecution case against the accused is tested in court. There are complicated rules of evidence concerning what can and cannot be said or submitted in writing to achieve the objective of proving beyond reasonable doubt, on the basis of the admissible evidence, that the accused committed the actus reus with mens rea and without a valid defence. However, the Children and Young Persons Act 1933 requires that the youth court should also have regard to the welfare of the child (see Chapter 8).

The result is that unlike the Children Act 1989, current youth justice legislation does not prioritise the child's welfare, but balances it against other considerations such as public protection, punishment and the prevention of offending (see Box below). Of course, for adult defendants, welfare is not a consideration at all. As a result, the English youth justice system finds itself at odds with the United Nations Convention on the Rights of the Child (1989).

The relevance of welfare

The Children and Young Persons Act 1933 section 44 states that every court 'should have regard to the welfare of any child who appears before it'.

The Children Act 1989 section 1(1) provides that when a court determines any question with respect to the upbringing of a child 'the child's welfare shall be the court's paramount consideration.' This does not include criminal proceedings but the Children Act section 17 places a general duty on every local authority to safeguard and promote the welfare of children in need and to take reasonable steps to reduce the need to take criminal proceedings against children and to encourage children in their area not to commit criminal offences. Many children who offend would come within the definition of 'children in need'.

The United Nations Convention on the Rights of the Child (1989) Article 3.1 provides that 'in all actions concerning children, whether undertaken by public or private social welfare institutions, courts of law, administrative authorities or legislative bodies, the best interests of the child shall be a primary consideration.'

The criminal justice system in action

In the following brief outline, the criminal justice process is followed from initial contact with the police in the street to appearance in the court room and some of the provisions which are particular to children are indicated. Youth justice services may have a role at each stage.

Contact with the police
Stop, search and arrest

The legal provisions regulating stop and search and arrest are basically the same as for adults with a few modifications under the provisions of the Police and Criminal Evidence Act (1984) and the accompanying Codes of Practice (Home Office, 2003d). Young people of 17 years of age are treated as adults and these modifications do not apply to them.

There is no longer any specific provision in the notes of guidance to the Code of Practice for the Exercise by Police Officers of Statutory Powers of Stop and Search (Code A) that children should not be subjected to voluntary searches. The wide powers of arrest without warrant given to the police under Police and Criminal Evidence Act (1984) (sections 24 and 25) apply equally to children and young persons except for the provision that they should not be arrested at school unless it is unavoidable. The parent or guardian should be notified immediately and the subsequent processes cannot begin without the presence of an appropriate adult, except in an emergency.

A child can also be removed from the street by the police for their own protection under the

Children Act 1989 (section 46) or under provisions in the CDA (sections 14 and 16):

(a) if they are under 16 (increased from 10 by section 48 of the Criminal Justice and Police Act 2001), unaccompanied and found in any locality where there is a child curfew scheme formulated or;
(b) if suspected of truanting.

There are also provisions in the Anti Social Behaviour Act 2003 (section 30) for the removal and escort home of under 16s found out at night in designated areas.

Detention and questioning

Suspects below the age of 17 must be held separately from adult detainees, an appropriate adult must be notified as soon as practicable and that person must be present during all interviews (Code of Practice for the Detention, Treatment and Questioning of Persons by Police Officers (Code C)) (see Chapter 11). The presence and consent of the appropriate adult may also be required at other stages in the investigative process such as during searches, fingerprinting and photographing. Bail should be granted in the same circumstances as for adults, although it can be refused when it is deemed necessary in order to ensure the welfare of the child.

Once the evidence is deemed to be sufficient, a decision is made by the police about whether to initiate a prosecution or to divert the child from prosecution.

Reprimands and final warnings

Section 65 of the CDA (1998) replaces the previous non-statutory practice of cautioning with statutory 'reprimands' and 'final warnings', each of which can be administered on one occasion only (see Chapter 12). These new measures, which may be administered to children and young persons under 18 are more rigid, less discretionary and more interventionist than both the caution they replaced and equivalent measures applied to adults. As in the case of adults, the police should consider that the evidence is sufficient for a realistic prospect of conviction, the offender must admit the offence and it must be deemed not to be in the public interest to prosecute. Unlike adults, children and young persons must also have no previous convictions. In these circumstances a reprimand may be given for a first-time, non-serious, offence and a warning for a more serious or second offence. In the case of serious offences, this part of the system would be by-passed in favour of prosecution. The seriousness of an offence is assessed on the basis of Home Office 'seriousness guidelines'. A final warning is followed by a referral to the YOT for assessment and participation in one, or several, offence-related programmes.

Prosecution

The decision to pursue a prosecution in the cases of children and young people is taken by the police in circumstances where the statutory reprimand/final warning scheme is not appropriate either because the offence is deemed too serious, the offence is denied, or because the young person has already exhausted these options. The Crown Prosecution Service retains the discretion to continue or discontinue criminal proceedings and makes this decision in accordance with the provisions of the Code for Crown Prosecutors issued pursuant to the Prosecution of Offenders Act 1985.

Which court?

The majority of criminal cases against children and young people are heard in the youth court, renamed from the juvenile court under the Criminal Justice Act 1991 when its criminal jurisdiction was increased to include all those under 18 years of age charged with criminal offences. The youth court is a part of the Magistrates' court and may comprise a bench of at least two lay magistrates or a single district judge, formerly known as a stipendiary magistrate. Unlike the adult magistrates' court, there is no right of access for the public and press reporting is judicially controlled. If a child is charged jointly with an adult he or she may appear before the adult magistrates' court. A young person appearing for a first offence who pleads guilty to a non-serious offence will in most circumstances be referred by the youth court to the newly created youth offender panel to determine the content of the sentence (see Chapter 16).

A child or young person charged with a serious offence may be committed to the crown court for

trial. This will always happen in cases of murder and may happen for a range of other serious offences known as 'grave crimes' (mostly offences where, in the case of an adult, a term of imprisonment of 14 years or more could be given). The Criminal Justice and Public Order Act 1994 extended the jurisdiction of the crown court to sentence children aged 10 to 13 to longer terms of detention. If the youth court considers that the appropriate penalty for an offence will exceed 24 months, the maximum custodial penalty available in the youth court, it may commit the case to be tried in the crown court. Decisions about which court a case against a child or young person will be tried in are taken solely on the basis of expected length of custodial sentence. This has caused problems for the courts in the case of 10 and 11 year olds, who cannot receive a custodial sentence in the youth court, and 12 to14 year olds who cannot be incarcerated by the youth court unless they are deemed 'persistent offenders'. It is not possible for children of those ages to be committed to crown court for trial to facilitate the imposition of a custodial sentence unless a sentence of two years or more is a likely outcome, even though the offence might otherwise be thought serious enough to warrant a custodial sentence. Unlike adults, children and young persons have no right to elect for trial by jury (Stone's, 2003).

Not surprisingly, most children and young people (and adults too) plead guilty so the offence just becomes the background against which sentencing takes place. The weakness of the system is displayed when children plead not guilty and the full rigour of the law is mobilised against them. It was the European Court of Human Rights, in the case of Thompson and Venables (V v UK and T v UK (2000) 30 EHRR 121), which forced some changes in the organisation of trials. Article 6 of the European Convention on Human Rights guarantees the right to a fair trial and childhood has been recognised as having an impact on fairness. As a result, when a child or young person is charged with a criminal offence, they should be dealt with in a manner that takes into account age, maturity and understanding. There should be less formality and attempts should be made to make sure the child understands what is happening and to make proceedings more child-friendly, or at least less child-frightening (Lord Chief Justice,

2000). The relevance of fairness to the concept of childhood has thus had a direct impact on the conduct of courtroom procedures, courtesy of European human rights legislation (Levy, 2001). However, the substantive criminal law and rules of procedure and evidence which apply to the trial remain largely the same for children as for adults.

Criticism from the United Nations Committee on the Rights of the Child

The UK ratified the United Nations Convention on the Rights of the Child (the Convention) (United Nations, 1989) in 1991 and undertook to comply with its principles and report to the United Nations Committee on the measures adopted to give effect to the rights in the Convention. The relevant principles prioritise the welfare of the child, commend diversion and minimal intervention and emphasise the protection of the child's legal rights. The UN Committee's second report on the UK's compliance with the provisions of the Convention had serious concerns about the worsening position of children in conflict with the law since 1994 (UNCRC, 2002; see Chapter 7). The Committee was particularly critical of the low age of criminal responsibility, the abolition of the presumption of doli incapax in the CDA, the trial of children in adult courts and increased incarceration. However, because the Convention has not been incorporated into domestic law, there is no procedure for enforcement.

Conclusion

Underpinning this chapter are a lawyer's concerns for the processes by which children and young people are dealt with in the criminal justice system in this country, reflected also in the concerns of the United Nations Committee on the Rights of the Child. Many of the problems are avoided in other European jurisdictions where the age of criminal responsibility is higher and the civil law is used to manage both troubled and troublesome children and young people. Those working in YOTs in England and Wales no doubt prioritise the child's welfare in their dealings with them but that does not alter the fact that services to children and young people are delivered on the platform of the criminal justice system. Pitting youngsters against the police in the streets and in the police station, even with the much criticised protection of the appropriate adult (see Chapter 11), is hardly an equal match. Delivering the losers into courtrooms, even with a lawyer in attendance, is also a contest, the real significance of which is likely to be lost on the child or young person. Prioritising the concept of fault, blame and responsibility sits uncomfortably with welfare and the concept of childhood.

The present government considers that there is no conflict between protecting the welfare of young people who offend and preventing their offending because, as the *No More Excuses* White Paper (Home Office, 1997b) suggests, prevention of offending promotes the welfare of the young offender and protects the public. This begs questions about whether the criminal justice system is the most appropriate forum in which to attempt to prevent offending by children and young people, whether it has negative consequences for the welfare of the young and whether it might be possible to find other means of achieving the desired goal.

Further reading

Ashford, M. and Chard, A. (2000) *Defending Young People*. 2nd edn. London: Legal Action Group

Goldson, B. (Ed.) (2000b) *The New Youth Justice*. Lyme Regis: Russell House Publishing

Muncie, J. (1999) *Youth and Crime: A Critical Introduction*. London: Sage

Newburn, T. (2002b) Young People, Crime and Youth Justice. in Maguire, M., Morgan, R. and Reiner, R. (Eds.) *The Oxford Handbook of Criminology*. 3rd edn. Oxford: Clarendon Press

Scraton, P. (Ed.) (1997) *Childhood in Crisis?* London: UCL Press

Part 2 The Principles of Youth Justice

7 Children's Human Rights and Youth Justice

Geoff Monaghan

Key points

1. Having ratified the United Nations Convention on the Rights of the Child and introduced the provisions of the European Convention on Human Rights into domestic law, the UK has a legal obligation to implement, and comply with, international standards with regard to children's human rights.

2. These international standards provide comprehensive principles designed to inform all law and practice relating to children, including youth justice law and practice.

3. However, the UK faces criticism by the UN for its worsening record of compliance with its legal obligations with regard to the youth justice system.

4. A rights-based statutory framework could help to ensure that law and policy vis-a-vis children is applied consistently and render it less vulnerable to the effects of party political priorities.

5. A youth justice system based on a culture of children's human rights is compatible with a recognition of their responsibilities, reductions in offending and improved community safety.

Whoever we are, wherever we live, these rights belong to all children under the sun and the moon and the stars, or in mountains or valleys or deserts or forests or jungles. Anywhere and everywhere in the big, wide world, these are the rights of every child.

(Castle, 2000)

Introduction

The Human Rights Act 1998 (HRA) incorporated the European Convention on Human Rights (ECHR) into domestic law. Subsequently, people have been able to challenge alleged infringements or denial of their human rights. Furthermore, those who work in public authorities must ensure that relevant aspects of their policies, decisions and actions do not infringe those rights. In introducing the Human Rights Act, the government noted that the Act:

. . . places new responsibilities on all of us who work in public authorities, which includes central government, the courts, the police, local government and many bodies who carry out functions which the Government would otherwise have to undertake. We all have a vital role to play in building a new human rights culture . . .

(Home Office, 2000)

But what does this mean for children? Although it applies to all human beings, the ECHR does not provide specifically for children. Indeed, the concept of legally binding children's human rights has a very short history. It was not until 1989, after 10 years of international debate and continual re-drafting that the United Nations Convention on the Rights of the Child (UNCRC) was adopted. The UNCRC is the first comprehensive statement of children's human rights, which recognises that children require special protection and establishes the rights of children as individuals rather than as appendages of their families or the subjects of their parents or other adults. The UK signed and ratified the UNCRC in 1991, thus formally accepting a legal obligation to implement its provisions. The Convention has now become the most ratified international treaty in history. It has been described as being potentially the first universal law of humankind (UNICEF, 1995) and only two states, the USA and Somalia, have not ratified it.

The UNCRC is supported by additional international guidance, rules, treaties and standards, relating to youth justice (see below). In some states, the UNCRC becomes enforceable in domestic legislation on ratification. In others, including the UK, new legislation is required to incorporate it. This does not mean that legal obligations do not apply to the signatories; the rights of the child, their responsibilities to respect the rights of others and the obligations on the government are, in international law, inalienable. It does mean however that they are not directly enforceable.

Nonetheless, the UNCRC has been recognised as a guide in some judgements in UK courts as well as in the European Court of Human Rights, particularly where the detail of ECHR law or domestic legislation is found to be wanting or ambiguous. For example, in the judicial review of the applicability of the Children Act 1989 to prison service establishments, brought by the Howard League in 2003, the judgement made reference to the UNCRC (Howard League v The Secretary of State, Home Department and Department of Health, 2003).

Few would dispute that some aspects of children's human rights have been crucial in helping to protect children from, for example, torture, abduction and trafficking, or participation in armed conflict. And few would wish to deprive children of the right to primary education, play and recreation or state sponsored care when separated from parents. Yet in the UK, there has been no systematic attempt to incorporate such rights into law, policy or practice, particularly in the sphere of youth justice.

Indeed, with regard to youth justice, there remains a considerable ambiguity of commitment to rights and a significant level of infringement and outright denial. There is for instance no statutory right to education for children in prison or secure training centres and, normally, no 'looked after' status under the Children Act 1989. In this sense, respect for children's human rights is selective and, arguably, discriminatory.

A core question for all who are involved in working with children in conflict with the law is whether, at least in principle, to subscribe to a rights based approach or not. Thus, decisions and judgements which are at all ambiguous or hinge on competing priorities or principles could be made in the light of a children's human rights framework. At best, every action should be considered within such a framework which would be relevant, for example, when considering issues of proportionality in devising an intervention or contract, where the question of publicly 'naming and shaming' arises, where a child might be removed prematurely from parental care or where

a planning review has not taken proper account of the child's views.

This chapter will consider the extent to which the youth justice system respects children's human rights and how those rights might be better embodied in law, policy and practice. But first, some of the more important conventions, rules and guidance are outlined.

A children's human rights framework

Rights can usefully be understood as falling into three basic categories:

- Absolute rights, which cannot be compromised (for example, rights to protection from abuse, sexual exploitation or cruel treatment).
- Limited rights, where the limitation is specified (the right to liberty under the ECHR does not apply to lawful detention after conviction by a competent court for example).
- Qualified rights, which are contingent upon 'proportionality'.

Qualified rights can be denied or infringed for a specific purpose. The UNCRC recognises, for example, that the right to freedom of association and free expression can be curtailed in order to protect the rights and freedoms of others or to maintain public order (this has particular relevance to recent anti social behaviour legislation in England and Wales). In such cases, the degree of denial or infringement of qualified rights must be proportionate to the risks posed. Thus, the Home Office, in its guidance to the HRA, notes that:

> *Any interference with a Convention right must be proportionate to the intended objective. This means that even if a particular policy or action which interferes with a Convention right is aimed at pursuing a legitimate aim (for example the prevention of crime) this will not justify the interference if the means used to achieve the aim are excessive in the circumstances . . . You must not use a sledgehammer to crack a nut. Even taking these considerations into account, in a particular case an interference may still not be justified because the impact on the individual or group is too severe.*
>
> (Home Office, 2000)

The concept of proportionality, so understood, is of obvious relevance to a variety of forms of intervention within the youth justice system. For example, the 'naming and shaming' of certain children by youth court magistrates, permitted by the Crime and Disorder Act 1998; inter-agency information sharing for the purpose of preventing offending; requirements or restrictions associated with 'anti-social behaviour' or interventions linked with the community element of detention and training orders may all, under certain circumstances, constitute infringements of qualified rights.

The duties of public authorities

The HRA places a duty on public authorities – which include youth offending teams (YOTs) and courts – to uphold ECHR rights. In so doing, it provides that such bodies may act contrary to regulations and standards (with the exception of unambiguous primary statute) where to do otherwise would deny or infringe an individual's human rights. Thus, for example, despite a court having made an order requiring reparation in a public place, the YOT might nonetheless be liable to legal challenge if the execution of this order resulted in an unnecessary infringement of privacy or was degrading.

Rights of different individuals may conflict (as in the rights of offenders and those of victims) and competing rights must be balanced. Hence, a young person's right to legal assistance or the presence of an appropriate adult at an interview might, in exceptional cases, be overridden by the need for limited questioning of a child in police detention to prevent immediate injury to another. A case in point would be where an act of dangerous vandalism on a railway was jeopardising the safety of rail travellers.

The HRA applies to children, protecting their right to a fair trial and privacy, for example, but it does not differentiate children from adults. The flagship of children's human rights is the UNCRC. It contains 54 articles which can be divided into four main categories:

- Rights to survival and to have one's basic needs met (e.g. food, health care).
- Rights to healthy development (e.g. education, freedom of thought, access to the arts and the child's own culture).
- Rights to be safeguarded (e.g. protection from abuse or exploitation, and the right to a fair trial).
- Rights to participate (e.g. having a voice and being taken seriously, freedom of assembly, access to information).

Although much of the Convention is concerned with specifying the rights of children, it also places responsibilities upon governments, governmental and other bodies and adults, and requires that progress in the implementation of children's rights should be monitored.

The UNCRC was designed to have global relevance, irrespective of wealth, cultural diversity, religion or tradition. Thus, although it contains many specific rights and provisions that lend themselves to direct application in law (for example, the right to be presumed innocent until proven guilty, the prohibition of capital punishment or the definition of a child as being someone under the age of 18), it is frequently aspirational in nature. So while the UNCRC could perhaps provide a blueprint for a 'bill of rights', it does not always provide the text for specific legislation. In this sense it might best be viewed as providing a framework of principles to be interpreted and utilised according to local circumstances.

For example, article 32(2)(a) obliges states to 'provide for a minimum age or minimum ages for admission to employment'. This clearly requires each state to establish a minimum in law, but allows flexibility to set it in accordance with the local school leaving age and the type of work available. At local level, this may permit part-time, weekend, employment or essential subsistence activities, while forbidding 'child labour' for long hours. On the other hand, some provisions are not easily defined – or enforced – such as that relating to standards of living.

Youth justice and children's human rights

Only article 40 of the UNCRC addresses itself exclusively to the administration of youth (or 'juvenile') justice. In a nutshell, the article is built around the requirement on states to:

> . . . *recognise the right of every child alleged as, accused of, or recognised as having infringed the penal law to be treated in a manner consistent with the promotion of the child's sense of dignity and worth, which reinforces the child's respect for the human rights and fundamental freedoms of others and which takes into account the child's age and the desirability of promoting the child's reintegration and the child assuming a constructive role in society.*
>
> (United Nations, 1989)

It goes on to detail a number of specific rights:

- The right not to be subject to penal action for behaviour that was not prohibited in law when it occurred (this could include 'preventive' intervention).
- The right to be presumed innocent until proven guilty according to law (this could include protection from any 'diversionary' or 'preventive' intervention based upon an assumption of guilt).
- The right to be informed promptly of any charges, via a parent/guardian where necessary and appropriate.
- The right to legal representation and other appropriate assistance.
- The right to have one's case processed without delay, in a fair hearing according to law. This right is not restricted to court proceedings and covers other judicial and quasi-judicial processes such as a Scottish children's hearing or a youth offender panel (see Chapters 3 and 16).
- The right to silence, the right not to incriminate oneself, the right to call witnesses and the right of review/appeal.
- The right of access to interpreters where necessary and appropriate.
- The right to have one's privacy respected at all stages of proceedings.

Article 40 also requires states to:

- Promote the establishment of a distinct youth justice system specifically for children.
- Establish a minimum age of criminal responsibility.
- Provide measures for dealing with children without resort to judicial proceedings, so long as rights and legal safeguards are respected.
- Provide a variety of dispositions as alternatives to 'institutional care' (including foster care, supervision orders etc.) that are proportionate not only to the offence, but to the circumstances of the defendant.

However, there is an inter-relationship between different provisions of the Convention which should be considered as a whole. In this sense, article 40 is by no means the only one that is relevant to the provision of youth justice and other articles are equally fundamental. Article 3, for instance, emphasises that the best interests of the child should be a paramount consideration in all actions by courts of law. The English translation of the convention states that:

> In all actions concerning children, whether undertaken by public or private social welfare institutions, courts of law, administrative authorities or legislative bodies, the best interests of the child shall be a **primary** consideration.

> (my emphasis)

This has allowed the British government to claim, in the case of young people who offend, that there may be other considerations which may also be regarded as 'primary', such as prevention of offending or the rights of victims. Critics argue that a more accurate translation from the original French would read: 'the best interests of the child shall be paramount'. If adhered to, this reading of the UNCRC would change the tenor of UK youth justice policy significantly.

Article 37 deals with the incarceration of children and young people and obliges states to ensure that:

- No child shall be deprived of liberty unlawfully or arbitrarily.
- The arrest (and holding), detention or imprisonment of a child shall be used only as a measure of last resort and for the shortest appropriate period of time.
- Every child deprived of liberty shall be separated from adults (unless this is not in their best interests) and has the right to family contact.

Elsewhere the Convention holds that: the child's views must be sought and given due weight, particularly in judicial proceedings (art. 12); that separation from families must only be undertaken in accordance with the law and only when such action is deemed to be in the best interests of the child (art. 9). It also requires that appropriate assistance should be given to parents (art. 18) and that children must be protected from cruel, degrading or inhumane punishment or treatment and from abuse within the youth justice system (arts. 37 and 19).

Each of the above rights (and obligations) should be provided, respected and assured without any kind of discrimination (art. 2).

The UNCRC is supported by an expanding body of international rules, treaties and guidance some of which focus specifically on youth justice.

These contain detail on diversion from formal justice systems, the administration of youth justice systems and the treatment of children in detention. The most significant are:

- United Nations Standard Minimum Rules for the Administration of Juvenile Justice (1985) (The Beijing Rules).
- United Nations Guidelines for the Prevention of Juvenile Delinquency (1990) (The Riyadh Guidelines).
- United Nations Rules for the Protection of Juveniles Deprived of their Liberty (1990) (the JDL Rules).

... and from sources other than the United Nations; *The Recommendations for Social Reactions to Juvenile Delinquency 1987* (The Council of Europe).

These documents contain guidance on the principles to be applied at each stage of a youth justice system which operates in accordance with children's human rights and international standards.

Children's human rights in practice

The UN Committee on the Rights of the Child (the Committee) is responsible for scrutinising states' compliance with the UNCRC. In its second report on the UK's record on children's human rights, produced in October 2002, it welcomed developments such as the implementation of the HRA, the Children (Leaving Care) Act 2000, the establishment of the government's Children and Young People's Unit (subsequently subsumed within the Children, Young Peoples and Families Directorate of the Department for Education and Skills), the development of multi-disciplinary YOTs and the increased use of restorative approaches.

However, considerable criticism was levelled at the youth justice system and the Committee took the view that the UK's record had 'worsened' in this context since its previous report in 1995. Subsequently, the Joint Committee on Human Rights (a Parliamentary committee of both Houses of Parliament tasked with advising the government on human rights issues) produced a report reflecting the Committee's concerns and making further recommendations for change (JCHR, 2003). To date, the government has given little indication that it intends to act on those

recommendations. Indeed, the youth justice annex appended to *Every Child Matters*, the green paper on children published in September 2003, makes no reference to the UNCRC and the proposals seem unlikely to address the majority of the Committee's concerns (Home Office, 2003j).

A coalition of children's charities and criminal justice organisations has summarised the committee's main concerns about youth justice policy and practice from a children's rights perspective in a recent report *Children in Trouble: Time for Change* (Monaghan et al., 2003). In particular, it is concerned that:

- The UNCRC is not incorporated into all law relating to children and, specifically, into youth justice legislation.
- The youth justice system does not comply with international rules and guidelines.
- The age of criminal responsibility is too low and should be raised 'considerably'.
- The primacy of the 'best interests of the child' is not reflected in all legislation and policies for children, notably in the youth justice system.
- Children can still be tried in adult courts.
- Deprivation of liberty is not being used as a measure of last resort and for the shortest appropriate period of time. It is being used for younger children, more children, and lesser offences and for longer periods than appropriate (see Chapter 25).
- Children may still be detained with adults.
- Young people of 17 years are still considered to be, and treated as, adults for the purposes of arrest and remand (the government has recently indicated that it will legislate to reverse this anomaly with regard to court remands (Home Office, 2004b)).
- There are numerous serious concerns relating to the treatment of children in detention.
- The principle of non-discrimination is not fully implemented and unequal enjoyment of rights still exists.

Indeed there is evidence that compliance with a children's rights agenda is worsening. The Children's Rights Alliance for England began a series of annual reviews of progress against each of the Committee's 2002 recommendations and, in the first, identified further deterioration against most of those relating to youth justice as a result of subsequent developments in policy and legislation (CRAE, 2003).

What future for a rights based system?

A starting point for policy makers and practitioners in assessing the extent to which the youth justice system is compliant with children's human rights might be to consider what a system which incorporated the main principles and provisions of the UNCRC would look like in practice.

Put at its simplest, it would be a system in which the age of criminal responsibility would be substantially higher than the present 10 years of age (if it were to be comparable with the age or criminal responsibility in most other European states it would be raised to 14). Where children under that age displayed problematic behaviour, they would fall within the purview of non-criminal justice welfare, educational or health agencies and legislation. This system for younger children would be sufficiently robust to provide for the most serious circumstances. At the same time it would require built in safeguards to avoid the risk of 'sentencing to welfare', such as that experienced in England and Wales with the 'criminal care order' arising from the Children and Young Persons Act of 1969 under which many children were institutionalised for periods that were disproportionate to the level of initial concern (see Chapter 8).

All youth justice law would reflect the paramountcy of the welfare of the child, as is presently the case in family proceedings cases dealt with under the Children Act 1989. Principles of proportionality, privacy, non-discrimination, participation and understanding would similarly be given statutory force and children would no longer be dealt with in adult courts. Wherever possible, children and young people would be diverted from the criminal justice process and dealt with informally through non-criminal justice agencies (see Chapter 37).

Remands to adult prisons would no longer be available for children and young people, who would face detention prior to conviction in secure child care facilities only as a last resort. Similarly, custodial sentences would be restricted to cases where detention was a genuine last resort with courts being obliged to consider a range of community alternatives before depriving a child of their liberty. Punishment would not be a primary aim of disposals in the system, which would focus instead on meeting the child or young person's welfare and educational needs and upon rehabilitation and restoration.

Youth justice practitioners would consider each intervention and programme of work carefully to ensure that the child's human rights were being fully respected, whether or not government policy and law supported such an approach. Qualified rights would only be infringed, where this was a proportionate response to the risk which the individual child posed.

Such a rights based framework could help to ensure that policies for children in trouble were more consistent and would help to insulate the youth justice system from the effects of party political priorities. Nor would a commitment to children's human rights undermine the related notion of individual responsibility. Children are responsible for their actions, subject to their age and level of development, and should reflect on the consequences of their actions if they infringe the rights and liberties of others.

There is too the question of whether such an approach would be consistent with the prevention of offending, protecting the public and satisfying victims. Provided arrangements for dealing with children below a raised age of criminal responsibility were sufficiently robust and youth justice interventions such as intensive supervision and surveillance and referral orders were maintained, there is no reason to suppose that the safety of the community would be compromised. Indeed the evidence suggests that a rights-based system – with its emphasis on diversion, informalism and participation, would be at least as effective in preventing offending as the current system with its 'worsening' record on children's human rights.

Moreover, perceived tensions between a rights based approach and preventing offending may not be insurmountable, providing the latter is viewed as a longer term, as opposed to immediate aim (Nacro, 2003i). Respecting children's rights and providing adequately for their welfare is in other words likely to reduce the risks that offending behaviour will persist into adulthood and is thus, in the longer term, compatible with preventing offending. Reconciliation of the two principles is, however, likely to require a reframing of the current approach to dealing with youth crime, probably enshrined in legislative change.

The promise of a rights based system is that it would enable proportionate intervention which targeted the problems underlying a young person's offending rather than politically expedient – and rapidly changing – responses, the effectiveness of which has yet to be demonstrated. In this context, establishing a culture of children's human rights is an urgent obligation for governments, youth justice professionals and all others working with children and families.

Further reading

Fortin, J. (2003) *Children's Rights and the Developing Law.* 2nd edn, London: Butterworths

Fottrell, D. (2000) *Revisiting Children's Rights: 10 Years of the UN Convention on the Rights of the Child.* The Hague: Kluwer Law International

Hodgkin, R. and Newell, P. (2002) *Implementation Handbook for the Convention on the Rights of the Child.* Fully revised edn. New York: Unicef

Monaghan, G., Hibbert, P. and Moore, S. (2003) *Children in Trouble: Time for Change.* London: Barnardo's

United Nations (2002) *Concluding Observations of the Committee on the Rights of the Child: UK.* Committee on the Rights of the Child United Nations (UNCRC/C15 Add.188)

8 The Welfare Principle

Sarah Curtis

Key points

1. The principal aim of the youth justice system is 'to prevent offending by children and young persons'. The youth court must also 'have regard' to the welfare of the child or young person but the welfare principle has never been defined.

2. The starting point for consideration of disposals in the youth court is the seriousness of the crime, not the welfare of the individual.

3. There is considerable overlap between children and young people appearing in youth courts and those who are the concern of family proceedings courts. The youth court's disposals are time-limited. It has no power to ensure that the long-term needs of children and young people who offend are met.

4. The number of young people in custody has increased and the minimum age for secure detention has been lowered since the crime and care jurisdictions for children and young people were separated.

5. The challenge now is to bridge the gap between justice and welfare approaches, ensuring the long-term needs of young people who offend are met without exposing them to injustice or diminishing their sense of personal responsibility for their offending behaviour.

Introduction

In the parliamentary debate on the Children Act 1908, which established separate courts for children, it was argued that 'the courts should be agencies for the rescue as well as the punishment of children'. The new juvenile court was a criminal court but it had a dual function, to deal with young law-breakers and with children found begging, destitute or in immoral company. The phrase 'the welfare of the child or young person' was introduced in the Children and Young Persons Act 1933 (Section 44(1)):

> *Every court in dealing with a child or young person who is brought before it, either as an offender or otherwise, shall have regard to the welfare of the child or young person, and shall in a proper case take steps for removing him from undesirable surroundings, and for securing that proper provision is made for his education and training.*

This 'welfare clause' has never been repealed. It was the guiding principle for the juvenile courts which, until the Children Act 1989 (CA 1989), considered both 'the deprived' and 'the depraved', as they were sometimes called. It remains in place for today's youth courts despite the fact that they deal only with those who offend.

The change to separate jurisdictions

The dual function of the juvenile court was increasingly seen as unjust. The stigma of criminality was thought to extend to children and young people who were the victims of adult abuse or neglect but whose future was determined in a court associated with crime, even if the court held separate sessions for care proceedings which were heard under a civil and not a criminal jurisdiction.

The juvenile court's most controversial power in criminal cases was to make a care order as a disposal for a young person who had offended (s1(3)(c) Children and Young Persons Act 1969 (CYPA 1969)), removing parental responsibility and putting the child or young person into local authority care until the age of 18, unless the order was subsequently discharged. In addition, the grounds for a care order in civil proceedings for children at risk included the so-called 'offence clause' (s1 (2)(f) CYPA 1969) that, 'he is guilty of an offence . . . and that he is in need of care or control which he is unlikely to receive unless the court makes an order under this section in respect of him'.

The care order, as a criminal disposal, and the offence clause in civil proceedings were seen as draconian and contrary to natural justice since, theoretically at least, after stealing a bottle of milk a child of 10 from difficult home circumstances could be placed in local authority care until the age of 18. Thus the consequences of their offending could last far longer for children than for those adults committing the same crime. It was argued that the response to criminal behaviour should be subject to due process of the law, with appropriate limited penalties, as in an adult court, and that the vulnerability of children should be examined separately, in a non-criminal context in which parents were represented.

A welfare approach, aiming to remove children from undesirable surroundings, and attributing responsibility for the crime as much to society as to the individual, was considered to be wrong in principle and punitive in effect. In 1974 over 8,000 care orders were made under criminal proceedings. As concern grew, the relevant legislation became used less frequently but the possibility of care as a consequence of crime became a symbol of the unacceptable dual nature of the juvenile court and a major argument in the campaign for establishing a family court which could deal appropriately with civil matters concerning children and their parents.

It is interesting to note that an early White Paper, before the CYPA 1969, mooted the idea of 'family councils' to replace courts altogether in dealing with delinquency caused by family problems, but the idea was never taken forward (Parsloe, 1978: 153). The high point of the welfare approach, stressing the causal effects of external circumstances rather than individual responsibility, was probably during the period leading up to the CYPA 1969, in which there was a proposal, still on the statute book but never implemented, to raise the age of criminal responsibility to 14.

In the family proceedings court today, the overarching principle is that 'the child's welfare shall be the court's paramount consideration' (s1(1) CA 1989), and before making decisions in care proceedings the court has to have 'regard in particular' to a welfare checklist (see Appendix). The seven items on the checklist include: the child's physical, emotional and educational needs;

their background; their ascertainable wishes and feelings in the light of age and understanding; and the capability of each parent, as well as any harm the child has suffered or is at risk of suffering. A child's record of offending may be put forward among the indications, for example, that they are beyond parental control, but it is not specifically itemised in the checklist. The family proceedings court is also enjoined to make no order unless one is necessary, and delay is seen as prejudicial to the interests of the child.

Youth courts, on the other hand, must only 'have regard' to the welfare of the child or young person, and the word 'welfare' has never been defined. The provision of the 1933 Act, 'in a proper case' to remove children from undesirable surroundings and to secure proper provision for education and training, is now seen as the brief only for family proceedings courts. In addition, the youth court's welfare duty has been complicated and modified by subsequent responsibilities. The most important of these are:

(a) The need to relate the penalty to the seriousness of the offence, as formulated in the Criminal Justice Act 1991 (see Chapter 9). Sentencers must look first at the offence and only then at aggravating or mitigating circumstances surrounding the offence or pertaining to the young person. This is sometimes termed the 'just deserts' approach, advocated as a correction to the injustice whereby intervention in a child's life could be longer and more fundamental than warranted by the crime committed.

This is reinforced by the need to observe the principle of 'proportionality' under the Human Rights Convention, the Human Rights Act 1998 and the UN Beijing Rules 1985 for the Administration of Juvenile Justice (see Chapter 7). In essence, these support the just deserts approach, that the penalty should be commensurate with the crime.

(b) The introduction, in the Crime and Disorder Act 1998 (CDA) of a 'principal aim' for the youth justice system, 'to prevent offending by children and young persons'.

The art of sentencing in the youth court is thus a balancing act between competing demands and, it could be argued, that ambivalent aims lead to confusion, particularly concerning welfare. It is agreed that it is in young people's interests, as well as those of the community, for them to stop offending but the means to help them to change, available to the youth court, are now strictly time-limited and, except for those appearing for the first time, consist of a mix of penalties (from fines to custody), restitution to victims, and programmes to address their offending behaviour and reintegrate them into mainstream activities (see Chapter 21). How, in the long term, to prevent offending is the key question.

Children in trouble and children in need

The separation of the youth court and the family proceedings court, implemented in 1991, prompts the question of whether the two courts deal with the same or different children and young people. The following statistics show the overlap between those who offend and those who live in difficult circumstances, and have educational, emotional and health problems:

- Over half the young people in young offender institutions in 2000–01 had been, or still were, in local authority care (HMIP, 2002).
- 15% of young people referred to youth offending teams (YOTs) in 2002/03 were excluded from school and 41% were regularly truanting; 60% had been assessed as having special educational needs.
- One in five was considered vulnerable to harm because of the behaviour of other people, specific events or circumstances in their lives.
- 9% of males and 15% of females were considered to be at risk of suicide or self-harm.
- Over half were recorded as having used cannabis and 42% said they were drunk at the time of their last offence. As many as a third of those sentenced to custody in 2001 had tried heroin or crack.
- Only 30% lived with both their parents (Youth Justice Board, 2003e).
- In a sample of young people in custody under the detention and training order (during the first year it was available), 17% were on the Child Protection Register.

YOTs collect data about personal and family factors on the ASSET form, an assessment tool introduced to calculate the risk of further offending (see Chapter 19). YOT staff use the evidence thus obtained, and from the young person and their family, to make recommendations to the youth court magistrates about the kind of intervention they think will be most effective. The ASSET form is related to, but shorter and different from, the core assessment records for children who may need protection by an order from the family proceedings court. The emphasis in the assessment for the criminal court is on the shorter-term likelihood of future offending, whereas the focus for the family proceedings court is on the needs of the child or young person and longer-term solutions. The YOT's report to the youth court gives magistrates the main findings from the assessment that the YOT thinks relevant to show the possible effect of different disposals. Defence lawyers use, in mitigation, facts about a child's unstable family circumstances and sometimes about the individual's capacity to understand the consequences of offending behaviour.

The consequences of the crime/care split

The establishment of family proceedings courts in 1991, by the CA 1989, has brought about many improvements for children and young people:

- The welfare of the child is the paramount concern of the court.
- The facts about what has happened to the child are established with legal safeguards.
- The child's wishes and feelings concerning the disposal are taken into consideration according to their age and understanding. The approach of the court is less adversarial and the aim is to arrive at solutions through mediation and conciliation.
- An independent 'children's guardian' is appointed with specialist knowledge of children and adolescents and appropriate communication skills. The guardian's report to the court covers the points in the welfare checklist, including an assessment of the child's developmental stage and needs.
- The child is separately represented in care proceedings and has the benefit of a lawyer who must have received specialist training in child care law and dealing with children.

- Parents are parties in the case and, as such, eligible for legal representation.
- Family court magistrates and judges receive some training in child development and other relevant issues.
- The structure of care proceedings in family proceedings courts has met with general approval and it is thought that delays and difficulties in appointing guardians would be eased if there were better organisation of the guardian service (CAFCASS, 2003).

There have also been improvements for young people who offend in the separate youth courts, especially with the provision of new disposals initiated by the Youth Justice Board.

- The function of the court is clear to children and parents: it is a criminal court dealing with offences.
- Penalties are laid down according to the 'level of seriousness' of the offence.
- The establishment of YOTs, multi-agency teams of specialist workers, has increased the viability and credibility of community-based rehabilitative schemes because of increased liaison with those responsible for providing education; social support and housing (see Chapters 5 and 17).
- Formal support for parents is offered through parenting orders, and only a minority see this as an unjustified punishment placed upon them rather than their offending offspring (see Chapter 31).
- Children and young people appearing in court for the first time, if they admit their guilt, are made the subject of referral orders which 'refer' them to panels composed of youth justice professionals and suitably trained and experienced lay people from the community. They and their parents – and sometimes the victims – discuss with the panel ways to enable them to repair the damage they have done and to change their life-style. The disposal takes the form of a contract, part punishment to exorcise the past and part plan to build for the future (see Chapter 16).
- A new emphasis on 'restorative justice', through reparation, action plan and referral orders, has the potential to give young people who offend better insight into their lives (and many victims more satisfaction, as well as insight into the complexity of youth crime) (see Chapters 28 and 33).

- Half of YOTs have limited access to specialist foster carers for young people on remand who otherwise might wait for charges or trial in custody. Pilot schemes for intensive fostering as an alternative to custody were introduced in Autumn 2004 (Home Office, 2002b; 2003f; 2004b).

There is, however, a debit side:

- The variety of penalties in the youth court is too great, and the rationale too complicated, for many children and their families, and the general public, to grasp. The 2003 Green Paper, *Youth Justice – the Next Steps*, suggested replacing the present non-custodial penalties with an expanded single community sentence. However, it did not say whether the new order would include the key requirement of the present supervision order for the supervisor 'to advise, assist and befriend' the child or young person who is the subject of the order.
- The formal proceedings of the court inhibit participation by young people and their families, particularly the significant number with educational and developmental problems. The importance of good communication and openness is now stressed but it will take time for sentencers to acquire such skills and to implement them in a court room setting.
- The government has not pursued the proposal in the 2002 White Paper, *Justice for All,* that the most serious trials (e.g. for murder and rape) now held in the crown court should be heard by a judge and youth court magistrates sitting in a youth court. It was suggested in *Youth Justice – the Next Steps* that judges in such cases should be selected and trained for work with young people, a welcome but less fundamental change. It appears that even this limited reform is not to be pursued (Home Office, 2004b), even though the Audit Commission, in *Youth Justice 2004: a review of the reformed justice system*, repeated the arguments for the more radical alternative.
- Custody is ordered more, rather than less, by youth courts in spite of the evidence that imprisonment is detrimental to the welfare of children and young people (see Chapter 24). The High Court ruled in November 2002 that the provisions of the CA 1989 apply to those in custody and the Youth Justice Board is now to fund the provision of local authority social

workers with a specific responsibility to safe-guard such children. It remains to be seen how much such provision can effectively promote the welfare of children and young people held in prison service custody.

- Youth courts are limited in making specific orders for drug treatment because of the shortage of such resources in the community for those under 18 years of age.

- The introduction of the final warning system, while ensuring positive intervention for early offending, has made less likely the possibility of diversion from court. The Audit Commission, in its 2004 review, suggested more diversion from court for minor offenders and less use of a 'tariff' in sentencing.

- With the abolition of the 'doli incapax' provision through s34 CDA, whereby it had to be shown that a child under 14 years of age understood the nature of wrong-doing, the emphasis has drifted away from consideration of the developmental stage of young people who offend (Bandalli, 2000).

- Lawyers in the youth courts do not have to be specially trained in the law concerning children and young people or acquainted with local resources.

- There is extensive training for youth court magistrates in the law but not as much on child and adolescent development, or the availability of resources in the community, as there was for juvenile court magistrates who heard both crime and care cases.

- YOTs, in their work with young people who offend, collect evidence that many of the children and young people have multiple prob-lems, which put them in the 'at risk' category. They also have good contact with statutory and voluntary community welfare organisations, and many of their interventions are intended to slot the child back into mainstream activities at the end of any formal order. However, their pri-mary responsibility is to prevent the likelihood of further offending and the supervision they can exercise is strictly time-limited.

- The youth court may be alerted to a child's long-term need through the information pro-vided by the YOT, but there is little it can do to ensure investigation and action under welfare jurisdiction.

Conclusion: towards effective crossover

Underlying any examination of youth justice lies the question of how much children should them-selves be held responsible for their offending and the proportion of responsibility resting with par-ents and society. The role of parents is recognised by the law which demands their attendance in court if the child is of compulsory school-age, and the concept of minority for young people puts them in a different category from adults in many ways. The youth court may impose a parenting order if it finds that a parent's lack of control has contributed to a child's offending but has no power to investigate the young person's long-term needs.

In addition, the rhetoric of the media and politicians heightens 'moral panic' and encourages short-term solutions from the courts. There is pressure to protect children and young people against external dangers but blindness to the damaging (and, except for the few who are violent and dangerous, unnecessary) imprisonment of children and young people. Custody for the under 18s increased from under 4,000 in 1992 to approaching 8,000 in 2001, with no comparable increase in crime by young people. Eight hundred children, aged 12 to 15, were sentenced to custody in 2001 following the introduction, under the Criminal Justice and Public Order Act 1994, of the secure training order for this age-group (Nacro, 2003j). In September 2002, there were 3,133 under 18 year olds, sentenced or remanded, held within custodial provision custody.

Custody is seen by the public (and youth court magistrates are not immune from public pressure) not only as a means to take a young robber or persistent burglar out of circulation for a period, but also as the only appropriate response by society to their crimes. Reconviction within two years of discharge from prison in 1998 was 80% for males aged 14–17 but, despite such evidence, custody is still considered by many to be the best deterrent to further crime. The public is not encouraged to wait for the effects of early intervention programmes like Sure Start or the Youth Inclusion and Support Panels, piloted from 2002 (see Chapter 32), or to consider the argument that it takes time to change an established life-style and to inculcate a moral sense. There is too little publicity in the press or through politicians about the Intensive Supervision and Surveillance Programme (ISSP), rolled out nationally in October 2003, to build public confidence in the comparative success of community programmes (see Chapter 22).

What can be done, for the benefit of young offenders caught in the middle of the argument, to bridge the gap between the justice and welfare approaches? It is clear that most have characteristics which would give them the label of being children at risk, if they had attracted the attention of the authorities by a different route (Goldson, 2002b). What can be done to give them the opportunity of receiving long-term attention to their needs without exposing them to injustice and without diminishing their personal sense of responsibility?

The radical solution would be to raise the age of criminal responsibility to 14, while ensuring suitable intervention at an earlier stage without the tariffs and stigma of the criminal court, but this suggestion is not on the political agenda at present.

A feasible alternative would be to enable transfer of appropriate cases from the youth court to the family proceedings court. This would ensure suitable investigation, honouring the welfare principle but avoiding the former dangers in juvenile court practice. For this to take place, it would be necessary for youth court magistrates to see the full ASSET assessment completed by the YOT and to set its findings besides the welfare checklist used in the family proceedings court. The youth court would then in appropriate cases direct the local authority to make enquiries to decide whether it should take any action 'to safeguard or to promote the child's welfare' under section 37 CA 1989, as suggested in the 2002 White Paper *Justice for All,* and appoint a children's guardian for the case.

A further improvement would be for youth court magistrates to be recruited, and district judges sitting in youth courts selected, specifically for work with children and young people. They should be trained in issues of child and adolescent development as well as the law, and to be familiar with local community resources. The 2004 Audit Commission review supported more specialisation for youth court magistrates who could perhaps be relieved of some of their adult court duties. In the opinion of this contributor, all youth court magistrates should also sit in the family proceedings

court but they should not necessarily sit in the adult court, an arrangement that used to be possible in Inner London where, in the past, the Lord Chancellor appointed juvenile court magistrates separately from other magistrates.

If supported by adequate resources in the community, such changes would help to prevent offending by children and young people more effectively and bring youth justice in England and Wales closer to good practice in Europe and to the United Nations rules for juvenile justice.

Appendix: the welfare checklist for family proceedings

(a) The ascertainable wishes and feelings of the child concerned (considered in the light of the child's age and understanding).
(b) The child's physical, emotional and educational needs.
(c) The likely effect on the child of any change in circumstances.
(d) The child's age, sex and background and any characteristics that the court considers relevant.
(e) Any harm the child has suffered or is at risk of suffering.
(f) How capable each of the child's parents, and any other person in relation to whom the court considers the question to be relevant, is of meeting the child's needs.
(g) The range of powers available to the court under this act in the proceedings in question.

Further reading

Curtis, S. (1999) *Children Who Break The Law.* Waterside Press

Curtis, S. (2001) Youth Justice Assessment Procedures. *Child Psychology and Psychiatry Review.* 6: 1

Goldson, B. (2000a) *The New Youth Justice.* Lyme Regis: Russell House Publishing

Parsloe, P. (1978) *Juvenile Justice in Britain and the United States: The Balance of Rights and Needs.* London: Routledge and Kegan Paul

9 Proportionality in the Youth Justice System

Spike Cadman

Key points

1. The principle of proportionality – that the penalty should fit the crime – has a lengthy history but was not formally enshrined in statute until the Criminal Justice Act 1991.

2. The historical role of the principle has been to restrict the use of capital punishment and excessive imprisonment. Within a youth justice context, the 'back to justice' movement was concerned to use proportionality to avoid over intrusive intervention based on welfare concerns.

3. The current sentencing framework for children and young people involves a complex balance between proportionality, the welfare of the child and the principal aim of the youth justice system to prevent offending.

4. The sentencing structure introduced by the Criminal Justice Act 1991 has been eroded in the intervening period. The youth justice reforms, in particular, pose a number of serious challenges to the principle of proportionality.

5. Proportionality is an essential element of consistent, fair and effective responses to young people who offend. It is important that policy and practice should be directed to retaining it as a cornerstone of the youth justice system.

Introduction

Simple theft is not so great an offence as to be punished by death.

(Sir Thomas More, 1487–1535)

The Criminal Justice Act 1991 (CJA 91) introduced a new statutory sentencing framework for the youth and adult criminal justice systems, founded on the principle of proportionality. The new approach was based on philosophy of 'just deserts' which the White Paper, preceding the Act, described in the following terms:

The severity of the sentence of the court should be directly related to the seriousness of the offence

(Home Office, 1990)

The anticipated result was the creation of a 'more coherent and comprehensive consistency of approach in sentencing'. The intention was that proportionality should be the guiding criterion for deciding sentence and that courts would be able to decide, the most suitable punishment within the constraints set by that criterion. Any restriction of liberty should be commensurate with the gravity of the offences committed.

Not that the idea of proportionality was new to the criminal justice system as a whole or the youth justice system in particular. Indeed, it had enjoyed a lengthy history as a principle which might inform decision making. The problem was that its relationship to other principles of sentencing was unclear. Some years earlier, the Court of Appeal had articulated the four aims of sentencing as being retribution, deterrence, prevention and rehabilitation, without giving any indication as to how these very different objectives were to be reconciled, nor which should take priority in the event of a conflict between them (R v Sergeant, 1974). Where young people were concerned, there was the additional problem of how the welfare of the child should impact on decision making (see Chapter 8). The CJA 91, with its commitment to 'an individualised, desert-based approach' was designed to provide a coherent philosophy against which criminal justice interventions might be measured (Haines and Drakeford, 1998). Moreover, although the current chapter deals primarily with sentencing, it is clear that proportionality goes 'deep down'. It is a principle which might be applied to all decision making points within the youth justice system.

Background

The history of proportionality has arguably been a largely progressive one. The author of *Utopia*, and 16th century Chancellor of England, Sir Thomas More's impassioned plea, cited above, for a more lenient approach to minor property offending, however, fell largely on deaf ears. During the reign of Henry VIII at least 72,000 persons, including More himself, lost their lives on the scaffold (Pettifer, 1992). Until the early 18th century, imprisonment was largely a measure of detention for those awaiting trial or execution, and courts had few sentencing options other than financial penalties (for trivial offences), transportation or the death penalty. The development of alternative forms of punishment, including custody, was largely motivated by philanthropic concerns which invoked a common sense appeal to proportionality such as that expressed by More, and given formal exposition in the writings of Kant and Hegel on retributive theories of punishment (Ashworth, 1997).

More recently, during the 1980s, the origins of what became known as the 'back to justice' movement were to be found in practitioner and academic responses to what was seen as the iniquities of the welfarist model for tackling youth crime, ascendant during the 1970s (see Chapter 1). Proportionality was adopted as an ally in arguments against over-intrusive intervention on welfare grounds that had overseen a large, unintended, rise in the use of custody and compulsory care for children and young people. The success of the movement was evidenced in tangible form by the incorporation of justice based principles into legislation during the 1980s (Haines and Drakeford, 1998). The Criminal Justice Act 1982 introduced statutory criteria, subsequently strengthened by the Criminal Justice Act 1988, which had to be met before any custodial sentence was imposed on a young person under 21 years of age. The criteria precluded the use of custody unless:

(i) The young person has a history of failure to respond to non custodial penalties and is unwilling or unable to respond to them; or

(ii) Only a custodial sentence would be adequate to protect the public from serious harm from him; or
(iii) The offence of which he has been convicted or found guilty was so serious that a non custodial sentence for it cannot be justified.

(s4.1 of Criminal Justice Act 1982 as amended by s123(3) of Criminal Justice Act 1988)

This appeal to proportionality underpinned the strategy of diversion and decarceration which characterised youth justice practice and policy during the 1980s, and achieved significant falls in the use of custodial sentencing without any associated rise in youth offending (Rutherford, 2002). The experience impressed government sufficiently to persuade them to extend the approach, both to adult offenders and to other forms of sentence. The adoption of proportionality in the CJA 91, as the basis of the sentencing framework, was accordingly a conscious attempt to reduce the use of custody across the board and to provide a mechanism for improving the public's and the court's confidence in community sentences.

Thus the Green Paper preceding the legislation proposed that the aims of sentencing policy:

> *Can often best be met by supervising and punishing the offender in the community . . . Imprisonment is not the most effective punishment for most crime. Custody should be reserved as punishment for very serious offences.*

(Home Office, 1988a)

Proportionality was again being used with progressive intent although, as subsequent events were to show, a just deserts approach proved to be equally consistent with rapid rises in the use of custody.

Proportionality in practice

The CJA 91 provides a structure, now contained in the Powers of Criminal Courts (Sentencing) Act 2000 (PCC(S)A), for the practical application of the principle of proportionality to the sentencing process. It does so by establishing thresholds that must be reached before certain penalties are deployed thereby, in effect, creating three 'sentencing bands':

- custodial sentences
- community sentences

- 'lower-level' disposals (discharges, financial penalties and reparation orders)

The thresholds operate by imposing restrictions on the imposition of penalties in the relevant band. Thus a custodial sentence cannot, in most cases, be made unless the court is of the opinion that the offending was 'so serious that only such a sentence can be justified for the offence'. Similarly, a community sentence cannot be passed unless the court takes the view that the offending 'was serious enough to warrant such a sentence' (Nacro, 2003k).

The assessment of seriousness is clearly not a precise science but involves a structured approach. The starting point is dependent on something inherent in the nature of the act that comprises the offence. Thus theft is generally less serious than robbery. Second, any individual offence will have factors associated with it which can increase (aggravate) the level of seriousness or reduce (mitigate) it. A burglary of a dwelling that is planned in detail, committed at night time as a member of a group when a house is occupied, involving aggression or threats towards the occupiers, with forced entry and the property ransacked, will be assessed as more serious than an offence involving a solitary person effecting entry through an open kitchen door and removing £5 from the kitchen table. Third, the court is required to consider whether the personal circumstances of the young person, unrelated to the offence, are such as to warrant mitigation.

The *Youth Court Bench Book*, produced by the Judicial Studies Board (2001), outlines the structured approach to be adopted by sentencers in the youth court. It provides a list of initial 'seriousness indicators' – ranked as high, medium or low – intended to be used as a preliminary marker for an average offence of the type described. The indicators however are designed to provide no more than a 'point of entry' and the assessment of seriousness is, therefore, an individual exercise on the basis of the facts before the court.

Certain features are always aggravating. The court is obliged to consider offending on bail as being more serious. Racial or religious aggravation also automatically aggravates the offence (upon implementation, the Criminal Justice Act 2003 will add offending motivated by discrimination on the basis of disability or sexual orientation). In addi-

tion, the court is able (but is not required) to take relevant previous convictions into account, and to consider the young person's response to any previous court disposals. Conversely, if the young person admits the offence, the court is obliged to consider the stage and circumstances in which the plea was entered. A timely guilty plea is generally regarded as mitigating, and can attract a discount on sentence of up to a third (Ashford and Chard, 2000).

Having determined the seriousness of the offence, the court is able to take into account the personal circumstances of the young person before determining the appropriate level of sentencing. It is important to be clear that such matters can only lead to a more lenient penalty than would otherwise be warranted by the nature of the offending. Individual factors, unrelated to the matters before the court, cannot be considered aggravating. Furthermore, the scope for personal mitigation to reduce the severity of sentencing is, in appropriate cases, significant. In particular, even where the criteria for custody are met, the court may determine that the circumstances of the young person are such that a penalty below the custodial threshold is more appropriate. The Court of Appeal, for instance, concluded in one case that:

> *Only a custodial sentence could be justified for this offence . . . That however is not the end of the matter . . . [T]he court is still required to consider whether such a sentence is appropriate having regard to the mitigating factors available and relevant to the offender (as opposed to such factors as are relevant to the offence).*
>
> (R v Cox [1993] cited in Ashford and Chard, 2000)

By the same token, it may be possible to argue for a lower-level disposal – such as a fine, discharge or reparation order – even where the matters would otherwise be serious enough to justify a community sentence.

The interaction between proportionality and other principles of sentencing

The principle of proportionality does not operate in isolation in a youth justice context. Courts are for instance obliged to consider the welfare of the child (see Chapter 8) and to have regard to the statutory aim of the youth justice system of preventing offending by children and young people (Home Office, 1998g). It is not obvious that the elements which combine to produce the statutory framework governing interventions with children and young people will always pull in a consistent direction. Indeed on the face of it, there may be considerable potential for tension between them.

For instance, a custodial sentence may well limit offending, at least in the short term, but is unlikely to promote the child's welfare and may not be warranted on the basis of the seriousness of the offending before the court. Similarly, a child's social circumstances may be such as to suggest that some form of long-term supervision would be beneficial in cases of relatively trivial offending where such an outcome would not be proportional.

In practice, therefore, using proportionality as a guide to decision making involves a sensitive balancing act. At the same time, it is possible to reduce tensions between the competing principles according to how they are interpreted. For instance, evidence suggests that responses to youth offending based on a punitive approach are likely to increase recidivism (McGuire and Priestley, 1995). Similarly, effective interventions are those which address the underlying social factors associated with offending behaviour (see Chapter 19). In the longer term, therefore, an increased resort to punitive measures, including incarceration, is unlikely to prevent youth crime in comparison with an approach which aims to promote welfare.

There is too, considerable evidence to suggest that early intervention in the criminal justice system or overly intrusive intervention may be associated with increased offending (see Chapter 37). Proportionality may therefore offer a sensible palliative to an unbounded needs-led approach by setting an upper limit to intervention in criminal proceedings on welfare grounds. (This is not to preclude the possibility of welfare services being provided to meet need outside of the criminal justice process.)

Significantly, in this context, Article 40 of the United Nations Convention on the Rights of the Child specifically conjoins issues of proportionality and welfare, suggesting that a children's rights focus may be able to resolve potential conflicts between the various principles which

inform the reformed youth justice system (see Chapter 7).

The gradual erosion of proportionality

The 'purist' justice framework of the CJA 91 did not long survive implementation, and the intervening years have seen a gradual erosion of aspects of the model. The first assault came in the form of the Criminal Justice Act 1993, which abolished unit fines and overturned the exclusion of offending history from the determination of seriousness.

The system of unit fines was intended to ensure that the impact of financial penalties on the individual for similar offences was the same irrespective of disposable income. Fines were imposed in terms of a number of units, the monetary value of which was determined following a means inquiry. This innovation, which had previously been successfully piloted, was repealed within 12 months of national roll out.

The CJA 91 required a focus on the seriousness of the current offence by requiring courts to disregard any previous convictions and, where there were multiple offences to be disposed of, to take account only of the most serious, plus one associated matter, in determining the appropriate restriction of liberty. The 1993 Act removed these restrictions and allowed the court to have regard to previous convictions and to consider the totality of multiple offences when assessing seriousness. It also made offending on bail a statutory aggravating factor. The Criminal Justice Act 2003 takes the matter one stage further by introducing a presumption – yet to be implemented – that previous offending should always lead to a more serious penalty unless the court determines it would be unreasonable to do so.

The Crime Sentences Act 1997 contained further breaches of the principle of proportionality, allowing courts to impose certain community sentences for offences which would not otherwise cross the community penalty threshold where the young person had previously failed to pay fines or had persistently committed petty offences.

Proportionality and the youth justice reforms

Perhaps more importantly from a youth justice perspective, reforms associated with the Crime and Disorder Act 1998 (CDA), and subsequent legislation, have involved a significant shift in emphasis away from a purely proportional model. The statutory principal aim of preventing offending by children and young people, introduced by section 37 of CDA, and the potential for conflict with proportionality, has already received some attention in the current context. Other aspects of the legislation also impact on the principle, none more so than the increased emphasis on early intervention to 'nip offending in the bud'. The final warning system, for instance, involves a statutory presumption that programmes of intervention will be delivered to large numbers of children and young people at the pre-court stage (see Chapter 12). Similarly, the referral order requires a minimum contract of three months intervention in many cases which previously might have been disposed of by way of a fine or discharge. The order, which in 2003 represented about one third of all disposals, also represents a significant modification of the sentencing framework described above since it is a mandatory sentence where the relevant criteria are satisfied. The length of referral is, however, determined on the basis of proportionality (see Chapter 16).

Two issues arise in relation to this focus on early intervention. In the first place, where assessment identifies a high level of welfare need and a potential risk of re-offending, the level of intervention is likely to be significantly higher than that which would otherwise be commensurate with the current offending behaviour. Secondly, it is clear that requiring intervention at an earlier stage can have the effect of lowering thresholds for more serious offending. The proportional approach enshrined in the CJA depends upon the determination of seriousness in order to access particular levels of intervention. That determination is not however an objective one; the thresholds are subject to fluctuation over time. As early intervention kicks in for minor misdemeanours, the level of seriousness considered necessary to access a community sentence, and thereafter custody, inevitably reduces. There is substantial evidence to suggest that just such a shift occurred during the 1990s and that as a result young people are being incarcerated for offences which would previously have resulted in a community penalty (Nacro, 2003a). There is a considerable danger that the focus on early intervention will accelerate that shift.

In an allied development, recent evolution in youth justice has increasingly encompassed a commitment to pre-emptive intervention on the basis of assessed risk. This has taken a number of forms. First, there is the development of a range of preventive measures, including for instance youth inclusion and support panels, for children who are, in some cases, below the age of criminal responsibility and those who are not adjudicated offenders (see Chapter 32). This model has attracted some criticism on the grounds that it premises intervention on what a child might do rather than what he or she has done' (Goldson, 2003). Whatever the merits of such a critique, it is clear that prevention in this form is not informed by a commitment to proportionality.

The same rationale has also given rise to the explicit possibility of harsher sentencing than proportionality would permit as a pre-emptive measure. The CJA 91 allowed for custodial sentences in cases of violent or sexual offending in order to protect the public from serious harm, even where the custody threshold would not otherwise be met. This exception is taken much further by the Criminal Justice Act 2003 which contains provision – to be implemented in December 2005 – for indeterminate sentences of detention for certain violent and sexual offences if the court considers the young person to represent a danger to the public. Extended sentences – which place the young person under extended supervision following release – are also made available in similar circumstances (Nacro, 2004b). These new sentences, too, pose a direct challenge to the concept of proportionality.

A further development at the heart of the youth justice reforms, and central to referral orders in particular, is the increased importance of restorative justice and victim involvement (see Chapters 28 and 33). Some accounts of restorative justice counterpose repairing the damage done to punishment and, in so doing, prioritise outcomes which are able to command the satisfaction of the various stakeholders rather than those which represent a proportionate response to the offending behaviour (Crawford and Newburn, 2003). In practice, little attention appears to have been given to the resolution of the inherent tensions and it has, in large part, been possible to avoid the issue because of the relatively low levels of victim involvement which continue to prevail (see Chapter 33).

Encouragingly, the development of principles for restorative justice is gaining momentum internationally and these specifically attempt to integrate proportionality into restorative models. For instance, the United Nations (2000) suggests that any agreements between parties 'should be arrived at voluntarily by the parties and contain only reasonable and proportionate obligations'.

Similarly, Recommendation No.R(99)19 on Mediation in Penal Matters, adopted by the Committee of Ministers of the Council of Europe in 1999, states that the principle of proportionality requires that there should be a broad correspondence between the burden on the offender and the seriousness of the offence.

Conclusion

The youth justice system remains formally committed to proportionality and one of its six key objectives remains the delivery of 'punishment proportionate to the seriousness and persistence of the offending' (Home Office, 1998g). That commitment is reinforced by the UK's obligations as a signatory to the United Nations Convention on the Rights of the Child. At the same time, the 'purist' model introduced by the CJA 91 has been subject to considerable modification, and the youth justice reforms pose further substantial challenges to the philosophy of just deserts.

There is good reason to restate the importance of proportionality as a principle fundamental to the fair and effective operation of the youth justice system. Although the experience of the 1990s in the wake of the CJA 91, a decade marked by a substantial shift towards a more punitive response to youth crime in general and ever higher levels of child incarceration in particular, demonstrates conclusively that proportionality is no guarantee of a progressive youth justice, it is nonetheless possible to argue that it remains a

necessary condition. The establishment of thresholds, for instance, has been historically important in limiting the use of custody and provides a baseline against which decisions of the court can be challenged, and consistency and parity promoted.

From the perspective of effective practice, proportionality – in conjunction with a commitment to promoting welfare – might also be regarded as crucial to reducing offending. The 'risk principle', underpinned by the *What works* research, confirms that over-intrusive intervention, not warranted by the seriousness of offending, can lead to increased recidivism (Andrews, 1995). In part, this is a question of how young people experience their treatment by the youth justice system. Outcomes are influenced by the extent to which young people regard disposals as a 'fair response' to their behaviour. A sentence which is not proportionate is likely to be perceived as excessive, and motivation to respond positively to any resulting programme will be undermined. Using proportionality to set limits to intervention – supplemented where appropriate by the delivery of welfare services outside of the criminal justice system – can thus be conceived as an effective mechanism for preventing offending.

Further reading

Haines, K. and Drakeford, M. (1998) *Young People and Youth Justice*. Basingstoke: Macmillan

Nacro (2000a) *Proportionality in the Youth Justice System*. Youth Crime Briefing. London: Nacro

Nacro (2003k) *The Sentencing Framework for Children and Young People*. Youth Crime Briefing. London: Nacro

Pitts, J. (2003b) *The New Politics of Youth Crime: Discipline or Solidarity*. Lyme Regis: Russell House Publishing

United Nations (2000) *Basic Principles on the Use of Restorative Justice Programmes in Criminal Matters*. Geneva: United Nations

Part 3 The Process of Youth Justice

10 The Policing of Young People

Alan Marlow

Key points

1. The police are the 'gate-keepers' of the criminal justice system and have discretion as regards the exercise of powers. The Police and Criminal Evidence Act 1984 provides accountability.

2. The Crime and Disorder Act 1998, through the creation of youth offending teams, required a multi-agency approach to the processing of young people who offend. Police are now participants in, rather than leaders of the process

3. The 'cautioning' system has been replaced by the more controlled procedure of reprimands and final warnings

4. There is an emerging emphasis on anti-social behaviour, which has implications for the relationship between police and young people. More anti-social behaviour orders are being granted.

5. There is a collaborative approach to dealing with the victimisation and abuse of young people. The police have developed dedicated units with high skill levels.

Chief Constable, I am alarmed that you report that 5% of young people under the age of 17 in the county have come to the notice of the police.

Perhaps, councillor, a better way to look at it is that 95% do not come to our notice.
(Exchange between a County Councillor and Alan Dyer, Chief Constable of Bedfordshire c.1990)

Introduction

As Geoffrey Pearson, in his classic historical study *Hooligan* (1983) so elegantly illustrated, each generation of young people tends to stimulate fears and anxieties amongst its parents' generation. The perceived association between youth and crime is a long-standing social phenomenon. Nevertheless, empirical studies indicate that for many young people, offending is a 'rite of passage' to a more settled adulthood (Graham and Bowling, 1995). It is not surprising, therefore, that young people are a constant focus of the day-to-day activity of policing.

Some commentators argue that, as a result of moral panics, the police tend to use discretion to focus disproportionately on offending by young people (Cohen, 2002). However, self-report studies by Graham and Bowling (1995) and Flood-

Page et al. (2000) indicate that young people account for a disproportionate amount of the types of crime that appear in police statistics. These studies show that the peak ages for volume offending occurred between the years 14 and 25. Up to a fifth of suspects detained by the police are aged 16 or under (Brown, 1997). Given that the offences admitted by the respondents in the studies are those most likely to be the cause of public concern (theft, burglary, robbery, violence and public disorder), the fact that young people who offend become a priority group for the police has empirical justification. Equally, many calls to the police will be the result of the apprehensions described by Pearson (1983), and the incidents in question may not involve a crime at all: one of the most frequent incidents to which the police are called will be 'nuisance youths'.

Arrest and detention

The police represent the key point of entry for young people into the criminal justice system. General powers of arrest, derived from common law principles, are codified in the Police and Criminal Evidence Act 1984 (PACE). The basis for lawful arrest is 'reasonable suspicion' that an 'arrestable offence' has been committed. The effect is to allow the police a fairly wide discretion as to whether or not to arrest.

Under PACE, detention is only permissible to secure or preserve evidence or obtain evidence by questioning. The custody officer, who although a police officer is independent of the investigation, has a duty to review the circumstances of the arrest, decide on the necessity of detention and safeguard the suspect's rights and welfare whilst detained. Reviews of detention are required at particular intervals. 24 hours is the maximum period for detention without charge except, in the case of an arrestable offence, on the authorisation of a superintendent when the limit is 36 hours. A further extension to 96 hours is possible with the consent of the Magistrates' court. Home Office guidance however, suggests that where the suspect is a juvenile, total detention in police custody beyond 24 hours would be exceptional unless the offence is a 'serious arrestable offence' (Home Office, 2003a). Some research studies have concluded that the length of time juveniles are detained without charge tend to be shorter than time spent in custody by adults (Brown, 1989; Dixon, 1990 quoted in Brown, 1997). In his review of research on the workings of PACE, Brown (1997) concluded that the Act is most effective in its regulation of procedures inside the police station.

Processing young people who offend

Whilst the youth justice system as a whole deals with young people up to the age of 18 years, for the purposes of police procedures, a juvenile is defined as 'a young person who appears not to have reached the age of 17'. One of the first duties of the custody officer in respect of a juvenile suspect is to secure the attendance of an appropriate adult (AA), usually a parent or guardian but in their absence, a representative of the youth offending team (YOT) (see Chapter 11). The purpose of the AA's presence is to:

• Advise the young person being questioned.
• Observe whether the interview is being conducted properly and fairly.
• Facilitate communication with the suspect.

The police have a duty to inform the AA of their function and the Home Office has produced printed guidance to assist this process (Home Office, undated).

Young peoples' rights to legal representation and other safeguards are not affected. The fact that an AA has been contacted does not vitiate the requirement to allow the suspect to have someone informed of their detention. Delays in attendance of an AA have tended to increase the time young suspects are held in custody (Brown, 1997).

The police and cautioning of young people

As Downes and Rock (1998: 349) point out, out of all the ideas in sociology, labelling theory has had a profound effect on criminal justice policy:

Translating labelling theory into practice consisted of variations on the theme 'delabelling'; decriminalisation, destigmatisation and decarceration.

Whether or not they appreciated the source of the ideas or were simply subject to their powerful influence, the police responded by the introduction of the principle of cautioning. It also reflected the liberal trends contained in the ill fated Children and Young Persons Act 1969. Although minor cases had long been disposed of by means of informal cautioning, the use of *personal* cautions for young people, commenced in the early 1970s, formed a radical policy shift. The rationale underlying this development was that, since one of the strongest predictors of future offending was early involvement in the criminal justice system, a mechanism for diverting young people from that system would reduce the likelihood of them embarking on a criminal career. Cautioning quickly became the preferred outcome for a first offence and involved the police assuming the power to dispose judicially of cases. The process usually took the form of a 'dressing-down' of the young person in the presence of parents, by a uniformed senior officer – none had been trained for the purpose. The caution had an element of paternalistic discipline about it.

The Home Office approved of the practice and recommended its extension. Not only did the personal caution fit with prevailing ideas on dealing with young people who offend, it was a cheap and demonstrably effective form of disposal.

Police forces expanded their role in the processing of young people. Juvenile Bureaux or Juvenile Liaison Departments were established whose purpose was to ensure that the most appropriate form of sanction was recommended on the basis of police enquiries into the family circumstances of the young person. A major criticism was that the more 'socially embedded' the young person, the more likely that a caution would result. Those with more 'dysfunctional' backgrounds had a greater probability of court proceedings as parental support was often seen as ineffective and the young person was less likely to demonstrate remorse. One response was the formation of inter-agency panels to consider appropriate disposals. Typically, these included representatives of police, probation, social services and education welfare. In the early 1990s attempts were also made to devise objective criteria for weighing the seriousness of offences without reference to the social background of the young person.

The cautioning principle was extended to include a new early stage in the process called 'informal warning' which allowed a non-formal disposal for minor matters. During the same period, the number of young people processed by the police declined dramatically (see Farrington, 1996). There is little doubt that one of the reasons was that officers took advantage of the informal warning option to avoid the extensive bureaucracy associated with the formal processing. This rather ad hoc accumulation of policy and practice resulted in the withering critique contained in the publication of *Misspent Youth* by the Audit Commission (1996) which concluded, in relation to pre-court measures that cautioning was reasonably effective on up to three occasions, but subsequent use was not only ineffective but brought the system into disrepute (Newburn, 2002b).

Despite the force of the critique, many of the recommendations were based upon selected good practice that had been developing in police forces. A new government, with an expressed intention for more 'robust interventionism' (Pitts, 2001c), drew from the Audit Commission's recommendations and through the instrument of the Crime and Disorder Act 1998 (CDA), produced a much more systematic approach to the police processing and management of young people who offend. At its core are three elements that had been developing within policing, albeit spasmodically:

- A rational and progressive approach to the use of pre-court measures.

- A multi-agency approach.
- A range of measures aimed to divert young people away from offending.

YOTs, in which the police are represented, were created to manage the process. Whilst a functional flexibility is expected of all team members, the police tend to have primary responsibility for victim liaison, the organisation of reparation work, and the supervision of bail conditions and orders. The present guidance (ACPO/Youth Justice Board, 2002) sets out standards by which police forces' efficiency is judged.

Reprimands and warnings

Cautions have now been replaced by reprimands and final warnings with the old informal warning restricted to exceptional circumstances (see Chapter 12). A reprimand or final warning can only be administered where there is:

- Evidence that the young person has committed an offence and if prosecuted, there would be a realistic prospect of conviction.
- There is an admission of guilt.
- No previous conviction.
- It would not be in the public interest for the offender to be prosecuted.

Both measures require the informed consent of the young person (Stone, 2003).

The Audit Commission (1996) had recommended the adoption of a practice, developed in some forces, which allowed a more objective assessment of the circumstances of offences against a matrix of weightings to improve consistency of decision making. The current guidance endorses this approach and each offence is accorded a gravity score, weighted to take account of aggravating and mitigating factors, which should determine the case disposal. The scoring system reflects the public interest principle in the Code for Crown Prosecutors.

The table in Chapter 12 illustrates the implications of the gravity score system when balancing the available options.

If the decision is to reprimand, the police may administer it without reference to the YOT who must, however, be notified within one working day. Those considered appropriate for final warning must be referred to the YOT for assessment.

Unless considered inappropriate, the team will devise an intervention programme to tackle the reasons for the offending behaviour. The Youth Justice Board (YJB) has set a target that 80% of warnings should be supported by interventions by 2004 although the Audit Commission has recently suggested that, given the relatively low re-offending rates for this group of young people, the target may be too high (Audit Commission, 2004).

Non-compliance is not in itself an offence but may be cited in any future proceedings.

Anti-social behaviour by young people

Lord Scarman (1981) in his report on the Brixton disorders recommended that the police make arrangements for local consultation. The proposal was given legislative effect in PACE. What surprised officers who undertook such consultation was that citizen concerns did not centre on crime in its more serious manifestations but upon the 'incivilities' of life, the minor disorders that confronted individuals once they left their front doors. A priority that emerged was nuisance caused by young people – albeit often exaggerated in its seriousness. The police were urged to take such matters seriously as they contributed to the fear of crime. A series of British Crime Surveys repeatedly demonstrated that the fear of crime was pervasive and far exceeded the probability of victimisation (Kershaw et al., 2000).

At about the same time, the influential American essay *Broken Windows* (Wilson and Kelling, 1982) was published. It suggested that attending to incivilities and disorders could halt the cycle of decline in problem neighbourhoods. A rather distorted interpretation of the principle led to what became known as 'zero tolerance policing' (Silverman, 1999). This implied that minor disorders should no longer be tolerated and that offenders should be prosecuted vigorously. The initiative was short lived: the frequency of street policing had declined; the Crown Prosecution Service was not enthusiastic to prosecute minor offences; and as the Audit Commission (1996) had concluded, the criminal justice process was largely ineffective and cumbersome in these circumstances. Nevertheless, the New Labour government considered that there should be some measures through which low level disorder and incivility

could be tackled. Their landmark CDA created the anti-social behaviour order (ASBO).

The order is a legal hybrid. It is a civil measure that contains prohibitions on behaviour necessary to prevent further anti-social conduct. Non-compliance however is a criminal matter, punishable in the case of a young person by a detention and training order.

An application for an order is subject to a two-stage test to establish whether:

1. The defendant behaved in an anti-social manner, and
2. The order is necessary to protect persons from further anti-social behaviour.

Following the judgement in the case of McCann (Association of Chief Police Officers/Youth Justice Board 2003), a criminal standard of proof is required to establish the anti-social acts alleged, but for stage 2 such a standard is unnecessary as it is a question of judgement.

The guidance concedes that the application process has proved protracted and expensive. A series of acts have to be proved to demonstrate a continuity of behaviour. Citizens are often reluctant to act as witnesses as they fear reprisal. However, the stage 2 test allows the involvement of practitioners. Some commentators (Matthews, 2003) have criticised the broad definition of anti-social behaviour arguing that it lacks precision. Nevertheless, after a slow start, the use of ASBOs is accelerating – nearly two-thirds of all those granted have been issued in the two years to March 2003. The acceleration is likely to continue as a consequence of the recently introduced power for courts to make an ASBO, in addition to any substantive disposal, of their own volition following a criminal conviction.

Anti-social behaviour can also be addressed by entering into a contract between the subject and either the housing authority or the police. This avoids formal involvement in the judicial process. 'Acceptable behaviour contracts' are voluntary and specify a range of behaviour in which the individual is not to engage. Any breach may be used in the application for an ASBO. Contracts were initiated by practitioners in Islington and elsewhere but have now become nationally accepted practice and are endorsed in government guidance (Association of Chief Police Officers/Youth Justice Board 2003).

Policing styles and preventing youth offending

During the 1960s and 1970s, polarised debates emerged about the role and function of policing. In essence, these centred on two ideal types: 'community policing' and 'crime fighting'. Community policing advocates stressed the importance of community involvement as a central tool of policing, with the officer as a facilitator of good order within local networks. The crime fighters, for their part, tended to see themselves as bastions of order confronting a sea of anarchy.

After the Scarman Report, community policing assumed orthodoxy amongst chief officers (Reiner, 2000). However, a new stress upon crime reduction through securing convictions and consequent performance monitoring since the Police and Magistrates' Act 1994, shifted the emphasis towards enforcement. A synthesis of the two models has generated a new orthodoxy based upon a 'problem-solving' approach. This implies analytical abilities to define the policing problem and the development of a wide range of 'evidence based' tactics for their resolution.

During the ascendancy of community policing, many forces developed programmes and diversionary initiatives aimed at reducing youth offending. Most had schools' liaison programmes, employing dedicated officers. Relationships were developed with schools' staff and pupils to tackle problems within and outside the school gates. Officers became involved in the curriculum and delivered lessons on the police role. Other initiatives included running activities during the school holidays, outdoor activities, and sports clubs. Officers also became involved in youth clubs. Some forces established volunteer cadet schemes. The variety of programmes depended upon the policies and commitment of the force concerned.

A criticism of these approaches was that they tended to attract young people who were unlikely to be at risk of offending. Those most at risk were the 'hardest to reach'. These activities continue but with much improved targeting. They now tend to be commissioned by or involve local community safety teams, YOTs and Connexions Service.

Nationally funded initiatives have been instigated. Safer Schools Partnerships are focused on schools in areas of high victimisation (Youth Justice Board, undated). They build on the police role in schools to reduce crime, create a safe environment, provide a full-time education for young people who offend and tackle problems through whole school approaches. Behaviour and Education Support Teams (BESTs) are government funded multi-agency behaviour improvement programmes that work with pupils 'at risk' of offending (DfES, undated).

A significant advantage of the final warning scheme is that young people who are demonstrably at risk are directed towards such appropriate activities.

Young people as victims

It is much easier to access information on young people as offenders than as victims. For example, the first British Crime Surveys did not generally include respondents under the age of 16. However, findings from the 1995 survey which did include a sample of younger respondents showed that 12 to 15 year old boys and girls are at the same risk of victimisation for some types of crime as adults. The majority of assaults on this age group took place at or near school and involved perpetrators of roughly the same age (Aye Maung 1995 quoted in Newburn, 2002b). Many such assaults are deeply distressing incidents of bullying which tend not to be reported by young victims and therefore, the school (and police liaison with it) is critical in preventing such conduct (see Chapter 38).

One of the most significant developments in the last 30 years, in terms of victimisation, has been the 'discovery' of the physical and sexual abuse of children and young people in families and institutions. Scandals provide powerful motors for change and there have been many in recent decades. The deficiencies of police investigation techniques were ruthlessly exposed in a 'fly-on-the-wall' documentary of the Thames Valley Police in the early 1980s.

The police response has been twofold: a collaborative approach through co-operation with other agencies under the auspices of local Child Protection Committees; and the development of higher levels of skills and expertise in the interviewing of children and investigation of alleged offences against them. All forces now have Child Protection Units (the title may vary according to local structures), staffed by specially trained officers.

Accommodation is available to facilitate sensitive interviewing and medical examination. Interviews are video-taped and vulnerable witnesses may give evidence at court by video-link.

All cases are subject to multi-agency case conferences and whether or not criminal proceedings result will be based upon whether:

- A criminal prosecution is in the best interests of the child.
- It is in the public interest that proceedings should be instigated.
- There is sufficient evidence to prosecute.

Notwithstanding the above arrangements, it is clear from the Climbié Inquiry (Laming, 2003) that failings still occur. The multi-agency approach brings a wide range of skills and information to a particular case, but confusion over responsibility may result. The government has appointed a Minister for Children and guidance associated with the implementation of the Children Bill, before parliament at the time of writing, is likely to require the appointment of a nominated case officer – which might include the police – to improve coordination.

Conclusion

The importance of the police as gate-keepers of the youth justice process cannot be overstated. All the evidence shows that early involvement may dramatically affect the life chances of young people who offend. Within the last 20 years, there have been some substantial improvements in the accountability process. PACE has proved to be a rigorous instrument. Causes-célèbres have also generated improvements, particularly through the stimulation of skills and facilities for dealing with the vulnerable. The CDA has encouraged innovative approaches to crime reduction through systematic multi-agency working and more coherent decision making in relation to young people who offend.

However, whilst the content of this chapter is accurate at the time of writing, there is a certainty that policies, practice and procedures will change. As Pitts (2001b) points out, the youth justice system is particularly volatile – not just because of detached considerations of justice, but as a consequence of the political ferment that characterises the criminal justice debate.

Further reading

Allen, R. (2002) Alternatives to Prosecution. in McConville, M. and Wilson, G. *The Handbook of the Criminal Justice Process*. Oxford: Oxford University Press

Association of Chief Police Officers/Youth Justice Board (2003) *A Guide to Anti-Social Behaviour Orders and Anti-Social Behaviour Contracts*. London: Home Office

Newburn, T. (2002b) Young People, Crime and Youth Justice. in Maguire, M., Morgan, R. and Reiner, R. (Eds.) *The Oxford Handbook of Criminology*. Oxford: Oxford University Press

Reiner, R. (2000) *The Politics of the Police*. Oxford: Oxford University Press

Waddington, P. (1999) *Policing Citizens*. London: UCL Press

Acknowledgement

The author would like to thank Constable Steve Robinson of Luton Youth Offending Team for his guidance in the preparation of this chapter.

11 The Role of the Appropriate Adult

Denis W. Jones

Key points

1. The appropriate adult role is potentially a very important safeguard for children and young people arrested by the police, but it has yet to be fully effective.

2. Research suggests that few appropriate adults actually make a difference. Parents often act as the appropriate adult, and are as likely to side with the police as with their children.

3. Social services departments and youth offending teams seem more concerned with *avoiding* their responsibility to provide appropriate adults than with providing them when requested.

4. Volunteer appropriate adult schemes can lead to an effective service, but volunteers need training and support if they are not to be co-opted by the police.

5. To achieve their potential, in this author's view, appropriate adults need to become a duty service provided by a statutory authority, with the parental role removed.

Introduction

Appropriate adults (AAs) were introduced by the Police and Criminal Evidence Act 1984 (PACE), as a safeguard for vulnerable suspects detained by the police. The provisions are set out in the Codes of Practice brought in under s. 60(1) (a) and s. 66(1) of the Act, now in their 5th edition (Home Office, 2003d). These provide for an AA to be present when a suspect with mental illness or learning difficulties is being interviewed, or a child or young person under the age of 17. The AA is present to support the suspect, assist with communication and ensure that the police act fairly. This chapter will only concern itself with children and young people. The reader interested in the literature relating to adults should see Palmer and Hart (1996).

The Codes of Practice define three potential sources of AAs. In the first instance, the police will request a parent or guardian. If this is not possible, then a social worker will be requested, and if both of these routes fail then an independent member of the public can fulfil the role. The 'social worker' role is now normally fulfilled by a staff member of the youth offending team (YOT) although police are precluded, and possibly probation staff – the law is unclear here. YOTs have a statutory duty to coordinate an AA service under s38(4) of the Crime and Disorder Act 1998 (CDA).

The presence of an AA is required at a number of key stages in the process of the police investigation:

- When the young person is informed of their rights.
- During a strip or intimate search.
- During any interviews.
- During taking of fingerprints or samples.
- At the point of case disposal.
- When the young person takes part in any identification procedure.

There are several excellent guides for those carrying out the AA role (Nacro, 2003b; NAYJ, 1996; CLC, no date; Littlechild, 1996) and this chapter will not attempt to replicate these. Instead, it discusses some of the research available, and controversies about the role.

The history of appropriate adult provision

Prior to PACE, there was no statutory provision requiring the police to take certain precautions when dealing with vulnerable suspects. The Judge's Rules existed, a set of guidelines under which judges had the discretion to exclude evi-

- Always request a solicitor.
- Know the codes of practice.
- And have the confidence and assertiveness to challenge the police when necessary, even in the potentially hostile setting of a police station.

Further reading

Evans, R. (1993) *The Conduct of Police Interviews With Juveniles.* RCCJ Research Study 8. London: HMSO

Littlechild, B. (Ed.) (2001) *Appropriate Adults and Appropriate Adult Schemes: Service User, Provider and Police Perspectives.* Birmingham: Venture Press

Nacro (2003b) *Acting as an Appropriate Adult: A Good Practice Guide.* London: Nacro

National Association for Youth Justice (1996) *Policy and Practice Guidelines for Youth Justice.* Leicester: NAYJ

Pierpoint, H. (2000) How Appropriate Are Volunteers as 'Appropriate Adults' for Young Suspects: The 'Appropriate Adult' System and Human Rights. *Journal of Social Welfare and Family Law.* 22: 383–400

Thomas, T. (1993) 'Appropriate Concern' in Community Care, 30 September 1993, pp. 2–3.

dence that they considered had been unfairly obtained, but research had found that the rules were usually stretched to allow evidence to be admitted (McBarnet, 1981).

It was the conviction of three youths for connected offences of arson and murder of Maxwell Confait, a transsexual prostitute, in 1972, that drew attention to the failure of the Judges Rules to protect vulnerable suspects. All three had learning difficulties, were denied legal advice, claimed that they were told that they would be allowed to leave the police station if they admitted to the murder, and were convicted on the basis of their confessions. Leave to appeal on the above grounds was denied, and it took a major campaign by Christopher Price, their MP, to get the case re-opened and a further appeal hearing in 1985, at which they were freed (see Price and Kaplan, 1977; Gudjohnsson, 1992). A judicial inquiry by Sir Henry Fisher (1977) still concluded that they had all been involved in the arson, and two of them in the murder. In a 'weak' report (McBarnet, 1978), Fisher accepted only that there was a technical breach of the rules. A subsequent Royal Commission on Criminal Procedure drew more helpful lessons and recommended the need for an adult to be present when children and young people are interrogated (Phillips, 1981): proposals eventually incorporated in PACE.

Fulfilling the role

If carried out effectively, the AA role could have been a major legal development (see Nacro, 2003b), giving a significant level of protection to the vulnerable suspect. Pearse (2001) describes it as the most important contemporary safeguard for juveniles, although he had earlier (Pearse and Gudjohnsson, 1996) called it 'a cosmetic and superficial exercise designed to satisfy legal etiquette' that could create conflict between the AA and the legal adviser. This is similar to Robertson et al.'s (1996) belief that the AA's presence could provide 'spurious reliability' for interview material. However, there is only one short account of good practice (Jones, 2001a) and most other literature is critical, for several reasons.

Debates on the Police and Criminal Evidence Bill ignored the AA role, and in subsequent guidance the main attention was given to police powers to stop and search, powers of entry, search

and seizure, and the new police complaints system (e.g. Driscoll, 1986; Christian, 1983). In the first edition of the Codes, the sole reference to AAs was in a note of guidance, and it only became a full part of the Codes in the 1991 edition (Home Office, 1991b; Littlechild, 1995).

The fact that the guidance suggested that a parent or guardian was the preferred AA also meant that the role of the social worker was relegated to 'second best'. The DHSS (1985) denied that there would be significant costs for local authorities of the introduction of PACE. This provided ammunition to managers in social services departments (SSDs) who were resistant to the development of the role on cost grounds, despite a strong Court of Appeal decision critical of a local authority pushing the responsibility back onto a parent when a young woman was clearly estranged from him (DPP v Blake, 1989). Articles in the social work press expressed concern that carrying out the role could lead to conflict between the police and social workers (Kay and Quao, 1987). Social work anxiety increased after a practitioner acting as an AA, following the instructions of her director, told the police that the suspect had confessed to a murder to her in private, and then became a witness in the case (Ogden, 1992).

An early opportunity to test the strength of the AA occurred in Tottenham during the investigation into the murder of PC Blakelock in 1985. Tottenham was one of the trial sites for the Codes of Practice, before they were to be implemented nationally. When a social worker acting as the AA tried to ensure that the police observed the Codes during interrogation of juveniles with learning difficulties, he was thrown out of the police station and replaced by a 'third-tier' AA. While the latter was a teacher, it subsequently transpired that she was also the girlfriend of the detective leading the investigation (see Jones, H, 1987; Gifford, 1989) who allowed the police to act unchallenged. It was these interviews that led to the wrongful conviction of Winston Silcott.

Blackwell (1990) has claimed that, as some social workers began to develop expertise in carrying out the AA role, the police would make greater efforts to get parents instead. It is true that in the early 1990s there was some evidence of attention to the role, particularly in youth justice teams in local authorities. There would always be workshops on the topic at National Association of Youth Justice and Nacro youth crime conferences, for example. Various commentators had pushed hard for training of social workers (Thomas, 1988, 1993; White, 2002) though most seemed to forget that in the majority of cases untrained parents acted as the AA. The Royal Commission on Criminal Justice (RCCJ) report on miscarriages of justice, in 1993, called for training and the development of a panel of people with expertise (RCCJ, 1993) and recommended that the Home Office carry out a comprehensive review of the 'role, functions, qualifications, training and availability' of AAs. Sadly, this review (Home Office, 1995b) added little to the debate, and the development of good practice in youth justice teams was shot in the foot by the decision of the highly influential Audit Commission to categorise the role as one of 'helping the police', and to then recommend that it should be carried out by volunteers (Audit Commission, 1996: for a critical account of this report see Jones, 2001b).

Research into the appropriate adult role

Most available research into the function of AAs has been commissioned by the Home Office. In a study of 5,500 custody records from 10 police force areas in 1987, Brown (1989) found that AAs were provided by a parent/relative in 77% of cases, by social workers in 17%, and by others in the remaining 5%. Irving and McKenzie (1989) raised concerns about a possible tension within the role concerning how AAs were to 'facilitate communication' between the police and the juvenile without detracting from the juvenile's right to silence – a conflict which has since been resolved by the partial abolition of the right to silence by the Criminal Justice and Public Order Act 1994.

Brown et al. (1992) considered 10,167 records from 12 police stations during 1990–91, observed over 500 cases being processed, interviewed 500 detainees, and analysed 814 questionnaires returned by custody officers. They noted an increase in the proportion of AAs being provided by social workers, to 28%, and criticised the failure of the police to explain the role of the AA to the juvenile.

Perhaps the most useful research has been that conducted by Evans (1993) for the RCCJ. He studied the processing of 367 juvenile suspects

and analysed 164 taped interviews. He found no clarification of the role of the AA on the tape, and noted that 75% of those carrying out the function made no contribution at all. In the 29 cases involving social workers, he noted only one contribution each from a social worker and a residential worker. He claimed that the police used 'persuasive and oppressive tactics' in a quarter of the interviews, even where a solicitor was also present.

Evans and Rawsthorne (1997) surveyed the provision of AAs in 18 SSDs in the North West of England, and interviewed 140 police officers and some social workers. They noted the poor quality of legal advice offered to juveniles by solicitors, suggesting that the AA needs to be able to advise and assist them and needs a good working knowledge of the Codes of Practice.

Social workers acted as AAs in 23% of the juvenile cases observed by Bucke and Brown (1997), in a much larger study involving adult detainees as well. They again noted the limited advice given by police to AAs about their function.

Finally, Brown (1997) raised concerns about the competence of AAs, one third of whom, in the study, were provided by social workers, and concluded that neither parents nor social workers played a significant role.

Is a parent an appropriate appropriate adult?

The problem that immediately faces any attempt to improve the provision of AAs, is that, in the large majority of cases, they are provided by a parent. Even when a YOT commits itself to developing a trained and experienced service, these only impact on a small proportion of those detained. Most juveniles will still be faced with a parent fulfilling the function.

Given the wider context of parental responsibility that now underpins youth justice, parents are likely to feel that they too are under suspicion. Even a confident, assertive parent will have little understanding of the role, and be very dependent upon the police or a solicitor if they have requested one, for guidance. Research demonstrates that parents are likely to be:

- uncooperative and unsupportive to the juvenile
- hostile to the juvenile

- indifferent to the juvenile
- on the side of the police
            (Bucke and Brown, 1997)

In one case researchers witnessed a parent ask the police to give their son 'the fright of his life', and, in another, saw a mother assault her son in the police's presence (Bucke and Brown, 1997). Other examples include the uncle of a 14 year old boy taking over the questioning from the police (Pearse and Gudjohnnson, 1996) and a mother promising to 'get my fist round his lug', which she later did, in front of, and to the approval of, the officers (Dixon et al., 1990).

This has led many to call for a rethink of the parental role (Law Society, 1993; Littlechild, 1995; Williams, 2000a). The Association for Youth Justice (1993) claimed that parents are the 'least equipped' to carry out the function. Dixon (1990: 118) raised concern that parents could well see their role as 'being to assist the police in extracting "the truth" from their children', using tactics that are forbidden to the police. Evans (1993) found that parents were as likely to be unsupportive of their children as supportive of them, and used their own oppressive and abusive tactics against the children. Where they did support their child, the police told them to be quiet. Brown et al. (1992) argued that 'in many cases parents are ill-equipped to fulfil the function' and noted that some took the side of the police.

A statutory duty and the use of volunteers

In 1997, a government consultation paper recommended that local authorities should have a clear duty to ensure an AA service in their area (Home Office, 1997a). While s38 of CDA incorporated this proposal, the government made it clear, during the Bill's passage, that it saw parents as normally fulfilling the role (Hansard, Lords, 1998), something reiterated in guidance (Home Office, 1998a).

At the same time, the recommendation of the Audit Commission to transfer the responsibility to the voluntary sector has been reflected in the encouragement, including grants, given to YOTs to develop volunteer provision (Home Office, 1998c; Youth Justice Board, 2001a). The police have also been enthusiastic, with HM Inspectorate

of Constabulary praising a volunteer scheme in Barnet (Littlechild, 1998).

Little has yet been published about the workings of volunteer schemes, though some concern has been raised about their use. Gloucestershire police used a volunteer to interview Frederick West who sat in on over 80 interviews and had several private meetings with him. After his suicide, she was called to give evidence of these interviews in the prosecution of Rosemary West, apparently without any support from the agency that supplied her. The Court of Appeal has suggested that the police owed her a 'duty of care' (Palmer, 1996). Another article, by a volunteer in Hounslow (Leibrich, 2000), suggested to this reader that she had been co-opted by the police and seemed to assume that all suspects were guilty (see my letter in response, Jones 2000).

Various voluntary organisations have contracted with YOTs to provide AA services, and initial experience suggests that they can offer quality provision and are developing the required level of training and support necessary for the role to be fulfilled effectively (see Pierpoint, 2000). However the arrangements frequently exclude child 'looked after' by a local authority, thereby put responsibility for them back onto untrained workers and foster carers.

Conclusion

The AA, as Hodgson (1997) argues, is 'an important safeguard . . . but one wh yet been fully realised'. The duty, in t everyone involved in youth justice crime' may be in tension with the 2000b), and the decision to characte one of assisting the police has clear a protection of the rights of suspe of statutory services is frequen avoid providing a service when

In my view, the full po safeguard will not be realise responsibility for their provis parents, and is made a statu authority, adequately funde ously be allowed to atten AA role. The duty solici obvious model to follow as an appropriate adu which would ensure t

12 Reprimands and Final Warnings

Sandy Pragnell

Key points

1. The final warning scheme introduced by the Crime and Disorder Act 1998 replaces cautioning for children and young people with a formalised system of pre-court disposals.

2. The scheme provides for a, relatively inflexible, three tier approach to police decision making: a first offence generally results in a reprimand; a second offence will receive a warning; a third offence automatically gives rise to prosecution – other than in exceptional circumstances – irrespective of the nature of the offending.

3. Concerns had been expressed about the previous inconsistent use of cautioning and so the final warning scheme is intended to limit police discretion. The use of a 'case disposal gravity factor system' to inform decision making provides for an additional level of objectivity.

4. Youth offending teams have a performance target; set by the Youth Justice Board, that 80% of warnings should be accompanied by a programme of intervention.

5. The system has led to unprecedentedly high levels of children and young people entering the court system and has, arguably, helped to fuel the increase in the use of custody.

Introduction

The scheme of reprimands and final warnings was introduced by the Crime and Disorder Act 1998 (CDA) as a replacement for police cautioning of children and young people. Cautioning had afforded the police relatively wide discretion to deal with young people who offended and cautions could be administered on a number of occasions if the police considered it appropriate. The final warning scheme, by contrast, limits police discretion by introducing a three-staged response to offending behaviour. A reprimand is given for a first offence and a warning for a second offence, providing the offences in question are relatively minor and the young person admits responsibility. Any further offending following a warning – no matter how trivial – will normally result in prosecution.

Final warnings also differ from cautions in that the police are under a statutory duty to refer the young person to the youth offending team (YOT) for an assessment and there is an expectation that this will result in a programme of intervention unless the YOT considers it unnecessary.

The replacement of cautions by the final warning scheme represents an attempt by government to inject greater rigour and consistency into pre-court disposals, and to confront young people with the consequences of their offending at the earliest possible point in their offending careers. The Youth Justice Board has set a target to ensure that 80% of final warnings are supported by an intervention (see Chapter 4).

By introducing the final warning scheme the Home Office was attempting to respond to the positive evidence that was being produced by 'caution plus' schemes. These were schemes that attached some form of intervention to the police caution. The Audit Commission (1996) asserted that such intervention was critical in preventing re-offending. However, according to the report *Misspent Youth* (Audit Commission, 1996), only 2% of young people cautioned at that time received intervention via a 'caution plus' programme.

An overview of reprimands and final warnings

Section 65 of the CDA replaced the pre-existing cautioning procedures for children and young people with the final warning scheme. Cautioning for adults still remains. The previous system had been criticised because of the inconsistency of its application by different police forces and, indeed, police divisions within service areas, resulting in large disparities in the rates of diversion from court. Concern was also expressed that multiple cautioning could bring the process into disrepute (Home Office, 1994). Moreover, in many areas little assistance was being offered to cautioned young people to prevent them re-offending (Audit Commission, 1996).

The introduction of the final warning scheme was intended to bring greater clarity to the system, encourage consistency in police decision making and provide a meaningful response to offending behaviour through early intervention by the YOT. In this sense, the scheme is intended to contribute towards the principal aim of the post-1998 youth justice system, to prevent offending by children and young people by diverting them from their offending behaviour before they enter the courts.

The objectives of reprimand and final warning schemes concern:

- Ending the use of 'informal action'.
- Ending repeat cautioning.
- Providing a progressive and effective response to offending behaviour.
- Providing appropriate and effective interventions to prevent re-offending.
- Ensuring that young people who do re-offend after being warned are dealt with quickly and effectively by the courts.

(Home Office/Youth Justice Board, 2002)

Responsibility for decisions about pre-court disposals remain with the police but the following criteria must be met if they are to issue a reprimand or warning:

- There is evidence that the young person has committed an offence.
- The evidence is sufficient for there to be a realistic prospect of conviction if the case were to go to court.
- The young person gives a clear and reliable admission to all elements of the offence.
- They must have no previous convictions (or pending court proceedings).
- It is not in the public interest for the young person to be prosecuted.

In addition, recent case law suggests that, to comply with the Human Rights Act 1998, a reprimand or warning requires the informed, and explicit, consent of the young person (Stone, 2003). This requirement has, however, yet to be reflected in guidance to the police or YOTs, and it is not clear to what extent it has impacted on police practice.

Schemes operate on a three-stage approach. Providing the relevant criteria are satisfied, a first offence will generally result in a reprimand, a second offence will attract a warning, and a third and any subsequent offending will result in the young person being prosecuted. The police decision also depends on the seriousness of the offence as well as the young person's offending history. Serious offences and in particular 'grave' offences (those which carry a term of imprisonment of 14 years or more for an adult) will usually lead to an immediate charge without the requirement to go through the first two stages.

In more formal terms, a young person may be reprimanded if they have not previously been reprimanded, warned or prosecuted, provided that the offence is not so serious as to require a warning or charge. No further reprimand can be given under any circumstances. A warning may be issued, provided the offence is not so serious as to warrant prosecution and the young person has not been previously warned or convicted. A young person may be given a second warning where the offence has been committed more than two years after the previous warning and the police consider the offence to be not so serious as to require a charge being brought. In no circumstances can a young person receive more than two warnings.

Assessment

In order to encourage greater consistency, and to lend an element of objectivity to the decision making process, the Association of Chief Police Officers has developed a gravity factor system which generates a score for the offence, between 1 and 4, on the basis of seriousness, and indicates the appropriate course of action, depending on previous offending history. Each offence type is allocated an initial gravity score that may be modified in the light of aggravating and mitigating factors specific to the particular offence committed by the individual young person. The scoring process is shown in Table 12.1.

Table 12.1: Police decision making

Gravity score	Police Action
1	Always the minimum response applicable to the individual young person – i.e. reprimand, warning or charge.
2	Normally reprimand for first offence. If the young person does not qualify for a reprimand but qualifies for a warning, then give warning. If the young person does not qualify for a warning then charge.
3	Normally warn for first offence. If the young person does not qualify for a warning then charge. Only in exceptional circumstances should a reprimand be given. Decision maker needs to justify reprimand.
4	Always charge.

Source: ACPO/Youth Justice Board 2002: 9.

Depending on local arrangements, and the individual circumstances of the young person, a reprimand may result in a referral to the YOT. In the case of a final warning, however, there is a statutory requirement for such a referral and the YOT is obliged to undertake an assessment, using ASSET, the common assessment tool for the youth justice system (see Chapter 19), to establish whether a programme of intervention would be beneficial. Guidance encourages the police to bail the young person before a final decision to warn is taken, in order to allow the YOT to explore what sort of programme might be offered and whether the young person is likely to comply with it. The assessment should:

- Identify any risk factors associated with the young person's offending behaviour such as homelessness, substance misuse, poor school attendance and/or unemployment.
- Consider the victim's views and the impact of the offence on the victim.
- Assess the likelihood of the young person taking part in any intervention.

There is a statutory presumption that a warning will lead to a programme of intervention unless the YOT considers it inappropriate. That presumption is reinforced by a performance target, set by the Youth Justice Board – and potentially linked to funding – that an intervention will be delivered in 80% of final warnings with a minimum level of contact of two face-to-face sessions. The programme should be designed to address:

- The circumstance of the offence(s).
- The impact of the offence(s) on the victim(s).
- Any risk factors that have been identified that lead to the young person committing an offence or that would increase the likelihood of their re-offending.

(Youth Justice Board, 2003a)

Implementation

Both reprimands and warnings can be given at the police station but legislation has been amended to allow delivery elsewhere. For instance, the YOT may be more appropriate in terms of the needs of the young person and the wishes of the victim. If a young person is under 17 years of age, they must be accompanied by an 'appropriate adult' and whenever possible this should be a parent or carer (see Chapter 11).

The police officer administering the reprimand or warning is required to point out to the young person the seriousness of the disposal and the consequences of future offending. Compliance with a programme of intervention is, in principle, voluntary but an unreasonable failure to comply with an intervention programme may be cited in any future court hearings, in a similar way to previous convictions. Furthermore, if a young person has received a warning within the past two years the court can only give a conditional discharge in exceptional circumstances.

A reprimand or warning remains on a young person's record for five years, or until they are 18 years of age, whichever is the greater. Although a reprimand or warning is not a conviction the record can be made available to a potential employer under certain circumstances. Offences of a sexual nature that have attracted a reprimand or warning may also be subject to the requirements of registration under the Sex Offences Act 2003.

Guidance emphasises that wherever possible the process should be a restorative one and points to the importance of involving victims in the final warning process and any related intervention (see Chapters 28 and 33). A restorative administration of warnings has the potential to increase victim satisfaction with both the process and outcome, and there is some evidence to suggest that it may also be more effective than the traditional method of cautioning in reducing re-offending (Hoyle et al., 2002).

Evidence of impact and effectiveness

The final warning system has resulted in a rigid and formalised process for responding to early offending by young people. It is intended to bring with it greater consistency and eliminate multiple pre-court disposals by placing clear limits on police discretion. It has created a stepped response to offending, based upon the seriousness of the offence and previous offending history. The Youth Justice Board has hailed the final warning scheme as a great success in helping to prevent offending, marking a considerable improvement over 'discredited repeat police cautioning' (Youth Justice Board, 2002b). However the available evidence indicates that the picture is more complicated than the Board's pronouncements suggest.

Whilst there may be merits in limiting the discretion of individual police officers in order to tackle discrimination, the scheme has also removed their professional assessment. In addition, it seems likely that the extent of repeat cautioning that was occurring has been exaggerated. Home Office guidance on the use of cautions indicated that one caution was appropriate before prosecution, unless the subsequent offence was trivial or sufficient time had elapsed since the first offence (Home Office, 1994). Unless the police were flouting the guidance, it seems likely that the majority of offences that attracted a second or subsequent caution were relatively minor. Indeed, research conducted during the early 1990s found that only 3% of juveniles cautioned over a single month had more than two previous offences (cited in Haines and Drakeford, 1998).

Nor has the new system proved a guarantee of consistency. Criminal statistics for 2002, for instance, indicate that the variation in rates of diversion between police service areas is only marginally narrower than the equivalent figures for cautioning in 1998; ranging from 65% of 15–17 year olds processed in Surrey, to 21% in Cheshire (Home Office, 2003b). This picture is confirmed by Youth Justice Board data for 2002–2003 which shows a regional variation in the proportion of all youth disposals resulting in reprimand or final warning of between 38% and 51% (Youth Justice Board, 2003b).

The inconsistencies also exist in the content and extent of any intervention attached to a final warning. The Audit Commission, in its review of youth justice reforms, reports that although the YJB target of 80% of cases receiving a YOT intervention is likely to be met, the intensity of these interventions varies enormously; between a single session on the consequences of offending to several weekly sessions, covering a range of topics such as drugs, alcohol and sexual health (Audit Commission, 2004).

Cautioning was criticised because the potential for multiple cautioning, irrespective of a young person's previous offending history, brought the cautioning system into disrepute. From an alternative perspective, this might be seen as a strength since its flexibility allowed a proportionate response to the current offence, taking into account any previous disposals for more serious matters. Thus, a young person, who may have previously served a custodial sentence for a serious violent offence, could be dealt with for a minor theft, committed a year after release, without recourse to court proceedings, thereby recognising the comparative severity of the two incidents. The final warning scheme precludes such flexibility.

A further consequence of the changes is that large numbers of young people with relatively minor offences are being processed through to court. The Audit Commission report points to a fourfold increase in the number of absolute discharges granted by youth courts between April 2002 and April 2003 and the fact that one in four referral orders are made for minor offences (Audit Commission, 2004). The rate of diversion from prosecution fell throughout the1990s and the final warning scheme has continued, and apparently, reinforced, this trend (Nacro, 2003j). (It should be noted however that a Home Office study using a small data-base (Jennings, 2003), concludes that there was a proportionate increase in police pre-court disposals from 65% in 1997 to 76% in the period January to March 2001.) Young people are thus entering court at a much younger age, arguably accelerating their progress through the system and contributing to the recent increase in the use of custody (see Chapter 25; Burnett and Appleton, 2004a).

This apparent reduction in the use of diversion has raised a concern that the final warning scheme may be 'widening the net' by drawing in young people who would not previously have come into contact with the formal criminal justice system. Some commentators have pointed to the potential for this process to impact negatively upon the life chances of those individuals and to increase the likelihood of their re-offending. While youth justice orthodoxy extols the virtue of intervening early in a young person's criminal career to 'nip offending in the bud', research reveals that:

> *Formal intervention with children and young people in trouble within the youth justice system can, and often does, have a negative impact in terms of their future involvement in crime and their adult life chances.*
>
> (Pitts, 2003a)

Available re-offending figures indicate that 70% of young people do not re-offend following a reprimand. Jennings (2003), like Hine and Celnick (2001), argues that reprimands and warnings have resulted in a reduction in reconviction rates compared with the system of cautioning. However, what these studies fail to take into account is that these new, younger, less problematic populations entering the system are the most trivial offenders, who are least likely to re-offend in any case and would in all probability have been dealt with informally in previous periods. Moreover, it is by now fairly well established that between 70% and 80% of young people do not re-offend following a first arrest in any event, irrespective of whether a formal intervention is made, and that they also avoid the stigmatising effects of a formal disposal which can subsequently be cited in court (Kemp et al., 2002).

There is an issue of proportionality at stake here since young people may find themselves propelled up the criminal justice tariff and, as a result, subject to more punitive responses and more intensive intervention than an adult committing a similar offence. Not only are there risks attached to intervening too early but it might also be wasteful of valuable resources.

An alternative approach

The final warning scheme was intended to eliminate the previously widely used measure of 'informal action', a disposal which 'fell short of a formal caution' (Home Office, 1994), on the grounds that it undermined a formal response to offending behaviour and encouraged inconsistency. Yet research suggests that informal action was highly successful in reducing re-offending (Kemp et al., 2002), and some police service areas have continued to make unsanctioned use of informal action prior to a reprimand.

Nacro and the Cambridge Institute of Criminology have conducted research into the use of informal actions in Northamptonshire. They conclude that, all things being equal, the greatest predictor of whether a young person would re-offend was whether they had been prosecuted, with those subject to court proceedings being significantly more likely to re-offend than those who had not. They observe that:

> *As far as young offenders are concerned, prosecution at any stage has no beneficial effect in preventing re-offending. On the contrary, prosecution only seems to increase the likelihood of re-offending.*
>
> (Kemp et al., 2002)

It is perhaps significant, and not a little ironic, in this context, that the Audit Commission, whose review of the youth justice system is widely credited with shaping the subsequent reforms, cited the Northamptonshire model as an exemplar of good practice (Audit Commission, 1996). *Misspent Youth* also noted that research suggested cautioning was effective up to three occasions. Given that the principal aim of the post 1998 youth justice system in England and Wales is to prevent offending by young people, it seems perverse that the re-vamped system allows for only two disposals prior to prosecution. The Audit Commission (2004), when noting the rise in the number of low-risk young people currently entering the court system, comments that this could be due, in part, to the removal of multiple cautioning. Nonetheless, rational debate on the issue appears to have been discouraged by policy makers. Hopefully, as custodial numbers mount, they will revisit the evidence and this 'veil of silence' will be lifted.

This is not to advocate a return to the 'benign neglect' associated with the 1980s where young people with considerable, and obvious, welfare needs were offered no support in the mistaken belief that the avoidance of official stigma was all that was required for them to lead successful and law-abiding lives (Pitts, 2003b). Informal action is not the same as inaction. Early identification of young people vulnerable to offending is to be encouraged. Once identified their needs cannot and should not be ignored. However, factors that make young people susceptible to committing offences also make them vulnerable to school failure, drug abuse, teenage parenthood and criminal victimisation, so why then intervene in a way that labels and stigmatises them as criminals?

Why can't we respond to a child in need who also offends outside the criminal justice system? As the *Every Child Matters* White Paper (2003) attests, rather than simply punishing them, we need to develop responses which focus upon the long-term interests and developmental needs of these troubled youngsters. Perhaps the 'rediscovery' of informal action would open-up the space necessary to offer appropriate intervention to vulnerable children without the stigmatising effects of a formal record. Such an approach has the potential to save considerable time and resources, while also reducing re-offending.

As part of the government's police reform programme to seek ways to increase the presence of uniformed officers in the community, a national task force, headed by Sir David O'Dowd, the former Chief Inspector of Constabulary was assembled. This Policing Bureaucracy Taskforce argued for legislative change to ratify a 'four stage approach' by allowing informal action prior to reprimand (Home Office, 2002a). The report concluded that such a development would not only reduce offending behaviour but, nationally, would save the police force alone an estimated £100 million pounds per annum. Of the 52 recommendations contained within the report this was the only one to be rejected by the Home Office.

Conclusion

Criticism of police cautioning was not unjustified. There were large disparities in the cautioning rate from one area to another and the wide discretion afforded to the police allowed too broad a role for subjectivity. In retrospect, it is unsurprising that

the system had, in some quarters, fallen into disrepute. A system that offered more objectivity and consistency was required.

The extent to which the introduction of reprimands and final warnings has brought about significant improvements is however open to debate. Youth Justice Board statistics show continued disparities in rates of reprimands and warnings; the application of the gravity factor system is open to interpretation with the result that scoring gives subjective decision-making an objective gloss. Unprecedented numbers of young people are being drawn into court in the face of evidence that such action can exacerbate offending.

Moreover, the relative rigidity of the system means that the search for objectivity in disposal has occurred at the expense of essential flexibility in responding to young people and their offending behaviour in a way that is understood by them and proportional to their actions. Pre-court diversion should provide an opportunity for young people to learn from their mistakes and offer non-stigmatising services designed to reduce the risk of further offending. Based on the evidence currently available, the final warning scheme does not offer this.

Further reading

Bateman, T. (2003) Living With Final Warnings: Making the Best of a Bad Job? *Youth Justice.* 2: 3

Home Office/Youth Justice Board (2002) *Final Warning Scheme: Guidance for the Police and Youth Offending Teams.* London: Home Office

Kemp, V., Sorsby, A., Liddle, M. and Merrington, S. (2002) *Assessing Responses to Youth Offending in Northamptonshire.* Research Briefing 2. London: Nacro

Pitts, J. (2003a) Changing Youth Justice. *Youth Justice.* 3: 1

Pitts, J. (2003b) *The New Politics of Youth Crime: Discipline or Solidarity.* Lyme Regis: Russell House Publishing

13 The Role of the Courts

Chris Stanley

Key points

1. A separate 'juvenile' court was set up for children and young people for the first time by the Children Act 1908.

2. The youth court is presided over by lay magistrates who are specially selected and trained. In a small number of courts district judges, who are paid, qualified, lawyers, sit.

3. The principles of child welfare, proportionality and preventing offending govern the decisions of the youth court.

4. The public are excluded from the youth court and procedures are less formal than those associated with adult courts.

5. Youth courts deal with the vast majority of young people who offend. A small number of 'grave crimes' are sent to the crown court.

The origins of the youth court

The Children Act 1908, or the 'children's charter' as it was described at the time, introduced a national system of juvenile courts to England and Wales. These courts were special sittings of Magistrates' courts, which dealt mainly with criminal cases involving children and young people aged between eight and 16 but also with those arrested for begging and vagrancy. Meanwhile, the Prevention of Crime Act of the same year imposed restrictions on custodial sentences for 14–15 year olds, and established borstals as a sentence for 16–23 year olds.

From their inception, the juvenile courts were required to consider both the criminal behaviour of children and young people and their welfare needs. Like the adult courts from which they derived, juvenile courts aimed to deter young people from offending and to punish them when they did so. However, they also proceeded from the assumption that children and young people, by dint of their relative immaturity, are less able to control their impulses, less capable of understanding the seriousness of their offences and less able to foresee the consequences of their actions. Linked to this was the belief that the culpability of many young people who offend could be further mitigated by the poverty, cruelty or neglect they

have suffered. These ideas were enshrined in law in the Children and Young Persons Act 1933 (CYPA) which established the principle that:

> Every court dealing with a child or young person who is brought before it, either as an offender or otherwise, shall have regard to the welfare of the child or young person, and shall in a proper case take steps for removing him from undesirable surroundings and for securing that proper provision is made for his education and training.
>
> (section 44)

This 'welfare' principle continues to inform decision making in the present day youth court. The 1933 Act also created, for the first time, panels of specialist magistrates, also known as Justices of the Peace (JPs), who were appointed to deal with both juveniles processed for offending and children and young people in need of care and protection.

In the 1960s, the Longford Report, *Crime: A Challenge to Us All* (1964), proposed that the welfare principle should become more central to the juvenile jurisdiction and that the juvenile court should be replaced by a welfare-oriented family council, not unlike what was to become the Scottish children's hearing system (see Chapter 3). But, these proposals were resisted by politicians, magistrates, lawyers and the probation service. Nonetheless, continued pressure for a greater emphasis on welfare resulted in the Children and Young Persons Act 1969 which, if fully implemented, would have raised the age of criminal responsibility to 14, restricted the prosecution of 14–16 year olds and replaced the court's power to make custodial sentences with care and supervision orders (Pitts, 1988).

The incoming Conservative government of 1971 failed to implement many of the measures introduced by the 1969 Act and this left youth justice legislation in a mess: an unsatisfactory mix of welfare and justice. There were demands for a unified family court, but the post-1969 Act statutory framework remained intact until 1992, when implementation of the Children Act 1989 created the family proceedings court which assumed responsibility for child welfare cases, leading to the separation of child care and criminal matters. As a result, specially trained magistrates began to sit in the two separate jurisdictions, although it is not unusual for some magistrates to sit in both. In the same year, the juvenile court was renamed the youth court by the Criminal Justice Act 1991 and its jurisdiction was extended to encompass 17 year olds.

The youth court

The majority of young people aged between 10 and 18, who are prosecuted for criminal offences are processed by the youth court. A small but growing number, who are alleged to have committed 'grave crimes' are tried by the crown court, and, if convicted, may be sentenced under sections 91/92 of the Powers of Criminal Courts (Sentencing) Act 2000 (see Chapter 25). In addition a young person may be 'carried' to the crown court if they are charged jointly with an adult.

Youth courts are presided over by lay magistrates or a district judge. Experienced lay magistrates, who undertake the role voluntarily and are not legal professionals, are appointed to a youth court panel and, after specialist training may sit in a youth court. Youth court magistrates usually sit in groups of three, with the most senior serving as the chair of the bench. The lay bench should consist of at least one man and one woman.

District judges (formerly stipendiary magistrates), who are lawyers appointed to sit as full-time magistrates, may also sit in the youth court. They can sit alone or with lay magistrates.

Magistrates in each petty sessional division elect the youth panel every three years. In selecting a panel, magistrates are required to appoint only those amongst them who have specialist experience of hearing cases involving children and young people. The Lord Chancellor has indicated that it is desirable for panel members to complete at least 13 sittings a year in the youth court so that they can retain their experience and use the training they have undertaken (LCD Circular AC (1992) (5)).

In 1991, the age of retirement for youth magistrates was raised from 65 to 70 years, the general retirement age for magistrates. Evidence from a recent study of magistrates appointed to youth courts (cited in Ball et al., 2002) indicates that they are an ageing population, with nearly 70% being appointed at or after the age of 45, and 13% being over 55 years at the time of their appointment. The study went on to question whether these magistrates were, in fact, 'especially qualified' to join the youth court, as the law requires, since the age of the majority of them necessarily distances them from the contemporary life-styles of children and young people.

Effective decision making requires that youth court magistrates should have as full an understanding as possible of the range of interventions available for addressing and reducing offending behaviour and effecting rehabilitation. This is facilitated by the twice-yearly meetings which youth court panels are required to have with other agencies involved in the youth justice system which have, since the establishment of youth offending teams (YOTs), invariably included YOT staff. One of the purposes of such meetings is to ensure effective communication between the bench and other court users about the programmes of intervention available in the local community. Recent research conducted on behalf of the Youth Justice Board, however, suggests that one in five magistrates considered the overall quality of the exchange of information between the court and YOTs to be unsatisfactory or poor (Bateman and Stanley, 2002).

The court process

Youth courts are guided by three central principles; prevention of offending, the welfare of the child and proportionality. Section 37 of the Crime and Disorder Act 1998 states that:

It shall be the principle aim of the youth justice system to prevent offending by children and young persons.

At the same time, the courts must have regard to the welfare of the child in accordance with section 44 of CYPA (see Chapter 8). While that legislation is now some 70 years old, the principle gains more recent reinforcement from the United Nations Convention on the Rights of the Child, Article 3 which states that:

In all actions concerning children, whether undertaken by public or private social welfare institutions, courts of law, administrative authorities or legislative bodies, the best interests of the child shall be a primary consideration.

The Criminal Justice Act 1991 established the principle of proportionality, which means that the sentence of the court should fit the seriousness of the crime. This is sometimes known as the 'just deserts' approach to sentencing:

The sentence for a given offence should reflect primarily the seriousness of the offence which has been committed.

(Home Office, 1991a)

The youth court sits at the lowest level of the court structure in England and Wales and all cases involving defendants of less than 18 years of age are processed in the first instance in that court unless the young person is jointly charged with an adult. Where an offence can carry 14 years or more in the case of an adult, the youth court magistrates can commit the case for trial at the crown court if they consider that a sentence of more than two years custody should be available to the sentencing court. In that event, the maximum sentence is that which would be available to adults. Having determined which court should have jurisdiction, the process in effect involves three forms of decision making:

- Where there is to be an adjournment the question of bail arises, and the court must adopt a structured approach to determining the most appropriate remand status for the individual young person (see below).
- The court must also determine the facts of the case. If a young person denies the offence this will involve a trial. The procedure is similar to that for adults: the prosecution is required to prove the charges against the defendant and will present evidence and call witnesses in an attempt to do so. The defence may then elect to present its case and the young person and any witnesses may give evidence. Both prosecution and defence are entitled to cross-examine each other's witnesses. In the youth court, magistrates determine the issue of guilt. Those young people tried in crown court are subject to jury trial.
- In the event of a conviction, the court decides on the most appropriate form of sentence, if necessary adjourning to allow the preparation of a pre-sentence or other forms of report by the YOT (see below).

Parents are generally expected to attend court if their child is under 16, and can be compelled to attend if the court thinks it necessary. In most cases the young person will be given legal aid and represented by a lawyer.

The court room

The youth court normally sits in a special courtroom, designed to be less formal than an adult court. Some will consist of a set of tables laid out in a square with lawyers, young people, parents, the court clerk (who is a legal advisor to the bench), YOT members and magistrates sitting around it.

There are restrictions on who may be present in a youth court. Members of the public and anyone under 14 are not allowed in the court unless they are defendants or witnesses. Those allowed in court are:

- officers of the court
- defence and prosecution lawyers (but only if they are part of the case being heard)
- witnesses concerned with the case
- YOT members
- trainee YOT staff
- victims
- representatives from newspapers and the media

Section 49 of CYPA, as amended, restricts the reporting of proceedings in the youth court, preventing any publication which might reveal or lead to the name of the young person concerned in the proceedings being revealed. There are however certain exceptions to this and the court may listen to representations before making an order to dispense with reporting restrictions if they deem this to be in the public interest. The 1998 Joint LCD/HO Guidance encourages the court to lift reporting restrictions in certain cases:

- If the nature of the young person's offending is so persistent or serious and has impacted on a number of people in their local community.
- If it alerts others to the young person's behaviour helping to prevent further offending by them.

Despite this circular, reporting restrictions have hitherto rarely been lifted by youth courts. However, the Criminal Justice Act 2003 removes the presumption of privacy where the court imposes a post conviction anti-social behaviour order as well as a substantive disposal, and the impact of this measure on court practice remains to be seen.

In recent years, following the issuing of a good practice guide by the Home Office and Lord Chancellor's Department (1998), efforts have been directed to 'opening up the youth court', making it more accessible to young people and their families, by improving the layout, attempting to engage the defendant and their family, using everyday language in an attempt to reduce formality and increasing victim involvement in the process, and encouraging feedback to sentencers. In addition, attempts have been made to improve relations with the media by lifting reporting restrictions in appropriate cases. Implementation appears to have been inconsistent. Not all youth courts have adopted the recommended changes and some still routinely sit in adult courtrooms. Nonetheless, where the good practice guide has been followed, court users have been relatively positive with over half considering that the impact had been beneficial. Moreover, some areas report a shift in sentencing patterns with a slight fall in the use of custody and an increase in conditional and absolute discharges as a result (Allen et al., 2000).

Delays

The New Labour government, elected in 1997, pledged to halve the time it took for 'persistent young offenders' to reach sentence. As a result those young people who meet the Home Office persistence definition (1997b), namely those who have been sentenced on three or more separate occasions within the last three years and are prosecuted for a further offence, are now 'fast tracked' through the system, with the police, the Crown Prosecution Service and the courts giving these cases priority over others. Indeed, it is not uncommon for such young people to arrive in court the day after their alleged offence. As a consequence of these measures, the pledge was met for the first time during 2001 with the period from arrest to sentence for 'persistent young offenders' being cut substantially from the baseline figure of 142 days to 64 days by June 2003 (Lowe and Gray, 2003). Although it is important that young people who offend get to court without delay so any penalty imposed by the court is seen as a direct consequence of their offence, there are other less beneficial outcomes.

In the past, when young people took longer to get to court, subsequent offending while on bail tended to be 'rolled up' into one court appearance where a single sentence was imposed. A speedier appearance in the court followed by sentence, followed by further offending will result in a quick succession of increasingly harsh sentences which will move the young person up the sentencing tariff very rapidly. There is also some evidence that the fast tracking of persistent offenders causes delays for non-persistent offenders.

Remand decisions
Bail

The powers to adjourn cases, and the length of the periods for which remands in care or custody or on bail may be granted by the youth court, are generally similar to those available to adult courts. A single magistrate may exercise these powers, although since the implementation of the Human Rights Act 1998, courts have been advised to involve at least two magistrates in remand decisions. Defendants can appeal to the crown court against Magistrates' courts and youth court remand decisions.

If a case is to be adjourned the court has, in effect, five options. It may remand the young person:

- On bail without conditions.
- On bail with conditions.
- To local authority accommodation with or without conditions.
- To local authority accommodation with a requirement that they be placed in secure accommodation.
- To custody.

(Nacro, 2003d)

There is a general right to bail, but it can be refused if the court believes that the young person would:

- Fail to attend court on the next occasion.
- Interfere with witnesses or obstruct the course of justice.
- Commit further offences on bail.
- Be at risk of self-harm (the welfare interests of the young person).
- The current offence was committed on bail.

Refusal of bail is only available if the risk that one of the above may occur cannot be addressed by attaching conditions to bail. Commonly used conditions include that the young person:

- Reside in a specified place.
- Report to the police station.
- Does not enter a specified area or place.
- Does not contact witnesses.
- Abides by a curfew.

YOTs are able to provide bail supervision and support programmes (BSS) that can address the courts concerns about the risks presented by young people and compliance with these programmes can be made a condition of bail (see Chapter 14). National standards require that such programmes should involve a minimum of three contacts a week.

Refusal of bail

Where bail is refused, the powers of the court depend upon the age and gender of the young person involved. 10 to 12 year olds may not be remanded to secure accommodation or custody and so refusal of bail will result in a remand to local authority accommodation. 12 to 14 year old boys and 12 to 16 year old girls cannot be remanded to custody and will therefore be remanded to local authority accommodation. However, if certain conditions are met, the court can attach a requirement that the local authority place the young person in secure accommodation – commonly referred to as a court ordered secure remand (COSR). 15 and 16 year old boys can be remanded into local authority accommodation, made subject of a COSR or remanded to custody. If the additional criteria, mentioned above, are met, the young person will be remanded to custody unless the court finds them vulnerable and a place is available in secure accommodation in which case they may make a COSR (see Chapter 14; Nacro, 2003h). 17 year olds are treated the same as adults for remand purposes and a refusal of bail will automatically result in a custodial remand.

Sentencing

Unless the defendant enters a 'not guilty' plea, the youth court grants an absolute discharge or it wishes to impose a custodial sentence, all young people appearing before the youth court for the first time for an imprisonable offence will receive a referral order (see Chapter 16). For any subsequent offending, or where a first offence is denied, the court has a broad range of sentencing options available to it, spanning fines, community sentences and custody.

Youth court magistrates are encouraged to employ a structured approach to sentencing and in arriving at their decisions they should consider each of the following factors:

- The seriousness of the offence.
- The welfare of the young person.
- What intervention is likely to reduce the risk of further offending.
- The range of sentencing options appropriate to the age and maturity of the defendant.
- Individual mitigating factors that may reduce the severity of the sentence.
- Whether the defendant has pleaded guilty (an early guilty plea will result in a one third reduction in a custodial sentence).
- Any ancillary orders which should be made against parents.

(Nacro, 2003k)

In some cases, particularly if the court is considering custody or a community sentence, the magistrates will adjourn the case and request that the YOT prepare a pre-sentence report (PSR) or sentence specific report (SSR) (see Chapter 18). In requesting a report, the court should indicate whether they consider that the case is 'serious enough' for them to be considering the imposition of a community penalty or 'so serious' that they are considering custody (see Chapter 9). The Youth Court Bench Book produced by the Judicial Studies Board provides offence indicators of seriousness which courts are encouraged to use as a starting point for their deliberations on the appropriate level of sentence (2001). The guide also contains a 'sentencing matrix' which relates the gravity of the offence and the risk of re-offending to a particular range of sentences, although it is important to understand that sentencing is intended to be an individual rather than a formulaic exercise.

There are currently fifteen sentencing options available for the youth court (though the Criminal Justice Act 2003 simplifies the sentencing framework for adults and there are proposals for similar legislation in relation to young people):

- absolute discharge
- referral order
- conditional discharge
- fine
- reparation order
- action plan order
- attendance centre order
- supervision order (with a variety of conditions)
- exclusion order
- community rehabilitation order (again with the possibility of conditions)
- community punishment order
- community punishment and rehabilitation order
- drug treatment and testing order
- curfew order
- detention and training order

(see Nacro, 2001a)

Prior to deciding on sentence, the court will hear representations from the young person's lawyer who will present mitigating factors which may reduce the severity of the sentence. The court may also speak directly to the young person and their parents. Mitigation will usually be concerned with factors such as:

- Cooperation with the police and credit being given for a guilty plea.
- The fact that the young person has shown remorse.
- The personal circumstances of the young person.

The court will also consider compensation and costs, a parental bind-over or parenting order (see Chapter 31) and in appropriate cases an anti-social behaviour order (Nacro, 2003c).

Conclusion

Do the courts and the sentences they impose help to reduce youth crime? Probably not. As Chapter 2 of this volume reveals, only 3% of offences result in a reprimand, a final warning or a conviction and, consequently, decisions of the youth court are unlikely to have a significant impact upon youth crime rates. It is also unlikely that sentencing will deter many young people since most offending is not pre-mediated, but committed on the spur of the moment and most young people assume that they will not be caught.

The Audit Commission (1996) found that the cost of processing young people through the youth justice system was over £1 billion per year, much of which was spent on young people, who offended repeatedly. The Commission therefore recommended a greater emphasis on early prevention and diversion from court. Recent research points to the effectiveness of diversion as a crime reduction strategy and suggests that, in most cases, prosecution is likely to have a negative effect on future offending (Kemp et al., 2002).

If this is so, we might usefully return to the Home Office guidance of 1985 which states that:

> *It is recognised both in theory and in practice that delay in the entry of a young person into a formal criminal justice system may help to prevent his entry into that system altogether. The Secretary of State commends to chief officers the policy that the prosecution of a juvenile is not a step to be taken without the full consideration of whether the public interest (and the interest of the juvenile concerned) may be better served by a course of action which falls short of prosecution. Thus chief officers will wish to ensure that their arrangements with dealing with juveniles are such that prosecution will not occur unless it is absolutely necessary.*

(Home Office, 1985)

Increasing the age of criminal responsibility would also decriminalise a large number of children who are currently treated as offenders, keeping them out of the criminal justice system and enabling their welfare needs to be addressed; arguably, a far more effective way of reducing their future offending.

There have been a number of calls recently for developing closer links between the youth court and the family proceedings courts (Butler-Sloss, 2003). This would enable youth courts to call for a welfare report from social services departments, and if this report revealed significant welfare needs then the child or young person could be transferred from the youth court to the family proceedings court.

On the face of it, this proposal is attractive. Children and young people with overwhelming welfare needs would end up in the court where help is on hand.

However, there are some problems with this approach:

- What happens to the criminal offence after transfer?
- Are there sufficient resources available via child welfare agencies to enable the family proceedings court to address welfare issues adequately?
- There is also the danger that being 'sentenced to welfare' could involve the young person in overly restrictive forms of welfare intervention in response to a relatively minor offence, as sometimes occurred in the 1970s and 1980s when care orders were frequently made for offending (Thorpe et al., 1980).

An alternative is for the Crown Prosecution Service to divert young people with pressing welfare needs who have committed criminal offences, away from the youth court to a multi-agency child welfare panel who, using the resources from a variety of child and youth-serving agencies, construct a comprehensive intervention that will address the child or young person's needs, in the manner proposed in the government's *Every Child Matters* Green Paper (2003b). This type of panel is currently being piloted under the auspices of the recently created Children's Trusts.

Further reading

Ashford, M. and Chard, A. (2000) *Defending Young People in the Criminal Justice System*. 2nd edn. London: Legal Action Group

Audit Commission (2004) *Youth Justice 2004: A Review of the Reformed Youth Justice System*. London: Audit Commission

Ball, C., McCormack, K. and Stone, N. (2002) *Young Offenders: Law, Policy and Practice*. 2nd edn. London: Sweet and Maxwell

Judicial Studies Board (2001) *Youth Court Bench Book*. London: Judicial Studies Board (Available on the JSB Website www.jsboard.co.uk)

Moore, T. and Wilkinson, T. (2001) *Youth Court Guide*. London: Butterworths

14 Remand Management

Sue Thomas

Key points

1. Decisions made at each stage of the remand management process can impact on whether or not the young person remains at liberty or in custody until the completion of their case. Action or inaction can have an effect on individual cases. Remand management services should mirror each stage of the pre-trial process and be offered pro-actively, systematically and without discrimination.

2. Remand management services should assess all available options and the most appropriate (least restrictive) should always be considered. The primary aim is to divert young people from unnecessary custodial experiences and to maintain them in the community prior to sentence.

3. Within the pre-trial process different agencies take a lead in making decisions about young people at different stages. There needs to be effective liaison between the police, those working in courts, local authorities and secure facilities. The availability of services should be promoted to court users to ensure that they are fully conversant with the range of non-custodial options available.

4. Bail programmes should be individually focused, address needs, ensure that risks are managed and the public safeguarded by minimising the likelihood of re-offending whilst on bail through the provision of proportionate and appropriate supervision and support. Young people should be encouraged to attend court at the appointed time, with assistance if necessary.

5. The situation and circumstances of young people should remain under review, until their case concludes. This is to ensure that full consideration is always given to the appropriateness of the remand status and that allowance is made for changes in circumstances or new information that may be relevant to further bail applications.

Introduction

Remand management is a generic term for the services that are provided to unconvicted young people that begin when they are arrested and charged with an offence and continue whilst the case against them proceeds until it is finally disposed of.

Whilst young people are awaiting a court appearance they will be remanded on unconditional or conditional bail, to local authority accommodation or to a secure facility (defined as a young offender institution, local authority secure children's home or a secure training centre). What happens to them will depend on; whether there are objections to bail, their age, gender, the level of seriousness of the offence, whether it attracts a custodial sentence, their situation and personal circumstances and whether, and the extent to which, there is advocacy on their behalf.

Not all young people who appear in court need remand management services. The majority of young people who are arrested and charged with an offence are bailed by the police and subsequently by the courts (87%). They are placed on unconditional or conditional bail and will live in the community whilst awaiting the outcome of their case (Youth Justice Board, 2003o). There is however a significant minority in respect of whom the Crown Prosecution Service (CPS) will object to bail on the grounds that:

- they may fail to appear in court at a future date
- they may continue to offend, and/or
- they are likely to interfere with witnesses or otherwise obstruct the course of justice if they remain at liberty or
- they meet the criteria for a secure remand because of the seriousness of their offence/s.

(Nacro, 2003d)

These young people form the target group for remand management services since they will be facing the possibility of a refusal of bail or a custodial remand. The evidence suggests that where YOTs offer intervention to this group of young people, approximately one third will be bailed and placed under supervision in the community (Youth Justice Board, 2003o).

The use of custody for young people has long been the subject of debate. There is extensive research that indicates that periods in custody can be disruptive to the family life, employment and education of the young person (Moore and Smith, 2001). Levels of intimidation and bullying are high, and vulnerable young people are likely to be further damaged by the experience of incarceration (Goldson, 2002d). There is a prevalence of those with mental health problems in prison service custody generally (HMIP, 2000) and the incidence of suicide and self-harm is particularly high among young people on remand (Liebling, 1996).

Prison custody, relative to other forms of intervention, is ineffective in terms of preventing or reducing offending. Young people subject to custodial remands are more likely to have a custodial sentence imposed upon conviction (Cavadino and Gibson, 1993). Moreover, the imposition of a community penalty following a custodial remand raises the issue of whether the remand was strictly necessary in the first place. Recent findings from Her Majesty's Chief Inspector of Prisons (2000) indicate that, in 1999, 47% of males on remand and 35% of women received a custodial sentence. Findings from the Children's Society National Remand Review Initiative indicate that approximately one third of young people received a community sentence following a period of remand in custody or secure accommodation (Goldson, 2002d).

The primary aim of remand management is to divert young people from unnecessary custodial remands and to provide a mechanism for effectively managing them in the community whilst they await trial or sentence. In addition, *National Standards for Youth Justice* (2004) identified the further aims of preventing offending on bail, (which is congruent with the principal aim of the Crime and Disorder Act 1998) ensuring young people attend hearings at the appointed time to avoid unnecessary delays occurring in the processing of cases through court.

An overview of the legislation

The legislation and the international standards which provide the framework for remand management are complex. They are contained in domestic criminal justice and child care legislation, the Human Rights Act 1998 and the United Nations Convention on the Rights of the Child.

- The Magistrates Court Act 1980 gives magistrates the power to adjourn a case and to remand a young person on bail or in custody until their next court appearance.
- The Bail Act 1976 sets out a presumption in favour of unconditional bail, the provisions for granting bail with or without conditions and the exceptions to the right to bail.
- The Criminal Justice Act 1988 clarifies the position with regard to making bail applications. Defendants can make two bail applications, which the court is obliged to consider. Beyond the second application, the court is not required to hear any arguments that it has heard previously, unless there is new information or a change in circumstances.
- The Children and Young Person's Act 1969 (as amended) provides the legislative base for remanding young people in (non-secure and secure) local authority accommodation.
- Section 23 of and the Criminal Justice and Police Act 2001 contains the provisions for electronic tagging as a condition of a remand on bail or to non-secure local authority accommodation.
- The UN Convention on the Rights of the Child (1989) requires that the deprivation of liberty and the removal of a child from its family should only occur as a last resort and that such deprivation should be for the minimum appropriate period of time.

It is important to note that government policy relating to remands of young people to prison service establishments has changed significantly in recent years. The Criminal Justice Act 1991 provided for the abolition of custodial remands for 15–16 year old boys as and when sufficient local authority secure accommodation became available. The proposed change was a response to widespread concern about the practice of remanding 15 and 16 year old boys to unsuitable custodial institutions, which resulted in the suicides of three vulnerable 15 year old boys in prison service custody during the early 1990s (Howard League, 1996).

Subsequently, the approach to young people who offend has become demonstrably more punitive and there has been a greater emphasis on the management of risk, protection of the public and the prevention of offending. A series of legislative changes have reduced the age at which children may be remanded to secure accommodation to 12 (s20 Criminal Justice and Public Order Act 1994); and limited the circumstances under which 15–16 year old boys may be remanded to secure accommodation as an alternative to custody (ss97–98 Crime and Disorder Act, 1998). As a consequence, by the time of its implementation, in 1999, a measure originally intended to phase out custodial remands for children under 17, had no impact on the prison service remand population but increased considerably those held on remand in local authority secure provision (Goldson, 2002d). More recently, the criteria for remands to custody and secure accommodation have been loosened (s130 Criminal Justice and Public Order Act, 2001). These changes have resulted in substantial increases in the juvenile remand population (Nacro, 2003a).

The key components of remand management

Remand management and diversion from custody is achieved by assisting the courts to make better informed decisions and through the provision of services to young people designed to encourage the courts to have the confidence to grant bail more frequently. The main forms of remand services for young people are:

Bail information

Bail information involves the provision of factual verified information to the court, which addresses the objections to bail, and may well satisfy such objections without requiring additional intervention. For example, the CPS may have concerns about offending on bail and non-appearance at a future date because a young person lacks a suitable bail address. Discussion with the young person and liaison with the family conducted as part of the bail assessment process (see below) may have

identified that there is an alternative address available in which the young person will be supported and supervised. This is information that the court would not necessarily have been aware of and making it known may allay its concerns about granting bail.

Bail supervision and support

Programmes of supervision and support can be provided for the young person as a condition of bail in order to address the court's objections to bail. The programme will specify how the young person will be managed in the community, the type of activities that will be undertaken with them and level of contact that will be expected of them. It will also show how their needs will be addressed and any risks they pose to themselves or others will be managed. Higher levels of intervention are also possible (involving 25 hours contact a week and additional surveillance) through a bail intensive supervision and surveillance programme (ISSP) where the relevant criteria are met (see Chapter 22).

Support can also be offered to young people on a voluntary basis – for example by providing assistance in getting them to court where there are known difficulties – rather than as a condition of bail.

Remand to local authority accommodation

When a young person aged between 10 to 16 years of age is refused bail they are remanded to local authority (non-secure) accommodation. There is a mandatory duty on local authorities to provide accommodation (for example with friends, family, in residential accommodation or with foster carers) for young people so remanded (s22 Children Act 1989). Youth offending teams and local authorities will share the responsibility for ensuring that the young person is cared for and fully supported, both in terms of their general welfare and obligations in respect of the criminal justice system (Nacro, 2003h).

Remand to the juvenile secure estate

Work in young offender institutions undertaken by the Howard League and the Children's Society in the past decade has indicated that young people remanded to custody should be reviewed immediately to establish if a programme of support could be offered at the next court appearance. The circumstances of those on remand should be kept under constant review in order to establish if a bail application could be made to avoid the continuation of a custodial remand when it may have become unnecessary. Courts have a duty to consider remand status at each hearing and, as a result, earlier decisions can be reversed. Youth offending teams now have a presence in some young offender institutions expressly to undertake what is known as remand review work of this sort. Such reviews should also form part of the care planning process for young people placed in local authority secure accommodation (Nacro, 2003i).

The remand management process

A successful remand management strategy cannot be developed in isolation. Effective practice requires liaison with the police, defence solicitors, the CPS, magistrates, clerks and the secure estate. This involves consultation with representatives from the many different agencies and organisations, and recognition that they will often have different perspectives on the young person and what should happen to them.

Effective remand management is systematic, involving a four-stage process:

Stage 1: referral

YOTs need to have mechanisms in place for identifying young people who will be appearing in court for whom an assessment will be required. There should be systematic daily checking by the YOT with the police to identify young people who have been denied bail and will be produced in court. Other methods include liaison with court personnel, checking court listings and liaising with secure escort companies to establish who is in the court cells (Thomas and Goldman, 2001). Additionally young people denied bail and held in secure facilities should be referred for remand management services to establish if a bail application can be made at a subsequent court appearance.

The aim of the early identification of young people (preferably before attending court), is to allow sufficient time to obtain background information and to conduct enquiries about those who

are specifically at risk of a custodial remand. The process will involve accessing YOT case records to provide any known information about the young person's background, current circumstances and previous responses to supervision on bail or otherwise. This process should identify what issues may need to be dealt with in court, assist in providing a preliminary view of likely YOT involvement, identify what resources may be required to manage the young person and the issues that might need be explored further with the young person as part of the assessment process.

Stage 2: targeting

At court, the CPS will decide whether to oppose or agree to the granting of bail. The role of the YOT is to liaise with the CPS and the defence solicitor to establish the circumstances of the case, clarify what submissions they will be making to determine whether further information or the provision of services could address the objections and areas of concern. This allows the YOT to prioritise and target those young people for assessment where there are clear objections to bail.

Stage 3: assessment

Having identified the target group, further information is required to establish if there are any community-based options that might assist the court to make a decision about the granting of bail or otherwise. The assessment process is essentially a filter through which all available options are considered and from which the most appropriate, and least restrictive option that will effectively manage the young person and any risks they present can be selected. The assessment process will involve interviewing the young person to establish risks and needs, gauging their motivation and attitude, and discussing the possibilities with them. It also involves gathering and confirming information from other available sources, which will include parents and family and statutory agencies with whom the young person has previously come into contact, such as the YOT and social services. The provision of bail information or a proposal for bail supervision and support can avert a bail refusal at this stage.

For young people who are remanded in custody or to secure accommodation, the process is broadly the same. However, action taken at the point of remand will need to be re-examined, and the reaction of the young person to the loss of liberty and their potential vulnerability in custody will need to be considered, when determining whether a bail application will be made at the next court hearing.

Stage 4: outcome

The assessment process should conclude with an agreement about what course of action will be taken – such as the presentation of a bail application that addresses the objections to bail and is agreed with the CPS and the young person's defence solicitor. This information is then laid before the court in the form of a verbal or written presentation of a proposal that outlines the individual programme of support and supervision with which the young person will be required to comply.

For those subject to a remand review in custody, any future action needs to be agreed with the defence solicitor and young person. Possible options will include whether a further bail application or an application to a judge in chambers should be made, if bail applications (under the Criminal Justice Act, 1988) have been exhausted.

Maximising the effectiveness of remand management

Practitioners who have specialist knowledge and expertise and an established presence in court will be more effective. Building effective working relationships with solicitors, magistrates, ushers and clerks is essential as is being viewed as part of the professional network. It is important that remand management services are promoted within the court setting on a regular and sustained basis in order to raise awareness and to remind magistrates of the non-custodial options available. Pre-court work must also be reliable in identifying young people at risk so that YOTs are aware of all young people due to appear in youth and non-youth courts. Where YOTs have taken the initiative in contacting the police on a daily basis this appears to be an effective mechanism (Thomas and Hucklesby, 2002).

Bail programmes that are based on a comprehensive assessment and are individually designed to focus on the needs and risks presented by the young person are more likely to gain the confidence of magistrates than those that take a less focused approach. High levels of court attendance are achieved by issuing reminders to young people and by accompanying them or providing transport if there are known difficulties. Identifying the factors that can prevent offending is more difficult. However, tightly focused one-to-one meetings with young defendants which explore their anxieties and problems and help them to develop strategies to deal with their behaviour appear to be effective. It is also possible to encourage and support those young people who wish to stop offending by providing constructive activities and occupying and supervising young people at times when they are vulnerable to offending.

It is difficult to quantify the impact of remand management services on the juvenile remand population due to changes in legislation, working practices and other influences that have either made bail more difficult to achieve or have had a diversionary effect away from custody. There is anecdotal evidence that the provision of bail information and bail supervision and support can successfully divert young people who might otherwise lose their liberty. This is as a result of systematic targeting, assessment and close supervision of young people in the community as they await trial. These factors have helped to ensure that courts have better quality information and are therefore more able to make an informed view when considering the options available.

The Audit Commission has reported that offending on bail has fallen from one in three to one in five cases (Audit Commission, 2004). The reasons for this are likely to be a combination of the impact of fast tracking, which has reduced the time available between arrest and sentence to offend, and the direct intervention of YOTs in providing focused supervision and support during the bail period. Baseline data on the levels of attendance at court by young people are not routinely collected, making it difficult to establish the influence of YOTs in this respect. However there have been significant improvements in the speed of operation of court processes and it is likely that efforts undertaken to promote attendance, closely monitor cases where there may be problems, provide assistance where there are known difficulties, actively following up those that do not appear, and to encouraging those on warrants to surrender have contributed significantly to this outcome.

An important limiting factor on effectiveness that is continually reported by those providing remand management services is the overall lack of suitable accommodation for young people involved in the criminal justice system. This can seriously undermine the objectives of remand management. Young people who do not have a suitable bail address and stable and supportive living arrangements may be remanded to custody as courts will be concerned that the likelihood of offending will be increased and bail conditions breached where stable accommodation is lacking.

There is a need for firmer evidence about the relationship between the lack of accommodation and vulnerability to custody, as much of what is reported is anecdotal and therefore difficult to quantify. However there are indications that significant investment is required to address the national shortage of suitable accommodation for young people, and that by expanding provision, an increased number of young people who are at risk of a custodial remand because of their social circumstances, rather than the risk they pose, may be diverted to community-based alternatives.

Further reading

Goldson, B. (2002d) *Vulnerable Inside: Children in Secure and Penal Settings.* London: The Children's Society

Nacro (2003d) *Bail as it Affects Young People in Court.* Youth Crime Briefing. London: Nacro

Nacro (2003h) *Remands to Local Authority Accommodation.* Youth Crime Briefing. London: Nacro

Thomas, S. and Goldman, M. (2001) *A Guide to the National Standards for Bail Supervision and Support Schemes.* London: Nacro Cymru and the Youth Justice Board

Thomas, S. and Hucklesby, A. (2002) *Remand Management.* London: Youth Justice Board

15 The Role of Family Placement in the Youth Justice System

Ann Wheal and Ena Fry

Key points

1. The Green Paper *Every Child Matters* and the accompanying *Youth Justice: The Next Steps* make a powerful case for alternatives to secure and custodial remands. The Anti-Social Behaviour Act 2003 will enable courts to include fostering as a requirement of a supervision order.

2. Preventive strategies, such as support care, can help families and young people cope with crises which might precipitate offending.

3. Research reveals that remand fostering is a positive experience for some young people and can contribute to a reduction in offending.

4. If they are to be effective, it is imperative that carers are well trained and well supported.

5. For family placement within the youth justice system to be successful, training that aims to change the attitudes of magistrates, judges and other youth justice system professionals is essential.

Introduction

This chapter charts the recent history of family placement schemes and indicates how they can benefit young people and families involved with the youth justice system by helping to prevent offending and re-offending.

'Family placement' refers to a family recruited and approved to look after someone else's child on a temporary basis and when utilised in the youth justice system may take one of the following forms:

- support care
- remand fostering
- intensive fostering

Background: the need for family placement

The Criminal Justice Act 1991 acknowledged the need to reduce the youth justice system's reliance on secure and custodial remands. In many cases, remanding children and young people into secure and custodial institutions contravenes the United Nations Convention on the Rights of the Child (United Nations, 1989), the Human Rights Act 1998 and the principles of the Children Act 1989 (see Chapter 7). Despite this, alternatives to secure and custodial remands are too infrequently used by the courts, not least because many sentencers appear to be unaware that alternative options are available (Home Office, 2003i).

The Green Paper *Every Child Matters* (DfES, 2003b) and the accompanying Home Office document, *Youth justice: The Next Steps* (Home Office, 2003i) make a powerful case for the further development of alternatives to secure and custodial remands and sentencing and the use, in particular, of family placement. Both documents point to the fact that family placements are not only cost effective, but also provide young people with a safe environment, help to ensure their appearance at court, prevent them from absconding and can reduce the incidence of re-offending during the period of remand.

In March 2003, the government published *Respect and Responsibility*, a White Paper outlining its views on the causes of anti-social behaviour and its preferred solutions (Home Office, 2003f). Children and young people and their families feature heavily in the debate on tackling anti-social behaviour. While many of the proposals in the White Paper, subsequently enacted in the Anti-Social Behaviour Act 2003, can be seen as placing an undue emphasis on enforcement, the introduction of intensive fostering as a requirement of a supervision order enhances the prospects of family placements being used as an alternative to custodial sentencing.

Intensive supervision and surveillance programmes provide 25 hours a week intervention during the most intensive phase (see Chapter 22) which in the case of some serious or persistent offending is insufficient to dissuade the courts from a custodial outcome. Intensive fostering, as described in more detail below, offers a more flexible disposal with the potential for supervision 24 hours a day, seven days a week.

The contribution of family placement

The development of family placements as a non-custodial option within the youth justice system is, we believe, justified on the following grounds:

- Managing offending young people in a residential or custodial setting can increase their offending and risk taking behaviours. This impacts adversely on other young people in placement as well as on the local community.
- Family placements, with an emphasis on changing behaviours and developing social skills, can lead to better outcomes.
- Foster carers act as agents for change by providing nurturing and care to young people, acting as advocates and contributing to re-establishing and strengthening family relationships.
- Fostering placements can involve offending young people in decisions and actions about their future.
- Fostering promotes equal opportunities and reduces the stigma attached to public care.
- Fostering has the potential to address discrimination within the youth justice system in respect of gender, ethnicity, exclusion and disability.

Support care

Support care is a tailor-made preventative service for families under stress. It aims to keep children and young people with their families by anticipating the crises that might precipitate offending and establishing the necessary support structures.

It may involve day care, home visiting by a part-time carer, or a young person being placed voluntarily with carers outside their own family for a limited period. Such placements tend to be very flexible, with the arrangements, and the duration, being agreed in advance with the child or young person and their family. In a youth justice context, support care aims to prevent the drift into crime and into 'care' and can also help young people reintegrate into the community after incarceration.

Support care offers a non-stigmatising service that takes account of the whole family not just the young person who is, or is at risk of, offending. Experience has shown that families see support care more as a 'befriending' service for parents and children, disproving the common perception that social services departments are only there to take children away from their families. It is a community-based provision so children and young people retain existing social, educational and health links. It also offers time out for children and young people to gain new interests and skills as well as giving a parent a break to spend time with other children in the family or just to 'recharge their own batteries'. It offers young people in single-parent families the opportunity to experience life in a two-parent family, which can be beneficial if, for example, the young person has no effective male role model.

Support carers are recruited, approved and trained by the local authority, which provides them with an allowance for each placement to meet costs. They come from widely diverse backgrounds and are able to offer placements which reflect the ethnicity and first language of the child. Similarly, where a young person is of dual heritage, having a carer of the same ethnic origin as the absent parent can be helpful.

The potential for developing support care in a more flexible manner has recently been enhanced since such placements are now legally available as a service to children and young people in need under section 17 of the Children Act 1989, without the necessity for the local authority to accommodate them under section 20. In practice, this means that young people who stay one night with carers will not be deemed to be 'looked after' children with all of the stigma that entails for the young person, family and friends. It also means that the administrative burden for those offering support care is considerably reduced as completion of the Looked After Children record keeping forms is not required. However, it is imperative that all the necessary checks are in place to ensure the young person receives appropriate care.

Currently, guidance is being sought from the Department for Education and Skills about when section 17 may be used in this way, to ensure consistency of care and that appropriate safeguards are in place.

The benefits of support care

Experience of support care to date suggests that intervention tends to be valued by the children and young people and their families because it helps them to 'stay together'. It enables troubled children of any age to receive help, care and advice on a temporary basis, thus preventing the potential damage of separating children from their families. It has proved easier to recruit carers to support care schemes than to mainstream fostering because it does not require a full-time commitment, although support carers do on occasion move into full-time fostering. On the other hand, support care also attracts experienced foster carers who can no longer offer full-time placements but are attracted to this type of service because they can continue to put their skills and expertise to good use. Support care is cost effective. For instance, during 2002, Birmingham's Neighbourhood Care Scheme offered 100 places and the total staff, carers, equipment and training budget was equivalent to the annual cost of three 'out-of-city' foster placements (Fry, 2002).

Remand fostering

Other forms of family placement used in the youth justice system aim to function as alternatives to custodial or secure remands or sentences (see Chapter 14). Remand fostering schemes were first established in the 1980s, during the heyday of 'progressive minimalism' (see Chapter 1) when the numbers of young people held in all kinds of institutions were declining rapidly. During the subsequent growth in the use of security and custody in the 1990s, remand fostering fell from favour, but with the secure estate now bulging at the seams, there is a renewed interest in its potential (Moore, 2000).

Remand fostering aims to provide a comprehensive fostering service for young people refused bail and remanded to local authority accommodation. In addition, a local authority might wish to use a family placement for a young person awaiting trial or sentence as part of a bail supervision and support programme (see Chapter 14). In some cases, remand fostering can be provided where the young person's family refuses to have them back home. Whatever the circumstances, the objectives are the same. The aim is to reduce the need for secure or custodial remands, to ensure attendance at court, prevent re-offending during the remand period and address other concerns which the court may have in relation to the granting of bail. Such placements thus offer the court a viable alternative to custodial or secure remands by providing a community option which does not involve the young person returning home. Ultimately, the intention is to assist the young person to return home after the conclusion of the court case or to move to other specialist provision where that is appropriate.

The effectiveness of remand fostering

In 1993, Fostering Networks (previously the National Foster Care Association) produced a report entitled *On Remand: Foster Care and the Youth Justice Service* (Fry, 1993). This survey based its findings on information provided by 16 agencies on:

- Recruitment and assessment of carers
- Support, management of offending behaviour and placement planning
- Outcomes
- Finance
- Staffing
- Involvement of carers and young people and future plans.

The overall conclusions were that fostering agencies had good links with the relevant professionals critical to the success of remand fostering schemes and that remand fostering represented a viable alternative to residential care/custody. The report noted that agencies were able to provide immediate placement from court; good and consistent support, rehabilitation back into their families for many young people, preparation for long-term placements, and that the service was also able to effect reduced levels of offending. However, the report also highlighted: a lack of alternative resources to enable young people to move on; problems of violence and absconding; delays in paying carers and meeting their insurance claims, when damage was done; and difficulties, with post-remand planning.

Research by Lipscombe (2003a; 2003b) revealed that remand fostering had been a very positive experience for some young people:

> *It gave me a bit of perspective on life, made me think about things. Before I was like, I thought life owed me, now I know that everything ain't going to come to me . . .*

> *It moves you away from the area, keeps you out of trouble . . .*

> *You've got someone who can give you attention, like look after you, sort you out and that, and it's better than if you're being in a jail with hundreds of other inmates.*

Most young people had contact with other professionals, such as their youth offending team officer, bail support worker, probation officer and social worker, during their remand foster placement but few were seeing counsellors or receiving mental health support, despite being in need of such assistance. Some young people were also unclear about the different roles played by various justice system professionals.

Some commentators have suggested that the present shortage of traditional foster carers may be exacerbated by the recent expansion in remand fostering, with remand foster carers tending to attract better remuneration and higher levels of support. The experience of the authors, however, suggests that many of the carers attracted to remand fostering are a different group of people who would not necessarily elect to become traditional foster carers in any event.

Intensive fostering

Section 88 of the Anti Social Behaviour Act 2003 allows courts, provided certain conditions are met, to include in a supervision order a requirement that a young person live with a local authority foster parent. The 'foster care residence requirement', to be piloted from October 2004 in Hampshire, Staffordshire and London, is designed to be an alternative to incarceration and is only available where the offending is so serious that a custodial sentence would normally be appropriate (or where the child is aged 10 or 11, would be

appropriate if they were older). In addition, the court must be satisfied that:

- The behaviour which constituted the offence was due to a significant extent to the circumstances in which the offender was living.
- The imposition of a foster parent residence requirement will assist in their rehabilitation.

The requirement allows placement, as part of a court disposal, of the young person for a maximum of 12 months with specially trained foster carers. There are a number of fundamental elements associated with such a placement:

- A core assessment is conducted to identify the child's needs with the resultant care plan subject to regular review (see Chapter 19).
- The young person will be required to undertake work and activities designed to address their offending behaviour.
- A range of support will be given to the young person's own family to prepare for the post-placement return home in most cases. A 'move on' with support will be negotiated if the plan is not for a return home.
- A wrap-around service of support is provided to each young person. (Carers receive high levels of dedicated training and support. Placements have access to a broad range of specialist services, including teaching, parenting intervention, psychological and therapeutic support, counselling and social work input. Wherever possible existing links with schools or other education providers are retained and strengthened; work with the young person's own family aims to build on relationships to ensure a planned return home; and the young person is provided with a network of constructive social activities.)

The Youth Justice Board has been tasked with the development of this new sentencing initiative and, as part of that process, the Board has commissioned a feasibility study undertaken by the Fostering Network and NCH Wessex Community Projects to explore the implications of fostering, as a sentencing option, and its links to a similar wrap-around service, treatment foster care, currently being piloted by the Department for Education and Skills.

Fundamental to the service is the prevention of

further offending, which is to be achieved through:

- Encouraging the development of normal and pro-social behaviours.
- Teaching young people new skills to improve and form better relationships with their family and peers.
- Providing close and careful supervision throughout the day.
- Limiting access to negative and delinquent peers.
- Encouraging the development of academic skills.
- Supporting birth families to increase the effectiveness of their parenting skills.
- Developing self-belief and a positive view of the future.

Service development in its early stages is informed by existing specialist fostering schemes in the UK which have focussed on providing foster care as an alternative to custody. These include Fostering New Links (FNL), a scheme established in 1997 by Coram Family, and operational until May 2004, and NCH's Community Adolescent Placement Schemes (CAPS) in Scotland (as well as MAPS, the Murray Adolescent Placement Scheme specific to that region). CAPS has recently been formally evaluated by the University of Glasgow (Walker and Hill, 2002). Both schemes have shown that, by offering intensive packages of support to young people in foster homes, they can provide a credible alternative to custody which can also be effective in retaining difficult young people within the community.

The 'intensity' of provision is assured through the service being 'wrap-around'.

Intensive fostering schemes need to be viewed in the context of other disposals available to the courts and linked to other forms of relevant foster care. Placement away from home, in a foster placement, can be a positive court outcome for serious and persistent offending providing it is combined with appropriate family work. Care and control are linked – good care implies control and vice versa.

The way forward

For a few young people incarceration is a necessity, but for the majority of those being considered for a secure or custodial remand, remand fostering and other community-based resources are more likely to prevent re-offending.

Clearly, in most circumstances, young people need help to prevent them re-offending. The court should be mindful of the benefits of living in a foster home as opposed to placement in some form of secure accommodation. There is still a lot to do. Early intervention is a must. Strategies such as support care and intensive fostering have a good deal to offer in preventing a young person offending or re-offending.

The use of family placements in a youth justice context is a relatively recent development which has the potential to impact positively on levels of custody and to prevent offending. Maximising that potential, by ensuring that family placements are fully integrated as part of the range of youth justice provisions, will, as Lipscome (2003a;b) suggests, be dependent upon improved information sharing among professionals and training, which aims to change the attitudes of sentencers and youth justice practitioners themselves, and engenders confidence in family placement.

Further reading

Beresford, A., Cook, S., Fry, E. and Wheal, A. (2000), *Specialist Fostering Scheme, Parts A, B, C.* London: Fostering Networks/University of Southampton

Buchanan, A., Wheal, A. and Barlow, J. (1995) *How to Stay out of Trouble: The Views of Young Offenders in Wiltshire on Their Offending.* Oxford: Barnardo's/University of Oxford

Dartington Social Research Unit (undated), *Taking Forward Specialist Services for Young Offenders: The Hampshire Young Offenders Community Support Scheme.* Devon: Dartington Social Research Unit

Gill, P. and Fry, E. (2000) *More Than an Address: A Good Practice Guide for Remand Foster Carers.* London: Nacro

Wheal, A. (Ed.) (2000) *Working With Parents: Learning From Other People's Experience.* Lyme Regis: Russell House

16 The Referral Order

Rod Earle

Key points

1. The creative potential of referral orders requires considerable time, effort and resources to fulfil.

2. When victims attend panels it can radically alter the dynamics of the meeting and enhance the potential of the order. Special resources or staff may help to assist victims to make a contribution to the panels.

3. Community panel members make the difference. It is a lot of work for them and they can make a lot of work for the youth offending team but without their unique contribution the referral order could not work.

4. The referral order co-ordinator must perform a delicate balancing act. Their job is situated at the interface between the needs of young people, volunteer community panel members, victims and the criminal justice system.

5. Close liaison with local courts is important in establishing appropriate lengths for referral orders and ensuring magistrates have confidence in a process they have little control over.

A brave new order?

The Youth Justice and Criminal Evidence Act 1999 (YJCEA), is the second of two pieces of legislation that have transformed the youth justice system in England and Wales. The first, the Crime and Disorder Act 1998, established a uniform organisational platform for those working with young people who offend. The principles of restorative justice found their first formal recognition in this legislation. The idea that when someone is convicted of an offence the impact of that offence should be considered by those most closely involved is not particularly new. For a long time, though, such an approach depended on the preferences, priorities and resources of local social services departments. The most daring departure from the past is that the YJCEA institutionalises such an approach as mandatory for most young people entering the criminal justice system. If they plead guilty and do not get a custodial sentence, they will usually be made subject of a referral order (see box below). Referral orders are thus the new standardised gateway to the criminal justice system. They account for nearly 30% of all sentences passed on 10–17 year olds (Youth Justice Board, 2003j).

The basics

A referral order is imposed on any young person aged 10–17, with no previous convictions, who pleads guilty in a youth or Magistrates' court. Magistrates may only impose another sentence of their choice if the offence is 'non-imprisonable'. Otherwise only an absolute discharge, a hospital order or a custodial sentence can be imposed.

Within 20 days of the order being imposed the young person is required to attend a youth offender panel (YOP) meeting. The panel is composed of at least two volunteer community panel members (CPMs) and a member of the local youth offending team (YOT). A parent/carer is required to attend with anyone under 16, and the court may order parents/carers to attend if the young person is over 16. The victims of the offences may also be invited to attend the panel meeting or asked to contribute to it in other ways if they wish to.

Panel meetings are held away from the court at times and places that suit those attending. A brief report, prepared by the YOT, is provided to panel members in advance. The panel is invited to consider how best to address the circumstances described so as to prevent any further offending and repair any harm inflicted by the offending. Participation of all those present is encouraged. The objective is to draw up a written agreement, or contract, on the best way forward that satisfies the needs and expectations of those present. The agreement is expected to include an element of reparation.

The court can impose a referral order for anything between 3 and 12 months but the period in question only becomes 'active' once a contract has been agreed. Progress in fulfilling the commitments made in the agreement is reviewed periodically by convening further panel meetings. If progress is deemed unsatisfactory by any such meeting, the case can be returned to court so that another sentence can be considered. If the agreement is fulfilled the conviction is considered 'spent' under the terms of the Rehabilitation of Offenders Act 1974. A final panel meeting is held to 'sign-off' the order.

Something old, something new

Although referral orders are a new and exciting development in England and Wales, they bear more than a passing resemblance to the Scottish Children's Hearing (see Chapter 3). For over 30 years north of the border, welfare principles have been a settled and accepted foundation to the Scottish response to young people who offend. This approach has deep historical roots that draw on Scottish ways of organising social and legal life (Lockyer and Stone, 1998; Paterson, 2000). There is a basic consistency in the Scottish system that has allowed it to evade the swings between punishment and welfare that characterise the English youth justice system (Newburn 2002; Pitts, 1988).

The referral order borrows from Scotland the idea of community volunteers sitting on a relatively informal panel to discuss, and decide upon, the appropriate response to a child or young person's offending behaviour. Implicit in the Scottish approach is that such behaviour represents a social and collective failure of care as much as it does any individual aberration. The Children's Hearings are not part of the formal criminal justice system but are run by local authority social services departments.

A socialised approach is also a characteristic of restorative justice, which is additionally distin-

guished by its inclusion of the victim (see Chapter 28). This approach has been influential in the radical restructuring of the New Zealand/ Aotearoa youth justice system. Much of the process, based upon the family group conference, occurs outside the formal court system (Swain, 1995). As with Scotland, the system draws on distinctive cultural resources that stand in contrast to those of the dominant Anglo-British model.

The referral order is more explicit in adopting a restorative justice perspective. However, unlike its two conceptual 'parents', there is something of a silence about the order's relationship to the wider culture in which it exists. It is not clear what consensus of values and what cultural resources, in the wider society of England and Wales underpin the order.

Although it is a new hybrid of two distinctive approaches, each of which circumvent formal criminal justice intervention for young people, the referral order remains anchored firmly within a very old criminal justice system. As such, it represents a characteristically uneasy compromise between the newly influential practices of restorative justice, the authoritarian tendencies of English law and order politics (Hall, 1980) and Scottish communitarian pragmatism (Hale, 2002; Wheatcroft, 2003). The tentative and exploratory aspects of this novel compromise are played out in the way that referral orders have come into operation.

An experimental order

From the summer of 2000, referral orders were piloted in 11 youth offending teams (YOTs) in England and Wales. Arrangements were made for an independent evaluation to provide reports and feedback on the experiences of all those involved (Newburn et al., 2001; 2002c). Although national implementation proceeded to a pre-established timetable, it is significant that three years after the order's introduction, some of those contributions have had some effect.

It became apparent during the evaluation that referral orders trigger a set of unique creative tensions (Earle and Newburn, 2002). By bringing together youth justice practitioners, community volunteers, victims, young people and their families or supporters, new frictions and energy are generated. Within two years over 5,000 volunteers have been recruited and trained as CPMs. Tens of thousands of panel meetings, each involving anything up to a dozen people, have been convened. Meanwhile, magistrates, solicitors and other professionals have been confronted with circumstances that marginalise their contribution to decision-making.

Discretion restored

In its original form the referral order removed from magistrates the discretion to decide the most appropriate response to the circumstances presented to them in court. For young people appearing in court for the first time and pleading guilty, it was almost a mandatory sentence. Although many magistrates and court legal advisers supported the order's restorative justice basis, the loss of discretion was less well received. Surveys conducted by the evaluation team, revealed that frustration with this aspect of the order grew with their experience of it (Newburn et al., 2002a). For some, the role and value of lay magistrates' contribution to the criminal justice system, itself voluntary, appeared to be undermined. For others, it simply seemed absurd to set up a relatively prolonged intervention when the incident to which it was a reponse was minor.

Magistrates particularly resented not being allowed to impose a small fine or conditional discharge. Although the evaluation revealed these occasions to be relatively infrequent, their impact disproportionately undermined the credibility of the order. The view was shared by YOT practitioners and magistrates and in August 2003, these frustrations were formally recognised when the legislation was amended to make 'the scheme more flexible' (Home Office, 2003c). Discretion to impose other sentences, where otherwise mandatory referral order conditions apply, is restored to magistrates if the offence is 'non-imprisonable'. Although this amendment applies to a limited number of offences, such as minor motoring matters, it remains a significant concession to what might be an emerging consensus on the shape the referral order should take. Maintaining and developing communication with magistrates about the enactment of referral orders can help them to exercise their discretion appropriately and foster their confidence in its viability.

Panel dynamics

A second issue, to which the evaluation drew attention, was the difficulty that pilot YOTs experienced in recruiting widely from the local community. Home Office guidance advises that CPMs should be 'properly representative of the community' (Home Office, 2000b). During the pilot, relatively few had backgrounds in manual work or were unemployed. Older, white and female volunteers were over-represented. Outside of the more metropolitan pilot areas, such as Nottingham City and West London, minority ethnic participation was limited. Being 'representative' is, of course, intrinsically problematic (Crawford and Newburn, 2002). The difficulty is whether any small group of volunteers can reflect the diversity and complexity of local communities without reduction to crude and simplistic categories. There is also a tension between restorative justice approaches that eschew representation in favour of addressing the immediate effects of the crime with those most directly involved.

'Representativeness' also suggests a process of accountability. If volunteers' actions on behalf of other parties are to be meaningful and authentic, they need to have elements of accountability to these parties and transparency to a wider audience (Roche, 2003). The evaluation found all those involved sensitive to the problem of the representative role but a pragmatic, work-in-progress, approach predominated. This meant that most pilot YOTs aspired to a model that sought to reflect the make-up of the local community, principally in terms of ethnicity and gender. Perhaps in recognition that the distinctiveness of the referral order hinges on this local participation, the Home Office commissioned follow up research on the composition of CPMs in 2003. Women were still over-represented in most areas, and the bulk of volunteers remained middle aged and fully employed. Although rates of minority ethnic participation corresponded to their distribution in the national census, many YOTs felt that these groups were under-represented and continued to target them for recruitment. Those most difficult to attract as volunteers were the young – particularly young men – whom the Home Office recommends as 'particularly well equipped to communicate with young offenders, and to understand their needs and motivation.' (Home Office, 2000b: para 1.16).

Evidence from the pilot, led the evaluators to speculate that there was a danger of certain, more willing or available, volunteers taking on the role of 'super-volunteer', attending a disproportionate amount of panels. This could dilute both the notion of being properly representative and risks the development of 'case hardening' or routinisation among volunteers and might reduce the potential for bringing a 'fresh', 'lay' viewpoint to bear on decision making (Crawford and Newburn, 2003). Becoming a CPM requires considerable commitment but the evaluation noted how quickly they established themselves as enthusiastic and energetic participants in the new process. As one YOT manager noted *'they are a very confident group of people. They are a force to be reckoned with'*.

For some YOT workers, such integral participation of members of the public provoked mixed feelings. They found it difficult to reconcile the current emphasis on evidence-based practice and risk assessment with transferring decision making power to unqualified members of the public. However two staff surveys revealed widespread, durable and emphatic support for the referral order (Newburn et al., 2001). Both YOT staff and volunteers appeared committed to forging a working partnership in largely uncharted territory. This partnership, though fraught with tension and uncomfortable at times, appears to be mostly creative and pregnant with possibilities (Earle and Newburn, 2002). The YOT worker who coordinates the delivery of referral orders is pivotal to the success of this process and must mediate a complex variety of demands, needs and resources. It is a challenging role to fulfill.

Shaping a new process

Much of the referral order's radical potential hinges on the active participation in the panel meeting of the young people subject to them, their parents, and, where possible, victims. Some commentators were concerned that placing a young person in a room full of adults would result in an oppressive experience and create unrealistic expectations about their contribution (Haines, 1998; Wonnacot, 1999; Ball, 2000).

The evaluation collected extensive monitoring data on those who attended panels and observed

panels to identify the dynamics at work. It was most common for a young person to attend a panel with a single adult, usually their mother. Only relatively rarely were other significant adults drawn in to the process. In this respect referral orders could be seen to be operating less inclusively than they might and the burden of participation is taken up disproportionately by women. Referral orders perhaps generate more 'shadow labour', those largely unacknowledged efforts that enhance the status and wellbeing of others. These efforts do not quite count as 'work' but are often crucial in getting things done. Like housework and childcare, this labour is heavily gendered and largely unpaid (Hochschild, 1983; 2001).

Observers recorded the extent of contributions within the panel meetings. As might be expected, given their role in structuring the meeting, CPMs contributed most and were most directive. Young people in the meetings were however far from passive. Nearly half (49%) made 'lengthy and full' contributions, while a further large proportion (40%) made 'short but several' contributions. Only 10% were noted as offering 'monosyllabic' responses. Parents were also observed to make frequent and meaningful contributions.

Over 80% of contract elements agreed at observed panels were 'actively' accepted by the young person. However relatively few contract elements were generated by parties other than the YOT or CPMs. This tends to suggest, perhaps unsurprisingly given the circumstances, that while young people and their parents/carers are not passive in the process they are more reactive than proactive. Allowing time for parents and carers to consider and generate their own proposals, either before or during the panel meeting might encourage a more proactive stance (Masters, 2003).

Absent victims

Throughout the pilot period, securing the meaningful participation of victims proved to be the single most challenging task facing YOTs. In only 13% of cases, where it might have been possible, did a victim actually attend a panel. Those that did attend were largely positive about the experience and even more supportive of the principle. Almost all the victims contacted, including those that did not attend a panel, described panels as a 'good idea'.

The presence of victims, where it occurred, was widely acknowledged as significant in altering the dynamics of the panel, usually in a constructive way.

The evaluation highlighted that unrealistic time constraints and the enormous task of launching such a complex order had contributed to the difficulties in securing victim participation. It pointed out that effective management of victim contact would need to be a priority for YOTs if they were to improve victim participation and that the provision of dedicated resources for this purpose could help achieve this. Some YOTs now report participation rates of up to 51% of viable cases.

Conclusion

Towards the end of the last century youth justice practitioners in some parts of the country, influenced by the labelling perspective, carried forward a programme that characterised the youth justice system as an area best avoided by young people because it tended to make a bad situation worse (Haines and Drakeford, 1998). The more they became involved in the criminal justice system the more their offending increased and their circumstances deteriorated. Thus the aim was to divert young people away from the criminal justice system by whatever means were available and appropriate.

The New Labour government has gone out of its way to discredit this strategy as one that simply excused young people's unacceptable behaviour (Home Office, 1997b). As an alternative, it has massively expanded the youth justice system. Stationed at the gateway of the new system are over 5,000 volunteers. Each year they will greet approximately 27,000 young people with a novel experience of justice. Volunteers, victims, family members and friends can join criminal justice professionals in an attempt to make a bad situation better. The question is whether by changing the architecture of the youth justice system the government will also change its values.

The models for the referral order, in Scotland and New Zealand, consciously draw on, and publicly affirm, fundamental social values anchored in history and struggle. These are not so readily identifiable in England and Wales where New Labour's past is projected as something from which it intends to escape.

Labour's criminal justice, and wider social policies, tend to promote a virile approach to responsibility riding under the banner of active citizenship. The policies are undoubtedly a response to powerful trends in modern society that compel people toward assuming ever-greater responsibility for their own circumstances (Giddens, 1991). But all too often those personal, material and historical conditions that constrain an individual's capacity to take on these new responsibilities (responsibilities often misrepresented as old and neglected) are obscured by the force of a moral rhetoric that emphasises only the virtues and rewards of assuming them, rather than their burden. When this rhetoric emanates from the more powerful and resourceful elements of contemporary society, it can be recognised as a process of 'responsibilisation', a devolving down of responsibility from above.

However, a similar, if reverse, orientation has characterised many of the progressive liberation movements of the modern world. The struggle for autonomy and self-determination from below, the re-appropriation and development of social capacities denied in the name of power and the accumulation of wealth has been called, by the Brazilian educationalist, Paulo Freire, a process of 'conscientisation'. Freire's concerns about the democratisation of culture focused on the process of dialogue in everyday encounters in which citizens take on the role of active agents conscious of their function in making and remaking their world (Taylor, 1993). Perhaps it is not too fanciful to see the evident appeal of referral orders to a wide variety of people as evidence of this process.

Further reading

Crawford, A. and Newburn, T. (2003) *Youth Offending and Restorative Justice: Implementing Reform in Youth Justice.* Cullompton: Willan

Johnstone, G. (2002) *Restorative Justice: Ideas, Values, Debates.* Cullompton: Willan

Lockyer, A. and Stone, F.H. (Eds.) (1998) *Juvenile Justice in Scotland: Twenty Five Years of the Welfare Approach.* Edinburgh: T and T Clark

Roche, D. (2003) *Accountability in Restorative Justice.* Clarendon Studies in Criminology. Oxford: Oxford University Press

17 Youth Offending Teams

Ros Burnett

Key points

1. Youth offending teams (YOTs) bring together social work, probation, police, health, and education staff into one inter-agency team which aims to prevent children and young people offending. YOTs must nominate members of staff as 'accommodation' and 'substance misuse' officers.

2. The 155 YOTs in England and Wales work to standards and targets set by the Youth Justice Board for England and Wales, which monitors their performance

3. Although YOTs are agencies in their own right, they are also open-ended organisations that utilise a range of external services to fulfil their tasks.

4. The sharing of skills and expertise should not be at the expense of maintenance of specialist roles. It is also important that some staff are permanent so that there is an accumulation of experience and 'practice wisdom'.

5. It is unlikely that the holistic approach to work with young people who offend will succeed unless the interventions to address 'risk factors' are supported by the development of a supportive and consistent relationship with the young person and their parents or carers.

Introduction

Youth offending teams (YOTs) are at the hub of each local youth justice system in England and Wales (see Chapter 5). They were brought into existence by the Crime and Disorder Act 1998 (CDA) which required all local authorities with social services and education responsibilities to replace social services youth justice teams with an inter-agency practitioner team with representatives from the local probation and police services, health, education and social services (CDA section 39). The Act specified that all those working in the youth justice system should have regard to the over-riding aim of preventing offending by children and young people (CDA section 37). Accordingly, 154 YOTs were established in 2000, 11 having been set up earlier as 'pilots', and by 2003 there were 155 YOTs in operation in England and Wales. They vary considerably in size and in the geographic area they cover. In addition to members from the five core services which make up the inter-agency teams, allowance was made for other services to participate, and most YOTs now have named 'accommodation officers' and substance misuse workers.

While YOTs are, in themselves, a multi-professional service, they are not self-contained units. They work in partnership with a range of services including the courts, the prison service, the voluntary and commercial sector and are involved in complementary inter-agency initiatives, such as child protection committees and community safety partnerships, in order to provide a 'joined-up', corporate, approach to preventing youth offending. Each YOT is overseen by a steering group which has responsibility for financial planning and strategic management and the agreement of an annual youth justice plan. The operation and standards of services delivered by YOTs are monitored by the Youth Justice Board (YJB) (see Chapter 4). Since April 2003 there has been an additional element of performance monitoring, via Local Criminal Justice Boards (LCJBs) set up in each of the 42 criminal justice areas in England and Wales. Although not solely concerned with the youth justice system, their aim is to increase co-operation between criminal justice agencies and, in particular, to target prolific offenders. Procedures for the inspection of YOTs, by a consortium of inspectorates led by Her Majesty's

Inspectorate of Probation, were introduced in 2003.

The origins, purpose and practice of youth offending teams

The origins of the YOT

Recently, inter-agency collaboration has been a key theme in UK policy. In youth justice, the idea of staff from different professions coming together to decide on the appropriate response to a young person's offending can be traced back to the multi-agency diversion panels established voluntarily in the 1980s, most notably in Northamptonshire. Indeed, it was the Audit Commission's visit to the Northamptonshire Diversion Scheme, during their review of the youth justice system, which is said to have provided the original idea for the YOTs. Many of the Audit Commission's recommendations (1996) were echoed in the subsequent White Paper *No More Excuses* (Home Office, 1997b) and the proposals in this White Paper were, in turn, closely mirrored in the CDA.

The purpose of the YOT

Three related aims underpin the YOTs:

1. *Youth justice workers should join forces with other professionals*
   The main argument for 'joined-up' services was that offending by children and young people is inextricably linked with a range of other problems, such as truancy, drug abuse and family breakdown, each traditionally dealt with by separate agencies. It would therefore avoid duplication of effort, inconsistencies and differences in emphasis if services collaborated in addressing these problems (Home Office, 1997b).

2. *All parties should share the aim of preventing offending*
   In *No More Excuses* the government stated its intention to break with the previous 'culture' of youth justice which, it claimed, excused young people's offending, focusing on their needs rather than their deeds. The paper pointed out that there had been 'confusion about the purpose of the youth justice system' and that approaches to youth justice had varied from area to area. It proposed a more consistent approach, focused on the clear aim of reducing crime by young people. For the representatives

of the agencies joining the YOTs this required a significant change of outlook:

> *Simply transferring existing practice would not be good enough. The police needed to recognise that arrest and sentence did not mean the end of interest in the offender. Social workers had to recognise that compliance was an essential pre-requisite of delivering justice. Education and health authorities had to recognise that offending and offenders were of direct relevance to their work*
>
> (Holdaway et al., 2001: 110)

3. *The principles of evidence-based practice should be applied*
   The Audit Commission review had pointed to the fact that much of the considerable expenditure on youth crime had little or no impact on youth offending and that the system was slow and wasteful. Guidance associated with the reforms stipulated the need for the system to be run according to the principles of 'evidence-based practice'. This would require the adoption of rigorous assessment procedures, systematic monitoring and evaluation and the delivery of interventions found to be the most effective in reducing offending.

The role of the YOT practitioner

The YJB set the following six objectives for YOTs in support of the principal aim of preventing offending:

1. The swift administration of justice so that every young person accused of breaking the law has the matter resolved without delay.
2. Confronting young people who offend with the consequences of their offending, for themselves and their family, their victims and the community and helping them to develop a sense of personal responsibility.
3. Intervention which tackles the particular factors (personal, familial, social, educational or health related) that put the young person at risk of offending and which strengthens 'protective factors'.
4. Punishment proportionate to the seriousness and persistence of the offending.
5. Encouraging reparation to victims by young people who offend.
6. Reinforcing the responsibilities of parents.

The core members of a YOT have to carry out a range of everyday tasks in order to achieve these objectives: they undertake detailed assessments; write court reports; and are responsible for the supervision of those who become subject to final warning interventions or court orders. Case-management responsibilities include developing supervision plans, accessing resources to address the needs related to the young person's offending, monitoring and reviewing progress and, not least, direct work with the young person. Some members of staff concentrate on designated responsibilities such as bail support work (see Chapter 14) or the supervision of referral orders (see Chapter 16), as well as, or instead of, core tasks. Each team also has attached workers who provide specialist services such as clinical psychologists or substance misuse experts. Core practitioners may also be involved in running group work programmes (see Chapter 27) and in representing the YOT by sitting on the committees for projects provided by partnership agencies. As an additional dimension to their work, YOTs are increasingly encouraged to engage in preventative work, including work with those under the age of criminal responsibility.

All YOTs have a manager and a steering group with representatives from each of the participating agencies, who agree a budget and oversee the partnership arrangements. With 'fingers in so many pies', and especially if a large geographic area is covered, determining an appropriate structure for a YOT may prove a challenge. Deciding whether it should be organised with units devoted to particular functions and areas of work (such as delivering intensive supervision order surveillance programmes or providing bail support) or dispersed across the region so that each area is able to provide the full range of services locally to young people's area of residence.

While YOT staff still work directly with young people and their families, the new working culture of evidence-based practice means that they spend a significant proportion of their working week on desk-work and behind a computer undertaking administrative tasks and completing ASSET forms (see Chapter 19). One of the main criticisms in the Audit Commission's 1996 review was that too little time was spent in direct contact with young people; an average of just one hour per week. It is ironic therefore that the Audit Commission's latest review (published January 2004) found

scarcely any increase on this, although for more persistent offenders the average amount of worker time with them amounted to 1.8 hours per week. The report recommends that:

> *In order to meet the diverse needs of individual young people more fully, a graduated approach should be developed in which the amount and quality of contact time is more closely tailored to their needs and risks.*
> (Audit Commission, 2004, para. 77)

The Youth Justice Board plays a significant role in establishing priorities for the YOTs and it has introduced a range of performance measures which set targets for YOT interventions, the achievement of which may be linked to funding (see Chapter 4).

Do YOTs work? From rhetoric to reality

Any professional who has experienced blocks and delays in obtaining information from another service is likely to find the idea of inter-agency work appealing. Breaking down the physical and bureaucratic boundaries between professions that share the same 'clients' seems like common sense (Crawford, 1994). But how easy and beneficial is it in practice?

Research on 'partnerships' and 'inter-agency co-operation' has shown relations between agencies are very complicated (Liddle and Gelsthorpe, 1994). The evaluation of the pilot YOTs found instances of latent and open disagreements between staff from different occupational backgrounds (Holdaway et al., 2001), and research on 'shadow' YOTs, found similar tensions arising from cultural differences and value conflicts, observing that 'the "shotgun wedding" of youth justice teams with colleagues from other agencies did not appear, on the face of it, to augur well for future collaboration' (Bailey and Williams, 2000: 70).

Other stress points flowed from tensions within the legislation, between speed and quality and punitive and restorative approaches, for example. There was also a 'sense of impermanence' among the staff because of their short-term contracts: some jokingly described the acronym YOT as meaning 'you're only temporary' (Burnett and Appleton, 2004b).

Despite these ominous rumblings, early studies revealed that YOT staff overcame their reservations and showed a 'pragmatic willingness' to make a go of it (Bailey and Williams, 2000). The evaluations of the pilots found that initial reservations were replaced by enthusiasm for multi-agency work. The speed with which the pilot YOTs were set up and 'developed the panoply of new relationships needed to deliver the new orders' was seen as 'a tribute to the general willingness of parties to implement the new youth justice provisions' (Holdaway et al., 2001: 110). Indeed, working in the multi-professional team was most frequently cited by practitioners as the 'best aspect of the work'.

This same spirit of goodwill and enthusiasm was apparent in a study by Burnett and Appleton (2004a; 2004b) which traced the development of a YOT over the first two and a half years of its operation. Practitioners found inter-agency working to be stimulating, enjoyable and the source of various benefits. Moreover, they commented on the absence of conflict and the relative ease with which people from different professional backgrounds adjusted to working alongside each other. But along with the benefits of inter-agency collaboration, some problems were also identified.

The benefits of inter-agency work in the YOT

Shared knowledge and skills

Working within the same team, often under the same roof, meant that information and expertise from staff from a range of different disciplines could be readily exchanged on an informal, ad hoc basis, as the need arose, instead of having to write off for information or wait for a return phone call.

Provision of a holistic service

Because representatives of all the relevant disciplines were now under one roof, it became possible to develop a holistic approach. When issues arose in a case which lay outside the expertise of the responsible officer, there was usually someone on hand with experience and knowledge in that area to solve the problem or make suggestions. It appeared that the multi-agency staff group bought the possibility of a 'seamless' youth justice service closer.

Improved referral

The availability of representatives from different services facilitated the referral of young people to those services. Specialist staff were expected to perform a brokerage function in relation to their parent agencies. Their attachment to the team could alleviate difficulties associated with lengthy waiting lists or complicated referral procedures, and increased the chances of 'having the right person in the right place at the right time'.

Areas of difficulty

Alongside the advantages of working together, some areas of difficulty were also encountered.

Cultural differences

Cultural differences between staff from different occupational backgrounds could be a source of misunderstanding or conflict. One such area concerned decisions and protocols which were perceived by one former youth justice worker as undermining the welfare dimension of the work; but such protests were regarded by management as examples of 'cultural hang-overs' from youth justice, indicating that the member of staff was 'frightened of change'.

Different conditions of service

One very practical source of difficulty that arises from YOTs being staffed by workers from different agencies concerned differentials in pay and conditions of service. Staff carrying out broadly the same tasks may receive very different rewards. Indeed, in some cases, operational managers might receive lower salaries than some of the practitioners under their supervision.

Identity confusion

In the multi-professional melting pot of the YOT, the professional identity of team members might get submerged under the mantle of 'YOT worker' with the result that practitioners lose sight of themselves as, say, an 'education worker' or a 'police officer'. While team members may value the sense of co-operation experienced when all are 'singing from the same hymn sheet', if they lose contact with their professional roots, they will be less able to bring their distinctive professional contribution. This problem has been exacerbated by the increasing numbers of unqualified YOT staff who, the YJB estimates, now represent one third of the youth justice workforce.

The lessons learned

The YOTs were developed by a 'modernising' government in a hurry. Objectives and standards were promulgated, tasks specified, organizational and administrative structures established and senior staff appointed. However, well before these new arrangements had bedded-down, yet more objectives, standards, tasks and structures were handed down to the YOTs. The funding offered by the YJB encouraged the rapid development of a broad range of services at the expense of attention to detail and the strengthening of the basic framework. Meanwhile, the YJB publicity machine was given to making inflated claims of success on the basis of anecdotal evidence. The provision of resources for specialised interventions outpaced the provision of resources for core provision, like interviewing rooms, administrative systems and staff. As Burnett and Appleton (2004a) observed in one YOT, there was plenty of 'caviar but not enough bread'.

The early experiences of YOTs have underlined the importance of the following factors in developing multi-agency collaboration in youth justice:

- An important skill for the strategic managers is to ensure that planning of youth justice services is co-ordinated with the plans of each of the partner agencies.
- A multi-agency partnership requires a *strategic* steering group not only at the time of its formation but on a continuing basis to ensure an adequate budget for forward planning, and to promote a sense of shared ownership and responsibility.
- Most obviously, services have to be delivered by a competent and committed staff, led by inspired and energetic managers.
- In a partnership arena that offers opportunities to expand and develop specialist services, there is a balance to strike between innovative growth and the resourcing and nurturance of basic core services.

Debates and controversies

A number of concerns have attended the introduction of YOTs which might usefully be addressed in the form of three questions.

Should team members be generalists or specialists?

YOTs exemplify both 'multi-agency' working, in which services come together to address a problem, and 'inter-agency' working, in which there is 'some degree of fusion and melding of relations between agencies' (Crawford, 1994). When practitioners from different professional backgrounds have their operational base in the same building and carry out the same tasks using similar skills, professional distinctions between them can become blurred. The creation of YOTs posed the question of whether staff should all carry out similar tasks using the same skills, so that they would become barely distinguishable from one another, 'like the ingredients in a fruit cake' or whether they should retain their professional identities and carry out work specific to their area of specialist expertise, 'like the ingredients in a fruit salad' (Hancock, 2000; Burnett and Appleton, 2004a).

Research suggests that the generalist-specialist distinction oversimplifies the reality (Burnett and Appleton, 2004a). Sometimes, staff identified themselves as generic 'YOT workers', while at other times, they found it useful to emphasise their particular area of expertise and 'play to their professional strengths'. Although successful multi-agency work requires the sharing of perspectives and expertise, this should not be at the expense of specialist contributions. Research conducted on behalf of the YJB has found that, in practice, many specialist health, education and substance misuse staff are under pressure to undertake generic youth justice duties. It suggests that this is both a reflection of the continued difficulty of obtaining specialist services from outside of the YOT and contributes to a dilution of specialist provision within it (Pitcher et al., 2004).

The multi-agency nature of the YOTs means that there should be a steady through-flow of seconded specialist staff. However this raises questions about what, exactly, the specialism of the permanent staff is supposed to be. Indeed, in some YOTs, permanent staff have sometimes complained that, while they spend a considerable amount of time teaching seconded specialists about the youth justice system and work with young people in trouble, their own status remains ambiguous. This suggests that permanent staff require more opportunities to update and extend their knowledge and expertise and that ways are found to validate their 'specialist' contribution, not least, because it is these workers who are the bearers of the accumulated 'practice wisdom' developed within the YOT. The recently unveiled YJB training framework may go some way to addressing this problem.

Has the formation of YOTs resulted in a 'dumbed down' workforce?

The changes in the working culture of youth justice, based on the micro-management of a centrally prescribed, 'evidence-based' practice agenda, has been seen by some as eroding the professionalism of youth justice workers, resulting in a 'dumbing down' of the workforce. The application of systematised procedures and the utilisation of formulaic practice methods conjure visions of a robotic workforce and routinised practice, graphically described by Pitts (2001a) as 'Korrectional Karaoke'. Such concerns have been fuelled by recruitment policies which have increased the proportion of unqualified staff, and funding which is contingent upon the achievement of tightly specified performance measures.

A more optimistic perspective could suggest that, rather than eliminating opportunities for professional discretion, evidence-based practice has provided tools which enhance professional skills by providing a consistent framework for developing programmes of intervention tailored to the requirements of individuals.

Has the emphasis on social work and social welfare in youth justice been supplanted by a justice-oriented 'corporatism'?

YOTs exemplify the 'joined-up' policies and practices which characterise contemporary public services. They may also be seen as an example of 'corporatism', described by Pratt (1989) as the 'third model of juvenile justice', between 'welfare' and 'justice' (see Chapter 1).

By corporatism, Pratt means 'the centralization of policy, increased government intervention, and the co-operation of various professional and interest groups into a collective whole with homogenous aims and objectives' (1989). One of the criticisms of corporatism has been its tendency

to 'spread the net of control' by incorporating a broader range of agencies, which previously had no criminal justice remit, into the criminal justice process, so drawing new and less problematic populations into the purview of the criminal justice system (Pitts, 2001a). From this perspective, an ostensibly benign organisational rationalisation may, in fact, be the Trojan horse of 'government through crime' which, some commentators claim, is gradually extending the reach of the criminal justice system into all walks of life (Hughes and Muncie, 2002). David Smith puts a more positive construction on corporatism in youth justice. He suggests that New Labour's reforms can be seen as a reversion to the principled pragmatism and co-operation promoted by the Home Office during the first wave of corporatist youth justice in the late 1980s and early 1990s prior to the 'punitive turn' from 1993, when custody began to rise in line with government rhetoric (Smith, 2000a). However, as Chapter 25 of this volume makes clear, measured in terms of children and young people incarcerated, punitive responses to youth crime are far from being a thing of the past despite recent efforts to reduce the custodial population.

Whatever the overall trend, research in one large YOT indicates that, practitioners did not appear to have been pushed onto a punitive bandwagon and that the social work ethic remained central to their work (Burnett and Appleton, 2004a). Moreover the severe problems in the lives of the young people appeared to require a welfare-oriented response which becomes 'grounded in the requirements of the job' (Eadie and Canton, 2002: 15). However, the Joint Inspectorate Report on *Safeguarding Children* was fairly critical of YOTs in general for being isolated from other services, failing to address the needs of vulnerable children and focusing on offending at the expense of welfare (Joint Chief Inspectors, 2002). Indeed, similar concerns have been noted by former YOT staff, not least because of decreased opportunities to make home visits and thereby gain greater awareness of welfare needs. Patricia Gray (Chapter 21) also points to the relative neglect of problems of social exclusion. Yet, the 'mélange of measures . . . [and] fundamental contradictions' (Muncie, 2001: 165) contained in the CDA has left scope for different interpretations and a variety of routes via which children and young people in trouble might be helped. While the focus on offending was accepted by the team investigated by Burnett and Appleton (2004a) as valid, the language of punishment was circumvented, and it was the restorative element of the work and the need to access other statutory services in order to meet welfare needs of the children and young people with whom they worked which they emphasised.

In the 1980s, when it was feared that the 'justice model' would sideline the 'welfare model', old methods of working were 'refurbished, brought up to date, remodelled' and new programmes were devised to provide 'an innovative way forward' (Pratt, 1989: 251). Twenty years on, YOT workers are adapting their practice, sometimes welcoming the expanded range of programmes and the improved access to resources while at the same time reasserting the best aspects of traditional practice. YOT workers appear to see themselves as a necessary anchor for young people caught up in the complexities of, and often in conflict with, the youth justice, welfare and educational systems. At the core of this role is the one-to-one relationship which they appear to regard as the *sine qua non* of effective work with troubled and troublesome young people (see Chapter 26).

Conclusion

Tackling the causes of youth crime effectively requires the mobilisation of a wide range of services. A multi-agency response is particularly important for young people who offend because 'the state and civil society have special obligations towards the nation's children and through them to its own future' (Faulkner, 2001: 220). The effec-

tiveness of YOTs can only be realistically measured in the longer term and it is therefore right to question the glib claims of success sometimes made by the YJB. However, some of the criticisms of YOTs may be unduly pessimistic and underestimate the propensity of frontline staff to 'play out' policy in ways which accommodate progressive professional goals. The emphasis on pre-emptive intervention (Pitts, 2003) and unprecedented increases in the use of custody suggest a 'punitive turn' in youth justice but, according to research reviewed here, it seems that alongside this, the social work ethic and a concern with welfare have been sustained within the working culture of practitioners.

Further reading

Bailey, R. and Williams, B. (2000) *Inter-Agency Partnerships in Youth Justice: Implementing the Crime and Disorder Act 1998.* Sheffield: University of Sheffield Joint Unit for Social Service Research

Burnett, R. and Appleton, C. (2004b) *Joined-Up Youth Justice: Tackling Youth Crime in Partnership.* Lyme Regis: Russell House Publishing

Eadie, T. and Canton, R. (2002) Practising in the Context of Ambivalence: The Challenge for Youth Justice Workers. *Youth Justice.* 2: 1, 14–26

Holdaway, S., Davidson, N., Dignan, J., Hammersley, R., Hine, J. and Marsh, P. (2001) *New Strategies to Address Youth Offending: The National Evaluation of the Pilot Youth Offending Teams.* Research, Development and Statistics Directorate, Paper 69. London: Home Office

Home Office (1999) *Inter-Departmental Circular on Establishing Youth Offending Teams.* London: Home Office

18 Court Reports

Tim Bateman

Key points

1. While written reports had as a matter of routine been provided to courts to assist the sentencing process, they had no basis in statute until pre-sentence reports were introduced by the Criminal Justice Act 1991.

2. While the role played by court reports in the sentencing process has expanded, the level of practical guidance contained in successive editions of national standards has fallen.

3. Pre-sentence reports were originally conceived as a mechanism for enhancing the use of non-custodial sentencing but the period since their introduction has witnessed a rapid escalation in the youth custodial population.

4. Court reports have considerable potential to influence to sentencing outcomes and in particular upon levels of custody.

5. In practice, the art of report writing consists in 'working towards a conclusion'.

Introduction

While the provision of reports to court was not uncommon prior to 1961, the publication of the report of the Streatfeild Committee in that year provided the first official recognition that sentencers might properly be furnished with:

> (a) information about the social and domestic background of the offender which is relevant to the court's assessment of his culpability;
> (b) information about the offender and his surroundings which is relevant to the court's consideration of how his criminal career might be checked; and
> (c) an opinion as to the likely effect on the offender's criminality of . . . [a] . . . specified sentence.
>
> (Streatfeild, 1961)

The Committee's comments were widely interpreted as indicating that criminal proceedings should henceforth include consideration of a written report (at that time known as probation reports but subsequently renamed social inquiry reports) in cases where fuller information to inform sentencing was desirable.

Nonetheless, social inquiry reports (SIRs) continued to have no basis in statute. There was little consistency in their format, content or quality and the extent to which courts availed themselves of written reports showed considerable variation.

The Criminal Justice Act 1991 (CJA 91) introduced a new sentencing framework, based around the principle of proportionality (see Chapter 9) and the government took the opportunity to look anew at the purpose and content of court reports within that context. Research conducted shortly before the new legislation had found that 59% of defendants sentenced to immediate custody following trial at crown court were sentenced without any form of written report (ACOP, 1989). A second study showed that black defendants were considerably more likely to be sentenced in the absence of an SIR than their white counterparts (Home Office, 1988b). Against this background, the CJA 91 required courts to consider a new form of report, called a pre-sentence report (PSR), before imposing a custodial sentence or any of the more intensive community sentences. For the first time, the provision of court reports was placed on a statutory footing and, associated with that change, came an increasing recognition of the importance of PSRs as an integral part of the sentencing process. The court report had in effect come of age.

The legislative provision inevitably resulted in a marked growth in the volume of reports prepared in criminal cases involving children and young people. By 1998, a PSR was requested on average for 41% of completed cases heard in the youth court (Audit Commission, 1998). When youth justice services were defined for the first time in section 39 of the Crime and Disorder Act 1998 (CDA), it was small surprise that the list included:

> . . . *the provision of reports or other information required by courts in criminal proceedings against children and young persons.*

Types of court report and when they are used

The PSR is the most important, and most frequently requested, type of report. It is defined in the Criminal Justice Act 2003 (CJA 03) as a written report produced, where the defendant is under 18 years of age, by a probation officer, social worker or a member of a youth offending team (YOT) 'with a view to assisting the court in determining the most suitable method of dealing with an offender' (s158).

There is a statutory presumption in favour of the court obtaining and considering a PSR before it imposes a custodial sentence or a range of specified, more intensive, community penalties. Although the court can, in the case of a defendant under 18 years of age, dispense with a PSR if it has access to a previous report, the circumstances and maturity of children and young people change rapidly over relatively short periods of time. In recognition of this potential, the Magistrates' Association has taken the view that it would rarely be wise to rely on previous reports (Magistrates' Association, 1995).

Although a PSR is not legally required for a supervision order or community rehabilitation order without conditions, it is frequently regarded as good practice for the court to request one. For other sentences, namely a drug treatment and testing order or a curfew order which can in principle be made without a written report, the court is obliged to obtain information as to the availability and suitability of the provision. The PSR is the obvious mechanism for provision of such information.

While the PSR is thus the most important category of court report, there are other forms. Courts are obliged to consider a written report, though not necessarily a full PSR, before imposing an action plan order. At minimum, that report must specify the requirements which the author proposes ought to be included in the order, the anticipated benefits of those requirements to the young person, and the attitude of the parents or carers to the proposed content of the order. Although there may be some advantages, in terms of reduced adjournments and resource input on the part of YOTs, there is also no provision, within the format suggested by the Home Office, for the report author to indicate that a form of disposal other than an action plan order is appropriate.

Similar considerations apply to reparation orders although these, unlike action plan orders, are not community penalties in terms of the statutory framework (see Chapter 6). A written report, but not necessarily a PSR, is again required, specifying the type of reparative activity that the author considers appropriate for the young person, and outlining the attitude of the victim to the proposed requirements.

Finally, 'stand down' reports are prepared for the court on the day, and may be presented verbally. They are generally used to supplement an existing PSR.

National standards: implications for reports

The format of court reports was not prescribed in any way prior to the introduction of PSRs. National standards were first published in 1992 to coincide with the implementation of the CJA 91, and have been subject to several revisions in the intervening period. The evolution of standards displays an interesting pattern, indicating a shift away from providing guidance on good practice towards an emphasis on minimum expectations, time management and quality assurance.

The first volume of national standards, which dealt with both adult and young people, stretched to some 122 pages, of which 19 focused on the production of PSRs (Home Office, 1992b). Considerable attention was devoted to what ought to go into, and be excluded from, the report and to how authors should arrive at an appropriate proposal. Standards were revised in 1995 with a reduction in size to 65 pages. There was an equivalent cutback in the space given over to court reports, which accounted for ten pages, although one and a half of these dealt specifically with PSRs for young people (Home Office, 1995a).

The biggest shift occurred however, in April 2000, with the publication of national standards to accompany the implementation of the youth justice reforms. These were, for the first time, specific to work with children and young people (Youth Justice Board, 2000d). The standards were characterised by a further reduction in size despite a considerable extension in scope: unlike their predecessors, the youth justice standards covered preventive work, assessment, restorative justice, appropriate adults, pre-court measures and parenting. Yet they were considerably shorter, 55 pages in total, with just two and a half allocated to court reports.

Revised youth justice national standards were issued early in 2004 (Youth Justice Board, 2004c). These are longer than the standards they replaced but the expansion is due, in part, to the inclusion of a number of new sections. There is a marginal increase in the length of the section devoted to court reports which now attracts three pages.

Current national standards then, provide relatively little practical guidance on the preparation of PSRs and other reports. What they do have to say on the issue can be summarised fairly shortly.

They require, first, that reports are based on information from all relevant sources, including a victim personal statement where available, an ASSET assessment (see Chapter 19), at least one interview with the young person and, where possible, an interview with the parent or carer. They should be: balanced; impartial; timely; focused; free from discriminatory language; verified and accurate; and understandable to the young person.

The standards also reaffirm that the purpose of a PSR is to assist the court to come to a decision as to suitable disposal. Reports must be produced within 10 working days where the young person meets the definition of a 'persistent young offender' or satisfies the criteria for an intensive supervision and surveillance programme (see Chapter 22). The time limit for all other cases is 15 days. Reports are to be prepared under the following headings:

- Sources of information.
- Offence analysis, including impact on the victim.
- Assessment of young person.
- Assessment of risk to the community, including the risk of re-offending and harm.
- Conclusion, including proposal for sentencing.

Guidance on action plan order and reparation order reports is similarly thin. The standards suggest that where a recent assessment in the form of ASSET is available, such reports should usually be available on the day of the request. Where an assessment has not previously been conducted, they should be prepared within five working days. It is not easy to see how a report prepared at court could properly address the views of the victim (as legally required in the case of a reparation order report), or adequately detail a range of requirements individually tailored to address offending behaviour (as expected of an action plan order report). Significantly, the original Home Office guidance on action plan orders anticipated that an adjournment, for ten working days, would usually be required to allow a proper assessment (Home Office, 2000e). Such a timescale seems more realistic if reports are to be of a high quality.

The standards make only a brief reference to stand down reports and indicate merely that YOTs may provide such reports either verbally or in writing on the same day as the court hearing, if a recent ASSET and 'other relevant reports/information are available' in order to facilitate the prompt conclusion of a case.

Practitioners wanting guidance on how to prepare good quality court reports will, it appears, need to look to sources other than the national standards (see, for instance, Nacro, 2003g).

The power to influence?

There is no doubt that PSRs were conceived as part of a package to reduce the use of custody. The sentencing framework contained in the CJA 91 was intended to enhance courts' confidence in community sentencing and to limit the use of incarceration to those committing the most serious offences. The government's explanation of the function of PSRs also showed clear decarcerative intent:

> The purpose of requiring courts to consider a report . . . when a custodial sentence is contemplated will be to provide the court with detailed information about how the offender could be punished in the community, so that option can be fully explored.
>
> (Home Office, 1990)

In the event, the anticipated fall in the use of custody did not come about. Instead, there was a rapid escalation in the number of children and young people deprived of their liberty from 4,000 during 1992 to 7,500 in 2002, with most of the rise concentrated in the period up to 1999 (Nacro, 2004c). The reasons for the rapid shift towards a greater use of detention are complex, but no doubt the impact of legislative change and the development of what have been called a 'new punitiveness', both made a significant contribution (Goldson, 2002b; Nacro, 2003a). A question also arises as to the role of PSRs in the process.

It might be tempting to think that the potential influence of court reports on final sentence is relatively limited. The legal framework provides that any restriction of liberty is determined primarily by the seriousness of the offending (see Chapter 9), and this might be taken to imply that the main function of the PSR is to assist the court in coming to a decision as to the most suitable disposal *within a pre-determined range*. From such a perspective, the scope for PSRs to have a significant impact on levels of custody might appear marginal. Indeed, in a recent survey, almost half of magistrates suggested that where a requested PSR was not available, they would sometimes go ahead with sentencing in any event (Audit Commission, 2004).

There is also evidence that PSR proposals are to some degree constrained by a 'local culture of sentencing practice', shared by all agencies working within the youth justice system and inevitably reflected in YOTs' recommendations to the court. PSR authors are, in other words, frequently engaged in a certain amount of 'second guessing' as to a court's intentions, so that proposals often reinforce rather than challenge local patterns of sentencing (Youth Justice Board, 2000b).

It would however be a serious error to underestimate the significance of a well argued court report. It is not at all clear, firstly, that magistrates in fact have a predetermined view of the outcome based upon the gravity of the offending. The sentencing framework allows for information about the young person's circumstances to mitigate sentence and the requirement on the courts to consider the welfare of the child ensures that the scope for leniency is greater in the case of a young person than it would be for an adult (Nacro, 2003k). More than 70% of magistrates report that their sentencing decisions are influenced by information about: behavioural prob-

lems; family background; and education. In addition, 80% consider the effectiveness of local community programmes to be a determinant and almost all sentencers point to the importance of mitigation in arriving at a disposal (Audit Commission, 2004). The PSR is often the primary source of information for each of these factors.

More concretely, research confirms a correlation between the level of custody in a particular area and the assessed quality of court reports. One study, for instance, found that PSRs in low custody areas achieved a higher 'score' in a quality audit than areas with a higher level of incarceration. More significantly, perhaps, the variation in scores could be largely accounted for by the differences in the assessed quality of the conclusion – considered in terms of the coherence and strength of the argument in favour of the proposal (Youth Justice Board, 2000b). A subsequent study also reported that PSRs in low custody areas achieved a significantly higher rating in terms of how well they provided information about the programme which would be delivered in the event that the court accepted the report's proposal (Bateman and Stanley, 2002). A logically structured, well argued, court report can thus exert a powerful influence of the sentencing outcome.

Of course, PSRs might also impact on sentencing outcomes in a more direct fashion by proposing custody or by failing to make an alternative proposal. There is some evidence to suggest that PSR authors have not been immune to the increasingly punitive climate that has characterised responses to youth crime. Rod Morgan, in an article written before he was appointed chair of the Youth Justice Board, points to a doubling of proposals for custody and an increasing number of reports containing no proposals in PSRs prepared by the probation service for adult defendants. He concludes that 'to the extent sentencers have moved up-tariff, so also have probation officers' (Morgan, 2003).

There may well have been a similar shift among youth justice practitioners. The Home Office evaluation of the first two years operation of Medway secure training centre (STC) found that for a full 22% of children sentenced to a secure training order, the PSR contained a positive and explicit proposal for that custodial sentence (Hagell et al., 2000). More recently, the Director General of the private security firm responsible for Medway and Rainsbrook STCs has suggested that 51% of PSRs written during 2002 for children subject to a detention and training order in those establishments, proposed custody either explicitly or implicitly. Only one in four of such reports contained a 'viable alternative to custody' (Stevens, 2002).

In this context, it is interesting that the question of whether court reports should propose custody has recently attracted attention in the wake of a finding by the National Audit Office that 48 out of 146 teams responding had a policy of not doing so (National Audit Office, 2004). A letter from the outgoing chief executive of the Youth Justice Board to YOT managers in response to the finding suggested that 'it is no longer acceptable to make no recommendation when a custodial sentence is appropriate' (Youth Justice Board, 2004b).

The Board has been concerned to reduce the population of the juvenile secure estate, reflected in a performance measure requiring YOTs to restrict custodial sentences to no more than 6% of all court outcomes. Indeed, the Board has a stated aim of reducing the number of young children unnecessarily held in custody by at least 400 over the next three years (Youth Justice Board, 2003e). Yet the Board's current antagonism to a policy of not proposing custody inevitably serves to obscure the fact that such proposals have played an inflationary role in the recent period. The problem is one of an *overuse* of custodial recommendations rather than the reverse. The Board's position also represents a failure to recognise the function of PSRs – as originally conceived – as a mechanism for ensuring that courts have access to information about what services can be offered in the community so that the choice of a custodial disposal is informed by full knowledge of what alternatives are available.

The danger inherent in promoting custodial proposals is further demonstrated by recent findings that more than 60% of magistrates consider detention and training orders to be effective despite a large majority reporting that they did not know whether custodial institutions were able to meet young people's needs in terms of mental health, education and addressing offending behaviour (Audit Commission, 2004). Given that YOTs have a markedly less optimistic view of the effectiveness of custody, the potential for PSRs to influence sentencers' views in this respect is considerable. Readily proposing custody would involve a failure to maximise that potential.

The practice of report writing

If there is one clear message from the foregoing overview, it is that court reports have an important, though frequently underestimated, part to play in the process by which sentencing outcomes are arrived at. The role is enshrined in legislation and the potential extent of the influence borne out by research. While it is beyond the scope of the current chapter to provide an account of the mechanics of preparing a high quality report, it may nonetheless be helpful to draw out some of the practical implications.

First, it is important to maintain the central role of the PSR as the court report of choice. The scope for influencing outcomes is substantially greater where the report author is able to marshal arguments for a particular course of action which may not always coincide with the initial inclination of the court. In particular, the use of stand down reports should be resisted where there is a risk of a custodial sentence or higher tariff community intervention.

Second, PSRs fail to exercise a positive influence on the levels of custody where they suffer from weak, poorly argued proposals. Good practice thus involves regarding the preparation of the report as an exercise in working towards a particular conclusion. The whole of the structure and content of the document should be determined by the requirement to achieve that end.

In concrete terms, an effective report will be one that contains:

- An analysis of the factors that are relevant to the young person's criminal behaviour, and an independent assessment of the seriousness of the current offending.
- An account of the young person's personal circumstances to the extent that they contribute to an understanding of the offending behaviour or have the potential to mitigate sentence.
- An outline of the risk of reoffending, and any resulting harm, framed in the context of what forms of intervention would be likely to reduce that risk.
- A description of a programme of intervention which is: commensurate with the seriousness of

the offending; addresses the young person's welfare needs and other factors highlighted in the offence analysis; and serves to reduce risk.
- A single proposal that matches the needs of the young person to the most suitable form of disposal within the range of penalties proportionate to the offending (Nacro, 2003g).

Preparing reports for court is a highly skilled activity and achieving the right balance is far from easy. The potential benefits however to young people in trouble, in terms of reduced levels of custody, and encouraging consistent and appropriate sentencing outcomes, more than outweigh the expenditure in terms of practitioner input.

Further reading

Bateman, T. and Stanley, C. (2002) *Patterns of Sentencing: Differential Sentencing across England and Wales.* London: Youth Justice Board

Nacro (2000) *Pre-Sentence Reports and Custodial Sentencing.* Youth Crime Briefing. London: Nacro

Nacro (2003g) *Pre-Sentence Reports for Young People: A Good Practice Guide.* 2nd edn. London: Nacro

Youth Justice Board (2000b) *Factors Associated With Differential Rates of Youth Custodial Sentencing.* London: Youth Justice Board

Risk and Protection

Jill Annison

Key points

1. Risk has become of increasing concern within society.

2. Risk assessment is now a key task for practitioners working with offenders.

3. In the field of youth justice, research has focused on the interaction of risk and protective factors.

4. The actuarial tool utilised within youth offending teams to assess risk is ASSET.

5. While risk assessment tools have provided a structured approach to risk assessment of young people who offend, the wider social, cultural and political context also needs to be considered.

Introduction

The notion of risk has had a significant impact upon youth justice in the recent past, reflecting developments in the broader criminal justice system as well as in everyday life. Social theorists have identified a growing apprehension in society about risk and they now speak about the 'risk society' (Beck, 1992), where individuals experience a heightened desire to control the future and to eliminate the threat to personal safety (Giddens and Pierson, 1998). In ordinary conversation the fine distinction between 'good' and 'bad' risks has all but disappeared, with the term 'risk' being used 'to refer almost exclusively to a threat, hazard, danger or harm' (Lupton, 1999: 8). This shift in usage has been mirrored in the criminal justice field, where the emphasis on 'risk' is now 'most often identified with loss, negative, unwanted or harmful outcomes' (Kemshall, 1996).

The increasing emphasis on risk, risk assessment and risk management has been characterised by Feeley and Simon (1992; 1994) as part of a 'new penology' which aims to manage the risks posed by those who offend rather than reform or punish them. Feeley and Simon identify three key changes:

1. The language of probability and risk increasingly replaces earlier discourses of clinical diagnosis and retributive judgment.
2. The formation of new objectives for the system, which increasingly focus on 'risk management'.

3. The deployment of new techniques which target, and aim to manage, risks presented by groups of offenders rather than bring about individual punishment or rehabilitation.

(Feeley and Simon, 1992: 450)

The appearance of these three strands is evident within the youth justice system in England and Wales. Major legal and policy changes have ushered in new organisational structures and established the Youth Justice Board for England and Wales (see Chapter 4) and youth offending teams (YOTs) (see Chapter 17). These new operational arrangements have in turn brought about change at practice level, particularly in relation to risk assessment tasks and the range and nature of interventions with young people who offend.

This 'paradigm shift' at practice level has led to the development and application of 'objective' assessment instruments and classification guidelines for use with young people who offend (Kempf-Leonard and Peterson, 2002). Thus, practitioners working in YOTs are required to assess 'risk of re-offending, risk of him/her causing serious harm to others (and) risk of him/her being harmed (vulnerability)' (Baker et al., 2002: 5).

The assessment of risk

Clinical approaches to risk and risk assessment

While concerns about risk have moved centre stage over the past ten years or so, this is not a new area of practice in the criminal justice field. Staff have traditionally made 'clinical' judgements of risk. These assessments have relied upon the professional experience and training of practitioners, rather than actuarial calculation, and focused on the particular circumstances, demeanour of, and background information about, individual offenders. The clinical approach rests heavily on the diagnostic skills of the individual practitioner and is dependent on the interaction between them and the offender (Kemshall, 1996). It has been criticised for being prone to 'subjective' interpretation or psychological bias with the resultant problems of mis-classification of risk – false positives which over-predict or false negatives which make the opposite error – or the erroneous 'framing' of risk (see Strathan and Tallant, 1997). Inconsistencies arising from such sources can, it has been argued, then lead to wide variations in the responses of different workers or teams (Baker et al., 2000). Nevertheless, in spite of these reservations, Kemshall suggests that the clinical assessment of risk in relation to offenders is still relevant because of its 'ability to explain behaviour, assess motivation to change, and match intervention programmes to the significant personality traits and situational factors related to the risk behaviour' (Kemshall, 1996: 9).

Actuarial approaches to risk and risk assessment

In contrast to clinical approaches to assessment, actuarial risk assessment tends to adopt what has been described as a 'technico-scientific' perspective (Lupton, 1999). Its origins can be traced back to the pioneering work of Burgess, undertaken in the 1920s, who attempted to devise statistical methods to assess risk in relation to parole decisions (Robinson, 2003). Actuarial risk assessments of individuals, within the criminal justice field, are based upon statistical calculations of probability. These are derived from information about the behaviour of, often large, cohorts of offenders with similar antecedents and characteristics. In the past few years, this approach has attracted increasing official endorsement within the criminal justice system (Feeley and Simon, 1992). As David Garland observes:

> Risk assessment and risk management are not new elements of penal practice, but they now have a

> *centrality and a formality which they have never had before.*

(Garland, 1997: 9)

With this intensified focus in the criminal justice system upon risk, there has been a rapid growth of what has been termed a 'risk industry' (Prins, 1999). This is because actuarial assessments demand the development and maintenance of extensive databases, and the accurate collation of complex information at both local and national levels. At their best, formal assessment and classification systems offer a framework which provides validity and consistency. They can, moreover, be seen 'to ensure fairness and consistency between the children and young people under consideration by making all decisions in accordance with the same explicit criteria' (Pitts, 1999: 147).

However, it is important to recognise that any type of risk assessment takes place within a context of uncertainty and that, as yet, no approach has been developed that offers 100% accuracy all of the time. As noted above, the main advantage of actuarial tools is that they are grounded in empirical data and their predictive value can be researched, developed and evaluated. Nevertheless, although actuarial approaches offer the possibility of more standardised and explicit responses to risk assessment, problems may arise in practice.

The problems of actuarial assessment

Gwen Robinson (2003) has highlighted four areas of particular concern about actuarial assessment. First, there is the potential for irregularities in the transfer of information in practice environments. For example, full and accurate information from the Crown Prosecution Service may not be available to the writers of pre-sentence reports (Williams, 2000). Second, actuarial tools focus on the probability of reconviction and not the probability of re-offending. Third, while they may predict the likelihood of a reconviction, this will not necessarily indicate the type or seriousness of any future offence. Finally, actuarial methods, which rely on static risk factors (such as age, gender and offending history), can only provide:

> ... *an estimate of the probability that an offender with a particular set of characteristics will be*

reconvicted within two years; it does not purport to make an accurate prediction for a specific individual.
(Robinson, 2003: 115–6)

These limitations are of critical importance, even though they may be viewed as somewhat esoteric by the public and the media. In the current highly charged political environment, professionals working in the spheres of social care, mental health and criminal justice have been faced with heightened expectations that risks will be identified and managed (Goldson and Jamieson, 2002). High profile cases where things have gone wrong have generated a 'culture of blame' (Kemshall, 2002) leading to a consequent tendency amongst professionals to over-predict risk and for risk procedures to become over-bureaucratic. As a counter to these tendencies, Hazel Kemshall has suggested that staff should endeavour to avoid the pitfall of defensive judgements and should instead 'apply the test of the 'defensible decision' to their decision making' (Kemshall, 1998: 68).

Risk and protective factors

With the rise of the 'risk factor' paradigm, we have also seen the emergence of the related idea of 'protective factors', which appear to insulate young people from criminal involvement or to ameliorate the risks:

> *In a straightforward sense, factors signifying the opposite or absence of risk will help to protect children and young people against involvement in crime, drug abuse and other antisocial behaviour. However, research has identified an additional range of factors that are 'protective' in the sense that they moderate the effects of exposure to risk.*
> (Youth Justice Board, 2001b: 21)

Any comprehensive assessment will need to balance both risk and protective factors. In youth justice in England and Wales, the risk factors identified by longitudinal studies of young people (see Rutter et al., 1998, Farrington, 2002) have informed the development of assessment tools like ASSET (Youth Justice Board, 2002a), which is discussed in greater detail below. Statistical analysis of the research findings has led to the identification of major risk factors in relation to juvenile offending in the following domains:

- Family
- School
- Community
- Personal or individual factors
(Youth Justice Board, 2001b)

ASSET aims to capture risks across these areas with sections on static risk – offending career; and dynamic risk – living arrangements, family and personal relationships, education, training and employment, neighbourhood, lifestyle, substance use, physical health, emotional and mental health, perception of self and others, thinking and behaviour, attitudes towards offending, motivation to change (Baker et al., 2000). While ASSET 'tots-up' risk assessment scores for each of these dimensions, it is unlikely to reveal the particular factor or factors underlying a particular young person offending. As the Youth Justice Board (2001b: 7–8) observes:

> *The tangled roots of delinquency can, more accurately, be found to lie in the way that multiple risk factors cluster together and interact in the lives of some children, while important protective factors are conspicuously absent.*

To date, protective factors have not received the same level of attention and scrutiny as those relating to risk. However, current research is showing that protective factors operate as a 'buffer against or mitigate the negative effects of risk exposure' (Catalano et al., 1998: 249). Michael Rutter and his colleagues have pointed to the interaction of multiple risk and protective factors and emphasise that 'their relative impact varies across different links of the causal chain as well as according to individual phases of development' (Rutter et al., 1998: 310). Protective factors can operate at individual or social levels and this has important implications for the development of effective preventive strategies (Farrington, 2002).

Research conducted for the Youth Justice Board identifies the following protective factors:

Individual level

- female gender
- a resilient temperament
- a sense of self-efficacy
- a positive, outgoing disposition
- high intelligence

Social level

- social bonding
- the promotion of healthy standards with family, school and community

(Youth Justice Board, 2001b: 115)

What is ASSET?

The ASSET assessment profile was developed in 1999 by the Centre for Criminological Research at the University of Oxford and came into operation with the introduction of YOTs in April 2000. It is an actuarial assessment tool utilised at all stages of intervention, from final warning stage, when preparing pre-sentence reports, or supervision planning (Youth Justice Board, 2002a). ASSET is designed as a 'working tool' and the National Standards for youth justice require workers supervising young people in the YOTs to update assessments at three-monthly and final reviews (Youth Justice Board, 2004c: Section 8.11). This has meant that 'for the first time, a common structured assessment profile was being used across the youth justice system in England and Wales' (Baker et al., 2000: 5).

The initial design of the ASSET format incorporated questions relating to risk and protective factors associated with youth offending which was derived from research in this area (Youth Justice Board, 2001b; Lipsey, 1995). As well as 'tick boxes' and a scaled assessment (from 0–4) of the extent to which the particular factor is considered to be associated with the likelihood of further offending, the form asks for a written summary of relevant evidence. Finally, there is a section entitled 'What Do You Think?' which is completed by the young person. This approach reinforces the participative nature of the assessment task and it is intended that, unless there are any concerns about harm to the young person, the completed assessments should be shared with them and their carers (Youth Justice Board, 2002a).

Practice applications

The promise of ASSET and other actuarial assessment tools is that they will allow practitioners to calculate the statistical probability of future offending and anticipate this risk by devising interventions which focus upon the relevant risk factors (Gelsthorpe, 2002). In this way, judgements of risk may be linked with plans for levels and types of intervention and the process of supervision. As Lord Warner, the first Chair of the Youth Justice Board has commented:

> *Our philosophy is very simple. You assess individuals to find out what causes them to offend or what risks exist in their lives to make the likelihood of offending greater. Then you take steps to put in preventative programmes that will tackle these risk factors.*

(Warner, 2003: 30)

This approach has important implications for the relationship between risk assessment and intervention, since the *What Works* initiative, which has permeated the criminal justice system in the recent past, suggests that higher-risk individuals require the most intensive interventions, whereas low-risk individuals may be safely assigned to less intensive alternatives (McGuire and Priestley, 1995). The crucial role now played by risk assessment in policy and the everyday practice of youth justice cannot be overstated.

A critique of ASSET and other actuarial tools in practice

ASSET is intended to be an evidence-based assessment tool which provides detailed, structured information upon which to base assessments of individual young people who offend (see Chapman and Hough, 1998). But it can also be seen to function at other levels. Information derived from ASSET can inform policy and practice development within YOTs and aggregated ASSET data can contribute to a national picture of youth offending in terms of the age, race, gender, and social circumstances of children and young people in trouble (Baker et al., 2000). Such an approach provides opportunities for a breadth and depth of analysis of offending data, not possible using clinical assessments.

Research on the first two years of ASSET reported that it has a predictive accuracy of 67% (Baker et al., 2000), a figure that compares favourably with other third-generation risk assessment tools like those currently being introduced in the probation service (see Merrington et al., 2003). The research also found reasonably good levels of consistency where different users undertook an assessment, suggesting that it can provide a 'meaningful indicator of the problem areas requiring intervention from youth justice staff' (Baker et al., 2000: 98). ASSET therefore appears to represent a reliable assessment tool within the youth justice field.

However, while meeting these methodological requirements, practical difficulties remain. The research undertaken by Baker et al. revealed a low completion rate for the evidence boxes and the care and criminal history sections on the ASSET forms. Moreover, the 'What Do You Think' forms were often not used to their full potential (Baker et al., 2000). These problems were due in part to ASSET being introduced at a time of considerable change and upheaval in youth justice and this may have affected the incorporation of the tool into day-to-day practice (Baker et al., 2000: 97). There also appeared to be some scepticism and resistance among practitioners about the use of actuarial tools. This mirrored the findings of a Home Office research study which looked at similar applications within the probation service (Aye Maung and Hammond, 2000). Such findings suggest that if an assessment tool is to fulfil its potential, implementation should be phased to allow staff time to understand its relevance to effective practice; its centrality to the assessment task should be underlined and the tool itself should not be overly time consuming and cumbersome to use. Thus 'a balance has to be struck between brevity (a feature much appreciated by users) and comprehensiveness' (Merrington et al., 2003: 33).

The wider debate

ASSET has become an integral feature of the structured assessment framework for young people who offend. However, it is just this precision and exactitude that has been challenged by some academic commentators and practitioners. Kevin Haines and Mark Drakeford, for instance, point to 'the danger of regarding risk assessment as a neutral, value-free, technical operation' (Haines and Drakeford, 1998: 217). They, and other authors (see, for instance, Muncie, 2000 and Pitts, 2001c), highlight the moral overtones and increasingly punitive political rhetoric which has formed the backdrop to these developments in relation to young people who offend, their families and their communities. In his discussion

of the theory of delinquent development, and the associated research findings, which have informed and underpinned the implementation of ASSET, John Pitts has highlighted the deterministic implications of this approach and the inherent difficulties in making quantifiable judgements in relation to complex social factors:

> *It (a criminal career) is not simply a tale of the inevitable unfolding of a developmental deficit. It is a story about a complex interaction of social, economic, cultural and developmental factors and burgeoning negative stereotyping. For the people caught up in this spiral, their worsening predicament is paralleled by the progressive erosion of their capacity to make any impact upon that predicament.*
>
> (Pitts, 2001c: 87)

Conclusion

These criticisms notwithstanding, ASSET can promote an approach to assessment and professional decision making which utilises explicit criteria, supports consistency and is open to scrutiny. However, operational pressures mean that information is often incomplete and practitioners are not fully engaged with the process and this can undermine the reliability of such assessments.

Hazel Kemshall (1996) has argued for a more holistic approach to assessment which combines the strengths of both clinical and actuarial approaches, thus encouraging practitioners to review actuarial findings in the light of their professional skill and experience. This would avoid the danger of assessment becoming a purely mechanical undertaking and increase the likelihood of it being used in a constructive way, utilising the range of professional skills available within the YOTs. As Kevin Haines and Mark Drakeford have pointed out:

> *The contribution which youth justice workers make to the sentencing process is to shine a light onto the before and after of a young person's actions, and to suggest ways to the court in which precipitating factors might be amended and responses tempered so as to lower future risks. This is what risk assessment should be all about.*
>
> (Haines and Drakeford, 1998: 228)

Nonetheless, there is an ever-present danger that structured assessment tools will be used as a way

of over-simplifying a complex social reality. They
are developed from samples taken from male,
usually white, correctional populations (Moffatt
and Shaw, 2000). This has raised particular concerns in relation to gender and diversity issues (see
also Bhui, 1999), with disquiet being voiced about
'issues of subjectivity, individual pathology, treatment proscription, and the "slippage" between
risk and need' (Moffatt and Shaw, 2000: 168).

To date, the fears and preoccupations of a 'risk
society' appear to have driven the youth justice
agenda, rendering the system more punitive and
condemnatory. In this respect the, 'technical fix'
offered by actuarial approaches draws attention
away from more complex, but fundamental, issues
of social inequality and human rights for young
people, their families and their communities.
Interestingly, the data gleaned by instruments like
ASSET could easily be utilised to counter this
punitive turn because they underscore the link
between young people getting into trouble and
social and economic disadvantage, and this could
then inform children's and youth justice policy at
local and national levels. This would, of course,
raise important political and resource allocation

issues. Nonetheless, this broader, more socially
inclusive, picture of children and young people in
trouble is an essential backdrop to any assessment
of risk and protection within the youth justice
sphere.

Further reading

Baker, K., Jones, S., Roberts, C. and Merrington,
S. (2000) *The Evaluation of The Validity and
Reliability of the Youth Justice Board's Assessment for
Young People Who Offend: Findings From the First
Two Years of the Use of ASSET*. London: Youth
Justice Board

Kemshall, H. (2002) *Risk, Social Policy and Welfare*.
Buckingham: Open University Press (Chapters
1, 2 and 6)

Lupton, D. (1999) *Risk*. London: Routledge

Merrington, S., Baker, K. and Wilkinson, B. (2003)
Using Risk and Need Assessment Tools in
Probation and Youth Justice. *VISTA*. 8: 1, 31–8

Youth Justice Board (2001b) *Risk and Protective
Factors Associated With Youth Crime and Effective
Interventions to Prevent it*. Research Note 5.
London: Youth Justice Board

20 Electronic Monitoring

Dick Whitfield

Key points

1. Electronic monitoring (EM) is a tool to monitor a curfew and not a programme in itself. Its most effective use is in conjunction with other forms of intervention.

2. EM is essentially a short-term option. Compliance rates decline sharply after three months.

3. The key to effective use is good targeting and clarity of aims. It may be useful in interrupting a pattern of offending, helping to deal with peer pressure, or as a short-term control measure.

4. Use with low risk individuals may be negative and the ability provided by the technology to detect all breaches, however minor, may simply accelerate young people along the path to custody.

5. Family pressures may be increased as a result of tagging and explanations and ongoing support to parents are important.

Introduction

The original inspiration for the electronic monitoring (EM) of offenders is usually attributed to Judge Jack Love of New Mexico who, it is said, spotted the idea in a Spiderman comic (Berry and Matthews, 1989). Once the idea was turned into a product, energetic marketing in the USA led to its widespread use (Ackerman, 1986). Although electronic monitoring of convicted offenders has been in use for over 20 years in the USA, it was not until 1995 that a pilot scheme for sentenced adults began in Britain, and a further two years before a pilot scheme for juveniles became available to courts. Since then, growth has been significant. Electronic monitoring is one of the most recent tools used in the community supervision of young people who offend. It allows us to verify whether or not a young person is complying with a curfew or other court order that requires them to be, or refrain from being, in a particular place at a particular time. This is achieved by fitting a small electronic device, or 'tag', onto the ankle of the subject. A monitoring unit in the young person's home then allows their presence there to be monitored for the time specified by the court. The law allows for curfews to be imposed for up to 12 hours per day (normally 7 p.m. to 7 a.m., but hours can be tailored to individual circumstances). Recent developments in monitoring technology also allow computer aided voice recognition, which allows checks from different locations, and, more recently, the possibility of satellite based technology which would allow continuous checks on movement and location.

The advantages of EM for youth justice agencies are that the electronic devices are relatively cheap, surveillance is easy to administer and electronic records ensure that evidence of breaches are clear and unequivocal. At present, the electronic tag, rather than voice verification, is the preferred technology for checking curfew compliance. Voice verification has its advantages, nothing has to be worn and checks can be carried out at any location where a landline telephone is installed, but early problems with the technology have engendered a lack of confidence while lack of knowledge about how best to use the technology has relegated voice recognition to a minor role in EM.

The uses of electronic monitoring in the youth justice system

There are currently five main applications of EM in youth justice systems in the UK:

- As a stand alone order.
- As a component of a community penalty. It may be combined with several community-based sentencing options, but is most frequently

used as part of an intensive supervision and surveillance programme (ISSP) (see Chapter 22).

- As a condition of bail, when it may be used either as a stand alone option, or in conjunction with a prescribed programme of bail supervision and support (see Chapter 14).
- In conjunction with a detention and training order; whether as part of early release arrangements or at the normal release date.
- In the case of Section 90/91 discharges from custody (very serious or life license cases), particularly in relation to early release under Home Detention Curfew.

The Youth Justice Board's aims in using EM are:

- To reduce offending.
- To reduce the use of custody.
- To support compliance with community penalties.
- To provide reassurance to courts and the community that penalties are being rigorously enforced.

(Burnham, 2003)

Since the first pilot projects in 1997, more than 8,000 juveniles have been tagged, the youngest being a girl of 12. Children and young people now represent around 14% of all tagged offenders in England and Wales. On any day, about 1,400 young people are monitored in this way. As noted above, the main use of EM in the youth justice system is currently to support ISSPs. The surveillance element of the ISSP can take the form of tagging, voice verification, tracking, checking by personnel from a surveillance agency and police checks. At their inception, about 70% of the subjects of ISSPs were tagged but by early 2004 this figure had risen to almost 90% (Waters et al., 2003).

The effectiveness of electronic monitoring

It is difficult to be clear about the effectiveness of any component part of a programme which may have many other elements. Since EM is usually employed in conjunction with other interventions such as work on offending behaviour, education and training, use of leisure and one-to-one supervision, it is problematic to isolate its individual

contribution. However, both the police and the courts appear to be positive about strictly monitored curfews supported by tagging, because they appear to offer a way of imposing some structure upon, often, chaotic and disordered young lives, while serving as a crime prevention tool in their own right.

However, effective use of the tag requires an understanding of its limitations. The tag, in itself, does not change behaviour. It can only monitor compliance with the terms of a curfew. It cannot tell us what the young person might be doing if they are at home, or where they might be if they are absent. There are however a number of benefits which can be claimed for tagging:

- EM imposes some structure on young people's lives which may help to break a pattern of offending behaviour and as a result . . .
- Can buy time for other programs, which address offending behaviour, to take effect. Although tagging is a short-term option, usually lasting no more than three months, this may be sufficient to break patterns and open up new pathways for the young person.
- EM exerts an impartial, remote, impersonal authority which young people in trouble may accept more readily than the personalised authority of youth offending team (YOT) staff or security professionals undertaking the same task.
- EM provides an early warning system of testing behaviour, or breaches. These tend to show up very early in minor infringements of curfew hours. A quick response from the monitoring company which demonstrates that the equipment really works, is often sufficient to ensure compliance.

Thus far, England and Wales are the only European countries using juvenile tagging on a significant scale and it remains unclear how effective it will be. As Figure 20.1 (below) indicates, several studies from around the world suggest that, in the case of adults, tagging can achieve high rates of compliance. However, the degree of compliance declines with the time spent having to wear a tag.

Periods longer than four months produce sharp falls in compliance, depending on associated programs. However, compliance, in itself, is of only limited use in assessing effectiveness. Studies of the impact of tagging on re-offending using

Figure 20.1: Period tagged and successful completion rates for adults

Up to one month	95% successful completion
One to two months	90% successful completion
Two to four months	80% successful completion

(Source: Whitfield, 2001).

matched samples of tagged and untagged adult offenders have concluded that the tag is 'offence neutral' (Dodgson and Mortimer, 2000) yielding similar re-offending rates for both groups.

Moreover, the evidence suggests that, by and large, penalties of all sorts, imposed upon children and young people are less effective in terms of re-offending than those imposed upon adults (Pitts, 2003b). It would therefore, be helpful to know whether, in the case of children and young people, tagging increases compliance with other interventions, such as offending behaviour programmes. Currently, the lack of research evidence about tagging means that the development of authoritative guidance concerning its most appropriate uses remains some way off.

Who should be tagged?

At present there are no types of young person and no types of offences, for which we can say that a tag would be 'effective'. There are however some indications from experience gained so far about the ways tagging and other forms of intervention might be usefully linked:

- EM may have some potential for young people who have difficulties with authority. The tag is completely impersonal; accepting it requires no personality clashes and no loss of face. It enables one of the barriers to effective supervision to be sidestepped.
- EM is the perfect 'opt out' for young people who need help to resist peer pressure to join risky or criminal activities.
- Flexible curfew hours can be imposed to help young people who need practical help to break a pattern of persistent offending, whether it be a problem of night-time burglary, daytime shoplifting or football related offences. The aim is to interrupt that pattern.

- The value of small, regular, frequent successes as a positive reinforcer has long been known and the tag offers this opportunity. Control room staff, who have frequent telephone contact with some young people being monitored, are particularly adept at using this to support young people towards successful completion of their curfew.
- For young people who have breached another order, but have nonetheless made progress, the tag offers sentencers an alternative to re-sentencing, where control can be increased but the progress already made can be built upon (Whitfield, 2001)

Adapting practice

The discipline EM imposes on the young person's life is paralleled by increased demands placed upon staff. So how have youth justice workers adapted to the demands and the opportunities that EM brings?

The short-term nature of tagging brings with it pressure to make the most effective use of what may be a limited 'window of opportunity'. Tagging is not a treatment in itself but, during the period in which control is most obviously exercised by the tagging company, there is a good opportunity for the supervisor to establish trust and a good working relationship with the young person, and to encourage and motivate them towards longer-term opportunities. There may be family issues to consider, as well as the impact that an externally imposed structure and boundaries are likely to raise. But good supervision can make use of these and can look for positive ways to use the 'space' they create.

In early work with adults, the aim was always to engage the offender in a formal programme — usually groupwork, centred on drug and alcohol abuse or offending behaviour — at least six weeks

---

before the tagging period ended. Getting established during this more structured period was the most effective way of developing a longer-term commitment to a programme which might help change behaviour. A number of programmes throughout the world adopt this method; the relatively short tagging period is overlapped with the main programme to give the latter the best possible start.

EM shifts the balance between help and control. For a short period, the focus of control is external; the tagging company and the supervisor can concentrate on positive interventions, building a relationship and working with the family. Experience so far suggests that good supervisors have been quick to take advantage of this.

Stigma

The introduction of tagging for children and young people was a controversial step, and for good reason. First, there could hardly be a more obvious 'label' than the tag and it would be virtually impossible to conceal it during a school day, particularly during sporting or gymnasium activities. As such, this makes nonsense of the anonymity supposedly offered by the youth court. On the other hand, there were fears that it could just as easily be brandished among peers as a status symbol and a way to achieve recognition of a most unhelpful kind. As the Penal Affairs Consortium (1997) argued:

> *Electronic tagging is at least as likely to provoke re-offending by juveniles as to prevent it, as well as being uniquely stigmatizing. The young people concerned will have to attend school with a tag attached to their wrist or ankle, branding them as an offender. Some children will undoubtedly boast about their tag and wear it as a badge of honour, adopting a 'hard' image to live up to it.*

Above all, there has been a fear that, in the volatile world of adolescent offending, the tag would accelerate the child along the path to custody by recording all breaches, however minor, and leading to an inevitable return to court. Finally, the impact on already troubled families, for whom the tag might be equally intrusive, is unknown and there has been considerable reluctance to add to existing pressures.

EM and the family

EM changes family dynamics, even if only in the short term, although the evidence of such impact is very mixed. Early Canadian studies gave some cause for optimism, indicating that there was no lasting impact in 50% of cases and that 20% of respondents claimed positive benefits, including bringing family members closer together (Mainprize, 1995). More recent work in England and Scotland has produced more pessimistic results (Dodgson, 2001; Lobley and Smith, 2001). In one English study, 20% of respondents said EM had produced specific problems in household relationships. In Scotland, parents spoke of being 'unpaid warders' and said they had no idea of the impact it would have on their lives. It is clear that if the tag is not to make the family's situation worse, skilled social work intervention is necessary in cases like these (Mainprize, 1995).

Supervising officers need to offer a clear and realistic explanation to parents and family members when the initial assessment is made, offering to discuss any tensions and pressures later, if the need arises. There are certainly welfare and health and safety concerns surrounding the tagging of children. These are addressed, in England and Wales, through special requirements being placed on the contractors in terms of explanations to parents; ensuring that a parent is available when the tag is fitted; and that all employees are subject to security checks in line with Department for Education and Skills' guidelines.

The future of electronic monitoring

'First generation' EM equipment, currently in use, while reliable, is relatively unsophisticated. However, there are great expectations of second and third generation systems which will use mobile 'phone technology, satellite tracking, or both, and will do much more than simply monitor a curfew at a fixed address.

Current developments in the UK are focused on producing a reliable tracking system which will monitor movement between locations and entry into areas from which a young person has been excluded because, for instance, they had often been in trouble there. The technology already exists and is used with adults in the USA. A UK pilot commenced in September 2004 and one of the pilot areas includes young people. There are, however, three main areas of difficulty to be surmounted before such a system could be used here. The first concerns the technology itself; it has proved difficult to develop adequate or reliable signal strength. Second, it requires the cooperation of the wearer to maintain the equipment, not least in the re-charging of batteries. What incentive they would have to do this remains an unanswered question.

Third, there is the question of the management of the information generated by the system. The capacity for 'real time' tracking offered by the technology is, in the overwhelming majority of cases, simply unnecessary. If a young person were so dangerous as to require this level of monitoring they would be unlikely to be at large in the community. However, downloading information at 12 hourly intervals, for example, offers very limited public protection, although it does offer certainty of detection, albeit at considerable cost. While it is likely to be a year or two before a fully viable system is available, it seems unlikely that, despite the seductive possibilities the technology appears to offer, it will play a significant role in the management of children and young people who offend.

Assessing progress

The Youth Justice Board oversees the largest EM initiative for juveniles anywhere in the world and the scheme has, not surprisingly, attracted enormous international interest. Given the fact that we now jail eight times as many children under 15 as we did a decade ago (Nacro, 2003a), it is perhaps no surprise that anything which seems to offer a credible and effective community option should be explored.

At present, the electronic monitoring of children and young people is primarily used in a support role in three ways:

- To improve compliance with other programmes and orders.
- To support parents and supervisors in providing a framework, through the nightly curfew, which will bring a more ordered pattern to often chaotic young lives.

- To support courts and others who want to avoid the damaging consequences of custody, yet feel that more control is necessary if community options are to be both credible and effective.

Evaluations of EM will need to take account of all three factors. Re-offending research will offer only partial answers, given the range of other programmes present in ISSPs, for instance, as well as the other, incalculable, changes that may occur in young people's lives during the tagging period. But if such evaluations demonstrate that a period of tagging correlates with better compliance and completion rates on other programmes, this will no doubt be taken as a positive indicator, not least because the 'average' tagging condition of two months adds only about £2,000 to the cost of an order; 'small beer' when compared with the cost of custody. However, if tagging is used for low risk young people and others who do not warrant that level of surveillance and control, it will not only ratchet up costs unnecessarily, it may well accelerate these young people along the path to custody because of its ability to record breaches, however minor. Clearly, cost-effective and positive use of tagging requires careful targeting.

Current estimates suggest continuing growth with an estimated 10,000 juveniles likely to be tagged annually by 2006. However, in a rational world, the urge to extend the use of tagging would be contained until the findings of current evaluations are available (Waters et al., 2003). If all we are doing is widening the net of control and exporting aspects of prison into the community, the impact of EM will be wholly negative. EM has the potential to offer much more positive help, but accurate targeting, sensible implementation and a sharp awareness of its possibilities and limitations by both sentencers and practitioners is the key to progress.

Further reading

Mayer, M., Haverkamp, R. and Levy, R. (Eds.) (2003) *Will Electronic Monitoring Have a Future in Europe?* Freiburg: The Max Planck Institute

Whitfield, D. (2001) *The Magic Bracelet: Technology and Offender Supervision.* Winchester: Waterside Press

21 Community Interventions

Patricia Gray

Key points

1. Community interventions within the reformed youth justice system tend to be guided by a narrow understanding of the risk factors associated with youth crime, interpreting them mainly in terms of personal deficits in young people's thinking, attitudes and behaviour which can be addressed through offending behaviour programmes based on cognitive-behavioural training.

2. The Home Office and Youth Justice Board's analysis of the research evidence tend to overestimate the effectiveness of offending programmes in enabling young people to desist from crime.

3. Many restorative interventions place a great deal of emphasis on 'responsibilising' young people who offend by holding them accountable for the consequences of their actions and less on repairing victim-offender-community relations.

4. The heavy emphasis on responsibilisation in many community-based interventions means that relatively little is being done to tackle the high levels of socio-economic disadvantage which often exclude young people who offend from full participation in mainstream community life.

5. Managerial constraints and inadequate resources often limit the ability of youth offending teams to take action to redress the social exclusion of those with whom they work.

Introduction

The Crime and Disorder Act 1998 (CDA) was influenced by the Audit Commission's report, *Misspent Youth* (1996), which criticised the youth justice system for being ineffective and inefficient. The Act attempted to address some of these criticisms by establishing the principle aim of the system as that of preventing offending. However, this new approach to crime reduction differed significantly from the welfare-based philosophies of the 1960s and 1970s, and the diversionary policies of the 1980s and early 1990s. Prevention was now to adopt what Pitts (2001b) describes as 'robust interventionism', entailing more intensive forms of intervention to 'correct' the inappropriate attitudes and anti-social behaviour of young people who offend. To this end, the legislation introduced a range of new community interventions for young people who offend and revamped the central focus of existing community measures.

An overview of youth justice community interventions

For the purposes of this chapter, the term 'community intervention' is used to describe that range of court disposals which are administered and supervised primarily by youth offending teams (YOTs). It therefore excludes financial penalties, discharges, attendance centre orders, curfew orders, community punishment orders and drug treatment and testing orders. At the same time, it includes reparation orders, and is therefore broader than the term 'community penalty' which has a distinct legal meaning (see Chapter 9). The referral order might legitimately be regarded as a community intervention, but it is not considered here because it is treated separately in this volume (see Chapter 16). Excluding the referral order, there are, therefore, six disposals which give rise to a community intervention:

- The **reparation order** was introduced by the CDA. It is not a community sentence in the legal sense but a lower level disposal within the same sentencing band as discharges and fines. The order requires a young person to make reparation, commensurate with the seriousness of the offence, to their victim(s) or the wider community. Any reparative activity may not exceed a total of 24 hours work to be completed within three months.

- The **action plan order** was also introduced by the CDA. It is intended as a relatively short and intensive response to the young person's offending. It places the subject under the supervision of the YOT for three months and requires them to comply with up to seven requirements, including an element of reparation, which together comprise the action plan.
- The **supervision order** was introduced by the Children and Young Person's Act 1969 but the CDA made amendments 'to improve its effectiveness'. The order can last for up to three years and a range of conditions can be attached. Since 2002, such conditions have been used as the basis, where the appropriate criteria are met, for the intensive supervision and surveillance programme (ISSP) (see Chapter 22).
- The **community rehabilitation order** (formerly known as a probation order) is available for those aged 16 years and over. It can last for up to three years and is intended to provide a form of supervision for young people who are older and more mature. Additional requirements can be attached to the order which may also be used as the basis for an ISSP.
- The **community punishment and rehabilitation order** (formerly known as a combination order) is again only available for those aged 16 years and over, and combines community rehabilitation with up to 100 hours unpaid work in the community.
- The **parenting order** was introduced by the CDA. It is available for parents/carers of young people convicted of an offence (and in a range of other circumstances). Parents/carers are required to attend weekly guidance or counselling sessions for up to three months. Additional conditions may also be imposed such as ensuring that a child attends school or avoids certain places.

The principles underlying community interventions

Government documentation (for instance, Home Office, 1998g; Youth Justice Board, 2002c) indicates that two fundamental principles should guide sentencing decisions about which community intervention is most likely to prevent further offending. The first is that of 'proportionality': that punishment should be proportionate to the seriousness and persistency of offending (see Chapter 9). The second principle reflects the current influence of what David Farrington (2000) describes as the 'risk factor prevention paradigm'. Research suggests that young people exposed to multiple risks, display a higher propensity to commit crime (Graham and Bowling, 1995; Farrington, 1996). Some of the key risk factors include inappropriate attitudes to offending, deficits in cognitive skills, inadequate parental supervision, unstable living arrangements, poor school performance and persistent truancy, exclusion from school or unemployment, association with delinquent peers, dependency on alcohol and/or drugs, and experiencing high levels of socio-economic deprivation. The increased emphasis on ensuring that community interventions are effective consists largely in developing programmes which target the risk factors identified during the assessment process (Baker et al., 2002a).

ASSET, the assessment tool developed for the youth justice system by the Youth Justice Board (YJB), requires YOT staff to rate each of thirteen risk factors to produce an overall 'risk of further offending' score. Recent research found that ASSET was 67% accurate in predicting reconviction (Baker et al., 2002b).

Three further principles, commonly referred to as the three 'Rs' (Home Office, 1997b; Nacro, 1997), have underpinned the development and implementation of community interventions. The first 'R' is 'responsibility', making the young person accountable for their behaviour. This is frequently achieved through offending behaviour programmes which adopt a variety of cognitive-behavioural training techniques to address perceived deficits in young people's reasoning, problem-solving and social skills. The Home Office has enthusiastically promoted the use of such programmes as part of its attempt to establish an 'evidence-based' practice in the youth justice system and argues that their effectiveness in reducing offending has been demonstrated through rigorous evaluation (Chapman and Hough, 1998; McGuire et al., 2002) (but see Chapter 39).

Parenting programmes (either voluntarily or as part of a parenting order) can also be viewed as mechanisms for reinforcing the responsibilities of parents to address their children's behaviour (Ghate and Ramella, 2002).

The second 'R' is 'restoration', associated with the concept of restorative justice (see Chapter 28), which has been defined as:

A process whereby parties with a stake in a specific offence collectively resolve how to deal with the aftermath of the offence and its implications for the future.

(Marshall, 1999: 5)

In England and Wales 'restoration' has generally been interpreted as meaning that young people who offend should be encouraged to make amends or reparation to their victims and/or the wider community as a way of repairing the harm done and reconciling victim-offender-community relations. Perhaps a significant reason why restorative justice is regarded as central to the reformed youth justice system is that it brings together two of the three core concepts underlying community interventions, because, in the process of making amends, young people also acknowledge responsibility for the consequences of their offending.

YOTs have developed a diverse range of interventions under the rubric of restorative justice that can be included in court ordered disposals. A national evaluation of restorative justice projects, conducted between 2000 and 2001 for the YJB (Wilcox and Hoyle, 2002), found that the three most common forms of restorative intervention were community reparation (35.7%), direct reparation (19.3%) and victim awareness training (20.5%). The first involved the young person participating in a work placement such as repairing criminal damage, improving the environment or providing some form of assistance to a charity. Direct reparation involved writing letters of apology or doing work of benefit to victims. Victim awareness training is essentially a form of cognitive-behavioural training to increase awareness of the impact of offending on victims. Only 13.5% of young people engaged in direct victim-offender mediation and a further 7.7% in indirect shuttle mediation.

The last of the three 'Rs' is 'reintegration', defined as 'young offenders paying their debt to society, putting their crime behind them and rejoining the law abiding community' (Home Office, 1997b: 32). But the broader connotations of reintegration are disputed. Raynor (2001), for instance, argues that the concept of enabling young people to reintegrate into mainstream community life is something of a misnomer since most were never integrated in the first place. Research has repeatedly shown that the majority of young people in trouble with the law have experienced acute levels of multi-dimensional, socio-economic disadvantage resulting in social exclusion and a denial of meaningful participation in the major social and economic opportunities generally associated with citizenship (Pitts, 2003d). Accordingly, Raynor (2001) suggests that a more appropriate strategy than reintegration 'would be to seek to involve them in a new set of pro-social linkages, resources and opportunities . . . a strategy for social integration or inclusion'.

The YJB has sponsored a range of innovative programmes designed to tackle social inclusion (see ECOTEC, 2002) and their development has been facilitated by the multi-disciplinary composition of the YOTs (see Chapter 17). There is also an implicit assumption that New Labour's social policies aimed at reducing poverty, will in the long run filter down to improve the life chances of marginalised, socially excluded, young people (Hughes et al., 2002; Matthews and Pitts, 2001).

The effectiveness of community interventions

Reconviction is often relied upon as the key measure of the effectiveness of community interventions although other, qualitative, outcome measures may be equally important in determining the success of community-based crime reduction programmes. A considerable number of studies have been commissioned by the Home Office and YJB to evaluate the new developments in youth justice some of which are relevant to the current discussion.

The Home Office evaluation of the nine 'pilot' YOTs, prior to the national roll out in 2000 (Holdaway et al., 2001; Dignan, 2000) provides an initial insight into some of the problems experienced by YOTs in delivering community-based interventions. In general, the research was positive about the potential of the new arrangements to reduce the likelihood of further offending.

● In the case of reparation orders, young people said that they had made them more aware of the harm caused to victims by their behaviour and had strengthened their resolve not to offend again. Most victims were satisfied with their experience of reparation, although many felt that their interests had not been adequately taken into account.

- Action plan orders were also positively reviewed by young people and parents, who felt that the discipline and structure of the order was likely to reduce the risk of further offending. Some YOT staff were however concerned that the order was not sufficiently tailored to the 'criminogenic' needs of those subject to it and victims were unhappy with the type of reparative activities on offer.

  A recent Home Office study suggests that there has been a fall in reconviction rates for most community interventions since the introduction of the CDA (Jennings, 2003). The research found a fall in reconvictions, within 12 months for those reprimanded, warned or convicted in the first quarter of 2001, of over 22% when measured against an 'adjusted predicted' rate, based on 1997 data. The largest improvements, by far, were associated with reprimands and final warnings (see Chapter 12). It might be noted that the reprimand, which achieved the highest reductions in offending, does not usually generate any form of YOT intervention.

- For those community-based orders aimed at young people whose offending is more serious or persistent, such as supervision and community rehabilitation, the differences were marginal, a point emphasised recently by the Audit Commission (2004).

Further evidence in relation to effectiveness derives from research which considers the extent to which the three 'Rs' discussed earlier have been realised in practice. For instance, a series of research studies to evaluate the effectiveness of offending behaviour programmes, particularly those adopting cognitive-behavioural techniques, provide an insight into the process of responsibilisation of young people who offend. Meta-analytical surveys, which aggregate the results of a large number of small-scale studies to produce an overview of the characteristics of effective programmes, suggest that community interventions can be successful both in altering attitudes and behaviour and in reducing reconviction. McGuire (2000: 97) argues that:

> *Taking all of these meta-analyses together, it can be demonstrated that the net effect of 'treatment' in the many studies surveyed represents on average a reduction in recidivism of approximately ten percentage points. But in studies meeting certain additional criteria, this figure ranges between 20% and 30% and is in some cases even higher.*

A report for the YJB, relies on such findings to argue that programmes utilising cognitive-behavioural techniques 'can make a significant contribution to reducing offending behaviour' (McGuire et al., 2002: 5).

Most of the data however derive from Canada and the USA and research in this country, primarily in relation to adults, has generated more variable results. Some studies show a marked reduction in reconviction by participants in cognitive-behavioural programmes (Vennard and Hedderman, 1998), while others have found no impact at all (Falshaw et al., 2003).

The national evaluation of YJB funded cognitive-behavioural programmes sheds further light on the extent to which such interventions have been effective in making young people accountable for their offending. There were indications that cognitive-behavioural approaches were considered to be constructive by both the young people and their parents. Nonetheless, this finding should be seen in the context of 'rather low completion rates and high reconviction rates as far as persistent young offenders were concerned'. Moreover, because of structural limitations and poor data, the evaluation was not able to assess the independent effectiveness of the cognitive-behavioural projects in terms of reducing offending (Feilzer et al., 2004). Similarly, parenting programmes appear to have been a responsibilising experience for parents with the majority of participants reporting 'statistically significant positive changes in parenting skills and competencies' (Ghate and Ramella, 2002: ii)

The national evaluation of YJB funded restorative justice projects (Wilcox and Hoyle, 2002), provides strong evidence to show that restorative interventions (particularly those which included a meeting between the victim and offender) were also effective in these terms. Young people participating in the programmes indicated that:

- restorative interventions had helped them to take responsibility for their offences (88%)
- given them a better understanding of the victim's perspective (71%)
- and had reduced or stopped their offending (69%).

Interviews with victims produced similarly positive feedback.

However, outcomes as measured by reconviction rates produced less promising results with 46.6% of the sample being reconvicted within 12 months of the start of the order. A subsequent study which extended the follow up period to 18 months generated a higher reconviction rate of 53.9% (Wilcox, 2002).

The research also echoed some of the concerns highlighted in the evaluation of the pilot YOTs, described earlier in this chapter, such as: lower than expected level of victim participation; over-reliance on community reparation as opposed to direct victim-offender contact; and a lack of any clear connection between the work undertaken and the nature of the offending. Frequently, the young people were unable to see how their activity benefited either the victim or the community. These findings call into question the extent to which the principles of restorative justice are fully integrated into these restorative interventions.

To date, research has shown limited interest in investigating the relationship between the principles of 'reintegration' or 'social inclusion' and young people turning away from crime. One exception involved a sample of young people and adults serving community penalties supervised by the probation service (May, 1999). It found that four social variables – accommodation, employment, drugs and income – had a significant effect on the rate of reconviction.

Within the youth justice arena, such research is limited. For instance, a report of a study commissioned by the YJB to investigate the main risk and protective factors associated with youth crime revealingly acknowledged that it was unable to investigate a number of social factors, specifically: low income and poor housing, disadvantaged neighbourhood and lack of attachment to neighbourhood, because 'the necessary work of piloting and validation would have taken too long' (Youth Justice Board, 2001b: 52). The authors concluded nonetheless that these factors contributed only 'indirectly', rather that 'directly', to young people's propensity to offend.

Yet there is evidence (albeit from American research) which demonstrates a direct relationship between young people's risk of offending and living with disadvantage (Wikstrom and Loeber, 1997; Sampson et al., 1997; Pitts, 2003d). Indeed,

the Board appears to have recognised the importance of education, training and employment (ETE) to reducing the propensity of young people to offend (ECOTEC, 2002). Moreover, considerable effort has been expended on developing services to integrate young people who offend into ETE. Yet there remains a distinct tendency to view the 'barriers' to effective achievement in these areas as being caused by personal deficits in the young people concerned rather than any shortfalls or inadequacies in service provision.

Some issues

A number of issues arise in relation to the implementation of community interventions within the reformed youth justice system:

- Firstly, there is the interrelationship with custody. There is a wealth of evidence demonstrating that custody is an ineffective response to youth crime which is likely to confirm young people in a criminal lifestyle (see Chapter 24). Between 1992 and 1999, custodial sentences imposed on young people rose by 90%. The implementation of the CDA has so far failed to reduce the level of custody significantly and between 1999 and 2002, its use has remained relatively stable at about 12% of disposals (Home Office, 2003b).

However, other research findings have revealed a more substantive cause for concern. Bateman and Stanley (2002) found that there were significant geographical variations in patterns of custodial sentencing. Although custody was generally reserved for relatively serious cases across all of the twenty YOT areas investigated, in 'high custody' areas, less use was made of lower tariff sentences, particularly reparation orders, and greater use was made of higher tariff community penalties. Conversely 'low custody' areas made significantly greater use of lower tariff disposals, particularly reparation orders. The end result was that they tended to use custody less frequently in cases which approached the custody threshold. The study suggests that these different sentencing patterns can in part be explained by the courts perceptions of the quality of youth justice provision and confidence in the YOTs. The findings suggest that 'justice by geography' still prevails and this is difficult to reconcile with the principles of 'proportionality' and 'parity' in sentencing.

- Secondly, community interventions have adopted a rather narrow understanding of the notion of risk, interpreting it largely in terms of individualistic shortcomings in young peoples' attitudes and lifestyles (see Muncie, 2001). This approach is manifested in the primacy accorded to the use of cognitive-behavioural offending programmes which focus on confronting young people with the consequences of their offending. The underlying philosophy also implies that deficiencies in young people's moral reasoning reflect inadequate parental discipline and so the responsibilisation of parents becomes a further target of intervention.

While the evidence suggests that offending behaviour programmes do challenge young people to think about their offending, the government is over reliant on such interventions as representing the most effective way of preventing young people from re-offending. However, as Pitts (2001b: 181) argues:

> *The apparent confidence in these measures appears to be rooted in a partial reading of the 'evidence' and an over-estimation of their 'promise'.*

None of the research demonstrates that cognitive skills training can, in isolation, lead young people to desist from crime. Indeed an alternative reading of the findings would lead one to question why reconviction rates remain so high and why such training 'works' for some young people under certain circumstances, but for the vast majority is apparently ineffective.

- The third issue concerns the introduction of 'restorative' principles into a system which retains an essentially retributive character. The end result is that many of the restorative programmes which accompany community interventions tend to pursue 'responsibilisation' at the expense of 'restoration' or 'reintegration'. Based on distinctions first developed by McCold (2001), Wilcox and Hoyle (2002) ranked interventions as being either 'fully', 'mostly' or 'partly' restorative. The most frequent forms of reparative activity undertaken by young people, community reparation and victim awareness training, are according to this framework only 'partly restorative'. Perhaps unsurprisingly, in this context, the research found that young people obliged to take part in such activities viewed them as a form of punishment of no direct benefit to victims. Similarly, while victim awareness training did increase sensitivity to the victim's point of view, it was the cognitive-behavioural elements of this training (the largest component), with its emphasis on holding the young people accountable for their behaviour which left the most lasting impression.

However, where young people were engaged in more direct forms of restorative intervention such as victim-offender mediation or writing a letter of apology, which would qualify as 'fully' or 'mostly' restorative, they, and their victims, expressed high levels of satisfaction; the former because it increased their awareness of the impact of their actions on victims, and the latter because it helped them to come to terms with the offence. But restorative justice is not simply about getting young people to take responsibility for their offending or the reconciliation of victim-offender relations. It also entails a commitment to an 'inclusionary' form of justice which provides opportunities for reintegration back into mainstream community life.

- The fourth issue concerns the controversy surrounding the neglect paid to the principle of 'reintegration' or 'social inclusion'. Research does not demonstrate any automatic correlation between making young people accountable for their behaviour and a reduction in offending. Rather, desistance 'is produced through an interplay between individual choices, and a range of wider social forces, institutional and societal practices which are beyond the control of the individual' (Farrall and Bowling, 1999: 261). The current emphasis on responsibilisation means that few community-based interventions do enough to address the broader socio-economic inequalities or constraints which often exclude young people who offend from participation in mainstream societal processes (Muncie, 2002).

One study which sought specifically to investigate this issue found that while the young people on the programme being evaluated were exposed to fairly acute levels of social exclusion, the intervention did relatively little to provide them with support to establish stable interpersonal relationships and housing, or to realise their aspirations in education, employment and training (Gray, Moseley and Browning, 2003). This lack of attention to the social constraints on young people's life chances is apparent in other research studies (Dignan, 2000; Newburn et al., 2002). Indeed, even when programmes take account of the effects of social deprivation, these factors are often framed as individual pathologies or deficits (Kemshall, 2002a). For example, a young person's inability to take advantage of opportunities is commonly blamed on their inappropriate attitudes rather than inadequate resources or structural barriers.

The evidence suggests, that to maximise their effectiveness, community interventions should expend more effort on enabling young people in trouble to break through the barriers to social inclusion. The current failure to do so may go some way to explain the relatively high levels of reconviction which are evident in the national evaluations sponsored by the YJB.

- The final issue is linked to the previous discussion. Theoretically, the composition and structural location of YOTs provide them with access to a range of expertise and resources required to address the social context of offending. Unfortunately, that potential is not always realised in practice. Many YOTs appear to have become preoccupied with meeting exacting national standards and the YJB's performance targets to the detriment of work with disadvantaged young people (see Crawford and Newburn, 2003). Faced with such 'managerialist' imperatives, there is a tendency to engage mainly in activities which challenge youth offending through structured, time-limited, correctional programmes rather than attempting to tackle the more nebulous and resistant social exclusion factors. YOTs will require greater discretion and increased resources if they are to effect the changes necessary to give young people a greater stake in mainstream socio-economic networks and incentives to desist from crime.

Further reading

Muncie, J. (2002) A New Deal for Youth? Early Intervention and Correctionalism. in Hughes, G., Mclaughlin, E. and Muncie, J. (Eds.) *Crime Prevention and Community Safety*. London: Sage

Pitts, J. (2001) The New Correctionalism: Young People, Youth Justice and New Labour. in Matthews, R. and Pitts, J. (Eds.) *Crime, Disorder and Community Safety*. London: Routledge

Youth Justice Board (2003q) *Speaking Out: The Views of Young People, Parents and Victims About the Youth Justice System and Interventions to Reduce Offending*. London: Youth Justice Board

22 Work with Young People whose Offending is Persistent: Intensive Supervision and Surveillance Programmes

Charlie Beaumont

Key points

1. 'Persistent young offenders' cannot be readily identified at an early stage on the basis of risk but assessments tend to indicate that their needs are more acute than those of their peers.

2. Young people who persistently offend represent a small minority of the overall youth offending population.

3. A commitment by the agencies in youth offending partnerships to sustained service delivery to young people who persistently offend is essential to the achievement of positive outcomes.

4. Programme design should focus on addressing the assessed needs of the young person as well as providing a clear set of boundaries, enforced in a consistent manner.

5. Evaluations of programmes for young people who persistently offend cannot rely solely on re-offending as a measure of success because their risk of future offending is high. Gradual improvements in behaviour, school attendance, desistance from drug misuse, or a reduction in the frequency or severity of offending, are also signs of progress.

Introduction

This chapter focuses on young people who, more than any other group, test the effectiveness of youth offending services. The term 'persistent young offender' evokes an image of a young person whose behaviour poses an affront to authority and whose offending is personally threatening and out of control. However those who come to know these young people quickly become aware that many of them have serious, deep seated, problems and unmet needs which may be either a cause or a consequence of their offending.

Providing non-custodial programmes for young people who offend persistently poses a particular challenge for youth offending services. They must achieve credibility with the public, the victims of crime, the police and the courts, without losing sight of the fact that they are also providing a service for children in need. Failure to do so increases the likelihood of a custodial outcome for these young people rendering them vulnerable to the negative effects associated with incarceration (see Chapter 25). At the same time, failure to respond successfully to their needs may well exacerbate their offending behaviour.

Who are 'persistent offenders'?

It is evident from aggregated data derived from ASSET assessments (see Chapter 19) that 'persistent young offenders' are not a homogeneous group. They defy early identification as the risks most commonly associated with their offending are also found amongst young people whose 'anti-social' behaviour is similar but who have little or no involvement with the youth justice system. However, it appears that youngsters with longer offending histories tend to score on a larger number of risk factors and these risks are often more intense.

Identifying those young people whose offending is persistent is no easy matter. Hagell and Newburn established that using slightly different definitions of persistence, one was likely to capture significantly different groups of young people. Moreover, persistent offending is relatively transient and few young people commit crime persistently over protracted periods.

As a consequence, the group whose offending is most problematic is a constantly changing one (Hagell and Newburn, 1994). Nonetheless, over the past decade, legislators and policy makers have endeavoured to devise a catch-all definition of persistence in order to target, and impose specially designed sanctions upon, the most troublesome young people. In practice, the complexity of this task has resulted in a variety of criteria being developed.

The secure training order was introduced, by the Criminal Justice and Public Order Act 1994, as a new custodial sentence for 12–14 year old children whose offending was 'persistent'. It could be imposed upon those convicted of three or more offences, who had also breached a supervision order or had been convicted of an offence committed while subject to supervision. The detention and training order, which replaced it from 2000, offered a far more flexible definition of persistence, requiring only that a child aged 12–14 years be deemed a 'persistent offender', a term for which no legal definition exists before a custodial sentence could be imposed. In practice, 'persistence' has been interpreted broadly by the courts. Indeed, it has been held that persistence can be established on first conviction for two separate offences even where there are no previous reprimands or warnings (Stone, 2003).

New Labour's pledge to halve the time from arrest to sentence for 'persistent young offenders' aged 10–17 required a more precise classification. For 'fast tracking' purposes, a persistent young offender is one:

> . . . who has been sentenced by any criminal court in the UK on three or more separate occasions for one or more recordable offences, and within three years of the last sentencing occasion is subsequently arrested or has information laid against him for a further recordable offence.

> (Home Office, 1998g)

Until recently, deprivation of liberty for a young person on remand required the court to determine that only such a remand would adequately protect the public for serious harm. Section 130 of the Criminal Justice and Police Act 2001 relaxed the criteria to allow a remand to custody or secure accommodation of those whose offending was persistent, defined in this case as a 'recent history of offending while on bail or remanded to local authority accommodation'.

Intensive supervision and surveillance programmes (ISSPs) are community-based interventions for those young people whose offending is sufficiently serious or persistent to place them at high risk of custody. Access to the provision is restricted to those meeting certain criteria. In terms of persistence, an ISSP is available where a young person has previously been:

> charged, warned or convicted of offences committed on four or more separate dates within the past twelve months and received at least one community or custodial penalty.

> (Youth Justice Board, 2002a)

Ironically, this definition is, in some respects, tighter than the criteria for the imposition of a custodial or secure disposal discussed above. For the purposes of bail, an ISSP is also available if the young person meets the criteria of persistence in section 130 of the Criminal Justice and Police Act 2001 (see above).

Persistence and seriousness

Persistence does not necessarily equate with the seriousness of offending or the degree of risk posed to others by the young person. Indeed, in the conclusion to their study of serious and persistent young offenders, Hagell and Newburn (1994) suggest that, for the most part, the serious are seldom persistent and the persistent seldom serious.

Thus, some children and young people, although they may have previously committed no or few previous offences, may commit a 'grave crime', one which could attract a penalty of 14 years if committed by an adult, and are therefore at substantial risk of a custodial sentence. It was for this reason that, in 2002, the Youth Justice Board introduced a grave crimes 'shortcut' to ISSPs for those young people with little or no offending history. In fact, the number of young people whose offending poses a serious threat is very small. The ISSP operated by Kent and Medway YOTs, for example, an area of over 160,000 10–17 year olds, has a projected throughput of 90 young people per year.

Intensive supervision and surveillance programmes

The Youth Justice Board decision to fund ISSPs in 2001 was prompted by a desire to reverse the upward trend in the use of secure and custodial sentences for children and young people in England and Wales, while simultaneously targeting the 3% of young people research pointed to as being responsible for a disproportionate share of youth crime. The resources of the juvenile secure estate were over-stretched and there was a need to reduce demand to a more manageable level. Outcomes from secure and custodial sentences, with respect to the prevention of further offending, were very poor and it was felt that community-based penalties could be more effective. The large numbers of young people held in young offender institutions (YOIs), managed by the prison service, were undermining effective implementation of the Board's planned reforms of custodial establishments to improve the quality of educational and offending behaviour programmes, and to enhance the likelihood of the successful rehabilitation of those leaving custody upon release.

However, the Board recognised that, politically, it was necessary to demonstrate that any community-based alternative to custody was sufficiently 'tough'. This was to be achieved through restricting the liberty of young people participating in ISSPs to a greater extent than was the case in other forms of statutory supervision in the community. The supervision element of the programme required minimum attendance of 25 hours a week, including activities at weekends. Supervision was to be supplemented by surveillance, including, in many cases, curfews monitored through electronic tagging (see Chapter 20). The conditions of ISSPs were to be rigorously enforced to ensure both consistency of application and a clear understanding amongst youth court magistrates and crown court judges of what would be expected of the young people subject to them. In addition, young people on ISSPs were to be required to attend programmes which addressed the problems associated with their offending such as drug treatment and education and training programmes.

The Board did not prescribe models for the delivery of ISSPs, although funding tended to be directed to programmes in which two or more youth offending services had developed them in partnership. The Board's decision to meet the full costs of ISSPs has encouraged innovation and the development of a wide variety of approaches to the delivery of services to young people who persistently offend.

Young people attending ISSPs may do so:

- As a condition of bail or of a remand to local authority accommodation;
- As a condition of either a supervision order or a community rehabilitation order;
- During the community element of a detention and training order.

The length of required attendance on the programme varies according to the stage at which it is deployed:

- For young people attending as a condition of supervision orders or community rehabilitation orders, the programme is divided into two periods, each of three months. The first 'intensive' phase requires a minimum of 25 hours weekly contact. The second phase involves a minimum of 5 hours per week.
- During 2004, as a consequence of changes in the Anti-Social Behaviour Act 2004, longer ISSPs with an intensive phase of 4 months, two months medium intensity (15 hours contact) and six months low intensity, are to be piloted.
- For ISSPs as a condition of remand or a detention and training order, programme duration was to be determined by the period of the remand or the length of the custodial order.

Prospects for success

Evaluations of earlier intensive programmes like ISSP have yielded mixed results. In a review of recent US research, Gendreau et al. (2000: 198) observed that:

> *when it comes to the matter of reducing offender recidivism, the conclusion is inescapable. ISPs have had little effect on offenders' future criminal activity.*

At one level, this is unsurprising since, as the evaluators of one of the forerunners to the ISSP note:

> *Most innovative programmes in youth justice are handicapped by unrealistic expectations about what can be achieved. Almost by definition, persistent*

*offending behaviour is extremely resistant to change
. . . it was unrealistic to expect that young people
convicted several times prior to beginning ISSP would
never be convicted during involvement with the
programme and in the 24 months that followed.*

(Little et al., 2004: 228–9)

At the same time, there have been more positive
findings. The evaluation of the Persistent Young
Offenders Project at Freagarrach, conducted by
the Scottish Executive Central Research Unit
found a 15% reduction in offending by young
people who participated on the programme
(Lobely et al., 2001). There is some evidence to
suggest that the variations in outcome are related
to differences in approach. Freagarrach, for instance, lays great store on personal engagement of
young people, playing to their strengths and the
provision of holistic support mechanisms. Similarly, in the review cited above, the authors concluded that programmes with a 'treatment
component' were more effective than those that
emphasised compliance and control (Gendreau et
al., 2000). This echoes, in slightly different terms,
the findings of Corbett and Petersillia (1994:77)
who conclude that:

*The empirical evidence regarding ISPs is decisive:
without a rehabilitation component, reductions in
recidivism are as elusive as a desert mirage.*

This body of existing evidence has important
implications for both the design and delivery of
programmes targeted at young people whose
offending is persistent.

Principles of programme design

Community-based programmes are less damaging to the young person and more effective in terms of reconviction than the secure or custodial alternative

One of the consequences of the Crime and
Disorder Act 1998 has been to draw children and
young people into the youth justice system at a
younger age and an earlier stage of their offending
careers. This means that they are more likely to be
viewed as 'persistent' by courts with a consequent
increase in the risk of custody. However, research
points to significantly lower re-offending rates if
custody can be avoided (Kemp et al., 2002; Nacro,
2003e). The Youth Justice Board has, as a result,

committed itself to a reduction in the use of
security and custody at all stages in the youth
justice process. The ISSP therefore represents an
important step in the establishment of a viable
alternative to incarceration for those young people
most at risk.

Programmes need to integrate care and control

Young people who persistently offend pose the
greatest challenge to practitioners whose professional ethic emphasises that the youngster in
trouble is a child first and an offender second
(Haines and Drakeford, 1998). The design of any
ISSP must necessarily establish behavioural
boundaries which are clear to the police, the
courts, the public and the young people attending
the programmes. Breaches must be enforced. At
the same time, programmes must also address the
personal, familial and social factors which under-
lie, and sustain, the young person's offending and
this requires access to a wide range of services for
young people who may be difficult to engage in
mainstream provision.

Programmes must be accountable to the community and victims of crime

ISSPs must be able to demonstrate that the risks
posed by young people who persistently offend
can be effectively managed in the community, if
they are to maintain confidence with victims, local
people, the courts and partner agencies. One way
this can be achieved is through the involvement
of victims. Victim care is a major government
priority, regarded as holding the key to the
restoration of public confidence in the criminal
justice system. Restorative justice, which requires
and enables young people to make amends, either
directly or indirectly, to those they have harmed
by their offending (see Chapter 28) is, accordingly,
integral to the development of effective ISSPs

Commitment to programme development and innovation

Because young people subject to ISSPs will
inevitably be known to YOT staff and partner
agencies, failure to achieve positive outcomes can
easily be laid at the door of the young person,
rather than the quality of the programme or the

manner of its delivery. This can offer an easy 'cop-out' and it is therefore doubly important that intervention is rooted in an evidence-base as to what forms of provision can reduce offending and contain the behaviour of challenging young people. It involves too a constant upgrading of the worker's skills through training and professional supervision.

Creating opportunities for 'quick wins', which enable the young person to experience success and a sense of progress at a very early stage of the order, are vital. That experience can provide the foundation for successful work in the future. Consistent commitment by the worker to achievable goals can motivate the young person. An ability to sustain motivation, to convey a positive outlook and to be flexible, informal and informative are essential qualities for staff working with the ISSP (Lobley et al., 2001).

If these are the qualities of the workers, effective programmes should benefit from:

- Clear managerial support, with front line staff receiving sufficient professional supervision to sustain their commitment in the face of the inevitable difficulties.
- The deployment of skilled staff able to engage effectively with young people who are challenging and hard to engage.
- The confidence of courts. Such confidence depends, in part at least, on effective court duty work, high quality bail assessments and pre-sentence reports, and regular feedback to decision makers on outcomes (Bateman and Stanley, 2002).
- The development of effective channels of communication at every stage in the process.
- Adequate and rapid access to the services provided by all the partner agencies.
- Consistency of delivery and enforcement.
- A commitment to monitoring, evaluation and user-friendly feed-back.

Programme delivery

Clarity about surveillance and information sharing

Workers should ensure from the outset that the young person understands how the surveillance element of the order will work, the implications for them and the possible consequences of any breach. Young people will also need to understand that the worker may be sharing information with the police and the YOT, particularly if the youngster is regarded as 'high risk'.

Compliance and programme content

The 25 hours per week programme attendance required of participants in the first three months is very demanding for young people whose lives may lack structure and who are unused to responding positively to adults in authority. To hold their attention a variety of activities which are fun, geared to their levels of skill and ability, offer new experiences and new opportunities to succeed, and have an obvious purpose and a short-term pay-off are essential to successful completion of this part of the order.

Anticipating reduced contact

During the intensive phase of the programme, the core elements of the plan for the second three months should be established. The young person should be prepared to manage with a much-reduced level of support and far less structure. This will involve the practitioner in stabilising the young person's living arrangements, ensuring they are involved in a relevant form of education, training or employment and establishing whatever forms of support are needed to maintain continued progress.

Unsettled family relationships and difficulties with accommodation are frequent among the ISSP population. Liddle and Solanki (Nacro, 2000) reported in their study of persistent young offenders that:

- 49% had experienced a breakdown of a 'care' placement
- 39% had parents who were divorced or separated
- 34% had lost contact with people in their lives whom they regarded as being significant
- 7% were or had been on the child protection register

As a result programme content at this stage should probably include training in the skills necessary to achieve some rapprochement with families, where possible, and the practical skills necessary for independent living.

Enforcement

Enforcement is a key consideration for the whole of the youth justice system (see Chapter 23) but it is particularly important in work with young people whose behaviour places them at risk of custody. On the one hand, the confidence of the court in programmes designed as high tariff alternatives to custody is built upon an expectation that failure to comply will result in a rapid and consistent response. At the same time, the establishment and reinforcement of boundaries is important for young people who are subject to such interventions. The Audit Commission has suggested that currently ISSPs experience high levels of breach leading in many cases to custodial outcomes (2004).

Effective enforcement should not necessarily focus on breach but can rather:

- Maximise opportunities for the young person to be engaged in effective supervision.
- Establish a sense of structure to provide a counterweight to the chaos that is characteristic of the lifestyles of many of those for whom the programmes are designed.
- Change behaviour leading to the achievement of positive outcomes through young people being clear about what is expected of them and understanding that there are consequences associated with non-compliance.
- Help to demonstrate an appropriate level of concern to young people about what they do and what happens to them through a consistent and rapid response.

It is inevitable that many of the young people involved with ISSPs will test boundaries. Others will have genuine difficulties complying with the rigorous nature of the programmes even where there is an overall commitment to comply with the requirements of the order to the best of their ability. Where young people are returned to court, therefore, this should be seen, in most cases, as a mechanism for encouraging future compliance rather than an indication of failure and an inevitable route into custody.

Monitoring and evaluation

The primary focus of programmes targeted at those whose offending is persistent is to reduce their criminal behaviour while maintaining them in the community. Monitoring of outcomes has the potential to fulfil three essential functions:

- Build evidence that the programme is effective as a prerequisite to increasing public and judicial confidence in community-based provision.
- Provide information on performance against targets which allows refinement of the programme on an evidential basis to improve the quality and effectiveness.
- Provide feedback on individual young people.
                                    (Merrington, 1998)

It is important, however, that expectations are realistic. In particular, evaluation of success should not be based solely or wholly on measures of re-offending since the chances of participants engaging in further criminal activity is, inevitably, quite high. Thus, frequency and seriousness of offending, before and after intervention, may be as important as measures of progress as desistance from offending.

There are a range of indicators, indirectly related to offending, that may be used to gauge success. These are likely to include progress in relation to the sorts of issues identified through assessment as being indicators of risk such as school attendance, family relationships and attitudes and beliefs. Gradual progress in these areas may indicate that the intervention is having a positive impact. Reviews of progress should also incorporate the views of young people and their parents, since YOT workers, even on intensive programmes, will only have limited knowledge about the young person's life and the ways it is changing as a result of participation in the programme.

Evaluations should also measure the extent to which ISSPs have made an impact upon custodial sentencing: an important measure of effectiveness. In addition it should have an eye to 'net widening', the process whereby more intensive programmes displace existing community penalties rather than diverting young people from custody. There is too a need to monitor the young people who continue to enter the secure estate, in order to ascertain what services are offered and whether different or additional services might be better matched to the risks they pose and their needs. This kind of information can enable ISSPs to re-configure their programmes to target those who still end up in custody.

Early evidence of effectiveness

The Audit Commission's review of the reformed youth justice system (2004) comments positively on introduction of ISSPs, citing encouraging findings showing that the programme offers significantly higher levels of support than that available to young people subject to a detention and training order (PA Consulting Group, 2003). The review also notes a 17% reduction in the numbers of young people receiving a custodial sentence between the first quarter of 2001 and the third quarter of 2003, a period which more or less coincides with the establishment of the programme. Despite that coincidence, however, the Audit Commission suggests that the fall may not in fact be attributable to ISSP.

Such a conclusion is reinforced by a subsequent rise in the custodial population and the publication of the initial evaluation commissioned by the Youth Justice Board which confirms that '*diversion from custody was not wholly dependent upon ISSP*' (Moore et al., 2004). The evaluation also indicates relatively low levels of completion (42% of supervision order cases) and high levels of reconviction over a 12 month period (85%), a rate higher than that predicted by ASSET scores. There were however reductions in both the frequency and seriousness of offending (though no better than that associated with supervision orders without ISSP).

It is, of course, important to remember the injunction about not having unrealistic expectations. In that light it is encouraging that ISSP had made clear inroads into tackling the underlying problems of young people who participated in the programme, especially for those who completed. But it seems clear that the full potential of intensive community supervision has yet to be realised. In particular, the rehabilitative content which Corbett and Petersillia (1994) regard as so essential to such programmes was not always in evidence.

> *While in the majority of cases young people's programmes were reasonably tailored to their needs, there was a significant number whose requirements were not being properly addressed. It would seem that particular attention needs to be paid to widening access to ... services including mental health, substance misuse and accommodation.*
>
> (Moore et al., 2004)

Conclusion

The evidence generated thus far suggests that, while there may be some way to go, intensive community-based programmes, such as ISSPs, which provide a broad range of services, tailored to the needs of, and the risks posed by, young offenders whose offending is persistent, can provide an effective alternative to a custodial sentence. Critical to the achievement of positive outcomes is the co-ordination and speed of response to identified need. The commitment of partner agencies, such as social services, health, education and Connexions are critical to enabling change by the young people.

Further reading

Crime Reduction Toolkit: Persistent Young Offenders Crime Reduction College (www.Crimereduction.Gov.UK/Toolkits)

Hagell, A. and Newburn, T. (1994) *Persistent Young Offenders.* London: Policy Studies Institute

Lobley, D., Smith, D. and Stern, C. (2001) *Freagarrach: An Evaluation of a Project for Persistent Juvenile Offenders.* The Scottish Executive Central Research Unit

Youth Justice Board (2003h) *Key Elements of Effective Practice: Intensive Supervision and Surveillance (Source Document).* London: Youth Justice Board

Youth Justice Board (undated) *Intensive Supervision and Surveillance Programme: A Guide To Good Practice.* London: Youth Justice Board

23 Enforcement

Rob Canton and Tina Eadie

Key points

1. Enforcement is not just about breach action. It is a process which begins when the pre-sentence report author discusses community supervision with a young person, and extends throughout the life of the order.

2. The purpose of enforcement is primarily to secure compliance and ensure the young person is effectively supervised, not to return them to court. However, breach action should be used as both a disciplined way of encouraging motivation and/or bringing the order to an end if this is thought necessary.

3. Professional discretion is required in balancing the need to 'stick with' and successfully engage the young person, as opposed to the need to adhere strictly to national standards. However, practitioners are accountable for their decisions about acceptable and unacceptable absences and these must be recorded.

4. Consistency within teams, between teams and across areas is important but does not mean treating all individuals in the sameway. Guidelines can suggest a consistent approach whereas professional judgement is essential in addressing diverse needs and circumstances.

5. Youth offending teams need to acknowledge and make use of the full range of expertise represented in their multi-agency composition to ensure that supervision is tailor-made for each young person subject to a statutory order.

Introduction

If community sentences are to be seen as a hard rather than a soft option, the terms of such orders must be clear, they must be directed towards addressing offending behaviour, they must be complied with, and the response to non-compliance must be quick and appropriate.
(Ellis et al., 1996: vii)

Enforcement in the context of this chapter is a generic term covering the methods by which youth justice practitioners work to ensure that young people subject to statutory supervision comply with the conditions of their order. The enforcement of orders includes making clear the circumstances in which breach action will be initiated and carried out. Children and young people in particular need to know what is expected of them and how their behaviour will be assessed. Any conditions attached to court orders, and the consequences of non-compliance, should be explained to the child or young person in a way that they can understand. The chapter suggests that enforcement also requires a creative and responsive approach to working with young people who offend, one that ensures firmness and

consistency but acknowledges individual needs and difference in complying with the sentence of the court.

The context of enforcement is the introduction and development of national standards for the supervision of offenders in the community (Home Office, 1992b; 1995a), leading more recently to standards that are specific to the youth justice system. Although the earlier standards included supervision orders for young people, most of the research undertaken on enforcement to date – and drawn on in this chapter – relates to the supervision of adult and young adult offenders aged 16 and over. Lessons learned from the probation context, however, can be transferred to youth justice and the central argument outlined here – that the mechanical application of a rigid breach policy will prove counterproductive as a means of offering a realistic alternative to a custodial sentence – holds true for both. Another important debate in both probation and youth justice is the extent to which a consistent approach towards enforcement can be achieved without the complete removal of practitioner discretion, and without treating all young people in the same way.

Introducing national standards

National standards have been described as the 'rock upon which effective service delivery is moored' (Hopley, 2002: 298) and are a relatively new concept to both probation and youth justice staff. They can, however, lead to the promotion of a number of different and sometimes competing objectives – see Box 1 below.

Box 1: Competing objectives for national standards

- To promote compliance with community sentences.
- To limit practitioner discretion.
- To make practitioner decision making more transparent and accountable.
- To discourage collusion between supervisors and offenders.
- To measure practitioner and organisational performance.
- To promote confidence in community penalties to ensure courts make use of them.
- To emphasise punishment and deterrence, in addition to rehabilitation.

(Adapted from Hedderman, 2003:186)

National standards were first introduced in 1989 for offenders aged 17 years and over sentenced to a community service (now community punishment) order. These were followed by national standards for the supervision of offenders (Home Office, 1992b), introduced to reinforce the statutory provisions contained within the Criminal Justice Act 1991. More like guidelines than requirements (Hopley, 2002: 299), these national standards set out expected levels of compliance by those subject to supervision. It was hoped that their introduction would achieve a measure of consistency which would help to reassure sentencers and the public that the order of the court was being strictly adhered to.

Interviews with probation and community service staff in the early 1990s suggested that most found the standards helpful in ensuring fair and consistent enforcement practice, allowing them to use discretion where necessary (Ellis et al., 1996:

ix). However, the same study found that the standards were subject to interpretation and were not followed strictly. Staff were failing to offer as many appointments as specified and were not responding quickly or firmly enough to non-compliance (ibid: 54). The study also identified considerable variation in enforcement practice within and between probation areas (ibid: 12).

Before the results of the research were published, the stage was set for the introduction of tougher guidance. High profile offending by young people in the early 1990s (see for example Pitts, 1999 5–6; Muncie, 1999: 286) and the accompanying media attention, resulted in an increasingly hostile climate towards offenders in general, and those who were young in particular. The political imperative to be 'tough on crime' led to revised standards (Home Office, 1995a). These took a more rigid line on enforcement, further reducing practitioner discretion and requiring line management authorisation for any deviation from the standards. Tightening up the policy towards enforcement, however, did not achieve the desired change in practice.

Enforcing national standards

Throughout the second half of the 1990s, probation areas were criticised by successive 'Quality and Effectiveness' reports for failing to offer appointments in line with standards or to enforce them rigorously (Hedderman, 1999; Hedderman and Hearnden, 2000). The lack of recording of decisions was regarded as a key failing and it remains the case that unless officers record their decisions, it is impossible to hold them to account or to form a view about the consistency of their practice. Far from reassuring sentencers that orders were being properly enforced, reviews of the standards seemed to highlight the lack of consistency in enforcement, resulting in further ministerial condemnation. The observation that it is one thing to promise uncompromising discipline but another to deliver it (Eadie and Willis, 1989: 414) was being realised. The official response however, in the form of the national standards 2000 (Home Office, 2000c) was increasing rigidity, further reduction of practitioner discretion and an even more punitive approach to offenders failing to comply with orders.

Youth justice

The tension between punishment and welfare in youth justice has been transcended by managerialist imperatives of efficiency and effectiveness (see Chapter 1). New Labour has extended and accelerated these trends through an unprecedented emphasis on organisational performance, assessed through quantifiable outputs (McLaughlin and Muncie, 2000: 182). The development of national standards for youth justice was central to this strategy. The production of a *Statement of Principles and Practice Standards* (ILYJS, 1995) in the mid-1990s became a precursor to the development of a set of national standards and principles for youth justice in England and Wales (see Pitts, 1999: 7–8). The creation of youth offending teams (YOTs) enabled the introduction of separate standards. These have been developed to help ensure that all youth justice agencies fulfil the principal aim of the youth justice system – to prevent offending by children. Enforcement requirements and related breach action are outlined in standards 8 and 9 which address court ordered interventions and Intensive Supervision and Surveillance Programmes (ISSPs) respectively (Youth Justice Board, 2000d; 2004c).

Breaching to promote compliance

Opinions differ regarding the extent to which breach action should be used to promote compliance. Taking a young person back to court for a warning or minor sanction can be a salutary reinforcement. On the other hand, if a threat is overused – or found to be empty – it becomes undervalued (Eadie and Willis, 1989: 417) and using breach to encourage compliance might lose its impact. The courts, too, may regard some breach action as over-zealous – a point made by a senior probation officer interviewed about enforcement (Whitehead, 2003):

> *I have returned someone to Crown Court, to have the judge send [the case] straight back to us, asserting the view that the problems the offenders presented with were the precise reasons he had placed her on supervision.*
>
> (25)

The threat may also turn out to be empty where the failure of the police to accord a high priority to the execution of warrants for breach effectively leaves an order unenforced (Smith, 2000b).

The debate has recently been refreshed by Tony Bottoms's influential paper *Compliance and Community Penalties* (Bottoms, 2001). Among its many insights and implications is an insistence on the importance of normative compliance. Legitimacy is a central aspect of this: people are more likely to comply when they are persuaded that the demands made upon them are fair and reasonable. Bottoms properly insists that prudential calculations – for example the prospect of further penalty for breach – have their influence, but at the point where the application of rules becomes so rigid as to be seen as unfair there will be a legitimacy deficit that will work against compliance.

Enforcement and the search for consistency

Failure to attend without an acceptable explanation is the most common reason for non-compliance (Probation Circular 24/00) and, consequently, for initiating breach proceedings. However, defining 'acceptable' and 'unacceptable' is not a straightforward process and has proved to be a major stumbling block in the quest for a consistent approach to the enforcement of orders. The youth justice standards state that general principles must be agreed in the YOT about what constitutes an acceptable and unacceptable reason for non-attendance. This opens up the possibility of regional variations, admirably demonstrated by Dersley's (2000) comparative analysis of thirteen probation services' policy documents on enforcement in which policy guidance regarding 'acceptable' absences ranged from two pages in one area to twenty-four in another (38). The danger of breach decisions turning into a 'simplistic and mechanistic response that further disadvantages individuals already disproportionately disadvantaged' (39) through treating everyone the same is highlighted in the example in Box 2 below.

Box 2: Case study

Darren is 15 years old. He missed an appointment with Karen, his supervising officer in the YOT. At the next appointment, Karen asked him to account for his absence. Darren said that he had forgotten. The YOT policy sees 'I forgot' as a clear cut case of an unacceptable absence. However, Karen asked Darren to say more. After careful and sensitive inquiry, she listened as Darren explained that, on the day before his appointment, his mother's partner had come home drunk. A row between him and Darren had turned into a fight and eventually the police had been called. Darren had finally gone to bed, bruised and terrified, at 3 a.m. He had overslept the following morning and had indeed forgotten all about his appointment. Karen was unwilling to record this as an unacceptable absence and reflected that her team's policy, if routinely implemented, could have led to a serious injustice in this case – as well as adding to Darren's disaffection and reducing the chances of his future compliance.

The importance of a reflective and questioning approach towards enforcement and breach decisions cannot be overestimated. Box 3 offers some suggestions as to how this can be achieved fairly and in a way which maintains the professional relationship and serves the best interests of the young person.

Box 3: Reflecting on enforcement decision making

- Take into account the young person's individual circumstances, any personal problems, and experience of discrimination when assessing failure to comply.
- How will breach impact on the welfare of the child?
- Be prepared to accept occasional transport difficulties – how many times has your bus or train arrived late?
- Is the young person demonstrating an overall willingness to cooperate with the order?
- Did the pre-sentence report note potential difficulties with achieving compliance (for example: substance misuse, unstable accommodation, mental health problems, poor school attendance) – good practice at

this stage can help make a case for recording an absence as acceptable.
- Recognise and acknowledge the difference between sustained absence at the beginning of an order and occasional absences weeks or even months apart.
- Ask yourself whether refraining from breach would be strongly in the interests of the order/preventing reoffending and be prepared to make a case to justify this.
- Inform sentencers as to whether the breach is technical – the result of enforcement requirements – or practical – a lack of engagement in the process of addressing offending behaviour/unacceptable behaviour in a group.

(NAPO news, 2000: 12)

Ensuring compliance

Evidence suggests that offenders who do not complete a programme of work are more likely to re-offend than those who do (Hedderman and Hearnden, 2000). Equally, the sentence of the court must be respected. Does this mean that enforcement must be more rigorous and more rigid? Hedderman (2003: 191) warns that increasing the likelihood of breach by tightening standards may lead to those who are most in need of effective supervision being breached and re-sentenced before they have a chance to be transformed into 'completers'. This might apply particularly to emotionally volatile young people needing to test boundaries to the limit. There is a point at which discipline becomes counterproductive and community orders cease being an alternative to custody but instead promote it (Eadie and Willis, 1989: 417). The Audit Commission confirms that high levels of breach of intensive supervision and surveillance programmes have just such a potential (Audit Commission, 2004).

The emphasis should be less on enforcement – at best a means to an end – than on ensuring compliance. This change of emphasis encourages an approach that is more imaginative, potentially more effective and certainly more demanding on the agencies involved. Bottoms identifies four principal mechanisms underpinning compliant behaviour: instrumental/prudential; normative; constraint-based, habit or routine (Bottoms, 2001).

These two latter mechanisms are referred to in Box 4 as practical facilitation (Hedderman, 2003, usefully speaks of 'designing out' non-attendance).

It should be noted that most of these practice proposals could be described as normative because they enhance the fairness of the demand made on young people by treating them as individuals and with proper regard to their circumstances and difficulties.

Managing the tension, holding the balance

The dual nature of care and control (Trotter, 1999) is even more important when working with children and young people. Interaction is unpredictable, demanding and potentially draining. Responses cannot be standardised without jeopardising the very purpose of the interaction. Pitts (1999) suggests that a youth justice worker will need to be:

- *A non-judgemental supporter who confirms their emerging adult identity.*
- *A critical ally who holds a mirror up to reality.*
- *An appreciative professional friend who celebrates their achievements.*
- *A solid adult who sometimes says no, but always explains why.*
- *A sounding board who helps them sort out their ideas, priorities and choices.*
- *An utterly reliable nagger who keeps on at them to do the things they do not want to do even though they are good for them.*
- *A tireless campaigner against the social and economic conditions which have limited their chances and choices in such a way that violence may sometimes become a problem-solving device.*

(87)

There will also be occasions when the youth justice worker will need to take breach action. This is part of accountable, professional practice.

Misgivings about the approach commended in this paper sometimes fail to distinguish between discretion and accountability. It is right that practitioners should be able to account for their decisions – and not only to their managers (Faulkner, 2001; Gelsthorpe, 2001). It is by no means clear that this entails restricting their discretion (see Eadie and Canton, 2002). Limiting discretion results in ignoring relevant differences and so leads to injustice. It can also reduce compliance by undermining legitimacy.

Conclusion

Community penalties will always pose difficulties of enforcement. This is because punishments in the community require young people to do something – report to an officer, undertake reparation, pay a fine – or at least refrain from doing something and this entails the possibility of default. Custodial institutions make no such demands. Since many young people might prefer not to do what the court has ordered of them, YOT officers must try to motivate and encourage as well as use negative inducements to secure compliance (see Smith, 2000b).

YOT staff must also make a judgement about whether (for example) a failure to attend is, in the circumstances, reasonable or not. Merely counting absences cannot answer questions of this kind. Assumptions that every missed appointment is wilful/reprehensible, or that a YOT worker's failure to return the young person to court is negligent or 'soft' are facile and unfounded. A fairer criticism would be that too little is known about the way in which such judgements are taken. It is a mistake to think that appropriate accountability is incompatible with discretion and sound professional judgement (Eadie and Canton, 2002). Practitioners should be prepared to account for enforcement decisions to their managers and managers should accept that it is their staff, not them, who 'know' the extent of leniency or toughness appropriate to the unique and ever-changing circumstances of each young person on their caseload. Enforcement decision making must be transparent – to the young people themselves and other criminal justice practitioners. To be otherwise risks an inconsistent and unjust response to already disaffected and socially excluded young people, and calls for an ever-increasing discipline code which will have the opposite effect of that intended.

Box 4: Ways of encouraging compliance

Practice	Compliance mechanism
• Request that sentencers stress the consequences of non-compliance at the point of sentence.	Instrumental; normative (increasing legitimacy)
• Have agreed times/days of the week for first appointments so that these can be formally announced in court at the time of sentence.	Practical facilitation
• Ensure the young person is clear about the first appointment before leaving court.	Practical facilitation
• Use appointment cards (and make these appealing to a young person).	Practical facilitation
• Set appointments to coincide with other important and/or regular events such as signing on.	Practical facilitation (habit)
• Set appointments on the same day each week at the same time.	Practical facilitation (habit)
• Remind the young person of the terms and conditions of the order at each appointment (and of the consequences of non-compliance).	Practical facilitation; instrumental
• Develop the relationship, including pro social modelling/positive reinforcement/motivating to secure attendance and willing participation.	Normative
• Make use of the different perspectives present in YOTs to ensure that supervision programmes are relevant (enjoyable even?) for each young person subject to a statutory order. But also prudential – carrot rather than stick?	Normative; prudential
• Ring up on the morning of the appointment to remind the young person of the appointment.	Practical facilitation; normative
• Involve the young person's wider family in the reporting requirements – to give reminders.	Normative; practical facilitation
• Revoke the order early for good progress.	Instrumental; normative
• Ring the young person's mobile number if more than ten minutes late for an appointment.	Practical facilitation
• Use a designated member of staff or volunteer to follow up missed appointments.	Normative
• Respond to missed appointments by asking what the agency can do to help the young person to comply.	Normative
• Give an initial or final warning.	Instrumental
• Undertake breach action and re-negotiate compliance at court.	Instrumental

Further reading

Bottoms, A.E. (2001) Compliance and Community Penalties. in Bottoms, A.E., Gelsthorpe, L. and Rex, S.A. (Eds.) *Community Penalties: Change and Challenges*. Cullompton: Willan

Eadie, T. and Canton, R. (2002) Practising in a Context of Ambivalence: The Challenge for Youth Justice Workers. *Youth Justice*. 2: 1, 14–26

Gelsthorpe, L. and Padfield, N. (Eds.) (2003) *Exercising Discretion. Decision-Making in the Criminal Justice System and Beyond*. Cullompton: Willan

The Use of Custody for Children and Young People

Ann Hagell

Key points

1. We have been imprisoning children in separate custodial provision for over 150 years. Many different types of custody have been tried, all found wanting at some point.

2. For the most part, these are the children with the most intractable and demanding behavioural problems. Rehabilitating them is never going to be easy, and attempts to do so take place within the context of tensions between their needs and those of their potential victims. Expectations should be realistic.

3. However, it is likely that large numbers of children who are in prison should not be there. The research evidence suggests that there are equally plausible alternatives for many of them if sufficient investment is made. High numbers of young people in custody are often a result of political expediency, public fear of crime and lack of confidence in the youth justice system, rather than a reflection of the children problems presented by themselves.

4. Custody works in the sense it stops committing crimes in their communities during the period of their sentence. However, it is unlikely that this reduces the overall rate of crime, unless effective work is done with the children while they are inside. This means addressing offending behaviour in a targeted way within pro-social regimes. In any event, the potential damage done by restriction of liberty should always be a consideration.

5. Because it is so ineffective, expensive, potentially dangerous, and – most importantly – a threat to human rights, custody should only ever be a last resort for a small group of children who pose a serious risk to society or themselves. It should always have a substantial rehabilitative component, and it should always be looking towards the time when the children are released and returned to their local communities. Custody for children will not work in isolation, only as part of a larger system aimed at turning children's lives around. We should never expect it on its own to be a magic bullet for youth crime. It may be a painful necessity for a tiny minority of children. That is all.

Introduction – who, why, where?

Children end up in custody in England and Wales via several routes. The majority are remanded or sentenced to custody in criminal proceedings (the 'youth justice' route), and it is they who form the focus of this chapter. Custody is the ultimate sanction of the youth justice system, as it is of the adult. At any one time in England and Wales, there are approximately 3,000 children (up to and including 17 year olds) in what has become known as the juvenile secure estate. At the time of writing this consists of prison service young offender institutions, private secure training centres, and local authority secure children's homes (where other children who have not offended may also be accommodated). The majority of 'beds' are in prison service provision and the accommodation

is very similar to that provided in adult prisons. Although a range of organisations are involved in provision, overall responsibility for standards and placement within the estate fall to the Youth Justice Board (see Chapters 4 and 25).

Although this chapter will not discuss them, it is worth noting the other two reasons for children being deprived of their liberty in addition to those arriving via the youth justice route: those held in hospital as a protection to themselves or to others because they are seriously psychiatrically ill (the 'health' route); and those looked after by the local authority and placed in secure accommodation on 'welfare' grounds, because they have a history of absconding and would be liable to injure themselves or others if kept in any other form of accommodation (the 'social care' route). These two groups are very small compared with those held in youth justice provision.

The legal framework for sending children to custody is complicated. The majority of the young people in custody arrive there as a result of having been given a custodial sentence – either a detention and training order (DTO), introduced by the Crime and Disorder Act 1998 (CDA) or, in the case of murder, manslaughter and other 'grave crimes', a sentence for long-term detention under sections 90/92 of the Powers of Criminal Courts (Sentencing) Act 2000, with the latter being available only in the crown court (see Chapter 25). A smaller, but still significant, number are remanded to custody or to secure accommodation, prior to sentence (see Chapter 14).

The use of custody for children and young people over recent decades has shown peaks and troughs, with the 1990s being characterised by a fairly rapid rise. 3,344 children aged between 15 and 17 years were sentenced to immediate custody during 1992, but by 1997 this had reached 5,365 (Home Office, 1998e). By 2002, there were 5,738 young people aged between 15 and 17 years old received into prison service accommodation under sentence, of which 545 were held under sections 90/92 (Home Office, 2003e). Moreover, from 1998 onwards, younger children under 15 years of age have also been received into the local authority secure children's homes and secure training centres, expanding further the numbers in custody (see Chapter 25). During 2002, a total of 7,500 children and young people were sentenced to custody (Home Office, 2003b). These figures exclude children remanded to custody. At the time of writing, the places available at any one time in the secure estate, for both remanded and sentenced young people, stand at just over 3,300.

Taken from the perspective of several decades, the current level of custody is relatively high. Exact comparisons are difficult because of successive modifications in the nature of custodial regimes and changes in jurisdiction; until 1992, 17 year olds within the criminal justice system were treated as adults. It seems clear, however, that the use of custody peaked in the early 1980s, fell until the early 1990s and has since risen to a level approaching the previous high point. The chart below shows those sentenced to custody *as children and young people* between 1980 and 2002. Part of the rise during 1992 can be explained in terms of the inclusion of 17 year olds for the first time in the latter part of that year.

The arguments for the custodial sentencing for children and young people

There are four arguments usually put forward for the use of custodial sentencing for young people: deterrence, incapacitation, rehabilitation and retribution. The *deterrence* argument has both general and individual forms: the former holds that the presence and use of custodial institutions will deter young people from committing crimes that *might* get them into custody. The individual form anticipates that custody will deter those who

Figure 24.1: Children and young people sentenced to custody 1980–2002

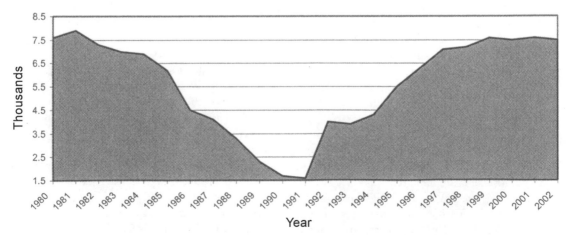

experience it from committing further offences in order to avoid further incarceration.

The *incapacitation* argument proposes that if you take young people who offend off the streets, they cannot offend and thus youth crime should be reduced. The *rehabilitation* argument holds that prison should be able to tackle the underlying problems in a way that is not possible when people remain in the community.

Retribution is sometimes posited as a rationale for the use of custody. The wrongdoer is made to pay for their wrongdoing. However, there is little point in punishment unless it changes people's subsequent behaviour. Nonetheless, punishment is very much part of the public view of what prison is for, and whatever the evidence as to whether or not it works, this is a central part of the debate about the role of custody for children.

On the other hand, there are also a number of arguments *against* using custody for children, and we will return to these below when we look at evidence on the impact of custody.

A brief historical survey

Was it always thus? Yes and no. There has always been a consensus, between the government, public and, for the most part, practitioners, about the need to incarcerate a small group of very persistent or dangerous children whose anti-social behaviour poses a serious physical threat either to themselves or others. Custodial institutions designed specifically for children emerged in the early 1800s, and marked an acknowledgment that children were more than simply small adults. To the extent that children might be different from adults, the theory was that custodial provision for them should also be different. Children's prisons thus arose, to some extent, out of welfarist considerations. However, the shape and extent of this alternative provision has been subject to considerable debate over the years.

It is not easy to provide a stratighforward account of the history of different types of custody and the children kept in them. There is a patchy research literature deriving in part from criminology, but also from sociology and child-care. Children have been locked up for different reasons over time. At the beginning of the 20th century, for example, they were being sent to custody for begging and being homeless, as well as the more familiar criminal offences (Home Office, 1922). Over time, definitions of 'children', 'in' and 'custody' have all varied considerably (Stewart and Tutt, 1987). This reflects our societal ambivalence about children who commit crimes; dealing with them sometimes through systems designed to care, sometimes through systems designed to punish and sometimes both at the same time (see Chapter 1).

The Box below provides an historical overview of some of the main types of custodial institutions that have been tried (and mostly discarded) over the last couple of centuries. Essentially, they can be grouped into two: one strand which is firmly rooted in provision based in the prison service, and a separate but related strand that originates in attempts to provide alternative, welfarist institutions.

A series of issues recur throughout this long and unsettled history of provision for children whom society believes warrant custody. It is evident, from the number of changes, that no one option has ever provided quite what everyone wanted. The conflict between what the public, the politicians and the practitioners desire for these children has resulted in constant policy innovation. While initial expectations are high, this honeymoon period is invariably followed by disillusionment. After a time regimes are perceived to be either too severe, or not harsh enough; establishments become regarded as too large, or too small, too specialised or not able to cope with the full range of needs encountered.

Managing these types of institutions is clearly a mammoth task with many challenges. Staff recruitment is difficult, retaining staff equally so. Difficulties in knowing how to train and support staff working with such difficult children persist. Today, the increasing clamour about the welfare and the human rights of the children in custody feed into an already fraught situation.

And, most relevant perhaps, reconviction rates are almost always poor. We might expect them to be so of course – the children sent to custody represent those with the most intractable and difficult behavioural problems. But can custody help at all? In the next section we look at the extent to which custody 'works'.

Historical overview of the principal institutions for detaining children who offend in England and Wales

The penal strand

Prison Hulks:

After the Battle of Trafalgar, HMS *Bellerophon* at Sheerness (1823) and *Euryalus* (1825) were deployed to house children who offend (under 16 years) separately from adults. Their cruel and degrading conditions were widely condemned and the last was closed in 1846.

Parkhurst:

Parkhurst was the first land-based government institution for juveniles, established on the Isle of Wight in 1838. The regime was based on the 'wholesome restraints of corrective discipline'. It was finally closed in 1864.

Borstals:

Conceived in the late 19th century (and given formal recognition in the Prevention of Crime Act 1908) as a halfway house between prison and reformatories, borstals were based on exercise and training and were often housed in wings of existing prisons. The sentence was indeterminate, between one and three years, and included a period of supervision in the community. By the 1920s the military style regimes were becoming unpopular, and they were remodelled on the English public school system. Borstals persisted until 1982 when they were transformed by the Criminal Justice Act of that year into youth custody centres.

Detention Centres:

Introduced in 1948 as the original 'short, sharp shock', junior detention centres catered for children aged 14-17 years whose offending was the most persistent. Sentence was initially for between 3 and 6 months, although this was later reduced to between 21 days and 4 months under the Thatcher administration. Provision expanded rapidly and, by 1965 detention centres provided 6,000 places. They were replaced by young offender institutions in 1988.

Youth Custody Centres:

Introduced in 1982 as a replacement for the old Borstal regime, the youth custody regime catered for those sentenced to terms longer than that associated the detentions centres. The focus was on security rather than rehabilitation.

Young Offender Institutions (YOIs):

Replaced both youth custody and detention centres in 1988. Still in existence, YOIs now cater for the majority of those subject to detention and training orders and all those remanded to custody.

Secure Training Centres (STCs):

Privately managed, relatively small, establishments introduced by the Criminal Justice and Public Order Act 1994 (but not implemented until 1998) to accommodate children aged under 15 years of age sentenced to a secure training order, a new custodial sentence for younger children. That order and detention in a YOI were both subsequently replaced by the detention and training order but STCs are still used for younger children sentenced to custody and a smaller number of those remanded to secure accommodation.

The welfare strand

Reformatories:

Established by the Reformatory Schools Act 1854, these institutions were intended to be an alternative to imprisonment. By 1870 there were 54 schools, but demand for places declined following a series of scandals and, in 1933, they were merged with Industrial Schools (originally a welfare provision rather than for adjudicated offenders) to create a new system of Home Office Approved Schools. These became, in due course, Community Homes with Education on the premises (CHEs), under local authority control.

Youth Treatment Centres (YTCs):

Established as a result of Home Office and Department of Health (DH) collaboration in the wake of public concern over two high profile murder cases involving child defendants, YTCs were intended to accommodate young people whose behaviour was considered too difficult for other types of establishment. Two centres were opened during the 1970s, each providing around 70 placements in a range of closed, semi secure and open conditions. There were increasing concerns about unacceptable practices in the centres during the 1990s and both were closed by 2000.

Local authority secure children's homes (LASCHs):

Approved Schools were not secure, and secure units (latter renamed local authority secure children's homes) developed as a response to children considered too difficult for non-secure provision, following disturbances at Carlton school. The first unit was established in 1964 and, in 1969, they came under local authority control. From the outset LASCHs provided for children secured through the social care route as well as those who offended. Those units which contract with the Youth Justice Board currently accommodate children sentenced to custody, those subject to court ordered secure remands as well as those secured through family proceedings. The remaining units provide accommodation primarily for welfare cases.

Derived from Hagell and Hazel (2001)

Evidence on the impact of custody

If we treat each of the objectives for custody in turn, we can start by stating that the evidence of a *deterrent* effect is weak. Individual deterrence is most effective when it involves a response that follows the crime closely in time, and when the sanction always happens in response to the same behaviour. Thus, having a high and almost certain risk of being caught in the act by a police officer is theoretically the best crime deterrent. Custody does not meet any of these criteria for effective deterrence. The chances of detection for most offences are relatively small and the youth justice process – despite recent progress in speeding up the system – relatively slow (Nacro, 2003e). Many young people who offend are not even clear exactly which act it was that resulted in any given custodial sentence. They routinely admit a large number of similar crimes that do not generate a custodial outcome.

What then of the argument for general deterrence, where others are said to be deterred just by the fact that custody exists, not through their own experience of it? Here too, there is a lack of supporting evidence. Indeed, to the contrary, there is some qualitative evidence that for some young people, acquiring a custodial sentence can be considered a mark of status.

The *incapacitation* objective is met in the sense that escapes from secure custody are rare, and security is usually not a problem. Generally speaking, dangerous young people *are* effectively incarcerated and it is unarguably the case that while they are in custody they are not on the streets offending. However, the incapacitation argument is more complicated than this. Estimates of the effect on overall levels of crime of locking up young people who commit offences indicate that a reduction in crime of just a few per cent would require the incarceration of huge numbers of children (Greenwood et al., 1994; Tarling, 1993). The incapacitation argument thus begins to fall apart.

Quite apart from questions of principle, the cost of locking up such large numbers of children would be prohibitive. In addition, young people may not offend during custody, but they may be learning about how to do so more effectively when they are released, thereby negating any positive effect in the longer term. This has long been a concern about custody for children, first raised with respect to the prison hulks of the early 19th century.

The *retribution* argument is predicated on the notion that punishment can, in some manner, restore a moral equilibrium within society. That argument is undermined, to an extent, by the fact that the public routinely underestimates the severity of sentencing (Mattinson and Mirrlees-Black, 2000). Moreover, the youth justice system has always proceeded on the assumption that children and young people are, by dint of their relative immaturity, less able to control their impulses and foresee the consequences of their behaviour. In those circumstances, it is difficult to sustain an argument for punishment unless it can be shown to reduce future offending.

That leaves us with *rehabilitation*, the best bet if custody is to make any contribution at all to combating crime. A number of reviews of effective treatment in institutional and community settings have been undertaken over recent years. Generally they suggest that some kinds of institutions could potentially have short-term effects on behaviour if the regimes contain the right ingredients. Research (Ditchfield and Catan, 1992; Losel, 1993; Hazel et al., 2002) identifies the key elements of effective practice in providing secure accommodation as including:

- An overall pro-social ethos.
- Good educational and work activities.
- Promotion of healthy peer group interactions.
- Provision of opportunities to develop self-esteem and responsibility.
- Assistance with resisting drugs.
- Assistance with maintaining and promoting links with families.

However, rather than introducing changes in the overall ethos, the prison service and hence YOIs have tended to concentrate on a more specific set of 'what works' programmes that address offending behaviour. The messages here about successful intervention suggest that these types of programmes are more likely to work (at least in the short-term) if they:

- Target specific behaviour (rather than offering counselling), and include social skills training and problem-solving.
- Are matched to the individual needs of young people who offend.
- Are well structured and planned.
- Are effectively supervised and monitored.
- Remain true to the original programme model (programme integrity).

We do not know, yet, quite how the individual components of regimes interact with the general ethos. It may not be enough to have a very good programme running for a few hours a week if the overall regime is unhealthy.

Research undertaken for the Youth Justice Board in 2000 highlighted the variation of provision across the three different types of institutions within the juvenile secure estate – YOIs, STCs and local authority secure children's homes (LASCHs) (Hobbs and Hook, 2000). The report argued that provision essentially represented three different models, from the formal programme-oriented approach of the YOIs to the much less formal, holistic and 'parenting' approach of the LASCHs. Earlier research, before the introduction of the STCs, had concluded that the secure accommodation model was most effective in achieving good outcomes for young people (Ditchfield and Catan, 1992). Hopes were high for the STCs, which seemed to represent the closest model to established good practice, in that they took a 'whole child' approach but also focused on specific behavioural changes, with a strong focus on education. However, early evaluations of their effect on subsequent behaviour were not particularly optimistic (Hagell et al., 2000).

Finally, but very importantly, custody also impacts at a very personal level on vulnerable young people. Most children in custody have a history of child care problems, abuse, educational exclusion, and generally not being wanted (Goldson, 2002d; Nacro, 2003e). When discussing the impact of custody, it is important to retain in the balance the high risks of mental health problems among young people who offend, the widespread prevalence of bullying and the high prevalence of self-harm and suicide attempts among incarcerated youth. While the public are safe from them, young people may not always be very safe themselves, and a distressed and injured child will not be able to put the effort required into resisting old influences when they go home. One famous American follow-up study concluded that custody can contribute to making it more likely that offending will persist (Sampson and Laub, 1993).

The key to success, if there is one, is the extent to which the regimes and the programmes can directly target the relevant behaviours in a systematic and focused way within a generally pro-social regime, without further damage to the child. The main conclusion is that there *may* be potential for something to be done to help some children who demonstrate serious and persistent offending and who are a real risk to the safety of others or themselves. However, common sense suggests that, for the relatively small number of young people for whom restriction of liberty is really necessary, a small and personal setting such as the local authority secure children's home, which can properly address the varied needs of the child, are more likely to meet these needs than prison service accommodation. In any event, historically, it has proved almost impossible to design and maintain the types of provision, which the research suggests, have the most chance of rehabilitating children.

Debates and controversies

The arguments for and against custody for children have remained surprisingly stable over time. Disagreements tend to focus on the size of the group who ought to be removed from the community and the type of provision to which they should be removed. Custody for children is such an emotive and political topic that it is

difficult to present a review of the evidence without entering into the debates and controversies right at the outset. The sections above have already touched on the conflict between punishment and rehabilitation; the right to individual liberty versus the need to protect the public; the extent to which seriously delinquent children are open to rehabilitation, and if so, the debates over the right way to achieve this, and the politics of punishment. It is clear from a range of statistics and research that levels of custody, and how we deliver it as a sentence, do not necessarily reflect levels of juvenile crime, nor do they particularly reflect evidence on its effectiveness (Nacro, 2003a). Fear of crime among members of the general public, fear of not appearing tough on crime amongst all political parties, and public concern that there are no alternatives, all contribute to the way in which we use this ultimate sanction with children.

These debates will continue to rage, and we will continue to struggle with these issues. However, we need always to be mindful of the UN Convention on the Rights of the Child (and other international agreements) which require that custody for children should only ever be a last resort, and that custody levels should be kept at the absolute minimum (see Chapter 7).

Further reading

Hough, M., Jacobson, J. and Millie, A. (2003) *The Decision to Imprison: Sentencing and the Prison Population*. London: Prison Reform Trust

Lyon, J., Dennison, C. and Wilson, A. (2000) *Tell Them so They Listen: Messages From Young People in Custody*. Research Study 2001. London: Home Office

Nacro (2002a) *Children Who Commit Grave Crimes*. London: Nacro

Nacro (2003a) *A Failure of Justice: Reducing Child Imprisonment*. London: Nacro

Stewart, G. and Tutt, N. (1987) *Children in Custody*. Aldershot: Avebury

25 Custody and Policy

Tim Bateman

Key points

1. The use of custody for young people has risen rapidly during the recent past. As a consequence, the United Kingdom is almost certainly in breach of the United Nations Convention on the Rights of the Child which requires that custody is only used as a last resort.

2. The legislative provisions by which young people are detained through the youth justice system are complex; involving a range of custodial sentences and remand options.

3. The Youth Justice Board assumed responsibility for oversight of the juvenile secure estate, comprising young offender institutions, secure training centres and young offender institutions, from April 2000.

4. The Board has delivered considerable improvement in custodial regimes, but significant problems remain, in large part associated with the predominance of prison service accommodation within the secure estate.

5. The scope for improving the effectiveness and humanity of custody, is constrained by the large numbers of children unnecessarily locked up. The potential for change depends on effecting a shift in the punitive ethos which has in recent years characterised responses to youth crime.

The Committee is deeply concerned at the high increasing numbers of children in custody generally, at earlier ages for lesser offences, and for longer sentences imposed by the recent increased court powers . . . [I]t is the concern of the Committee that deprivation of liberty is not being used only as a measure of last resort and for the shortest possible appropriate period of time, in violation of Article 37(b) of the United Nations Convention on the Rights of the Child.

(United Nations, 2002)

Introduction

The suggestion by the United Nations Committee on the Rights of the Child, that the number of children locked up as a result of criminal proceedings in the UK may be indicative of a breach of international convention, requires some explanation. There is after all widespread agreement amongst politicians and justice system professionals that the use of custody for children and young people is frequently damaging to those deprived of their liberty and often counterproductive as a measure for reducing offending (see Chapter 24). Indeed, the government's stated policy is to 'limit the number of young people who are in custodial provision' (Home Office,

2002b). The Youth Justice Board, too, has taken the view that for most young people community sentences are 'more effective in reducing offending and are better value for money' (Youth Justice Board, 2003f). Consistent with that position, among the performance targets which the Board has set for youth offending teams (YOTs) are two which aim to limit the demand for custody (see Chapter 4).

The roots of the United Nations Committee's concerns lie in a dramatic expansion in the use of detention from the early 1990s until the latter part of the decade. While the youth custodial population has been broadly stable since the implementation of the youth justice reforms associated with the Crime and Disorder Act 1998 (CDA), those changes have failed so far to effect any significant fall in the use of custody which remains at unacceptably high levels.

Between 1992 and 2002, the number of 10–17 year olds sentenced to custody rose by almost 90%, while detected youth crime fell by more than a quarter. Nor has the rapid escalation in incarceration been uniform. For younger children aged 10–14 years, custodial sentences have risen four fold; for girls the equivalent increase is 600%, albeit from a relatively low base (Nacro, 2004c).

The over-representation of black young people among those deprived of their liberty is a continuing cause for concern, with children classified as black or black British accounting for 15% of those remanded to custody or secure accommodation, 11.3% of all custodial disposals and more than 20% of all those sentenced to long-term detention (Youth Justice Board, 2003o). Furthermore, the over-representation of black young people held within the juvenile secure estate has increased significantly since the introduction of the youth justice reforms from 1998 onwards (Audit Commission, 2004).

Notwithstanding a recent fall, one estimate has suggested that the level of child incarceration in England and Wales, relative to the under 18 population is four times that in France, ten times that in Spain and one hundred times that in Finland (Nacro, 2003a). At the same time, the period for which young people are locked up has also increased: average sentence length for boys aged 15–17 years rose between 1992 and 2002 from 9.2 to 12.2 months (Home Office, 2003e). The concerns of the United Nations Committee would appear to be well founded.

The range of custodial measures

Children locked up in the youth justice system fall into two categories. The first comprises those detained whilst on remand; the second includes all those who receive a custodial sentence. Although there is an inevitable fluctuation between the two constituencies, the remand population accounts for roughly one quarter of all young people held in custody at any one time.

Remands

The legislation governing bail and its refusal for children and young people is extremely complex (see Chapter 14). It affords two routes by which young people can be deprived of their liberty. A remand to custody is available for all 17 year olds and 15–16 year old boys. It results in placement in a young offender institution (YOI) administered by the prison service. A remand to local authority accommodation with a security requirement, more commonly known as a court ordered secure remand (COSR), is available for 12–16 year old girls, and vulnerable 15–16 year old boys for

whom a relevant placement is available. A young person subject to a COSR is placed in a local authority secure children's home (LASCH) or, less commonly, a secure training centre (STC).

Remands to custody increased significantly during the early part of the 1990s and remained high despite a fall in the latter part of the decade. Thus the number of 15–16 year old boys, held on remand in YOIs, rose from 72 on 30 June 1992 to 245 in 1997, falling to 213 in 2002 (Home Office, 2003e).

The COSR was initially conceived as a measure for the abolition of custodial remands for 15–16 year old boys. However, a series of legislative amendments, prior to implementation, expanded the group of children for whom it was available. The changes ensured that when the order was finally implemented in June 1999, the new provision had little impact on the number of children held on remand in YOIs, while generating a significant increase in the numbers of 12–16 year olds remanded to secure accommodation (Goldson, 2002d). Between 1992 and 2003, the population held on remand in LASCHs expanded from 73 to 95 (DfES, 2003a).

The remand population is, in any event, significantly lower than it might otherwise have been as a consequence of moves to halve the time from arrest to sentence of those young people who meet the definition of a 'persistent young offender'. The time from arrest to sentence for this group fell from an average of 142 days in January 1997 to 66 days in February 2004 (Lowe, 2004). The reduction in the average length of remand periods has a corresponding impact on the remanded population, without any necessary decline in the numbers of young people deprived of their liberty.

Custodial sentences

Custodial sentences for young people also take a variety of forms. The mainstream custodial penalty, available in the youth court, is the detention and training order (DTO) which, on implementation in April 2000, replaced secure training orders (for 12–14 year olds) and detention in a young offender institution (for 15–17 year olds) (Nacro, 2000b). The order must be made for a set period of four, six, eight, 10, 12, 18 or 24 months and, by default, is served half in custody and half in the community, with provision for early or late release. There has however, since May 2002, been a presumption of early release at the earliest possible stage, subject to an electronically monitored curfew (Nacro, 2003f). This measure too has operated to reduce the numbers held within the secure estate at any one time.

The DTO was intended to be a more constructive custodial disposal than those that it replaced based on assessment-led planning of 'purposeful activity' and a focus on continuity of intervention between the custodial and community phases of the sentence. Shortly after its introduction, the Youth Justice Board described the DTO as a 'better sentence for young offenders' (Youth Justice Board, 2000a).

However, the Board's evaluation of the order, conducted over the first two years of its operation, found that one in five YOT supervising officers reported having no information on what work had been undertaken by the custodial establishment to address offending behaviour. The evaluation also suggested that, once full data became available, re-offending rates following release from a DTO would probably resemble those associated with previous custodial penalties for young people (Hazel et al., 2002). The Board has subsequently become less upbeat about the potential of the order as an effective mechanism for dealing with young people who offend.

The DTO accounts for the large majority of sentences of detention for young people, but the crown court also has *exceptional* custodial powers to impose a sentence above the maximum generally available, where a child is convicted of a 'grave crime'. Section 90 of the Powers of Criminal Courts (Sentencing) Act 2000 (PCC(S)A) deals with murder and requires that children convicted of that offence are sentenced to be detained 'during Her Majesty's pleasure', the functional equivalent of a mandatory life sentence in the case of an adult. The sentence is indeterminate and, in administrative terms, has two parts: the young person must first serve a minimum period, or 'tariff', determined by the sentencing court; once the tariff has expired, the young person will remain in custody until the Parole Board considers it safe to release them into the community, under licence for the remainder of their lives. The number of children committing murder is extremely small and during 2002, only 20 sentences under section 90 were imposed.

Other serious offences, primarily, but not exclusively, those which can attract 14 years imprisonment or more in the case of an adult, can also be subject to the grave crimes procedures, under section 91 of PCC(S)A. The maximum sentencing powers, in such cases are generally those which apply to adult defendants. The use of long-term detention for such offences has increased dramatically in recent years from less than 100 orders imposed in 1992 to 706 in 2002 (Nacro, 2004c). This does not necessarily imply a corresponding growth in the incidence of serious youth crime, however. A succession of legislative changes has brought an ever greater number of offences within the ambit of section 91. At the same time, there is convincing evidence to suggest that shifts in sentencing practice have led to the grave crimes provisions being used in cases where standard custodial powers or community sentences would previously have been considered adequate (Nacro, 2002a). For instance, the proportion of residential burglaries tried and sentenced in the crown court which attract a sentence of long-term detention has risen from 2.8% in 1989 to 7.2% in 2000 to 10% in 2002 (Home Office, 2003b).

Finally, the Criminal Justice Act 2003 introduces new custodial provisions, available in the crown court for young people convicted of certain sexual or violent offences who are deemed to be 'dangerous'. The new orders, 'detention for public protection' and 'extended detention', are additional to and distinct from existing custodial powers. In particular, they are 'preventive' sentences aimed at reducing future risk rather than providing a proportionate response to current offending. They can, accordingly, last beyond the maximum sentence which would otherwise be available.

Detention for public protection is an indeterminate sentence which can be imposed for sexual or violent offences which carry a maximum penalty in the case of an adult of ten years or more imprisonment. It is available where the court is of the opinion that there is a significant risk to members of the public of serious harm from further violent or sexual offences committed by that young person. Administratively, it differs very little from a discretionary life sentence imposed under section 91 of PCC(S)A.

Extended detention involves a period in custody with an extended licence period, of up to five years in the case of a violent offence, or eight years for a sexual offence. The sentence is available for young people who have committed a violent or sexual offence which, in the case of an adult, carries a sentence of two years imprisonment or more, where the court considers that there is a significant risk of serious harm to the public.

Both orders are to be implemented in December 2005. At the time of writing it is not clear how widely they will be used but the potential for an increase in the number of young people subject to lengthy custodial penalties is obvious.

The juvenile secure estate

One of the most significant changes associated with the CDA (1998) was the establishment of the Youth Justice Board with a national remit for the oversight of the youth justice system. From April 2000, the Board assumed responsibility for commissioning custodial places within, what has become known as, the juvenile secure estate, comprising:

- Local Authority Secure Children's Homes (LASCHs) which also accommodate children placed in secure accommodation on welfare grounds.
- Privately managed Secure Training Centres (STCs), dedicated, relatively small, custodial institutions for children and young people under 18 years of age.
- Prison service Young Offender Institutions.

In the interim period, the Board has expended considerable effort and finance in improving the performance of the custodial sector, based on its vision of an effective secure estate (Youth Justice Board, 1998). Substantial change has indeed ensued; most of it for the better. Perhaps most important has been the creation of a separate 'estate' within the prison service for those under the age of 18 years, but other significant improvements have been achieved through the establishment of performance targets and expected minimum standards integrated into the service level agreement with the prison service and the contractual process with other secure establishments.

As indicated above, young people on remand are allocated placements on the basis of their legal status: whether they are subject to a remand to custody or a COSR. Custodial sentences however can, in principle, be served in any part of the juvenile secure estate. Allocation to a particular type of establishment is determined by a range of factors, with a primary focus on age and gender.

Thus, the Board's placement strategy indicates that:

- Children under 12 years of age will be placed in a LASCH.
- Children aged 12–14 years of age must be placed in a LASCH or STC.
- 15–16 year old girls should be given priority for places in non-prison service establishments.
- 17 year old girls will be allocated to a LASCH if places are available.
- 15–17 year old boys will usually be placed in a YOI although vulnerable 15–16 year old males should be considered for placement outside of the prison service where places are available.

(Youth Justice Board, 2002c)

In practice, the scope for discretion is extremely limited because YOIs account for the large majority of available places: 2,860 of the total 3,348 at November 2003 (Youth Justice Board, 2003m). Considerable numbers of vulnerable children are inevitably placed inappropriately in prison service accommodation because of a lack of alternative provision. Detailed figures are not available, but Lord Warner, then Chair of the Youth Justice Board, told the Home Office select committee in December 2002 that between 15 and 20 vulnerable boys were being placed in prison service establishments each week as a consequence of overcrowding in the rest of the secure estate (Community Care, 2002). This is almost certainly an underestimate. YOT assessments, leading to the ascription of 'vulnerable' status, are mediated by an understanding of the limited availability of secure placements, inevitably leading to a process of prioritisation. The number of children deemed vulnerable, in other words, represents the end of a spectrum of those young people whose needs are most pressing. Demand is in effect constrained by supply.

The same constraints impact in other ways. For instance, the Board, in recognition of the importance of maintaining family and community ties while young people are in custody, set a target in March 2001 that 90% of placements within the juvenile secure estate should be within 50 miles of home. The target has never been met and, in November 2003, 28% of young people were detained further than 50 miles from their home address, just 2% less than in April 2000.

This mismatch between need and provision is a longstanding problem. In March 1991, the government announced that all 15 and 16 year old girls would be placed in local authority provision rather than prison service custody by April 2000. It did not happen. In April 2001, the Youth Justice Board renewed the pledge, to be effected by mid 2002, but an increase in the overall custodial population during that year led to a further revision of the target date. The Board eventually announced that there were no 15 year old girls in prison service establishments during March 2003 and removal of 16 year olds was effected by December of the same year (National Audit Office, 2004).

The restricted potential for placing young people according to their needs was also highlighted when, following a damning critical inspection by Her Majesty's Chief Inspector of Prisons, the Board determined that it would conduct a phased withdrawal from Ashfield YOI with the juvenile population capped at 212. The Board acknowledged that overcrowding elsewhere in estate precluded a more rapid response (Youth Justice Board, 2003b). Conversely, a lack of spare capacity to cope with the high level of demand is cited as the principal reason for the fact that, in the ten months from April 2002, there were more than 2,400 moves of young people within the secure estate (National Audit Office, 2004).

The predominance of prison service provision has other negative consequences. The regime associated with each type of establishment varies considerably. Considered from a financial perspective, the cost of a place in a LASCH is more than three times that in a YOI, reflecting wide differentials in levels of staffing, expenditure on education and other programmes, and the minimum requirements of establishments to which Children Act 1989 standards apply. Anticipated outcomes, unsurprisingly, also vary considerably. Less than 20% of YOTs consider that YOIs meet the educational, health and welfare needs of those detained within them 'well' and almost 50% believe that they do so 'poorly'. This compares with equivalent figures for LASCHs of nearly 70% and less than 10% (National Audit Office, 2004). Since less than 15% of children in custody are placed in LASCHs or STCs, it is reasonable to assess the effectiveness of custodial regimes as a whole on the basis of the conditions prevalent within prison service establishments. Despite the considerable improvements of recent years, those conditions leave much to be desired.

In December 2002, the High Court was called upon to comment on the state of YOIs in a case bought by the Howard League. Mr Justice Munby, reviewing recent reports by Her Majesty's Chief Inspector of Prisons, concluded that the findings:

> . . . *shame us all. They ought to be – I hope they are – matters of the very greatest concern to . . . society at large. For these are things being done to children by the State – by all of us – in circumstances where the State appears to be failing badly and in some instances failing very badly, in its duties to vulnerable and damaged children.*
>
> (R v Home Department, 2002)

The judgement captures succinctly the glaring contradiction which exists between the welfare needs of the vast majority of young people whose offending leads to them being locked up and the capacity of custodial institutions, and YOIs in particular, to deliver a service that can adequately address those needs. Indeed, in most cases, custody simply serves to damage further already very vulnerable children. The damage done is reflected to some degree in one set of figures that can stand proxy for a more detailed account. Between January 1998 and January 2002, there were 1,111 reported incidents of young people harming themselves while in a YOI. Given the nature of official recording, it is reasonable to assume that a considerable number of lesser injuries went unreported. More telling still, is the stark fact that 12 boys took their own lives while in custody during those four years (Nacro, 2003e).

The potential for change

It is clear that the scope for improving custodial regimes is severely constrained by the numbers of children detained. The Youth Justice Board has recently announced a reduction in the number of places that it purchases from the prison service, following a fall of some 13% in the custodial population over the past year (Youth Justice Board, 2004d). At the same time, it has received criticism for also reducing the number of placements which it commissions within local authority secure provision (Donovan, 2004).

An important question concerns the extent to which the recent fall in the numbers of locked up children represents a sustainable reversal of the trends noted earlier in this chapter. The increases in custody of the 1990s are in part explicable in terms of successive legislative changes which made it easier to remove young people from the community. The maximum custodial sentence available in the youth court, for a single offence, increased from six months to two years; mainstream custodial sentencing was made available for children aged 12–14 years; the grave crimes provisions were extended to encompass a larger range of offences and to apply to younger children. The recent development of incarceration for preventive purposes, to guard against what young people might do, marks a radical new, and disturbing, departure. Remand provision has followed a similar trajectory. In 2002, the principle that no child would be locked up, pre-trial, unless they posed a risk of serious harm, was undermined by section 130 of the Criminal Justice and Police Act 2001, which allowed incarceration on the basis of persistence (Nacro, 2003a)

But what triggered the statutory changes which led to this custodial bonanza in the face of falling youth crime? In 1993, in the wake of the murder of two year old James Bulger by two truanting ten year olds, John Major, the prime minister, exhorted society to 'condemn a little more and understand a little less' in its dealings with children who break the law. This utterance proved to be the precursor of a seismic shift in attitudes towards children and young people in trouble resulting in legislation which made custody more readily available to courts.

The Youth Justice Board attributes the recent 13% fall in the custodial population primarily to the impact of intensive supervision and surveillance programmes (see Chapter 22; Youth Justice Board, 2003b). However, the Audit Commission has been more circumspect, suggesting that ISSP alone is unlikely to have much impact upon the level of youth custody (Audit Commission, 2004). Consistent with that assessment, the custodial population began to rise again just as the national roll out of ISSP took effect (see Chapter 22).

Conclusion

Unless the predominantly punitive ethos which fuelled the 'rush to custody' is reversed (Rutherford, 2003), there must be a risk that child incarceration will remain at historically high levels. At present, the major obstacle to securing change in the use of custody is ideological rather than administrative, political rather than legal or logistical. In the recent period, governments have effectively placed being tough on youth crime at the heart of political debate. In so doing, they have encouraged and reinforced punitive populism. The results in terms of outcomes for young people in trouble are predictable. Thus New Labour's expressed commitment to reduce the use of custody is frequently undermined by rapid legislative change designed to criminalise ever larger numbers of children and marginalise a concern with their welfare.

Further reading

Goldson, B. (2002d) *Vulnerable Inside: Children in Secure and Penal Settings*. London: The Children's Society

Hodgkins, R. (2002) *Rethinking Child Imprisonment: Report on Young Offender Institutions*. London: Children's Rights Alliance for England

Nacro (2003a) *A Failure of Justice: Reducing Child Imprisonment*. London: Nacro

Nacro (2003e) *Counting the Cost: Reducing Child Imprisonment*. London: Nacro

National Audit Office (2004) *Youth Offending: The Delivery of Community and Custodial Sentences*. London: National Audit Office

Part 4   Face to Face Work in Youth Justice

26 The Young Person-Worker Relationship

Susan Batchelor and Fergus McNeill

Key points

1. Contemporary developments in youth justice have placed a disproportionate emphasis on the role of effective programmes, whilst neglecting evidence supporting the significance of effective relationships in working with young people who offend.

2. Young people who offend often have a range of social and personal difficulties, other than just their offending. Youth justice workers need to acknowledge and address these difficulties if they are to help prevent further re-offending.

3. Commitment to desistance from crime on the part of a young person appears to be generated by personal and professional commitment on the part of workers, whose reasonableness, fairness, and encouragement is seen by young people to demonstrate an understanding of, and genuine concern for, them as people.

4. Desistance from crime ultimately depends upon the young person recognising for themself the need to change. Workers can help develop intrinsic motivation using a technique called 'motivational interviewing'.

5. Another effective way in which workers can have an impact on desistance is by modelling pro-social behaviour. This involves identifying, rewarding and modelling conduct to be encouraged and the identification, discouragement and challenging of that to be changed.

The young person-worker relationship in context

Recent debates about 'what works' in intervening with people who offend have tended to concentrate on the characteristics of related programmes and, in particular, on cognitive-behavioural programmes (McGuire, 1995; Vanstone, 2000). However, critics have expressed concerns that the narrow contemporary focus on programmes is flawed, in that it ignores or minimises the importance of the wider social and environmental context of offending (Farrall, 2002), and that, in prescribing particular modes and foci of practice, it contributes to the deprofessionalisation of workers (Eadie and Canton, 2002; Pitts, 2001b). Furthermore, some authors have argued that the over-emphasis on programmes is such that the service user-worker relationship has come to be seen as almost incidental to the process of promoting change (Barry, 2000).

More broadly, for some commentators, the shift of emphasis from individualised rehabilitative interventions, to correctional programmes for 'groups' or 'types' of offenders is symptomatic of a wider transformation of the penal realm. This transformation is described broadly as entailing a shift away from penal welfarism towards a new penology, characterised in part by the 'responsibilisation' of offenders, by the exclusionary exaggeration of their 'other-ness' from law-abiding citizens and by the development of technologies and approaches for the assessment and management of the risks they pose to the public (Garland, 2001).

As a result of such critiques, recent years have witnessed a renewed focus on effective processes of intervention and on the characteristics of effective working relationships between those who offend and those who are charged with encouraging them to stop (Svensson, 2003; McNeill, 2003). A growing number of research studies have highlighted the significance of relationships with supervising officers in developing and mobilising offenders' intrinsic motivation to change (see for example, Trotter, 1999).

The social and familial context of offending

Relationships are important in work with young people who offend because they are both part of the problem and part of the solution. Studies of young people show that they see relationship problems as the main cause of the mental distress they experience (Armstrong et al., 1998) and that they often offend because they have been damaged by relationships. Relationships can also be central to the alleviation of young people's difficulties, including offending behaviour (Hill, 1999).

The need for connection with others – defined as 'interaction that engenders a sense of being in tune with self and others, of being understood and valued' (Bylington, 1997: 35) is a primary motivation of human behaviour. Positive connections grow out of relationships where interaction and discussion are encouraged, and where members share mutual respect and empathy (Swift, 1998: 259). However, the relational experiences of most young people who persistently offend are characterised by disconnection and violation. According to a recent study of persistent young offenders in an outer London borough (Liddle and Solanki, 2002), only 14% of the young people lived with both biological parents, 66% lacked a good relationship with one or other parent, 22% had suffered bereavement, 39% family breakdown or divorce, 34% had lost contact with significant people, 44% had experienced neglect or physical, sexual or emotional abuse, or had witnessed violence against other family members, 22% were being 'looked after' by social services and 27% had been previously 'looked after'.

Where these difficult circumstances entail a lack of experience of mutual and empathic relationships, youth justice workers, in addition to tackling the young person's offending behaviour, often have to deal with problems relating to poor parenting, abuse, neglect, and damaged relationships, along with association with delinquent peers, poor school performance and persistent truancy, substance abuse or dependency, high levels of impulsiveness and aggressiveness, poverty, poor housing and/or homelessness (Farrington, 1996).

Given this range of difficulties, it is perhaps not surprising that recent studies of adult probationers

and parolees have shown that offenders tend to value supervision that tackles their social and personal difficulties rather than just their offending, which they often regard as a consequence of these other difficulties. For example, the most commonly mentioned aspect of 'good social work' cited by probationers in McIvor and Barry's (1998) research was finding out what their problems were in order to get to the root of their offending. Likewise probationers in Rex's (1999) study said that what they most appreciated about supervision was problem-solving advice (i.e. rather than direct intervention). In both studies, probationers recognised that dealing with their difficulties was something that they had to do themselves. Just as workers cannot stop young people from offending, they cannot solve all their problems either. Young people's own social networks – their friends and family – are often better at resolving their difficulties than professionals (Hill, 1999).

The potential of young people's own social networks for resolving difficulties is highlighted by 'resilience perspectives'. In contrast to a risk factor model of offending, which focuses on young people's social problems and personal difficulties, resilience perspectives consider the 'protective factors and processes' involved in positive adaptation in spite of adversity. In terms of practice with young people, such perspectives entail an emphasis on the recognition, exploitation and development of their competences, resources, skills and assets (Schoon and Bynner, 2003). Workers should strive to develop the young person's strengths – at both an individual and a social level – in order to build and sustain momentum for change.

Studies have revealed three general categories of protective factors that may impede or halt the impact of adverse experiences: qualities of the young person; characteristics of the family; and support from outside the family (Garmezy, 1984). Some of these are detailed in Table 26.1.

Desistance from offending

Within criminological research, many of the insights of resilience perspectives are echoed in available evidence which suggests that processes of desistance from offending are aligned to young people's social and situational circumstances. Jamieson et al.'s (1999) study of young people in

Table 26.1: Protective factors

Qualities of the young people	Family characteristics	Social support outside the family
• Sense of self-esteem and confidence • High aspirations • Even temperament (especially a sense of humour) • Empathy • Sense of self-efficacy • Problem-solving skills • Above average IQ • Good school performance • Hobbies • Social competence	• Stable and supportive family environment • Consistent discipline • Warm relationship with parent • Parents show interest in young person • Established routines in the home	• Adult mentor for young person outside immediate family • Extra adult help for caretaker of the family • Support for young person from friends • Support for young person from mentor at school • Support for family from church • Support for family from workplace

Scotland demonstrated a number of age and gender related differences in desistance. For younger research participants (aged 14–15 years) desistance was associated with the real or potential consequences of offending and with growing recognition that offending was pointless or wrong. Young people in the middle age group (18–19 years) related their changing behaviour to increasing maturity, the transition to adulthood and related events such as securing a job or a place at college, forming a stable relationship or leaving home. For the older participants (22–25 years), stopping offending was linked to the assumption of family responsibilities or to a conscious lifestyle change. In general, young women tended to attribute their decision to desist to the assumption of parental responsibilities, whereas the young men focused on personal choice and agency.

Graham and Bowling's (1995) research found similar gender differences. Whereas the young women in their study tended to stop offending quite abruptly as they left home, formed partnerships and had children, the process for young men was much more gradual and intermittent. This led Graham and Bowling to speculate that life transitions 'only provide opportunities for change to occur; its realisation is mediated by individual contingencies. Males may be less inclined to grasp, or be able to take advantage of such opportunities, as females' (1995: 65). This highlights not only the importance of objective changes in a young person's life, but their subjective assessment of the value or significance of those changes (see also Maruna, 2001).

The role of supervision in supporting the decision to desist from crime was addressed by Sue Rex (1999) in her study of probationers. Rex found that offenders who attributed changes in their behaviour to probation supervision described it as active and participatory. Probationers' commitment to desist appeared to be generated by the personal and professional commitment shown by their probation officers, whose reasonableness, fairness, and encouragement seemed to engender a sense of personal loyalty and accountability. Probationers interpreted advice about their behaviours and underlying problems as evidence of concern for them *as people*, and 'were motivated by what they saw as a display of interest in their well-being' (Rex, 1999: 375). Such encouragement seemed especially important for younger probationers involved in recidivist offending, who were more willing to receive critical advice than probation officers were to give it.

Put together, these findings suggest that work with young people who offend must be grounded in an understanding of the wider social contexts both of their offending and of their individual processes of and strategies for desistance. It is vitally important to young people that they are treated as 'ordinary human beings', not just as 'clients' (de Winter and Noom, 2003), and as whole people rather than as instances of some 'problem' or 'disorder' (Hill, 1999). As we shall see in the section that follows, one of the most effective ways in which workers can have an impact on desistance is by building and encouraging motivation (Farrall, 2002). However, unless such work is based on a demonstrated understanding of young people themselves and of their situation, it may miss its mark.

Effective approaches

It is now widely assumed that individual casework as the dominant method for working with offenders came off badly in meta-analytical reviews of 'what works' (see Chapter 21). Criticism focused on 'unstructured' or 'overly didactic' methods of traditional one-to-one work in favour of 'active, participatory approaches' (Chapman and Hough, 1998). However, the principles derived from such reviews of the available research themselves at least imply the importance of relationships and by no means rule out individual work (Burnett, 2003). For example, the principle of 'responsivity' suggests that effective interventions take account of and respond to offenders' particular learning styles. Moreover, the principle of 'multi-modality' suggests that effective interventions address a range of problems and employ a range of approaches. By implication, the relationship between the young person and their 'case manager' assumes even more significance (Holt, 2000).

Important lessons can thus be drawn from a brief exploration of approaches to individual interventions that emphasise the importance of the young person-worker relationship. Here, we focus on two such approaches: 'motivational interviewing' and 'pro-social modelling'.

Motivational interviewing

Desistance studies highlight the significance of motivation. Depending upon which stage the young person becomes involved with services, they may not be ready, willing or able to desist. In order to target interventions appropriately, and thereby avoid setting young people up to fail, workers need to assess, explore and develop readiness for change.

One way in which workers can attempt to engage young people in this process is by using 'motivational interviewing' (MI). This technique has been widely studied as a method of substance misuse treatment, but has also been found to have a beneficial effect on the attitudes of offenders (Harper and Hardy, 2000). Miller and Rollnick (2002) define motivational interviewing as a client-centred approach that strategically directs clients to examine, explore, and resolve the ambivalence they have about their behaviour. It works on the assumption that ambivalence is a normal part of the decision making process and that people have implicit attachments to the behaviours they engage in. In order to assist clients to change, therefore, workers need to utilise a range of strategies to help resolve ambivalence and override attachment.

The main objective of MI is to promote intrinsic motivation, that is, motivation that comes from within the person rather than from outside (e.g. from YOT staff or court mandates). Whilst extrinsic motivation is initially important in getting the client through the door, it is up to workers to help the individual shift perspective so that they recognise *for themselves* the need to make changes and then commit to act on this recognition. The worker's style of practice is central to this process.

Key factors in successful styles of practice include:

The ability to express empathy

One of the characteristics clients value is the ability to convey empathy (Barry, 2000; Rex, 1999). Young people respect workers who show real interest in them, listen to what they have to say, demonstrate a genuine willingness to understand their point of view, and who are non-judgemental (Bell, 2002; Hill, 1999). This does not necessarily mean approving of or colluding with an individual's perspective or actions; it is about accepting the person, not the behaviour (Williams, 1995).

The ability to develop discrepancy

Developing discrepancy involves the worker helping the young person to develop an awareness of the conflict between their present and desired behaviour, through 'evocative' questioning and the use of feedback. Workers reflect any conflict they hear back in their own words. The aim is to get the young person to articulate the need to change themself.

The ability to avoid arguments

Counselling which is confrontational tends to increase resistance (marked by the client arguing, changing the subject, interrupting, and denying), while counselling that is supportive decreases it.

The ability to roll with resistance

Resistance is regarded as a normal part of the change process and as something that should be worked *with*, rather than against. Workers reframe resistance with empathy, focusing on getting clients 'unstuck' by identifying and exploring sources of ambivalence.

Supporting self-efficacy

Self-efficacy relates to clients' belief in their own ability to carry out and succeed in a particular task. Research shows that people who are optimistic about their ability to desist from offending have greatest success in doing so (Burnett, 2000). Workers have a responsibility, therefore, to emphasise personal accountability, offer role models of effective change, and convey belief in the young person's ability to change.

To date, the available evidence for the effectiveness of MI is more convincing in the field of substance misuse than in work with young people who offend.

Nonetheless, Harper and Hardy (2000) found MI techniques had a beneficial effect on attitudes of offenders, especially those with substance misuse problems. They reported statistically significant improvements in the attitudinal scales amongst offenders whose supervisors had been trained in MI compared to those who were not. Though this study did not include reconviction data, other studies have demonstrated some relationship between such changes in attitude and reductions in reconviction (Raynor, 1998).

Promoting pro-social behaviour

Perhaps the best-known model of intervention focused on the supervisory relationship is Trotter's (1999) pro-social modelling. Although it would be possible to conceive of pro-social modelling as a form of individualised programme, it is perhaps better described as a style of or approach to practice. Its central principles include:

Role clarification

In work with young people who offend, where the roles and relationships are complex and inclined to become confused, effective workers need skills in clarifying their role. They should have frequent and open discussions about the purpose of the intervention, the dual role of the worker in terms of control and welfare, the client's expectations, the use of authority, negotiable and non-negotiable aspects of the intervention, and the limits of confidentiality.

Problem-solving

Effective workers make use of collaborative problem-solving processes. The great advantage of such an approach is that it allows each of the parties an opportunity to identify issues of concern and exert some control over what is eventually decided. Research suggests that there is only a partial overlap between the ideas of young people and social workers, and between probation officers and probationers, about what problems warrant intervention (Farrall, 2002). Consequently, an exclusive focus on 'the problem' as defined by workers may divert attention from young people's concerns and hinder their engagement with the change process (Hill, 1999). In helping young people to solve problems, effective workers help their clients to exert some control over, and make choices about, their own lives. This is particularly important for young people who often experience control as something imposed upon them from outside (Pitts, 1999).

Modelling and reinforcement

Collaborative problem-solving needs to be balanced by a process of 'modelling'. This involves identifying, rewarding and modelling comments or actions to be encouraged and the identification, discouragement and challenging of those to be changed. Examples of pro-social comments include remarks by a violent offender that recognise the harm that has been done to the victim. Examples of pro-social behaviour might include turning up for appointments, completing tasks between appointments or acting and reacting differently towards others.

There is evidence from work with various types of involuntary clients that workers who *model* appropriate behaviours are more likely to be effective (Andrews et al., 1979; Trotter, 1999). This means being a stable presence in the young person's life and someone they can rely on; keeping promises, being available, being punctual (Bell, 2002; Hill, 1999).

Relationship skills

Relationship skills are essential to achieving positive outcomes and these involve the worker being open and honest, empathetic, able to challenge rationalisations, non-blaming, optimistic, able to articulate the client's and family members' feelings and problems, using appropriate self-disclosure and humour (HMSO, 1995; Shulman, 1991; Trotter, 1999).

Trotter's (1996) empirical research tested the hypotheses that clients of probation officers who made use of these principles would be more likely to experience reductions in their problems and would be less likely to offend. Clients supervised by probation officers trained in the approach were significantly more likely to report reductions on their problems and re-offence rates were also significantly lower than those in a control group. The model was *most* effective with young, high-risk, violent and drug using offenders.

Conclusion

Contemporary developments in working with young people who offend can be criticised for an undue emphasis on the characteristics of effective *programmes*, and neglecting the evidence about the importance of effective *relationships*. A brief review of the evidence around resilience and desistance suggests that relationships are implicated in the problems that young people experience but that they are also integral to processes of change.

In many respects, these arguments may seem obvious, particularly to experienced practitioners. That they now seem to require re-stating, perhaps merely underlines the extent to which programme talk has become dominant in discourses around evidence-based practice. Excavating the reasons for this dominance is beyond the scope of this chapter, but a case could certainly be made that the emphases on programmes rather than processes, on packages rather than people, on tools rather than relationships, on external and academic as opposed to professional expertise, and on (supposedly) technical as opposed to ideological or moral questions, sit all too comfortably with the requirements of managerial control, modernisation and penal populism (McNeill, 2001; Robinson, 2001).

Young people have complex problems which require complex responses rooted in supportive relationships characterised by partnership, participation, respect, loyalty and trust. Developing such qualities with young people who offend, many of whom have been damaged by previous relationships, requires considerable investment of professional time and skill. The complexities and uncertainties of this more nuanced approach to understanding and supporting change that the evidence requires may seem unattractive when set beside the latest alluring 'kite-marked' programme, but, the future development of effective practice may depend more on internal investment in educating, developing and supporting youth justice staff (and the young people with whom they work) than on external investment in experts, tools and programmes.

Further reading

Hill, M. (1999) What's the Problem? Who Can Help? *Journal of Social Work Practice.* 13: 2, 135–45

McNeill, F. and Batchelor, S. (2004) *Persistent Offending by Young People.* London: National Association of Probation Officers

Miller, W. R. and Rollnick, S. (Eds.) (2002) *Motivational Interviewing* 2nd edn. New York: Guilford Press

Trotter, C. (1999) *Working With Involuntary Clients.* London: Sage

27

Group Work with Young People who Offend

Tim Chapman

Key points

1. Group work mobilises the members' capacity for mutual aid or support.

2. Group work offers participants opportunities for support, learning, helping others and problem-solving.

3. Effective group work requires:
   - members and workers to share a common purpose;
   - a planned process or set of tasks designed to achieve the purpose;
   - the cultivation of relationships between members which facilitate progress towards the achievement of that purpose;
   - effective facilitation and leadership.

4. Group work has been found to enhance participants' personal strengths and enable them to gain access to resources.

5. Group work can be used as a central component of multi-method approaches to work with young people who offend.

Groups and young people who offend

Young people spend much of their time in and out of school in groups, and when they have nothing better to do they also like to hang out in groups. Having friends, being popular, belonging, loyalty, territory and common values and beliefs are important aspects of growing up and developing an adult identity. Peer groups are a form of refuge and resistance against the perceived lack of understanding and interference of the adult world. However, for others the peer group can be a problem, because of scapegoating, bullying or rejection.

Many young people also get into trouble in groups and membership of certain types of groups, like gangs, is a significant risk factor in serious offending. Young people are more likely to take risks in groups as a way of gaining acceptance or status or of demonstrating loyalty or courage. Moreover, peer groups based upon community or ethnicity can clash violently.

The basics

What is group work?

Group work, at its simplest involves a group of people working purposefully together. In group work, the work is done not only in a group but also by the group. The group is not just a collection of individuals working under the direction of a worker or leader in the same space.

Why do group work?

At their best, groups bring people with common problems, needs or issues together and offer them the opportunity to pool their intelligence, creativity and compassion and in doing so become more effective at problem-solving than the sum of their parts.

Yalom (1995) identifies the following therapeutic factors in group work:

- A sense of not being the only one with the problem.
- Being able to talk openly about issues that are usually repressed.

- Learning through exchange of information, discussion and imitation.
- The installation of hope.
- The opportunity to help others.
- The opportunity to confront basic issues of life.

Shulman (1979) adds to this list of potential benefits: problem-solving, rehearsal, and 'strength in numbers'. Thus group work offers participants an opportunity for support, for hope, for learning, for helping others and for solving problems.

What kinds of groups are there?

Groups can take many forms. 'Formed groups' are created by professionals who wish to work with young people who share common problems, needs or issues. However, it can also be very effective to work with so-called 'natural' peer groups. Recognising the power of peer pressure, the worker may attempt to mobilise it to influence the attitudes or behaviour of a gang or group of young people who go around together. Group members need not all have problems or needs. Some groups will include young people with needs and young people who are mentors or peer educators. PHAB groups would be an example of young people with different capabilities working together.

In what circumstances is group work appropriate?

It is frequently assumed that effective practice with young people who offend requires group work. This is not the case. Meta-analyses of 'what works' have found that effective interventions are characterised by a 'multi-modal' approach. This implies a legitimate role for individual work, family work and other forms of intervention. Programmes for young people who offend limit their effectiveness by sticking to a single approach.

Indeed, research into the effectiveness of group work vis-a-vis individual work is generally inconclusive, suggesting that one approach is no more or less effective than the other (McRoberts et al., 1998).

It is more helpful to pose a more concrete question – when is it likely to be more effective to employ group work? This means considering:

- Which young people?
- With which needs?
- To achieve what objectives?
- Through which methods?

It would be ineffective to insist that all young people should do group work merely because they are subject to statutory supervision. The research would suggest that it is detrimental to mix 'low risk' young people with young people who are at a high risk of re-offending. Similarly young people object to being in groups which address issues, such as drug use, which they do not connect with their offending. Young people are unlikely to be highly motivated to participate in a group whose objective is to talk about personal problems in front of peers. A very structured learning programme is likely to put off young people who hate school.

Generally, group work can be more effective in raising awareness of problems due to the 'all in the same boat' perception and the opportunity to share different experiences and perspectives. It also allows for collective problem-solving and the rehearsal of skills and strategies. One-to-one work is usually more appropriate for personal disclosure and working through complex personal problems. There may also be more time in individual work to apply the awareness and skills learnt in groups to real life situations.

Group work needs facilitation and leadership

Effective group work requires:

1. A common purpose.
2. A process or set of tasks designed to achieve the purpose.
3. Relationships between members which facilitate progress towards the achievement of that purpose.
4. Effective facilitation.

The potential for mutual aid exists in most groups. But it does not happen spontaneously or by chance. There are many obstacles to the process caused by past negative experiences of destructive groups, of promises of support which were not kept, and of humiliating experiences of learning, and the stereotypes people have of each other. Most groups need a group worker to create the conditions for support and learning to happen.

The group work method

Purpose

The purpose of the group is a product of negotiation between the goals of the individuals within it and the goals of the agency responsible for running it. While the overall aim of agencies working with young people who offend may be to prevent offending, different groups can have more specific objectives such as drug education, anger management or resisting peer pressure.

The early phases of the group will focus on clarification of purpose. The effectiveness of group work is undermined if purposes are unclear. Young people should be involved in group work on the basis of an understanding of each individual's needs and goals, a clear explanation of the purpose and process of the programme and clear expectations of roles, rules and performance.

Process

One way of looking at group process, or development, is in terms of Maslow's hierarchy of needs. For young people who offend the primary need is for safety and security. They are usually aware of their capacity to hurt each other and may have experienced authority's power to humiliate and oppress them. Only when they feel safe will they seek to meet their need for belonging and acceptance. Once accepting relationships have been negotiated, the group is more likely to choose to work towards its objectives.

Tuckman (1965) has described the process of group development as moving through the stages of:

- forming
- storming
- norming *and*
- performing

Forming involves enrolling the members into the group and clarifying purposes, roles and rules. One can expect a 'honeymoon period' during which individuals are checking each other out, trying to work out what the real rules are, where authority really lies and what threats to their security may emerge. This may lull the inexperienced worker into a false sense of confidence that does not prepare them for the next stage, *storming*.

Storming is likely to break out in the early phase of group work when the first major issue, which usually concerns authority and control and the worker's ability to set limits, comes up. This will require the worker to re-state the boundaries or ground rules they have established. The ground rules of the group are designed to protect the safety of each member and the integrity of the group. They should obviously have been clearly communicated and explained at the outset, but however effectively this is done the group will almost certainly test boundaries and the worker's ability to enforce them. It may appear that young people want to subvert the rules of the programme. However, it is more likely that they are anxious that the rules and the worker might not be able to offer them sufficient protection. When a challenge to the worker's authority occurs, they should confront it, reminding the group of the expectations upon them and explaining how the rules are intended to maintain everyone's safety and to support the work. Enforcement should be consistent and fair and only result in exclusion as a last resort.

Norming. Once issues of authority have been resolved, and this is not to suggest that they may not re-emerge, questions of belonging and being valued emerge in the form of norming. The role of the worker at this stage is to enable the members to work out how they will work together. This can be achieved through observing how the group is behaving, communicating, relating, or working together and reflecting back these observations to participants. The reflections should provide information which the group can use and not judgements against which the group is inclined to defend itself. The next section goes into more detail on the quality of relationships necessary for effective group work.

Performing. Now the group can start performing, which means progressing towards the achievement of the group's purpose and the goals of each individual. The role of the worker at this stage is to keep the group's focus on purpose and task, breaking this down into manageable steps, enabling reflection upon and clarification of issues, increasing members capacity and confidence, and providing positive feedback.

Communication

A major function of the worker is to facilitate constructive interaction among members of the group. This can entail participation in exercises and activities such as art, drama or outdoor activities. However, all group processes involve verbal communication. The process of effective group conversation requires different contributions from different members. Kantor and Lehr (1975), writing about family work, note that a conversation requires a *mover*, someone who initiates an issue or focus for the conversation. A *mover* needs a follower who supports and possibly develops what the mover has said. Unless someone challenges this perspective or opinion the conversation may not fully develop and generate new information or ideas. Thus, a conversation also needs an *opposer*. Finally, there should be a *bystander* who often does not say much but can provide observations rather than taking a stand on the issue. In group work it is important that each of these roles is recognised and that the less vociferous or forceful players are supported to participate in group discussion.

The *mover* need not be the group worker. It is easy for the group worker to make the mistake of perceiving any initiative that is not strictly in the session plan as irrelevant, or subversive, and consequently to repress the *mover*. Similarly one might feel irritated by an *opposer* and try to silence, or defeat, them. Participants who are quiet may be seen as lazy, bored, or lacking in confidence. The group worker may urge the *bystander* to speak more or not to speak at all. The skilful worker will bring such a person in at the appropriate times and with the appropriate questions.

Ending

The final stage of group work is the ending, or a transition into a new phase of work. The worker should be preparing the group well in advance for this. By now the group will have settled into a pattern of work. Any particularly disruptive members will have given up their resistance, dropped out or have been excluded. However, the group will have become used to the routines, relationships and structures of its operation and may be reluctant to finish. Workers should expect a regression to 'acting-out' behaviour, which may be symptomatic of anxiety at the ending or a demonstration that the progress made has been reversed and so the group should continue. This should be dealt with sensitively but firmly. Young people should be leaving a group with a viable exit plan. This might involve further work on other needs, a plan to maintain change, or a relapse prevention strategy.

The role of the worker

Schwartz (1961) argues that the group worker has 'two clients', the individual and the group. The function of the worker is to mediate the engagement between these two clients.

Figure 27.1:

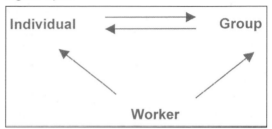

This dual focus is what makes group work so challenging. It is clear that the worker is an important part of the group process and its dynamics but is not the same as the other members. These differences are important to the effectiveness of group work. They are also areas of potential confusion and conflict over role and authority:

- The worker has a responsibility to control the process so as to maintain safety and to facilitate progress towards goals.
- The worker is different in that the group does not serve the worker's needs.
- The worker makes demands of the members to work towards goals even when it is difficult or uncomfortable.
- The worker does not have all the answers or solutions; the group has to take responsibility to work at these.

While being aware of these issues and dealing with them when necessary, the worker also pays attention to the relationships between group members and their patterns of communication. The group worker must also model values and behaviours which are considered critical to both the purpose of the group and how members should relate to each other if they are to achieve their purpose.

> ## Some characteristics of effective group workers
>
> - self awareness
> - empathy
> - creativity
> - commitment
> - responsibility
> - intensity of purpose and focus
> - honesty
> - respect
> - belief in change

The structure of relationships within groups can be determined by both external and internal conditions. External factors include the agency's purpose for the group, its resources, policies and staff knowledge, skill and style. Internal conditions include relationships between members, their culture and personalities. Groups can have informal leaders who structure the interaction between members in such a way as to help or hinder the performance of the group.

Some types of group work with young people who offend

There are a broad range of interventions which can be undertaken in a group setting with young people who offend. The following gives a brief outline of some of the most common approaches.

Social learning

The purpose of a social learning is to increase understanding of the consequences of a problematic behaviour and/or to learn skills. It is often associated with the 'what works' approach to effective practice and tends to link offending behaviour with interpersonal and cognitive deficits. Sessions are usually highly structured and are frequently based on a programme manual. Social learning is very task-oriented, based on exercises and role plays and, as a consequence, places less emphasis on group process and the development of relationships. The group worker accordingly adopts the role of trainer.

Forum theatre

Forum theatre is a drama-based approach to group work which aims to examine issues, explore moral dilemmas or choices, and to generate alternative strategies. Interventions of this sort often conceptualise offending in terms of the 'masks' or the 'front' used by young people to cover their real thoughts and feelings.

Forum theatre enables the group to àct out a real situation leading to an offence. The scenario can then be replayed to explore other choices and their consequences. From a young person's point of view a drama-based approach has the advantage that personal issues can be addressed in role so that individuals do not feel over-exposed and subject to personal judgements.

Once the initial anxiety about the performance is overcome, it can also be good fun.

On the other hand some young people may resist acting, associating it with embarrassment or childish games. At the same time, many practitioners do not feel sufficiently competent or confident to use this method even after training.

Dialogue

The purpose of this approach is to generate new solutions to recurring problems. Rather than skilfully leading the group towards a set objective, the facilitator enables participants to suspend their assumptions and listen with renewed respect to each other. Group members are treated as colleagues on a common quest. This allows deeper questions to be explored and new insights and solutions to emerge through the dialogue.

Solution-focused group work

The aim of solution-focused work is to release group members' own resources and strengths to solve their problems or to provide support to each other in dealing with the oppressive pressures of the outside world. The principles underpinning such an approach include an emphasis on change and possibilities, creating goals and preferred futures, building on strengths, skills and resources, looking for what's working, being respectfully curious, creating co-operation and collaboration, and using humour and creativity.

Peer education

Peer education is a form of group work facilitated by young people who have similar backgrounds to the members of the group. The peer educators may have experienced similar problems to the group and may thus be in a better position to engage young people more effectively than older professionals.

Self-help

The first formal self-help group was probably Alcoholic Anonymous. Self-help groups bring together people with common problems or experiences of stigmatisation or oppression to provide each other support and advice. They are based upon the assumption that those experiencing problems have the knowledge and strengths to solve them. They require minimal facilitation by professionals. Examples of this type of group are more common among young people who have been looked after or are recovering from mental illness. Young people whose offending is linked to the experience of oppression, such as young women or young black people, could benefit from the support of their peers in such a group.

Social action groups

The facilitators of social action groups work to enable a group of disadvantaged or oppressed young people to understand the circumstances which gave rise to their problems and to take collective action to change or improve these circumstances (Mullender and Ward, 1991). This approach has been used with young people in Northern Ireland, who have been involved in car crime, to make statements about paramilitary punishments (Chapman, 1995).

Irrespective of the particular model employed, individual group sessions require a structure which ensures that participants understand the purpose of the activity, identifies the problem to be addressed, provides for learning opportunities and allows for reflection on what has been learned and how it might be applied outside of the group. In general, it is helpful to think of a typical session as including the following elements:

- Clarification of the objectives for the particular session and connecting those to the group's overall purpose.
- Providing a context for the session by connecting it with any previous work undertaken by group.
- 'Icebreaker' exercises.
- Developing a concrete example of the problem or issue to be addressed.
- Enabling the group to reflect upon the issue.
- Developing capacity to deal with the issue more effectively and generate alternative responses.
- Considering the application of learning to real life situations.
- Reviewing what has been achieved in relation to the objectives for the sessions.

Encountering, and dealing with, difficulties

Working with young people who offend can present particular challenges, given that those subject to interventions within the youth justice system frequently display demanding behaviour and that participation in any programme is generally involuntary. Within a group work setting, problems can take a wide variety of forms but it is possible to outline some of those which most commonly arise.

Rates of attrition for group work programmes can be high and in some circumstances can undermine the viability of the group. Given that attendance for young people in trouble is often a requirement of a court order, the issue of motivation is key. Workers need to be able to convince participants of the relevance of the group to their needs in the early stages, in order to turn what will, in all probability, be attendance based on *extrinsic* motivation into cooperation with the programme which is reinforced by *intrinsic* motivation; where the young person attends because they recognise the value of – and perhaps even enjoys – the intervention.

In terms of the operation of the group itself, certain forms of behaviour can appear, from the workers' point of view, to represent obstacles to the smooth running of the process. Young people might for instance, complain that the group is irrelevant, boring or a waste of time or contest the ground rules. Alternatively, young people may make unrealistic demands of the group, which has the potential to reinforce a perception that change is impossible or that the service provider is unable to address the needs of the group members.

Similar problems can be experienced where individual participants persist in creating distractions from the task, by cracking jokes, wanting to go to the toilet or attempting to annoy other participants. Dominant group members can monopolise sessions, making it difficult for learning to take place. Alternatively, group members might engage in withdrawal or non-participation which is sometimes a mechanism for passive resistance in circumstances, or in relation to issues, which young people experience as threatening. These two problems are frequently related since the dominance of one or more young people is likely to be matched by the withdrawal of others.

More obviously, aggression towards the worker, sometimes motivated by challenges to authority, or towards another group member, frequently associated with scapegoating, can interfere with the effective functioning of the group. In developing a repertoire to deal with such behaviour, it can be helpful for staff to consider that 'acting out' in this way may be a mechanism for gaining peer approval or for demonstrating loyalty to a value base which rejects authority. It might also be intended to provoke an oppressive reaction from the worker and so confirm their attitudes towards authority. In these circumstances, group workers' responses should avoid overreaction.

Indeed, many of the difficulties in group work tend to arise from the group worker's perception of group members' resistance. Resistance is typically caused by feelings of being threatened. The worker can often make things worse by reacting aggressively and confirming the threat.

Workers can also make matters worse by seeing resistance as arising in the individual as a pathological symptom. Pathological explanations of resistance may also strengthen the group's antipathy to being judged negatively or 'psychoanalysed'.

More effective strategies for dealing with such difficulties are usually developed from a standpoint of understanding resistance through a framework of context and relationships. Firstly, it is important to consider *from the individual's point of view* whether the group's goals, rules, methods and relationships have been effectively clarified and implemented.

Secondly, workers will need to appreciate what the positive intention could be behind this behaviour, what it may be saying about the group dynamics and what group/individual strength it reveals. Problems may arise from blocks in communication, from confusion over purpose or meaning, or from issues of authority or control.

Thirdly, responses to any identified positive intention should be framed in a way that encourages or enables positive participation. This may be to clarify again an objective, method, rule or relationship. Alternatively, it may require asking the individual what is causing the obstacle to active participation and what would need to be done to get over it.

A number of general principles inform effective responses to problematic behaviour within groups. Group leaders should:

- Try to understand before making judgements.
- Avoid taking sides – focus on the problem in relation to group progress.
- Affirm strengths and any sign of motivation.
- Ensure that the group feels safe, respected and supported.
- Move at a pace appropriate to each group member.
- Ensure that negative behaviour is not allowed to attract more attention than positive behaviour.
- Regularly review progress with the group in relation to objectives and purpose.
- Use supervision to explore their own feelings and perceptions, and to develop a skills base which contains a repertoire of responses.

Conclusion

Group work is not easy. It is not necessarily a more efficient use of staff time since effective work requires preparation and debriefing, and sometimes recovery! But it can be effective in developing positive working relationships with young people, identifying the characteristics and strengths of individuals and speeding up the learning or problem-solving process. Like one-to-one work, to be effective it must be done skilfully. In group work the worker is making hundreds of critical decisions very quickly. Training helps. But there is no substitute for experience and practice. You will make mistakes. But that's how you will learn. As the Native American saying goes:

> *Good judgement is based upon experience; experience is based upon bad judgement!*

Further reading

Sharry, J. (2001) *Solution-focused Groupwork*. Sage: London

Shulman, L. (1979) *The Skills of Helping Individuals and Groups*. Illinois: Peacock

Restorative Justice and Youth Justice

Guy Masters

Key points

1. Having first emerged in Canada in the mid-1970s, interest in and the use of restorative justice (RJ) has steadily grown. In England and Wales, the development of RJ has been accelerated by the mainstreaming of restorative processes as part of the youth justice reforms. At least four different models of restorative practice are now widely used internationally; victim-offender mediation, family group conferencing, restorative conferencing and community panels.

2. Central to RJ is the belief that victims, offenders, and those close to them have the right to be meaningfully involved in the decisions that are made following an offence or offences.

3. There is a well established evidence base supporting restorative practice. There is no question of whether RJ 'works' or not, but the question is how to make it work on a local level. Evaluations have shown that the majority of victims appreciate taking part, and that when delivered well, restorative processes can reduce re-offending rates.

4. Good restorative practice within the youth justice system is the provision of a flexible model in which practice is chosen from several options. These decisions should be guided by the wishes of victims, and the capabilities/needs of the young people concerned.

5. A large number of victims will participate when projects have staff committed to working with victims, adequate resources, and the support of local agencies.

Introduction

At the time of writing, there is considerable interest in restorative justice (RJ) in England and Wales. This follows the publication of the government's consultation document on developing RJ within the adult criminal justice system (Home Office, 2003g), which seeks to build on the considerable investment in restorative practice within the youth justice system since 1998 (Liebmann and Masters, 2000). These current developments represent something of a *renewal* of interest in RJ in England and Wales, as there was substantial experimentation in the 1980s (Marshall and Merry, 1990), but they are also taking place at a time of significant international growth in the RJ field (JUSTICE, 2000). This chapter covers three key areas. Firstly, it places this renewal of interest in context by detailing how the main restorative practice models have developed in various countries. Secondly, it considers how RJ has been implemented recently within the new youth justice system in England and Wales (though little attention will be paid to referral orders as these are covered in detail in Chapter 16). Finally, it discusses some current issues relating to the implementation of restorative practice within the new youth justice system.

Models of restorative justice

Model 1: victim-offender mediation

The first practice model to develop is now commonly referred to as 'victim-offender mediation' or 'victim-offender dialogue', though it was originally described as 'victim-offender reconciliation'. The term 'reconciliation' reflects the motives of the Canadian Mennonites responsible for its initial development; they were seeking to introduce a Christian response to offending into the criminal justice system (Peachey, 1989). Successful, but ad hoc, attempts to bring offenders and victims together to discuss offences and reach agreement on how amends could be made by the offenders (usually under a probation order) led to a formal project beginning in 1975.

This first project offered victims and offenders the opportunity to communicate through mediators, who were usually trained volunteers or probation officers. This communication could be done 'indirectly' or at a 'face-to-face' meeting. The project quickly demonstrated the feasibility of having victims and offenders communicate about an offence in a respectful manner, and that many offenders were willing to make amends for the harm they had caused (financially or through material work). However, while a key aim of the project was to achieve reconciliation between victims and offenders, evaluation (Coates and Gehm, 1989) established that this was only important to a minority of victims. Rather, victims valued the opportunity to be listened to, to ask questions, to explain how they had been affected, to ask for reparation, to see that the offender was remorseful and that the offender got some help. Offenders, on the other hand, valued being listened to by their victims, and being able to negotiate how costs could be reimbursed.

Very few of those participating in the process were dissatisfied with their experience, though many found it difficult. The vast majority of victims who took part said that they would enter mediation again if they were revictimised (Coates and Gehm, 1989).

As information about the project spread, similar initiatives began in the United States in the late 1970s and in various European countries in the early 1980s (in particular Austria, Germany and England). The results from the English projects, as with similar experiments in Europe and North America, were encouraging (Marshall and Merry, 1990; Umbreit and Roberts, 1996). For some victims, the impact can be quite profound; for example fear of further victimisation can be halved (Umbreit and Roberts, 1996), and desires for revenge also greatly diminished (Strang, 2000). For a significant minority, mediation appears to provide an ending to a bad episode in their life, sometimes achieving very powerful outcomes, such as victims being able to sleep again or being confident to leave their home.

Common mediation practice is that mediators contact the victim both to explore the impact of the offence on them and to ask whether they have questions about or for the offender. Some victims value the opportunity to meet the offender, perhaps for the first time in some cases, or to see the offender in a different context. However, for other victims, just meeting with the mediator initially (and not the offender) can also be beneficial, valuing the attention and the opportunity to speak their mind, and have some questions answered.

For offenders, contact with mediators provides an opportunity for them to actively take responsibility for their actions, by offering explanations to questions, showing some remorse, and the possibility to make amends in some way. Following preparatory work with all parties, meetings are conducted under agreed ground rules, with both parties receiving 'uninterrupted time' to express their views before a general discussion takes place. Unless required to intervene to preserve the ground rules, mediators attempt to remain silent during any meetings, which are considered to belong to the participants rather than the professionals (see Quill and Wynne, 1993).

Systematic attempts to use mediation in youth justice in England began in the early 1980s predominantly as part of 'caution plus' programmes (see Chapter 10). From 1985–1987, the Home Office funded four pilot victim-offender mediation projects to work at different stages of the criminal justice system (diversion from prosecution and diversion from custody) with both adults and young offenders. The results from these projects were broadly encouraging (Marshall and Merry, 1990), though were not without some justified criticisms. Davis (1992) argued that some arrangements effectively used victims to benefit offenders, offering mediation in cases where the 'system' wished to divert the offender from prosecution or to reduce their sentence, rather than because mediation had been assessed as likely to be beneficial. Following these criticisms, practice generally changed to offer mediation as a *voluntary* process following all case disposal decisions. This meant that victims could be confident that offenders were genuine in motivation, not benefiting in any way through participation.

Though government support for mediation projects ended in 1987, various projects continued, or came and went, until the recent investment made by the Youth Justice Board (YJB) (see Liebmann and Masters, 2000 for a full review of the development of mediation across the UK).

Model 2: family group conferencing

While mediation emerged through the work of local practitioners wishing to develop new practice, family group conferencing was introduced in New Zealand through legislation (the Children, Young Person, and their Families Act 1989), following some piloting. This legislation created a diversion-based youth justice system in which only those young people whose offending was the most serious or persistent were to be prosecuted, with custody becoming a very last resort (Maxwell and Morris, 1993).

New Zealand remains the most ambitious example of how restorative practice can be used to completely reform a system. In practice 80% of young people who offend in New Zealand are dealt with through a police caution which cannot be cited in court. Unless the offending is of a serious nature, young people will receive multiple cautions. However, over half (58%) of young people diverted in this way, are still involved in some form of 'active penalty', such as mediation with the victim, community work, or paying compensation (Maxwell and Morris, 1996). Of the 20% that are not dealt with informally, a further 10% are still not prosecuted, but referred for a *diversionary* family group conference (FGC). For the 10% that are prosecuted, once they have admitted guilt, or guilt has been found, then the court cannot pass sentence until an FGC has taken place. The only exceptions to this are for manslaughter and murder charges.

An FGC is convened by an independent coordinator. The young person attends accompanied by their immediate and extended family network, plus other 'supporters', such as friends and other adults that are significant to them. Any victims of their offences will also be invited to attend, with supporters if they desire. Also attending will be professionals who can advise the FGC about programmes available to help the young person. At the FGC, discussions take place about the offence, with victims invited to speak as in mediation. However, a wider discussion then takes place about the likely causes of the offending, and other issues of concern. The FGC will consider various options for addressing these concerns, as well as how the young person might make amends for the offence(s). A key aspect of FGCs is that decision making power largely rests with the young person, their family, and the victims (including recommendations of custody). The professional workers are there as advisers, not decision makers. Following the discussions between the victim and the offender, and the information given by professionals, the young person and their supporters are then left alone, for as long as they need ('Private Planning Time') to produce a plan that should address all concerns. When the plan is ready the full FGC reconvenes to discuss and finalise the plan.

In FGCs used to divert young people from court, providing that the plan is acceptable to the police, then the young person will not be prosecuted. For FGCs held following conviction, the FGC plan is then considered at court and judges can only disregard the plan if they believe it will leave the community at risk from the young person. In New Zealand, FGC plans are created at 95% of conferences, which are unchanged by courts in 80% of cases. Nationally, victims attend 50% of conferences, with 60% of those who attended saying that they benefited from participation (Maxwell and Morris, 1993). The overriding message from New Zealand is that the young people and families in the most challenging of circumstances do produce plans that impress the court when given the opportunity. Longitudinal research in New Zealand has demonstrated that FGCs reduce re-offending where practice is to a high standard (Maxwell and Morris, 1998), and in some areas of New Zealand re-offending has been reducing by a third annually (JUSTICE, 2000). Compared to mediation there have only been a small number of attempts to use youth justice FGCs in England (Liebmann and Masters, 2000; see Chapter 29). One project, the Essex Family Group Conferencing Service, which mimics New Zealand by only working with the 'top 20%' of young people who offend has been extensively evaluated and shown to significantly cut re-offending amongst this group (Essex County Council, 2002), while directly involving over 60% of victims (Masters, 2002a).

Model 3: restorative conferencing

Restorative conferencing (also known as diversionary conferencing) is well known in England and Wales due to the pioneering work of, and publicity stimulated by, Thames Valley Police,

Nottinghamshire Police, and Surrey Police. This model was first developed by police in New South Wales, Australia, but can be considered a development of victim-offender mediation *rather* than FGCs. In this model, the young person and their supporter are brought together with the victim and their supporters. Unlike in mediation, restorative conferences are 'scripted', with the facilitator (often a police officer) using standard set questions in a prescribed order. This script has been constructed to ensure that all present are enabled to explain their involvement in the incident, how they have been affected, and what they would like to see happen from the incident, including reparation agreements. The process is designed to bring about discussion of the emotions caused by the actions of the young person. Unlike in FGCs, there is no private planning time, and agreements do not generally involve other services becoming involved with the young person. As with mediation and FGCs, the satisfaction rates of participants are high (Masters, 2002b), and recent research in England suggests that this model can halve the likelihood of 're-sanction' within one year (Hoyle et al., 2002).

Model 4: community panel meetings

The fourth practice model to emerge in England and Wales is that of the community panel meeting which is a legislative requirement following the imposition of a referral order. This model has quickly become established as the most commonly used restorative process, used in around one third of all outcomes, and it is the only one required by statute. The referral order and its relation to RJ are treated separately in Chapter 16 of this volume.

Defining restorative practice

What makes these processes 'restorative' is that they seek to directly involve victims and offenders in opportunities to *communicate* with one another about what has happened, and to *reach their own decisions* about what action should follow. In mediation or restorative conferencing this may mean reaching an agreement about how the offender can compensate the victim or community in some way. In FGCs and panel meetings, agreements may also involve substantial plans

about services the offender will access, or what they are going to do differently in the future to avoid re-offending. Within RJ there is thus a very strong emphasis on victims having the right to be consulted with the *option* of direct involvement, and on offenders having an *obligation* to make amends for any harm done by their actions. In short, it is the nature of the process followed which defines practice as restorative or not, rather than the outcome.

This definition raises the interesting question of how restorative justice relates to the principle of proportionality. From a restorative justice perspective, two offenders who have committed very similar offences could easily end up with significantly different outcomes. This rests very uneasily with the principle of proportionality, that similar offences warrant similar outcomes (see Chapter 9). There is no easy solution to this dilemma. However, most jurisdictions that have sought to mainstream restorative practice require restorative processes not to agree any sanction disproportionate to what a court might pass in sentence. In England and Wales, community panel members are given guidance recommending different amounts of reparation based on the length of the referral order. My own experience of panels in practice is that when young people are asked how much reparation they think they should do, they usually suggest amounts higher, often substantially so, than the recommended amounts. New Zealand has perhaps the most rigorous 'proportionality' check in cases where an FGC has been convened following prosecution, as the sentencing court can amend whatever reparation was agreed at the FGC. However, it seems inevitable that proportionality will always remain a difficult issue to square with restorative justice.

Some implementation issues in the new youth justice system

The descriptions above will have hopefully made it clear that any restorative process can be used in very different ways. New Zealand uses FGCs both to divert offenders from prosecution and to significantly inform the sentences passed on the minority who are prosecuted. Alternatively, practice can be developed to *support* an existing youth justice framework, which is what has largely happened in England and Wales. The two major pieces of legislation associated with the reform of the youth justice system (the Crime and Disorder Act 1998 (CDA) and the Youth Justice and Criminal Evidence Act 1999 (YJCEA)) establish clear procedures for deciding whether a young person is to be diverted from court or prosecuted (see Chapter 12).

While the decision to divert a young person through a reprimand or a final warning remains that of the police, guidance (Home Office/Youth Justice Board 2002) greatly encourages the use of restorative justice as a means of 'effectively' delivering the warning or reprimand. This development draws significantly on the experience of Thames Valley Police and their partners in using restorative conferencing to support pre-court disposals. Though it did not explicitly legislate any restorative practice, the CDA established a presumption that 'reparation' should feature as a key component of community disposals such as the action plan order, supervision order, and obviously the reparation order. While many YOTs have established a variety of innovative community reparation projects, the involvement of victims in restorative encounters, *nationally*, remains low to date. Jim Dignan's (2002) comprehensive assessment of four pilot reparation areas found direct reparation was made to a victim in just 12% of eligible cases, with 9% resulting in mediation. The national figure for referral orders is similarly low (Newburn et al., 2002) and the national evaluation of YJB funded RJ projects pointed to, what it termed, an over-reliance on community reparation (Wilcox and Hoyle, 2004).

These low figures for victim involvement pose a difficult issue for the YJB who have clearly indicated their support for YOTs to develop restorative practice. The YJB had set a target for youth offending teams (YOTs) to use some form of restorative practice with 80% of YOT clients. Even if community reparation activities are considered to be restorative, then 80% remains a very difficult target for YOTs. Whether community reparation can be considered restorative is an issue worthy of more debate then can be provided here. Community reparation can be considered a restorative activity when, as above, it involves the young person in a process through which they can appreciate that some harm has been caused by their actions, and that they have a moral obligation to do something to rectify this. I would also advise

that the young person's views on what they should do are taken very seriously. This process may or may not involve victims. While some may argue that only processes that involve victims can be restorative, this would exclude any young person who has committed a victimless offence from inclusion. In my experience it is also a common occurrence for a victim to not wish to be involved in any communication with the offender, but think it highly appropriate the offender carries out some form of community work. This, in my opinion, can constitute restorative work. As stated previously, it is the *process* through which it is achieved that defines an activity as restorative in nature.

However, low levels of victim involvement do not necessarily reflect a general reluctance amongst victims to participate, as two English projects, one primarily undertaking mediation and another family group conferencing, routinely involve over 60% of victims. Masters (2002a) argues that the key to their success has been their relatively high level of resourcing, with staff and all partner agencies committed to delivering restorative outcomes. Similar results have been found in New Zealand (Morris et al., 1993).

Two different pieces of research examining the involvement of victims in YOT work identified very similar issues relating to the low levels of participation; Dignan (2002) and Newburn et al. (2001). Firstly, both studies identified 'cultural resistance' amongst some YOT staff, for whom involving victims was simply not a priority. In his evaluation of the piloting of reparation work Dignan (2002) found that only two thirds of eligible victims were contacted. While this evaluation was carried out in 1999 when reparation was a very new activity, Newburn et al. (2001) found a similar rate in relation to the piloting of referral orders – contact was only being made with victims in 70% of cases. The method used to contact victims also impacts significantly on participation rates, with 'opt-out' letters proving far more successful than 'opt-in' letters. These are issues that can be addressed through training. It is noteworthy that less than a quarter of YOT staff involved in contacting victims and preparing them for community panel meetings reported having had any relevant training (Newburn et al., 2001: 55). Undertaking sensitive victim contact work is a specialised, labour-intensive activity, which many

YOTs do not have the staff resources to undertake.

Two other issues that have hampered victim contact relate to data protection and time-frames. In some areas, interpretation of the Data Protection Act 1998 has led police forces to refuse to supply the necessary contact details of victims to reparation staff unless victims have first given the police their informed consent. This results in difficulties when the police in any one area are unable or unwilling to contact victims to elicit consent in a sensitive manner. This issue may now have been addressed with the issuing of new guidance by ACPO (Home Office, 2003g: 71). The second system difficulty relates to a clash between the objective of speeding up the youth justice system, in itself a laudable aim, and effective victim involvement. With tight deadlines for the preparation of court reports (particularly when a reparation order may be made on a stand-down basis (see Chapter 18) and a National Standard of 20 days for the initial youth offender panel meeting to be convened, victim consultation has been seen by some YOTs 'as an optional extra that should only be tolerated where it does not hold up the proceedings' (Dignan, 2002: 79). Clearly all of these factors also impact upon one another, and a YOT experiencing difficulties in receiving victim details, with no specialised or experienced staff, which is working to National Standards will find involving victims virtually impossible.

Almost certainly in recognition of some of these factors, YJB targets have now been changed to require YOTs to contact at least 75% of all victims eligible, and there is now no set target for how many young people should be involved in a restorative process. Some may consider this to represent an important shift in emphasis for the YJB and YOTs, as this target now reflects services YOTs should be offering to victims, rather than how they should be working with young people who offend.

The mainstreaming of restorative practice

There is potential that these changes could effectively mainstream restorative practice throughout the new youth justice system in England and Wales. YOTs are now being encouraged to use mediation, restorative conferencing, or FGCs in any case where they are considered suitable following assessment (Youth Justice Board, 2003l). A flexible approach is recommended, with the most appropriate practice model being selected in the circumstances. For example, mediation or restorative conferencing may be used as part of a reparation or action plan order, while an FGC might be selected to plan for a young person's release from custody, or perhaps as part of an Acceptable Behaviour Contract. The government has also recently published a consultation document examining the potential use of restorative practice in the adult system (Home Office, 2003g).

However, the key challenge for this mainstreaming to be successful has already been discussed in some detail; the provision of adequate resources to effectively engage with victims. Unless these resources are made available then community reparation will remain the most common (partially) restorative practice. In addition, the provision of training is also essential to ensure that practice is to a high standard, so that practitioners, and the public, can have faith in restorative methods. Newburn et al. (2001) commented on the lack of public debate or awareness about restorative justice or youth offender panels to be a further hindrance to involving victims. It will be important for a positive media strategy to inform victims of this option, and give them the confidence to participate.

However, the mainstreaming that is underway is leading to a reconsideration of restorative practice in several significant respects. Firstly, early mediation projects would often only approach victims if a young person had been assessed as remorseful and willing to apologise. This should be changing to services being offered on a universal basis to victims, who are often interested in participating for reasons other than receiving an apology. For example, they may wish to inform the young person how the offence has affected them, or to 'put a face' to 'their offender' so they can regain trust of other young people. However, in all cases, good practice requires that the motivations of victims for participating are explored and that they are given honest feedback on the likelihood of expectations being met.

Secondly, early mediation practice stressed that participation for young people should be voluntary (as it remains for victims). This issue has been blurred by the introduction of the referral order, which raises questions for wider restorative practice. Victims have a right to attend a panel meeting as long as this has been assessed as being safe. The fact that the young person may simply not wish to meet the victim no longer prevents a meeting going ahead, though suitable preparation work should be undertaken with all parties, and the victim informed of the young person's views. Participation by the young person is thus moving from a voluntary option to an obligation, as it is in New Zealand. While this change may leave some practitioners feeling uncomfortable, many believe it is necessary for restorative practice to become commonplace; no longer an *addition* in a minority of cases, but an *expectation* for the majority.

Conclusion

Internationally, restorative practice has been increasing significantly since the early 1990s. The recent consultation paper (Home Office, 2003g) looks set to expand dramatically the use of restorative practice in England and Wales following gradual 'grassroots' development. There now exists a very strong evidence base for the efficacy of restorative practice. The question is no longer *whether* restorative justice can work, but *how* it can be made to work within local frameworks.

Further reading

Crawford, A. and Newburn, T. (2003) *Youth Offending and Restorative Justice: Implementing Reform in Youth Justice*. Cullompton: Willan

JUSTICE (2000) *Restoring Youth Justice*. London: JUSTICE

Mediation UK (2001) *The Rough Guide to Restorative Justice and the Crime and Disorder Act*. Bristol: Mediation UK

Quill, D. and Wynne, J. (1993) *Victim and Offender Mediation Handbook*. London: Save The Children (Available From Mediation UK)

Zehr, H. (1990) *Changing Lenses*. Ontario: Herald Press

29 Family Group Conferencing in Youth Justice

Peter Gill

Key points

1. Family group conferencing is a process, generally associated with restorative practice which aims to facilitate decision making by the family. The role of professionals is to provide the space to facilitate the development by the family and significant others of a plan to address their child's need and to provide services to support those plans.

2. Although the potential for the widespread use of family group conferencing in a youth justice context has been demonstrated, particularly in New Zealand, development of the model for use with young people who offend has generated relatively little interest in England and Wales.

3. This lack of attention to family group conferencing can be seen as part of a broader tendency for restorative approaches to focus on 'responsibilising' young people or requiring reparation as opposed to an emphasis on reintegration.

4. The existing evidence base suggests that family group conferencing can be an extremely effective model for decision making in relation to children and young people in trouble.

5. The emerging policy context, and in particular the proposed development of Children's Trusts, may provide fertile ground for promoting a renewed interest in family group conferencing as a model of restorative practice which empowers families and communities.

Introduction

A family group conference (FGC) is a decision making process whereby families and the state work together to safeguard and promote children's welfare. The process can be used in a range of circumstances, including where a child or young person is in need, at risk, at risk of separation from their birth family or involved in offending behaviour. Crucially, families and other relevant members of the community retain responsibility for planning. The function of the conference is to provide space to develop a family plan to address the identified need. The rationale behind the approach is that decisions about a child should be made by those who are best placed to provide on-going protection and support long after the state's involvement has ceased. The state's responsibility is to facilitate the conference, and provide services to support the plans agreed within the FGC, intervening only where the proposed plan would not be sufficient to keep the young person safe.

FGCs have been 'mainstreamed' in New Zealand where they provide the primary model of working in both the child welfare/protection and youth justice systems. In England and Wales, however, the adoption of FGCs has been less uniform. Their use has become fairly common in relation to child welfare cases but remains relatively underdeveloped in the youth justice sphere.

Family group conferences – origins

Restorative justice has usefully been defined as:

> *a process whereby parties with a stake in a specific offence collectively resolve how to deal with the aftermath of the offence and its implications for the future.*
>
> (Marshall, 1999)

Family group conferencing is frequently considered to be a form of restorative practice, particularly when victims are engaged and participate in the process. In successful FGC projects, where programme integrity and the effective application of principles into practice have been central to the approach, very high levels of victim involvement have been achieved.

FGCs were developed in New Zealand in the early 1980s (see Chapter 28) where the Children and Young Person Act 1989 formalised conferencing as the primary decision making mechanism for children and young people in both civil and criminal matters. As a result, an FGC must be called if there are significant child welfare issues and the family must consider what is to be done by way of an action plan to address the issues. The conference is charged with deciding if the child is 'in need of care and protection' and advice and information are made available on the services available to support the family in implementing their plan. The procedure is intended to reinforce family ties, enabling and empowering the individual family unit to meet its responsibilities towards its children.

The FGC is also at the heart of the New Zealand youth justice system. Young people can be referred to the conferencing service by the police as a diversionary measure, or from court following conviction. All but the most serious offences are dealt with by FGCs although no case is automatically excluded on seriousness grounds. The conference provides a framework for facilitating a direct meeting between the victim and the young person with the aim of securing a resolution of the offence for all parties, potentially involving an element of reparation. By way of the family plan, the young person and other family members take responsibility for the offence and, with the support of available services, seek to re-integrate the young person into their community and the locally available informal support networks. Where the FGC is court ordered, there is the possibility of returning to court to sanction the family plan.

Following, the implementation of the legislation, there was a reduction in the number of children and young people in state care and in the use of custody for young people, both of which have been attributed to the introduction of the new approach (Maxwell and Morris, 1996).

In England and Wales, following recognition in the early 1990s of family group conferencing as a model of practice that encourages participation and empowers families in key decision making processes, its use has become quite widespread in child welfare and child protection work. According to the Family Rights Group, more than 50% of social service departments have access to family group conferencing or use it as *the* planning meeting in all referrals for these services. Indeed, family group conferencing is specifically mentioned in *Working Together to Safeguard Children*, the government's guidance on ensuring child safety, as an effective model of practice having the potential for increasing participation in decision making processes (Department of Health, 1999).

In youth justice the picture is rather different. The use of FGCs was pioneered by a handful of projects in the mid-1990s. A number of national conferences championed its development and training in how to use it grew. Recent legislation, particularly the Crime and Disorder Act 1998 (CDA) and the Youth Justice and Criminal Evidence Act 1999, has encouraged victim involvement, parental responsibility, programmes of reparation and confronting young people with the consequences of their offending. This has led to the widespread development of restorative practice, including letters of apology, reparation, direct/indirect victim-offender mediation (see Chapter 28), but the adoption of family group conferencing has been much more limited, with only a small number of youth offending teams (YOTs) using this model of practice.

Following implementation of the CDA, the Youth Justice Board established a development fund for projects aiming to change young people's offending behaviour. Over 250 projects were awarded grants, including 46 within the ambit of restorative justice, using a variety of restorative approaches (Wilcox, 2003). Of these, only 20 included family group conferencing in their portfolio and after two years funding, seven of these projects had failed to complete any conferences. Only five projects had managed to complete six or more FGCs (Wilcox, 2003) The cessation of funding appears to have led to a further reduction in the use of FGCs, with only a small number of areas – including Essex, Gloucestershire and the Manchester Youth Justice Trust – continuing to use conferencing for young people who offend.

Yet it seems clear that the model has much to offer in the youth justice arena. Research tells us that the clusters of risk bearing upon young people with whom YOTs work, are strikingly similar to those of children in need (see Chapter 8) and it is with these high risk groups that FGCs tend to work best, since the model focuses on harnessing the services necessary to address need and support the plan. Moreover, the emphasis on mobilising informal familial and community resources operates to empower parents and can thus help them take responsibility for their children's behaviour.

Family group conferences in practice

There are four distinct stages involved in putting family group conferencing into practice in youth justice (Morris et al., 1998).

Stage 1: the referral

- A need for a planning and decision making meeting is identified. Experience suggests the greater the level of need or concern, the higher the probability of family engagement.
- An independent co-ordinator is appointed to work directly with all participants and set up the meeting. This person should have no other responsibility for work with any of the participants.

Stage 2: preparation for the meeting

- The co-ordinator, with the child and immediate carers, identifies the appropriate family network and significant others who should be invited to the conference.
- The co-ordinator, in consultation with the victim, decides who should be invited as a supporter.
- The co-ordinator is responsible for sending out invitations and for all practical arrangements. They will contact all potential participants in advance to explain the purpose of the conference, how it will operate and to discuss, and attempt to allay, any concerns which they may have.
- The co-ordinator ensures that there is full consent to continue with the process from all those who are to attend so as to extract the maximum benefit from the conference.

Where FGCs are used in a youth justice context, it will also be important that any obligations placed on the young person in the family plan, are proportionate to the seriousness of their offence (see Chapter 9) (Nacro, 2000a). The notion of a proportionate response to the offending, rightly features prominently in the Youth Justice Board

guidance on the operation of referral orders (Home Office/Youth Justice Board, 2001) and as restorative practice develops internationally, the United Nations Congress on Crime Prevention and the Treatment of Offenders has also considered this principle. Moreover, recommendation No R(99)19 adopted on 15 September 1999 by the Committee of Ministers of the Council of Europe on Mediation in Penal Matters, states that:

> *The proportionality requirement means that there should be correspondence between the burden on the offender and the seriousness of the offence.*

This is a further issue which will need to be explored with the participants in advance of the conference as part of the process of preparation by the co-ordinator.

Stage 3: the conference

The meeting itself consists of three distinct parts:

- *Information sharing*: the facts of the offence are established, victims have the opportunity to explain how the offence affected them and the young person is given the chance to make an initial response.
- *Private family planning time*: the family have the opportunity to talk alone and are given space to devise a plan of action to address the concerns raised during the information sharing process.
- *Agreeing the plan*: all participants reconvene. The young person presents the plan and apologises to the victim. The services and support required to make the plan work are negotiated and agreed by professionals present. All agree how to check the plan is working, how to monitor any commitments made and what action to take if the plan is not followed.

Stage 4: reviewing the plan

- A review FGC, or sub-group of the original meeting, meets to review progress/completion of the plan, to make revisions to the plan where necessary or, in some instances, to devise a new plan.

Family group conferences – the principles

There are a number of key principles which underpin the FGC model. Three in particular appear to be fundamental to the effective operation of the approach and where practitioners have departed from them, integrity is lost and outcomes are likely to suffer (Restorative Justice FGC Project, 2002).

The nature of participation

Involvement of all parties must be on the basis of consent since voluntary participation is a prerequisite of the commitment required to develop and sustain the plan, which is the main outcome of the process. The role of the co-ordinator is essential to ensuring that all those involved are properly 'signed up' to the process and maintain appropriate levels of commitment in advance of the meeting itself.

For this reason, it is important that the coordinator is the same person throughout and that he or she allows each individual concerned adequate time and attention so that they are thoroughly prepared. Mere inclusion is insufficient. The importance of preparation and support in advance of the conference, to empower each of the parties participating in the process, is becoming increasingly acknowledged. Imparting information about how the conference will work, its purpose, and the awareness of the underlying mechanisms, is an essential part of preparation for a successful FGC and can be time consuming.

Given the skilled nature of the task, and the centrality of the role in enhancing participation, it is essential that all co-ordinators should be fully trained in family group conferencing as well as in the wider principles of restorative practice.

Empowerment

The primary aim of the FGC is to provide a framework which involves and empowers young people and their extended families to take responsibility for future planning about how appropriate support will be provided. Independence and impartiality of professionals involved in the process – and in particular, the co-ordinator – is essential for the realisation of the aim. The co-ordinator should not therefore have had any previous involvement with the family other than as part of the preparation for the conference itself. The model attempts to alter the power imbalance

between families and professionals, putting both sides on a more equal footing, and locating decision making power clearly with those most directly affected.

Practitioners sometimes have difficulty with this approach and it does not sit easily with some perceptions about how the youth justice system ought to operate. The introduction of referral orders as a mainstream part of the sentencing process, however, has established the principle that there should be no impediment to the community being involved in deciding upon the content of judicial orders (see Chapter 16). In that context, and given the international experience, there is no insuperable conflict between the principle of empowerment which underpins FGCs, and their incorporation into youth justice processes.

Partnership

Once the family has developed the plan, they must be given the support necessary to implement and sustain it. Professionals at the conference must be authorised to agree access to, or the provision of, services to meet the diverse range of needs of the young people concerned. This requires a partnership approach by a variety of agencies. Partnership is key too, to the process of negotiating with the family within the conference itself as to what provision will be offered to support the young person and family in implementing the plan. Given that the plan is devised by the family alone during their private time, the FGC model implies a new way of working for many service providers in which partnership, with those who would otherwise be perceived as clients, plays a significantly greater role.

Family group conference outcomes

The apparent lack of interest in developing FGCs within a youth justice context is particularly surprising given the positive outcomes that are frequently achieved by those projects which have adopted the model. The Family Rights Group has summarised some of the key outcomes from research and evaluations of FGC projects (both child welfare/protection and youth justice) in England and Wales (Tapsfield, 2003). They are said to:

- Successfully engage the wider family in making plans for children.
- Produce plans that agencies agree to support in the great majority of situations. One study found that over 90% of professionals agreed or strongly agreed that agencies cooperated well in relation to supporting plans developed within an FGC (Restorative Justice FGC Project, 2002).
- Make safe plans for children.
- Achieve high levels of victim participation and victim satisfaction in youth justice conferences. Where sufficient time and effort is put into victim engagement, attendance of victims has reached 94% (Restorative Justice FGC Project, 2002).
- Be effective in reducing offending, particularly where victims attend.
- Make more use of family and community resources than plans made at meetings where agencies dominate.
- Reunite children with their families more securely.
- Secure a placement in the wider family for those children who cannot live with their birth parents.
- Be valued by children and families who attend.
- Provide a service that is respectful of cultural difference.
- Provide an effective forum for the direct voices of children and young people to be heard.

Given the research evidence, there are grounds for supposing that devoting further attention to the use of FGCs as an effective method of intervention with young people who offend might bear considerable fruit.

Fresh impetus – the emerging policy context

Interest in developing the use of FGC in the youth justice context, in contrast to other restorative approaches, has been limited to date. Moreover, that interest has apparently waned since the ending of the Board's injection of monies to YOTs through its development fund. If as Nacro has suggested (1997) restorative justice entails three core values; responsibility, restoration and reintegration – it could be argued that the underuse of FGCs is symptomatic of a broader lack

of attention to a third of these values (see Chapter 21).

Evaluations of the Board funded restorative justice projects and of youth offender panels have noted that while most of the young people who come to YOTs' notice, experience moderate to high levels of social exclusion, there was a relative lack of service provision available to facilitate reintegration (Dignan, 2002; Newburn et al., 2003).

Family group conferencing as a model of restorative practice is one in which the primary focus is on addressing social exclusion, and the available evidence suggests that it does so with some success. It is noticeable in this context, that in terms of the typology of restorative practice developed by McCold (2000) classifying interventions as 'fully', 'mostly' or 'partly' restorative, FGCs would be partly restorative even where the victim does not attend.

Since the mid-1990s, there has been substantial debate about the most appropriate location for FGCs within the youth justice system. Some commentators have contended that it should be used primarily as a diversionary measure and others that it should be reserved for relatively heavy end offending, where it may have the potential to function as an alternative to custody. Arguably, such debates have acted as an obstacle to the development of FGC as a model for youth justice intervention.

In principle, there is nothing to prevent the use of conferencing at any stage in the criminal justice process where all participants consent voluntarily, the level of need and risk is sufficient to secure active involvement and the young person admits the offence. But to a certain extent, the debate has now been pre-empted, temporarily at least. In February 2004, the Youth Justice Board announced funding to allow five trial areas to pilot FGCs, linked to Youth Inclusion and Support Panels (YISPs) (see Chapter 32), aimed at preventing children aged 8–13 years of age from becoming involved in offending (Youth Justice Board, 2004a). For these pilot areas, FGCs will be firmly located at the front end of the system, working with children deemed at risk of offending.

This initiative takes place when the prospects for a renewal of interest in FGCs as a youth justice measure may however be brighter than they have been for a number of years. The pilot was announced shortly after the White Paper, which prefigured the Anti-Social Behaviour Act 2003, referred to the use of FGCs as an effective way of dealing with offending behaviour (Home Office, 2003f). At a press conference on 14 October 2003 to outline the proposals, Tony Blair stressed the need for a re-investment of power in local communities, to provide the most effective response to anti-social behaviour. Family group conferencing as a practice model may be ideally placed to deliver such an outcome.

Significantly, the Green Paper on children, *Every Child Matters* (DfES, 2003b) and the companion document *Youth Justice: The Next Steps* (Home Office, 2003i) both make explicit reference to family group conferencing. In the former, it appears as one of the potential specialist parenting support services:

> . . . *to support families to get together and develop a plan with an independent facilitator, which may be triggered by child protection or youth offending concerns.*

In the latter, the reference is made in the context of strengthening whole family approaches to tackling youth offending and is related to the YJB target of ensuring that restorative processes are used in 80% of youth justice interventions (see Chapter 4).

The coming period will see the integration of local health, education, Connexions and social services within Children's Trusts, which will also be able to include youth offending teams (DfES, 2003b). It is intended that the Trusts will be characterised by improved information sharing, joint working, multi-agency service delivery and the identification of a lead professional for any child where more than one service is involved. Family group conferencing fits well with such a model of service delivery and would benefit from ready access to the range of services which will fall under the Trusts' umbrella. The move towards the integration of children's provision might accordingly foster the further development of the conferencing approach in both the child protection and youth justice arenas and provide a springboard for expanding the use of FGCs to tackle more serious offending than that currently targeted in the Youth Justice Board's pilots.

Further reading

Family Rights Group Website at *www.frg.org.uk*

Morris, K., Marsh, P. and Wiffin, J. (1998) *Family Group Conferences: A Training Pack*. London: Family Rights Group

Restorative Justice Project Family Group Conference, *Research Outcomes and Lessons Learned*. Essex FGC Service, Oct 2002

Restorative Justice Consortium (undated) *Standards for Restorative Justice*

30 Mentoring in Youth Justice

David Porteous

Key points

1. Mentoring involves pairing a young person with an older volunteer who acts as a role model and friend, sometimes in the context of other activities or services.

2. Mentors and mentees typically meet for around two hours per week and do things like meet for a coffee, go to an ice rink or work on schoolwork or obtaining a job.

3. Not all matches will work but successful relationships may be sustained for one year or more.

4. The key to successful mentoring relationships is mutual trust and respect.

5. It may take up to two years for a mentoring scheme to become established.

Introduction

Mentoring schemes have become increasingly popular in work with young people at risk and those who offend in recent years. Since being highlighted in the influential report *Misspent Youth* (Audit Commission, 1996) as a promising form of intervention and subsequently promoted by the Youth Justice Board (YJB) as part of its youth crime prevention strategy, mentoring projects have proliferated such that there must now be few youth offending teams (YOTs) that do not include mentoring amongst their range of services. Mentoring is also to be found in young offender institutions, pupil referral units, youth inclusion projects and Connexions offices. In just ten years, mentoring has become a core feature of the new youth justice.

Essentially, mentoring involves the pairing of an older volunteer role model with a young person deemed at risk of offending or with an offending history so that the former can befriend, advise and support the latter towards an agreed set of objectives. The project coordinator's task is to recruit and train volunteer mentors and subsequently to match them with young people referred to the project by other workers and agencies. What mentor and mentee do together will vary according to the context and the needs of young people but will usually combine leisure activities with some form of education, training or pastoral support. Mentoring is frequently linked to other forms of intervention such as bail supervision, or drugs advice, with the mentor's role being to support the young person accordingly.

Forms of mentoring

One of the attractions and benefits of mentoring projects is their adaptability. Even within the context of youth justice, schemes differ according to the model of mentoring offered (e.g. adult to young person, older to younger peer, group mentoring), the age of mentees and their circumstances (i.e. from being designated at risk of offending through to being in prison), who has responsibility for the project (e.g. a national voluntary agency, a YOT, a local community group) and the framework in which it is delivered (i.e. as part of a wider 'mentoring plus' project or as a 'stand-alone' mentoring scheme).

Moreover, the nature and focus of any mentor-mentee relationship will also vary dependent on need and the characteristics of the individuals involved. For both those working with young people and young people themselves, therefore, mentoring comes in different shapes and sizes.

Probably the best known mentoring scheme in England and Wales is that first piloted by Crime Concern in Hackney in 1994, the Dalston Youth Project. Here, mentoring is one component of a wider programme that also includes two residential courses and education, training and careers advice. Matching takes place following the first residential which includes outward-bound activities, action planning exercises, games, videos and so on. The education and careers component includes a college 'taster' course, a pre-employment training programme and classes on interpersonal skills. Mentors and mentees are encouraged to meet on a weekly basis for approximately two hours over the course of a year. Meetings may involve trips out or simply chatting in a café; essentially the role of the mentor is to encourage and support the young person to realise the goals they have set themselves within the context of the broader programme.

Clearly, this 'mentoring plus' model requires significant resources over and above those involved in establishing mentoring relationships and there are many schemes that simply deliver the mentoring component of the model, arranging matches and providing ongoing support and supervision to mentors and mentees. In such projects, mentors may still be expected to support young people in specific activities. Within YOTs for example, participation in a mentoring scheme may form part of a wider package such as a bail supervision and support programme (see Chapter 14) or a final warning intervention (see Chapter 12), and part of the mentor's role could be to attend court with a young person, to facilitate their joining a sports project or to support their reintegration into full-time education.

Mentoring schemes are available to young people at different points of an 'offending career', and they may be geared towards both prevention and rehabilitation. On the one hand, young people excluded from school and thereby deemed to be at risk of offending, may be referred for mentoring so as to try and ensure there is no deterioration in their behaviour. At the other end of the scale, there are now several schemes established within young offender institutions where the aim is to assist the young person in finding work, somewhere to live and other essentials of resettlement when they leave custody. At the 'Trailblazers' project at Feltham, for example, volunteers visit young people on a two weekly basis towards the end of their sentence and then continue to meet with them for up to six months post-release.

The multi-faceted nature of mentoring can be seen in a different way in mentees' comments about what they like about their mentors. The quotations in the box below, drawn from various research studies (Porteous, 1998a; Skinner and Fleming, 1999; St James Roberts and Samlal Singh, 1999), describe a range of possible roles: parent, confidant, friend, teacher, counsellor, role model, expert, even emergency hot-line number.

Young people's descriptions of mentors

She spends money on me. She's like a mum.

I can talk to her, with other adults I can't talk about some things but I can with her.

I know she won't judge me and that's important, other adults do.

I'm getting better at my schoolwork, especially using the computer, that's because my mentor and I often go the internet café, where I learn to use the computers. It's also been good, because I want to be an air hostess and we've been able to look up on the computer what I need to do at school.

She makes things better, shows me the way to find the answer. I've learnt to control my feelings; not to get into a tantrum. She teaches me to count to ten.

Someone who will actually listen to what you have to say, someone in the job you'd like to go for 'cause they can give you a lot of advice and that. Me mum and dad felt it was really good, it got me motivated in a way that they couldn't.

We can phone him at any time – he is very accessible. If we have a problem we can phone him late at night or early in the morning, he is there for us.

Key components of mentoring schemes

Central to all mentoring schemes is the project co-ordinator and this is the role most likely to be performed by professional youth justice workers. Their core tasks and responsibilities will include:

- Developing and maintaining project systems and records and liaising with management and steering groups.

- Establishing links with partner organisations and managing the referral process.
- Recruiting, training and providing on-going support to mentors.
- Assessing clients' needs and organising the matching process.
- Liaison with families and carers and with other professionals with whom clients are working.
- Supporting and monitoring mentor-mentee relationships and managing the end of relationships.

Those with experience emphasise that the project co-ordinator's own mentoring role, vis-à-vis. volunteers, is both very demanding and critical to the success of schemes (cf Benioff, 1998; Porteous, 1997). Whereas the mentors will typically have one mentee, the project co-ordinator may have between 10 and 20. As well as providing individual supervision, co-ordinators run support group meetings, organise on-going training and other events and offer a first point of contact should difficulties arise. It is worth noting that most volunteers will have relatively little experience or knowledge of working with young people and rely heavily on project co-ordinators and on each other for practical advice and emotional support.

A flurry of handbooks and guidance on setting up mentoring projects has been produced in recent years, some of which are listed at the end of the chapter. In the broadest terms, the implementation of a mentoring project involves three phases:

1. *Establishing the structure and organisation of the scheme*: setting up partnership arrangements, recruitment of staff, definition of aims, objectives and activities, developing office space and so on, defining procedures and designing forms for assessment, referral, and monitoring.
2. *Recruitment, selection and training of mentors and mentees*: involving on the one hand advertisement, open days, interviews, screening including police checks and initial training and on the other, developing links with referral agencies, securing parental consent, undertaking needs assessments, running introductory sessions.
3. *Matching, on-going training, support and related activities*: the matching process may involve residential weekends and the initial meeting between mentor and mentee will be facilitated by the project co-ordinator. The mentoring relationship will often take place in the context of a wider programme of activities for mentees, involving education and/or training, structured leisure time, health awareness and prevention.

The box below shows the 'key indicators of quality' identified by the Youth Justice Board in its mentoring guidance. About the guidance, the Board says 'It is to be used by managers to monitor the performance of their services . . . This evidence should then be used to identify strengths and develop an action plan to address any weaknesses' (Youth Justice Board, undated b: 4). The guidance is sufficiently general to allow for alternative versions of mentoring. At the same time, it usefully identifies certain minimum standards for practitioners to work towards.

The effectiveness of mentoring

Given the enthusiasm with which mentoring has been promoted by the British government in recent times, one might think that the evidence of its success had been firmly established. However, whilst there is now a good deal of research showing that mentoring can indeed work for some young people, there remains uncertainty about which kind of young person this might be and there is increasing recognition that for every successful match, another will fail.

First, the good news. The most frequently cited evidence that mentoring works is Tiernay et al.'s (1995) evaluation of the long-standing Big Brothers/Big Sisters organisation in the United States. Drawing from a pool of 959 10–16 year olds who had applied to the project, the researchers compared outcomes for a randomly assigned 'treatment' group of young people – those who were matched with a mentor – and a 'control' group who were placed on a waiting list. After 18 months, young people in the first group were found to be 46% less likely to use drugs and alcohol, 52% less likely to miss a day at school and 27% less likely to hit someone.

Few other evaluations of mentoring schemes have been able to replicate the experimental approach used by Tiernay et al., or the size of the sample. Nonetheless, research comparing the progress of, and outcomes for, young people who have been successfully matched with those who have not has consistently shown positive results amongst the former group. For example, Delaney

The Youth Justice Board's 'Key Indicators of Quality' for mentoring schemes

Assessment
- There are clear guidelines for identifying the young people the programme aims to recruit.
- Potential mentors should be screened to identify those that have the greatest understanding of the role, and the interpersonal skills and commitment to put it into practice.

Individual needs
- The framework and structure of programmes should depend on the young person's age, maturity, and developmental and cultural needs and any local issues.
- The specific factors that determine the structure of programmes should be established early on in the mentoring relationship and should be reviewed and adapted regularly.

Communication
- There should be a regular meeting between the mentor and the young person.
- Simple, clear, age-specific, culturally sensitive literature should be developed to explain mentoring programmes to young people. This literature should take into account the language and the literacy levels of the young people the programme is trying to engage.

Service delivery
- Goals for the programme should relate specifically to the young person, be owned by them and be SMART (**S**pecific, **M**easurable, **A**chievable, **R**ealistic, and **T**ime-bound).
- Regular, structured group activities, monthly/bi-monthly group trips and activities with a residential element should be provided.

Training
- Mentors need to be trained to work to the aims and objectives identified for the young person within the programme.
- Training for mentors should focus on communication skills, motivation skills, ideas about relationship building, interaction with young people, setting boundaries, child protection issues, goal setting, and values and diversity awareness.

Management
- Matching mentors to young people should be clearly managed and criteria for this should be developed and consistently applied.
- The relationship between the mentor and the young person should be supported, as intensively as possible, by a case manager who is in contact with the parents/carers of the young person, the young person and the mentor.

Service Development
- A local protocol for working with young people that covers staff selection, staff skills, staff training, on-going support and, for those working in the secure estate, security, should be developed.
- Clear referral procedures should be developed and should be consistently followed.

Monitoring and Evaluation
- Effective and efficient case recording systems should be established and maintained. In principle, they should monitor meetings between staff, mentors and the young person they are working with.
- Mentoring should be fully monitored and reviewed. Where appropriate, it should be independently evaluated. All monitoring and evaluation should be against a series of established benchmarks and indicators of effectiveness.

and Milne (2002: 6), describing two pilot projects developed in Sydney, Australia, observe that 'all young people involved in 'performing matches' of six months and more reported reduced offending, increased community involvement, improved self esteem and communication skills and more motivation' ('performing matches' emphasised).

Qualitative evidence of the beneficial effects of mentoring is not hard to find. In their evaluation of the Dalston Youth Project Part II (which targeted 11–14 year olds still in school), Tarling et al. (2001) quote a parent's endorsement of the scheme's impact on their son:

> *Having a mentor has been so good for him. She has had the time to discuss things with him and listen to him. She even got him doing subjects that he wouldn't do before.*
>
> (p56)

In my own research (Porteous, 1998a, 2002), case studies of successful matches have also provided evidence of improved family relationships, greater self-confidence, and desistance from offending and new friendships. Successful relationships are characterised above all by friendship and mutual respect. This can only develop over time. In getting there, mentors stress factors and qualities such as the need for honesty and trust, agreement over boundaries, patience, and the ability to listen and not to judge. Whilst it is impossible to demonstrate empirically that it is the introduction to their lives of a mentor which has enabled young people to achieve positive changes, the testimonies of project workers, mentors, mentees and their parents, strongly suggest that the combination of practical and emotional support which mentoring brings has been a decisive factor.

The Trailblazers Project (2002) reports that only 17% of the 210 young offenders they have worked with have re-offended so far. However, such claims, common enough in promotional literature, cannot be verified as the means by which re-offending has been measured is not stated. The results from published evaluations by independent researchers are less impressive. In their study of the Dalston Youth Project, Tarling et al. (2001) note that whilst eight of the 80 young people referred to the project had a prior record of offending, 32 (40%) obtained a caution or conviction whilst on the project or thereafter.

Overall, they say, 'there appeared to be little association between whether a good relationship had been formed and whether or not the (mentee) subsequently committed an offence' (p61). A more promising picture is obtained by comparing the offending rate of those who were successfully matched with others, but this has to be set against the fact that only 21 matches resulted in 'successful' relationships being established.

A relatively high 'drop out' rate is also noted by Delaney and Milne who observe of the projects they evaluated that whilst 'most referrals were appropriate' in the sense that they met the agreed criteria, 'most young people were unsuitable for mentoring or not interested' (2002: 9). They do not specify what they mean by 'unsuitable' but other studies suggest, as the Youth Justice Board (1999: 9) puts it, that, 'Some young people . . . may have multiple problems so deeply entrenched that a volunteer mentor proves ineffective.' Indeed, some researchers (Porteous, 1998a; Crimmens and Storr, 1998) have found that the 'at riskiness' of young people is negatively correlated with the success of the mentoring relationship – the more problematic the young person's circumstances, the less likely the relationship is to work. The theory that mentoring can enhance personal development is born out by the evidence. The evidence that it can make a significant impact upon problematic behaviour is more circumspect.

Conclusion

The European Mentoring Centre describes mentoring as 'a means of achieving development and personal growth' (EMC, 1999: 1). Implicit here is the notion that *everyone* can benefit from having a mentor. In the context of youth justice, however, we find a different emphasis. Here, the promise of mentoring has tended to be linked to a perception that some young people more than others *need* a mentor. To quote the Dalston Youth Project:

> *Mentoring offers at-risk young people . . . a positive, non-judgmental and supportive role model. For the first time in their lives, these young people will have the undivided attention of an adult, trained to listen to them and take their concerns, problems, hopes and accomplishments seriously.*
>
> (Dalston Youth Project Information Leaflet, 1997)

In this version, mentoring is seen as a way of making good the deficits of a young person's past, a lack of love, care and attention and/or inferior opportunities in terms of education and employment. There is, we might note, some irony in the fact that the original mentee, Odysseus' son Telemachus, was the son of a king. On the other hand, there is also, one suspects, an underlying assumption behind this theory of mentoring that absent fathers are a significant part of the problem.

My point is not that mentoring cannot work with young people at risk or known to have offended. On the contrary there is growing evidence that it can. However, there is no reason to believe that it works better with disadvantaged young people than others and, by investing undue optimism in schemes' potential to 'turn around' troublesome youngsters, there is a danger of setting them up to fail. As John Pitts has argued, there is a clear difference between 'emancipatory' mentoring, 'born of a critique of an inequitable social order', and 'correctional' mentoring which 'finds the origins of such 'social exclusion' within the person being mentored' (2000: 56). The former model emphasises the voluntaristic nature of the mentoring relationship and effectively discounts the possibility that mentoring can fail in the sense that there is nothing to lose. It also suggests that mentoring projects working with young people who offend and those at risk should think of their clients as being there not because of what they *have done* but because of what they *could do*.

Further reading

Crime Concern/Youth Justice Board (2000) *Mentoring for Young People at Risk and Young Offenders*. London: Crime Concern/Youth Justice Board

DIVERT Trust (Undated) *DIVERT Mentoring Handbook*. London: The DIVERT Trust

Skinner, A. and Fleming, J. (1999) *Mentoring Socially Excluded Young People*. Manchester: National Mentoring Network

Tarling, R., Burrows, J. and Clarke, A. (2001) *Dalston Youth Project Part II (11–14), An Evaluation*. Research Study 232. London: Home Office (Summary available at www.homeoffice.gov.uk)

Tierney, J, P, et al. (1995) *Making a Difference: An Impact Study of Big Brothers/Big Sisters*. Philadelphia: Public/Private Ventures (Available at www.mentoring.org)

31 Working with Parents

Carole Pickburn, Sarah Lindfield and John Coleman

Key points

1. Parenting is one of the most challenging tasks an individual undertakes. The risk and protective factors of family life have featured consistently in the research into possible predictors of offending and anti-social behaviour.

2. Involving parents and supporting parents in the parenting task should be a continuous thread running through practice when working with young people.

3. The quality of the relationship between worker and family is a key factor in the success of any intervention provided to parents and young people.

4. Recognising the unique nature of families in all their diversity is crucial to providing inclusive and effective parenting interventions.

5. Monitoring, reviewing and evaluating the parenting support intervention contributes to evidence based practice. Evidence based practice leads to the provision of effective services to support young people and their families.

Introduction

Since the 1970s research has consistently shown that the presence of risk factors and the absence of protective factors in family life is associated with the likelihood of young people engaging in offending or anti-social behaviour. While these risk factors frequently include environmental factors such as poverty and deprivation, almost without exception the role of parents and carers of young people – and parental attitudes and behaviours – feature strongly in these studies:

> *Family risk factors include; poor parental supervision and discipline, family conflict, a family history of criminal activity, parental attitudes that condone antisocial and criminal behaviour, low income, poor housing and large family size. These risk factors can first be identified at the pre-natal and perinatal stages and persist in influence throughout childhood and adolescence.*
>
> (Youth Justice Board, 2001b)

(When discussing parenting, it is of course, important to acknowledge the different ways families are constituted. The combinations of family structures are almost limitless. The factors that contribute to the diversity of family life must be considered e.g. race, culture, gender, sexuality, disability, faith, class, age, absent parents, non-biological parents. Acknowledging the realities of family life and increasing our awareness of the range of diversity increases our opportunities to work in real partnership with families. In this chapter, therefore when we use the words 'parent' and 'parents' and occasionally, 'carer', they are intended to reflect all those possible family structures.)

Research in the USA has also highlighted the parenting and family factors that can protect young people from becoming involved in offending behaviour:

- The use of positive discipline methods.
- Active monitoring and supervision.
- Supportive parent–child relationships.
- Families who advocate for their children.
- Parents who seek information and support.

(Kumpfer and Alvarado, 1998)

Greater understanding of the key features of family life associated with youth crime influenced the reforms of youth justice introduced by the Labour government from 1997. The Audit Commission report, *Misspent Youth*, published in 1996, recommended the provision of assistance to parents to develop their parenting skills to prevent youth offending. The government consulted on this and a range of other reforms of the youth justice system during 1997 and built the results into the Crime and Disorder Act 1998 (CDA). The Act established the Youth Justice Board and required local authorities to set up youth offending teams (YOTs) to carry forward the youth justice reforms which included the parenting order. The Youth Justice Board (YJB) also made 'reinforcing the responsibilities of parents' one of the six key objectives of the youth justice system.

The Anti-Social Behaviour Act 2003 extends the statutory basis for work with parents with the introduction of parenting contracts and free-standing parenting orders.

Legislative background

The Crime and Disorder Act 1998 (CDA) (as amended by the Criminal Justice Act 2003) and the Anti Social Behaviour Act 2003 (ASBA) are the statutory basis for parents to be provided with support. A short description of the relevant pieces of legislation follows. However, it should be noted that the introduction of a statutory basis for working directly with the parents in the youth justice arena 'triggered an equally significant growth in the provision of support on a voluntary basis and we will return to this point later.

The guidance for parenting contracts and orders outlines the intended principle behind the legislation:

> *Help and support for the parents of young people who become involved in crime is part of a wider programme of action to support families. Parents have an important role to play in preventing their children offending; they have a responsibility to the child and to the community to supervise and take proper care of them. Some parents may need help, support, encouragement and direction. Such assistance may be provided at an early stage by or on behalf of social services or a local education authority or by a voluntary agency and could be in the form of group work or one to one counselling.*

> (Home Office/Youth Justice Board/Department for Constitutional Affairs, 2004)

The parenting order was introduced by the CDA and is available in any proceedings where the child of the parents has been convicted of a criminal offence. It can also be made where a child safety order, an anti-social behaviour order, a referral order or a sexual offences prevention order has been imposed, or where the parents themselves are convicted for failing to ensure their child's school attendance or have failed to attend a youth offender panel held in respect of their child.

The order can last between 3 and 12 months and is intended to support parents to prevent further offending or anti-social behaviour by their child. The order requires parents to attend guidance or counselling sessions for up to three months and may include other requirements, such as ensuring the child's school attendance, ensuring that their child does not associate with disruptive youngsters or providing effective supervision of the child during certain times of the evening, for up to a year. Failure to comply with the order is a criminal offence and parents who are found to have breached the requirements can be fined up to £1,000 or be given a discharge or a community penalty.

The ASBA introduces *free-standing* parenting orders which can be made, on the application of the YOT, in isolation from any order made in respect of the child. (Local education authorities can also apply for free-standing orders on the basis of different criteria. Such orders are not considered in any detail here.) The order is available where the court considers that it would contribute to the prevention of further offending or anti-social behaviour by that young person. The YOT must have evidence of criminal or anti-social behaviour by the young person, and courts are likely to require a criminal standard of proof but there is no requirement for a previous criminal conviction, thereby enabling earlier statutory intervention than allowed by the parenting order hitherto. It is anticipated that an application for a free-standing parenting order would usually only be considered where attempts to engage the parents on a voluntary basis and/or by means of a parenting contract, described below, have proved unsuccessful.

The ASBA also introduces parenting contracts. These provide a more formal framework for work carried out on a voluntary basis with families by the YOT:

> *Parenting contracts are not intended to replace all voluntary work with parents but to provide an additional option backed by statute.*

> (Home Office et al., 2004)

A parenting contract is a voluntary written agreement between the YOT and the parents of the young person. The YOT may enter into a parenting contract when there is reason to believe that the young person has, or is likely to, become involved in criminal conduct or anti-social behaviour. The parenting contract requires a statement made by the parents or guardians of a young person that they will comply with whatever is negotiated and agreed in terms of the support required. Contracts will usually include a requirement to participate in a parenting programme. The YOT also provides a statement agreeing to provide the support outlined in the contract. (The legislation also gives schools and the local education authority power to initiate a parenting contract but these provisions are again not considered here.)

Support to parents was available in many YOT areas on a voluntary basis prior to the establishment of parenting contracts, but the legislative changes provide a statutory basis for such involvement. The YOT now has a statutory power to initiate negotiations with parents with the intention of agreeing a contact, and in return is required to provide services to help parents deliver their part. While there is no direct penalty for parents who fail to enter into, or comply with, a parenting contract, a possible consequence of failing to cooperate is that courts can take this into account when considering whether to make a parenting order in the future.

Service delivery

Parenting support in the youth justice context is commonly designed as a programme of activities which address areas of the parent–child relationship such as:

- Dealing with conflict and challenging behaviour.
- Constructive supervision and monitoring of young people.
- Setting and maintaining boundaries and ground rules.
- Communication and negotiation skills.
- Family conflict in general.

Interventions should address the parenting risk and protective factors discussed earlier and should be based on a sound assessment of the parents'

needs. Initially, most service provision by YOTs focused on groupwork, but after three years of development in the field there is now a broad range of support interventions available reflecting the wide diversity of parents and their individual needs. The level and type of service provision varies significantly across the 155 YOTs and we discuss below how this variation is being addressed.

A menu of services should be made available to families so that the best 'match' can be achieved, rather than YOTs pursuing a 'one size fits all' approach. A portfolio of provision might include any of the following:

Family therapy

There are a number of different models that can be offered to families including:

- Individual family based therapy such as that offered by Child and Adolescent Mental Health services.
- Multi Systemic Therapy is an intensive therapeutic approach that addresses issues in the interconnected systems of the family, education, peer relationships and social care.
- Functional Family Therapy involves the whole family to improve communication and levels of support between family members.
- Solution Focused (Brief) Therapy is a short-term intervention assisting participants to explore future solutions rather than past problems.

Group work programmes

These can be provided in a variety of ways by either the YOT itself or a partner agency and may be targeted to provide support to different groups of parents:

- Group based programmes, attended either voluntarily or as the result of a parenting order, targeted at parents/carers of young people who have offended.
- Group based programmes designed for a wider client group of parents/carers of young people considered at risk of offending or who are behaving 'anti-socially'.
- Group based programmes delivered on a universal basis and designed for any parent/carer of a pre-teen or teenager.

Multi-media cognitive behavioural programmes

Many of these programmes can be delivered either individually or in a group environment. They can include programmes using video scenarios, interactive CD ROMs, audiotape and so on.

Parent adviser

The adviser builds a relationship with the parent/s and offers counselling and guidance in the home.

Parent mentor

This involves the linking of a parent/carer with a volunteer mentor who can provide guidance and support in the development of skills and knowledge. This can sometimes be a parent who has participated in a programme previously and wishes to share their experiences, skills and knowledge with other parents.

Many of these models of intervention require specialist expertise and training and it is unlikely that they will all be provided directly by the YOT. The YOT can, however, play an important role in the local coordination of parenting services to ensure that access is readily available and is not limited by a lack of interagency cooperation and partnership. As indicated above, provision remains patchy and the next key stage of development in this field is to ensure greater consistency across YOT areas so that parents in any part of England and Wales can access services that are designed to meet their particular needs and which are of a consistent and high standard of quality.

To assist in that process, the YJB has published *Key Elements of Effective Practice*, intended as part of an overall quality assurance framework to guide the development of parenting support work across YOTs (Youth Justice Board, 2002d). The Board has also introduced a parenting related performance measure requiring YOTs to 'ensure that 10% of young people with final warnings supported by intervention and community based penalties receive a parenting intervention and 75% of parents who attend are satisfied' (Youth Justice Board, 2003d). This should help to ensure that parents' support needs are addressed as a routine part of YOTs' core work. At the same time, the govern-

ment has provided £1.5 million additional funding through the Anti-Social Behaviour Unit to support YOTs to resource their work with parents (Youth Justice Board, 2003a).

Impact and effectiveness

Whilst the research into parenting risk and protective factors is extensive, the research into the effectiveness of programmes in the UK that support families is limited. Research into programmes for the parents of older children or teenagers is even more so, in part because until implementation of the youth justice reforms, parenting support programmes for the parents of teenagers were scarce.

The initial research into some of the new programmes in the youth justice arena provides some promising early findings, but this is limited by the short-term nature of the research, the lack of comparison groups and the low numbers involved in each study.

Despite the limitations of the current research base, the early evidence is that there are some positive benefits for parents and their young people from participating in parenting support interventions. In their report *Positive Parenting*, Ghate and Ramella (2002) describe their evaluation of 34 parenting projects based in YOTs, or partner agencies, with data from around 800 parents and 500 young people. The findings from a sub sample of 200 parents showed statistically significant changes in their parenting:

- Improved communication with their child.
- Improved monitoring and supervision.
- Reduction in conflict.
- Better relationships.
- Parents feeling more able to influence their child's behaviour.
- Parents feeling better able to cope with parenting in general.

Nine out of ten parents also reported that they would recommend the parenting programme to other parents:

Our relationship is much better – we talk more.

We no longer have situations where [child] is aggressive and verbally abusive as we (parents) will not even go down that path with him.

These sessions should be made essential for anyone in similar circumstances ... I may have had a breakdown without them.

Ghate and Ramella (2002)

The evidence of impact on young people whose parents participated in parenting programmes was drawn from questionnaires completed by 78 young people as well as a study of the official reconviction rates of nearly 300 young people. Young people reported slight improvements in:

- Communication and mutual understanding.
- Supervision and monitoring by their parents.
- Reduction in frequency of conflict.
- Better relationships.

The reconviction and re-offending rates of young people whose parents attended parenting programmes were also found to have dropped in the year after the programme, by one third and one half respectively. Although the parenting programme may have contributed to these effects, its impact cannot be separated out as there was no control group involved in the study. Other change programmes the young people were involved in and/or other factors affecting their development may have contributed to this reduction (Ghate and Ramella, 2002).

YOTs have an opportunity to contribute to the growth of the evidence base in this field by systematically monitoring and evaluating the parenting services they provide. Their findings would also help to inform the development of their practice. However, the resourcing of longitudinal studies, designed to include comparison groups, would enhance the findings from local evaluations carried out by YOTs and their partner agencies and create a stronger evidence base in the UK.

Issues

The delivery of parenting support in the youth justice system has raised a number of policy and practice issues. We will focus on the following: that support for parents of teenagers is predominantly offered through the youth justice system; engaging parents in this context; and the lack of services delivered to black and minority ethnic parents and to all fathers.

Support for the parents of younger children has been available for quite some time and is accepted by both professionals and parents in many areas of social and health care practice. The role of parenting support in early childhood years is seen as a preventative strategy by agencies as part of an overall package to families. The National Family and Parenting Institute (2002) conducted a national audit of family services in the UK in 2002. It found that the families of children under five were three times more likely to be provided with services than the families of young people aged 11–15 years. However, parents themselves reported that they found the teenage years most difficult, highlighting concerns about substance misuse and young people's behaviour.

The experience of many parents of teenagers in trouble is that they have asked for support at the first signs of difficulty and not received it. Yet support for the parents of teenagers is a relatively new development for both parents and professionals and one that has been received with a mixed response. If parents identify the teenage years as the most difficult, why then has parenting support for these families been ignored by policy makers for so long and then been received by parents and professionals with such mixed feelings? The answer may partly lie in the majority of provision for this group of parents being introduced as a result of legislation.

The total population of teenagers in the UK is 7.5 million and the percentage of young people who are involved in offending behaviour is approximately 2.37% of that total (Coleman and Schofield, 2003). In using parenting orders as a vehicle to launch support for the parents of teenagers, the focus has been on the parents of young people who have offended, a tiny minority of parents of teenagers overall.

Parenting orders have been condemned as a process of 'blaming' or 'criminalising' parents. Both workers and parents can view parenting orders as a punishment for the perceived failure of parents in their parenting role. Media reports have consistently talked of parenting support in terms of 'punishing' either feckless parents who have shirked their responsibilities or parents who are victims themselves of an over zealous youth justice system.

The model of the generic support offered to the parents of younger children is a useful counterpoint. Here the focus is on offering parenting support such as information giving, informal support networks, structured programmes linked to children's education, and therapeutic interventions provided by a range of professionals. If we cannot offer the equivalent of the generic support available for the parents of younger children, if the focus remains on the parents of teenagers identified as experiencing difficulties, there is little wonder that parents can be reluctant to associate themselves with programmes that they perceive as targeting those considered to be 'failures'.

Discussions about the provision of support for the parents of teenagers are often overshadowed by the debate about parenting order legislation. Misgivings about the compulsory elements of parenting support still exist for parents, practitioners and for critics of current government policy. However, there is a body of thought amongst parenting professionals that without parenting orders there would be no services for the parents of teenagers to discuss.

It appears, moreover, that many parents on orders can be successfully engaged in parenting programmes and find them beneficial despite their initial anger and frustration (Ghate and Ramella, 2002). The key features of programmes provided in the youth justice arena, that successfully engage parents have been documented (Ghate and Ramella, 2002; Elliott et al., 2002). Parents frequently reported that it was the relationships they established with the programme workers that made the difference in their experiences and helped to overcome initial reticence associated with compulsory attendance. Parents described the following skills and qualities in parenting practitioners as most helpful:

- *Being a good listener*: workers that actively listened and took notice of what was being said, looked interested, and remembered what parents had said were particularly valued.
- *Having a positive approach*: parents wanted workers who were relaxed, calm, and in control and who were knowledgeable about teenage behaviour. They felt supported by workers who had been through the difficult times themselves and could share this with humour.
- *Not judging negatively*: parents said they could tell by the way people talked to them that they were not being judgemental. They valued belonging to a safe and supportive group in group work interventions.

- *Establishing trust*: setting clear boundaries for confidentiality in both group and individual interventions was important, as was being able to offer some counselling when a crisis occurred.

(Elliott et al., 2002)

A further noticeable feature of parenting programmes delivered in the youth justice context has been that the majority of participants are white mothers (Ghate and Ramella, 2002). Box (2001) has identified that despite the growth in programmes for parents of teenagers over the last few years, there are low numbers of black and minority ethnic families participating in them. A lack of materials and culturally sensitive programmes have been identified in a number of reviews (Smith, 1996; Roker and Coleman,1998; Butt and Box, 1998) which may be seen as a contributory factor to low levels of participation. Funding from the Family Policy Unit (DfES) has helped in the development of new materials and programmes such as the *Strengthening Families, Strengthening Communities* programme developed in the UK by the Race Equality Unit to better serve the needs of black and minority ethnic families.

The low numbers of fathers participating in both statutory and voluntary parenting support programmes may in part be a reflection of a wider societal view that a father's role in parenting is less significant than that of the mother. Evidence from research, however, suggests that such a view misrepresents the importance of the father's role (Fathers Direct et al., undated). As a consequence, practice has been developing in the direction of attempting to involve fathers routinely when assessing families' needs and by providing services that are relevant to both fathers and mothers. Clearly courts also have an opportunity to consider the participation of fathers when they are contemplating making parenting orders.

In any event, it is clear that youth justice and parenting support professionals need to explore how they can engage effectively with all aspects of the diversity of families and family life when providing parenting support services.

Conclusion

The government has outlined a proposal to focus on supporting parents and carers on three levels as part of its strategy to develop comprehensive services for families (DfES, 2003b). The first level will be to provide universal services to parents through schools, health and social services. These universal services will form part of a preventative strategy. The second level is to provide targeted and specialist support for the parents of children requiring additional support. The third level of the government's strategy is to use statutory powers as a last resort to reinforce the responsibilities of parents.

The use of compulsion in the parenting support arena remains an issue, as does the increased level of state intervention in family life. However we view these issues, it should nonetheless be acknowledged that there has been a dramatic change in the level of provision for parents of teenagers in the last few years, a previously much neglected area of family support services. The advent of the Parenting Fund over the next few years will also help voluntary sector organisations to develop more services for parents. Greater availability of voluntary parenting support across the spectrum should help larger numbers of parents to access services when they need them and also help to promote a shift in how seeking help is viewed. The more routinely services are offered to parents at all stages of their parenting journey, the more ordinary it will become to seek and receive support.

A parallel shift can be seen to be taking place in the youth justice sector. Many workers in the field have historically focused their work on young people, yet parents have the potential to be the greatest positive influence on a young person's development. So engaging effectively with parents to offer support in the parenting task will in many cases be the most effective way for youth justice practitioners, of supporting young people. Through an increased understanding of the relevance of parenting risk and protective factors, YOT staff are beginning to broaden their focus to include parents and families of young people they are working with. The more they are able to identify parents' needs early on and to provide strength-based parenting interventions, the more likely they will be to provide opportunities for parents that form one element of a local comprehensive parenting strategy.

Further reading

Barrett, H. (2003) *Parenting Programmes for Families at Risk*. London: National Family and Parenting Institute

Coleman, J. and Roker, D. (Eds.) (2001) *Supporting Parents of Teenagers*. London: Jessica Kingsley

Ghate, D. and Hazel, N. (2002) *Parenting in Poor Environments, Stress, Support and Coping*. London: Jessica Kingsley

Ghate, D. and Ramella, M. (2002) *Positive Parenting: The National Evaluation of the Youth Justice Board's Parenting Programme*. London: Youth Justice Board

MacFarlane, A. and McPherson, A. (1999) *Teenagers, the Agony, the Ecstasy, the Answers*. London: Little, Brown and Company

32 Preventive Work in Youth Justice

Howard Williamson

Key points

1. All young people need support in making an effective transition to adulthood, and young people at risk of offending need it particularly.

2. Preventive interventions need to address the immediate causes of a young person's offending or anti-social behaviour

3. They also need to offer positive opportunities and experiences to 'disadvantaged' young people and address their social circumstances.

4. Youth crime prevention is a multi-agency responsibility.

5. Preventive strategies can be deployed at any point in the system.

Introduction

'Prevention' comes in three main forms. Primary prevention which stops things happening in the first place, secondary prevention which nips things in the bud and tertiary prevention which stops things in their tracks and creates a foundation for reversing adverse developments. An early Welsh substance misuse prevention strategy put it more simply, suggesting that prevention spans 'stopping people starting' through to 'starting people stopping'. The analogy might be applied equally to youth crime and justice.

Since 1998 the prevention of offending by young people has been the principal aim of the youth justice system of England and Wales, yet developing preventive practice and 'proving' its effects remains a professional and political challenge. There is a wealth of evidence that effective preventive strategies will involve policy domains beyond the criminal justice system; education, health, social services and youth support services. Preventive interventions can be deployed at every stage in a young person's offending 'career' and, if implemented effectively, can halt more serious involvement in crime and serve as a platform for redirecting young people in a positive direction.

For the sake of clarity, it may be useful to think of prevention as a strategy to be deployed at five key stages in a young person's offending career:

- pre-offending
- early offending
- regular offending (on the cusp of custody)
- in custody
- post-custody

This chapter will focus on the earlier stages in that career.

Youth justice sits, somewhat awkwardly, between the 'correctional services' of the criminal justice system and the 'children's services' provided by education, health and social services. As Sarah Curtis argues (see Chapter 8) little distinction was made, historically, between adult, and younger offenders but, in the 20th century the 'welfare' imperative has gradually colonised the youth justice system, marking a recognition that the individuals concerned are 'children first and offenders second'. However, this remains a politically contentious area, not least because of continuing uncertainty about what we should do with the significant numbers of relatively 'petty' but persistent teenage offenders whose offending is neither a trivial 'one-off' nor of pathologically serious dimensions (see Chapters 12 and 37). During the 1960s, a powerful 'non-interventionist' lobby composed of practitioners, politicians, academics and lawyers argued that the best strategy was to 'leave the kids alone'. Most young people in trouble, it was argued, simply 'grew out of crime' anyway and greater damage would be done by labelling them and processing them through the criminal justice system (Schur, 1973). That was, however, at a time of a buoyant youth labour market and greater social cohesion. What might then have been considered to be 'benign neglect' would today be viewed as 'malign indifference', because of the evidence of the impact of youth crime on its victims and a recognition that, today, youth transitions to adulthood are more complex and more problematic (Drakeford and Williamson, 1997). It is now fairly widely accepted that young people in general need greater support, advice and direction and that disadvantaged young people, those at heightened risk of offending, need significantly more. As the rhetoric of the Connexions service in England puts it, there is clear evidence for a 'universal support service differentiated according to need'. But how is this to be achieved?

Recent developments in preventive work in the youth justice system

Following the Crime and Disorder Act 1998, the government created the Youth Justice Board (YJB) and, in each local authority area, statutory inter-agency youth offending teams (YOTs) (see Chapter 17). The YJB was initially responsible for monitoring the operation of the youth justice system. Later, in 2000, it also took on a commissioning responsibility for placements for all under 18s within the 'juvenile secure estate' (see Chapter 4). These new arrangements have been variously depicted as an arm of the 'new correctionalism' (Pitts, 2001b) and as having driven through 'miraculous' improvements in the quality and effectiveness of interventions with young people who offend, admittedly often from a very low base (Hodgkin, 2002). YOTs have been responsible for the implementation of this new agenda. And while there were immediate political targets, such as fast-tracking 'persistent young offenders' to halve the time between arrest and sentence, there has been growing attention to preventive work. As Jill Annison notes (Chapter 19) research suggests that all young people will be subject to a range of 'risk' and 'protective' factors which will heighten or reduce the likelihood of their becoming involved in crime. The youth justice policy challenge, put simply, is to address and reduce the factors that place young people at 'risk' of

offending and to develop and strengthen those factors that 'protect' them against involvement in offending. If this is the strategy, what is the nature of the interventions required and how can the youth justice system's capacity to deliver be maximised?

The YJB has endeavoured to improve preventive provision for young people who offend. In doing so, it has had to steer a course between the 'opportunity-focused' and 'problem-oriented' policies directed at young people. It has sought to promote interventions of immediate benefit to young people; in education, in the assessment and treatment for substance misuse, in the field of mental health and in the development of 'purposeful activity' programmes. At the same time, it has endeavoured to maintain the confidence of politicians and the courts, by respecting calls for 'just deserts', ensuring appropriate reparation for harm done, and recognising the need for 'victim satisfaction'. As Rob Allen notes (Chapter 4) the media spotlight can easily undermine effective, but politically difficult, measures, as evidenced by the perennial allegation that the youth justice system is merely about providing 'treats for the bad kids' (the 'Safari Boy' episode of over a decade ago is, it appears, indelibly etched in the minds of many *Daily Mail* readers!).

Within the constraints of *realpolitik*, the YJB has introduced a range of new measures designed to prevent offending. These have included new sentences such as referral orders (see Chapter 16), a robust 'alternative to custody' in the form of intensive supervision and surveillance programmes (see Chapter 22), improved programmes within the juvenile secure estate, and more robust post-custody resettlement schemes as part of the community-based element of detention and training orders. Although academic research and government inspections continue to highlight areas of weakness or operational failings in this fast-developing strategy, most commentators concede that these developments are on the right track (Audit Commission, 2004).

Within this broader strategy, the prevention committee of the YJB has tried to give a sharper focus to the Board's prevention strategy by concentrating on three key areas:

- pre-crime prevention
- post-crime reduction
- post-crime detection

The YJB is committed to a targeted approach to its work, making the best use of the resources available. This does not deny the value placed upon 'universal' provision for young people, which it regards as a valuable supplement to its more focused interventions. Its prevention strategy has focused to date on pre-crime prevention (Youth Inclusion and Support Panels) and post-crime reduction (Youth Inclusion Programmes). Two further initiatives (Safer Schools Partnerships and SPLASH programmes) lie on the bridge between the two, addressing both concerns.

Youth Inclusion and Support Panels

One of the most recent preventive initiatives developed by the Board has wide-ranging aspirations, even if crime prevention remains at their core. *Youth Inclusion and Support Panels* (YISPs) are aimed at children below the age of criminal responsibility, and up to 13 years of age, whose circumstances are indicative of high risk of future offending. YISPs require more robust recording and much closer information sharing between the police, social services and YOT than before, if services and support are to reach the children most in need. Current evidence suggests that such systems are patchy, though protocols for more effective practice are presently being put in place. Rather predictably, this initiative has been lambasted by some academics and children's charities as the 'criminalisation of social welfare', and legitimate concerns have been expressed about labelling, stigma and 'net-widening'. The view of the YJB, however, is that the children who are to be targeted by YISPs are already vulnerable to exclusion, underachievement and an absence of opportunity, which need to be rectified if pathways into offending, and other marginal destinations, are to be forestalled. Indeed, parents whose children have been the recipients of pilot interventions have usually been delighted with the learning and personal development opportunities they have presented. Participation in available programmes is currently voluntary, even though the underpinning philosophy is to ensure that children identified as 'at risk of offending' are offered appropriate support at home, in school and during their leisure time to reduce the possibility/probability of subsequent offending. YISPs are still at an embryonic

stage; pilots were established in 14 areas from February 2003, and best practice is still to be developed.

Safer Schools Partnerships

The YJB Prevention Committee has also recently encouraged the establishment of *Safer Schools Partnerships* [SSPs], originally conceptualised as 'police in schools'. There is strong evidence that attendance and achievement in school are a pre-eminent protective factor against offending by young people, and that truancy and absenteeism is a significant risk factor in terms of crime, substance abuse and psycho-social disorder. Yet some schools really are 'concrete jungles' where the capacity to learn, and even attend, is undermined by threats and fear. Piggy-backing on the government's street crime initiative, the YJB has argued that some schools within the ten street robbery areas merited a stronger police presence. Notwithstanding some newpapers' depiction of 'cops with Kalashnikovs in the corridors', the idea was that a dedicated police officer could provide a reassuring presence to the majority of children while simultaneously being on the spot to deal with 'low level' nuisance and crime within and around the school. As John Pitts argues (Chapter 38) there is growing evidence that a great deal of bullying and intimidation takes place not just inside school but on the routes to and from school. It seems clear that 'safe places are learning spaces' and, as the mental health charity Young Minds has observed, young people who are distracted by anxiety and fear are not likely to be fully engaged with their education.

SPLASH

A proven initiative pioneered by the YJB is the highly successful holiday SPLASH scheme which has been running for the past three years in over 140 high crime, low-income, neighbourhoods. Evaluations of SPLASH show reductions in youth offending in the areas concerned. Impressive though these findings are, these reductions cannot be attributed to SPLASH alone, not least because SPLASH does not, and cannot, address individual offending. However, the success of the scheme in engaging 'disaffected' young people has led to it merging (in England) with other summer and holiday programmes under the new 'Positive Activities for Young People' initiative (located within the Department for Education and Skills). This has brought together different funding streams to provide a year round programme. Such developments underline that preventing youth crime cannot be easily dissociated from the longer term endeavour to create high quality leisure and recreational provision for young people in disadvantaged neighbourhoods, which enhances their social learning as well as their personal development. It could be argued that the YJB, because it can command political attention and Treasury support, has served as a 'stalking horse' for the development of the kind of high quality youth provision that other sectors, like education and the youth service, have cried out for in the past. Youth crime prevention and reduction may be but one of the positive outcomes of such provision.

Youth inclusion programmes

Whereas SPLASH and Safer Schools address 'whole populations', a community or a school, Youth Inclusion Programmes (YIPs) are targeted at a core group of 13-16 year olds, deemed to be most 'at risk' within the 70 neighbourhoods where the schemes are operating. The core group is identified through a multi-agency consultation process, but a broader group of young people within the neighbourhood are also encouraged to participate in the activities. YIPs utilise a range of methods including 'street work', outdoor activities, football tournaments and fashion shows in order to make and sustain contact with what is often a multiply-disadvantaged, and very 'hard-to-reach', population. Each project aims to reduce arrest rates among the target group by 70% and ensure that 90% are in appropriate education training or employment.

Some issues raised by prevention

The renewed political emphasis on 'prevention' is welcome, although it has been 'bubbling under' within the Blair administration ever since the publication of the *Report of Policy Action Team 12*, the Social Exclusion Unit's analysis of the position and condition of young people in 'deprived neighbourhoods' (Social Exclusion Unit, 2000). However, the problem for 'prevention' is twofold:

proving that it has been achieved, and securing the resources to deliver preventative interventions. Education authorities may be willing to establish robust 'alternative curriculum' programmes that reduce youth crime or substance misuse, but they are very likely to want the youth justice system or the health authority to contribute to the costs because they are a heavy burden for education authorities to bear alone. Conversely, criminal justice agencies and health authorities do not always see why they should pay for 'education'. There is still a long way to go before the rhetoric of 'joined-up thinking' becomes a reality.

As we have noted, youth justice systems must always balance the accountability of the young person for their offending with a concern for their personal and social circumstances. There is little doubt that the majority of young people who commit offences persistently are both troubled and troublesome and, as the Children Act 1989 reminds us, a child in trouble is, very often, 'a child in need'. Because of this, the Welsh Assembly is currently producing an *All Wales Youth Offending Strategy*, rooted in a commitment to primary prevention and based on the philosophy of preventing youth crime by 'extending entitlement'. *Extending Entitlement* (National Assembly for Wales, 2000) is the Welsh equivalent of the Connexions strategy in England but it proceeds from a different premise. Rather than considering the attitudes and behaviour of 'difficult' teenagers in isolation, it explores the opportunities and experiences that are routinely provided for young adults who have remained in education and training and not become involved in longer term offending and problematic substance misuse.

Extending Entitlement identifies, amongst other things, a high quality educational experience, access to relevant information and new technologies, sporting and cultural opportunities and 'away from home' experiences as 'protective' factors. The majority of children and young people access such experiences 'organically', as a result of parental interest and encouragement, good schooling, extra-curricular activities, membership of youth organisations and travel, if only on package holidays abroad. Some young people do not have such opportunities, including many, and probably most, young people who offend. *Extending Entitlement* indicates that where young people do not access such opportunities organically, they should be made available, through public policy measures which aim to extend the entitlement to all. This is the essence of an effective preventive strategy and the practical legacy of political exhortations to be 'tough on the causes of crime'. It does, of course, demand more rigorous information sharing protocols for the most positive of reasons – to ensure that the 'disadvantages' of young people are spotted early and that appropriate early intervention is secured. This should be the primary rationale for the information sharing and assessment (ISA) systems currently developed in England and the analogous Keeping In Touch (KIT) systems in Wales.

There is, however, the further question about being 'tough on crime', for those within the criminal justice system, where primary prevention has not been effective in diverting them from committing offences. Historically, solely *retributive* measures appear to have had only very limited impact upon re-offending while 'welfarist' rehabilitative measures could be said to have excused offending. As a result, current *restorative* approaches should be welcomed (see Chapter 28). They seek to ensure that young people are held responsible for their behaviour and expect them to 'make good' the harm that they have caused, to the satisfaction of their victims. It is intended that, whenever possible, involvement of victims will enable the young person to recognise the impact and consequences of their actions. All too often in the past, the victim has been an anonymous and therefore, in the eyes of the offender, a 'legitimate' target.

Restorative and preventative measures go hand in hand. The former, beyond connecting the offence to the 'punishment', helps to maintain the confidence of the courts and the public. The latter produces the possibility of re-engaging the young person in more legitimate, mainstream, routes to adulthood. Such interventions demand an individualised approach informed by an understanding of 'what works', for individuals, on issues such as 'anger management' and 'personal development'. Although sometimes perceived as 'soft options' within the media and some sections of the political establishment, such an approach should be viewed as progressive when set against either non-intervention or retributive intervention strategies of the past which had little positive impact.

Further reading

Crawford, A. and Newburn, T. (2003) *Youth Offending and Restorative Justice: Implementing Reform in Youth Justice*. Cullompton: Willan

Haines, K. and Drakeford, M. (1998) *Young People and Youth Justice*. London: Macmillan

Pitts, J. (1999) *Working With Young Offenders*. 2nd edn. London: Macmillan

33 Working with Victims in Youth Justice

Brian Williams

Key points

1. The Crime and Disorder Act 1998 and other legislation associated with the youth justice reforms is aimed at promoting a cultural change in youth justice, partly with a view to giving victims of crime greater centrality within the system. This has enormous implications for service delivery.

2. Alongside the introduction of court orders which require consultation with victims, the legislation also increases the extent to which the youth justice system becomes involved with first and minor offences. At the same time, the government is requiring the system to process cases more quickly, which is not necessarily compatible with victims' interests. Thus, work with victims has been promoted at a time of considerable change and expansion in the youth justice system.

3. The early evidence on the effectiveness of these changes is mixed. Referral orders have been successful in certain respects, often at the expense of the other types of court orders, which are made relatively rarely since the introduction of referral orders.

4. Direct victim participation in youth justice is not as common as might have been expected.

5. In most cases, the involvement of young people in reparation has been coerced rather than voluntary, an approach unique to England and Wales despite the success of voluntary participation in other countries.

Introduction

Prior to the late 1990s, hardly any youth justice practitioners in England and Wales worked directly with victims of crime at all. Only a few years later, victim work has become something of a specialism in many youth offending teams (YOTs) and it also impinges, to a greater or lesser extent, upon the work of all youth justice workers. This rapid transformation has occurred largely as a result of two pieces of legislation; the Crime and Disorder Act 1998 and the Youth Justice and Criminal Evidence Act 1999. The former introduced the Youth Justice Board for England and Wales (YJB) and the YOTs and created a range of new sentences for young people who offend. Most of these new disposals included opportunities for direct or indirect reparation, and encouraged or required young people to make some kind of recompense to the victims of their offences. The YJB vigorously promoted the notion of restorative justice, providing funding for many experimental projects. Even before the Crime and Disorder Act was fully implemented, the Youth Justice and Criminal Evidence Act introduced new arrangements for dealing with all young people appearing in court for the first time – other than those committing the most minor and the most serious offences – via referral orders (see Chapter 16), and victim involvement was built into these; at least in theory.

Thus, youth justice workers who had seen their role as primarily concerned with assisting, and responding to the behaviour of, young people in trouble, have had to get to grips with work with victims and to encourage young people to reflect upon the impact of their offending upon them. In many areas, working with victims presents 'deep-rooted difficulties for YOTs,' whose staff are not accustomed to doing so (Crawford and Newburn, 2003: 238). Although a new group of victim specialists has emerged over the period, in most areas, responsibility has been shared by other members of YOTs. The emphasis in the 1998 Act upon early intervention, particularly in the shape of referral orders, but also through final warnings, action plan orders and reparation orders, has drawn many more young people into statutory supervision, and it has required workers to consider and routinely consult the victims of their offences.

Working with victims in youth justice

YOTs come into contact with victims of crime, or have to deal with issues of victimisation in the course of preparing pre-sentence reports (PSRs), when supervising final warnings, referral orders, action plan orders, reparation orders and supervision orders and, in some parts of the country, when they are involved in family group conferences (see Chapter 29). These interventions may require direct reparation, involving contact between victim and offender, or indirect reparation which may take the form of a written apology or some form of community service. In very serious cases (defined by law as 'grave crimes') the probation service takes responsibility for keeping the victims, of offences committed by young people, informed during the course of long custodial sentences. For the great majority of incarcerated young people, however, this is the responsibility of YOTs.

The final warning is a formal pre court intervention imposed upon children and young people who re-offend having previously been the subjects of a police reprimand. The YOT is responsible for devising intervention programmes to accompany the final warning, and in many cases these include a restorative element (see Chapter 12).

Pre-sentence reports are required by the National Standards to take account of the effect of an offence upon the victim (see Chapter 18). This does not usually require direct contact by report writers with victims: rather, the information can be obtained by reading the documentation about the offence provided by the Crown Prosecution Service, where available. Nonetheless, the YOT may consult the victim to explore the possibility of reparative options in advance of sentencing. Where the likely disposal will be an action plan order or a reparation order, a full PSR is not legally required; instead, shorter specific sentence reports (SSRs) which address the proposed components of the order may be sufficient. Courts do, however, have the discretion to request full reports in all cases.

The referral order is the primary sentence available in the youth court in the case of first court appearances, and involves a young person being referred to a youth offender panel (see Chapter 16). Panels are composed of a representative from the YOT and two trained volunteers recruited from the local community. The young person is required to attend with at least one parent and the victim is invited to attend or to be represented, and can also bring one or more supporters.

Although the young person's attendance is compulsory, the outcome is more likely to be successful if they feel that they have been able to participate as fully as they wish, if they feel they have been treated fairly, and if they genuinely 'own' the terms of the contract which is agreed between the panel, the victim and themselves at the initial meeting (Crawford and Newburn, 2003). Inevitably, panel meetings can be very emotional encounters and no matter how well they are managed, both the victim and the young person are likely to be apprehensive and to need help in preparing for the meeting. The management of this process by YOT staff is clearly important. Each party needs an understanding of what the meeting is about, how it will run and roughly what is expected of them. Once the preparations have been made, the meeting itself also needs careful and tactful management.

The reparation order, as its name suggests, requires the young person to undertake direct or indirect reparation to their victim for up to 24 hours. It is not a community sentence in legal terms (see Chapter 9) and there is a presumption that such an order will be imposed in all cases unless there are good reasons why not, or the court intends to make another order with a reparative element.

As with all forms of reparative activity, where the proposed reparation is directly to a victim, their consent has to be obtained, and the task of obtaining this falls to the YOT worker involved. Meetings between the young person and victim may be relatively informal but both parties still require considerable preparation. In some cases the victim may be a corporation or business and so, for example, the 'victim' may be represented by a manager from the chain store from which a young person may have stolen goods.

The action plan order is a community sentence intended to provide short-term interventions by the YOT. The order can include any combination of up to seven requirements and there is a presumption that reparation, either directly to a victim or to 'the community at large' will be one of these.

Supervision orders are imposed in cases where the court feels that a young person needs more intensive supervision by the YOT, and they can last up to three years. A range of conditions can be added to the orders and the Crime and Disorder Act provides for a requirement that the young person undertake direct or indirect reparation for up to 90 days. The use of this requirement, however, appears to be relatively uncommon.

Family group conferences (FGCs), unlike the interventions described above, have no statutory basis in England and Wales (see Chapter 29). They involve intensive intervention with young people in trouble and their families at any stage of the youth justice process as a way of empowering those at the conference to make decisions about what should happen to the young person. They are not part of the repertoire of most YOTs, and where they are used; they tend to be reserved for the more serious cases. An FGC brings together the young person and their family and supporter/s, the victim or their representative and a similar number of supporters, a trained, neutral, facilitator and any relevant professionals. The meetings can be quite large, and sometimes more than one young person and more than one victim can take part in the same conference. Meetings require careful preparation, and can take some time to set up. The aim is to reach agreement, rather than an enforceable contract, in order to resolve the conflict between the offender and the victim. Conferences are forward-looking in that, having confronted the young person about their offence and its consequences, the emphasis changes to how the young person will behave in the future.

The intellectual rationale for FGCs is that meetings are a ritual which triggers a process of 're-integrative shaming' (Braithwaite, 1989). This involves encouraging the young person to express how they feel about the offence and the victim, often involving an apology, and hearing their expressions of remorse. Victims have an important role in decisions about the form that reparation should take but the young person's views are also heard. The YJB funded a number of experimental projects in its early days, but by 2004 almost all of these had disappeared as a result of losing their funding.

The impact of the new orders and of working with victims

The changes introduced in the late 1990s were a response to criticisms that the youth justice system ignored the needs of victims, failed to respond quickly enough to, and colluded with, offending by young people, used resources inefficiently and spent too little time in face to face contact with young people (Jones, 2001a; 2002). Whatever one may think of this critique, it has had a powerful impact on both the administration and practice of youth justice in England and Wales in the 21st century.

While one of the unintended consequences of the youth justice reforms, with their heavy emphasis upon monitoring and evaluation, has required many practitioners to spend more time in front of computers than in face to face work with young people, it has also brought them into contact with the victims of crime. Youth justice workers are now engaging with victims and bringing victims and young people who offend together in considerable numbers. While those numbers continue, as we note below, to fall short of the targets set by the YJB, victim perspectives are being incorporated into youth justice practice to an unprecedented degree. This has effected a significant cultural shift towards an acceptance by professionals that the impact of youth offending should be a major focus of their work and that, inasmuch as it is possible, the victims of youth crime should be partners in the resolution of youth offending.

The multi-agency nature of the YOTs has mobilised new resources for young people, and made it easier to collaborate with agencies like Victim Support and local mediation services. Initially, this collaboration was driven by the need to implement a large number of new court orders very rapidly and so the onus of collaboration was upon staff training. However, longer term relationships have been built on this basis to the benefit of the victims of youth crime.

Youth justice has certainly been speeded up since 1998 in response to the government pledge to halve the time it took to process 'persistent young offenders'. Whereas in 1997 the average time from arrest to sentence was 142 days, by August 2001 it had halved to 71 days. Further reductions have since been achieved. Whatever its other merits, however, this has not necessarily been a welcome development in the case of victims of crime who would often prefer more time to ponder whether, and to what extent, they wish to be involved in restorative encounters. At the same time, if it is the case that the reduction in court delays has contributed to a reduction in re-offending rates, this is obviously in the interests of victims in general (see Audit Commission, 2004).

The impact of victim involvement

The impact of interventions with the victims of youth crime has been mixed:

Pre-sentence reports

As indicated above, a problem with requiring the victim perspective to be addressed in PSRs is that the necessary documentation often fails to reach YOTs in time to be included. Many PSRs therefore involve a superficial and/or one-sided account of the victim's perspective. In some areas, specialist YOT staff makes direct contact with victims in order to obtain up-to-date information about the impact of the offence and to ascertain the potential for reparative activity. The victim may have supplied information to the police already for a Victim Personal Statement, but these documents tend to go out of date quickly in more serious cases (although, theoretically, there is the possibility of updating them) and they are often not passed on by the police to the other agencies which could benefit from having access to them.

Referral orders

Within a year of their implementation in 2002, referral orders had become the most frequently imposed court order, making up one third of all youth court disposals and eclipsing other court disposals like reparation and action plan orders (Home Office, 2003g).

The orders have been implemented with some success, but the extent to which victims have been involved in the making of contracts has varied from place to place, and overall levels of victim involvement have been low; only 13% of cases in the Home Office pilot projects (Crawford and Newburn, 2003). Panel members are expected to introduce a victim perspective in cases where the victim is not present, but the evaluation of the pilot projects found that even this did not occur in over 20% of meetings where the victim was not represented (Crawford and Newburn, 2003).

Given the strong emphasis placed upon the restorative nature of the referral order by government, and the fact that most definitions of restorative justice stress the importance of victim involvement, these are important findings. The YJB is now emphasising the need to achieve greater levels of victim involvement in, and satisfaction with, panels, and has provided additional funding to assist YOTs in meeting these targets (YJB, 2003k).

Reparation orders

These have been very successful in terms of reconviction rates: young people placed on reparation orders were reconvicted within a year in 51.2% of cases in 2001, which was 'the lowest reconviction rate for a non-custodial court disposal for juvenile males' (Home Office, 2003g: 16). Given the much higher reconviction rate for all custodial sentences, this makes it the most successful court order by this measure.

The YJB evaluation of the pilot YOT areas was published in time to influence practice in the rest of the country (Home Office, 2001a), and some valuable lessons appear to have been learnt (Dignan, 2000). In many cases, these lessons were incorporated into the relevant National Standards. The need for careful preparation before bringing young people and victims together was perhaps the most important of these lessons, along with the need to avoid placing any pressure on victims to take part (Dignan, 2002).

The YJB commissioned research on the implementation of this and other new orders, and although there were serious design and methodological problems with this research (Wilcox, 2003), the findings suggested that most victims who did decide to take part in direct reparation found it a positive experience. Of those who completed satisfaction questionnaires, 62% indicated that they would recommend the experience to others and 70% said that they thought the young person had a better understanding of the impact of the offence upon them as victims as a result of the encounter (YJB, 2002b).

Action plan orders

These orders were successful initially, in terms of reconviction rates, with only 52.8% of young people placed on them being reconvicted within one year. However, reconviction rates are normally measured over at least a two-year period, which allows for more reliable comparisons. In any event, they are limited by the fact that they measure only recorded and detected crimes (see Chapter 2). The reconviction rates for low-tariff disposals such as referral orders and action plan orders also need to be seen in the light of the likelihood that the young people concerned have committed relatively minor offences and are often younger than those receiving (for example) custodial sentences, in which case lower reconviction rates would be expected anyway.

Action plan orders allow focused, relatively short-term intervention by the YOT, and they open up the possibility of reparation as part of a package of responses to an individual young person's offending. They have been criticised, however, for their potential for net-widening (Morris, 2002) and because they can be made without recourse to a full pre-sentence report (Monaghan, 2000). They also carry the danger that once a young person has been given an opportunity of undertaking reparation as part of the order and this has broken down, subsequent court appearances will result in harsher sentences because of the perceived failure of a reparative approach. In some areas, the reparation component of action plan orders has been criticised for being implemented in a mechanistic way, with most reparation being indirect and much of it unconnected with the nature of young people's offending.

Supervision orders

By their nature supervision orders are designed to provide longer-term supervision for young people with more serious and intractable problems. Supervision orders with reparation conditions are made relatively infrequently, and little is known about the outcomes of such cases. However, even where orders do not include a specific requirement there is nonetheless a presumption that reparative activity will form part of the intervention. In some cases, the victims have suffered seriously as a result of the offence, and YOT staff might involve them indirectly in the young person's supervision, for example by facilitating a letter of apology.

Family group conferences

Although a number of experimental projects were funded by the YJB, few survived beyond the point where the funding ran out. It appears that although projects struggled to find sufficient referrals, both victims and young people found involvement in such intensive interventions beneficial in a majority of cases. In the few areas where they remain in place, FGC projects are now adapting to the changed environment.

The principles of effective practice

Initially, some people believed that the government's failure to adhere to the principle that involvement in restorative justice should be voluntary on the part of all involved, would sabotage the experiment with restorative interventions (Williams, 2001). In fact, practitioners, courts and the YJB have taken a flexible approach which recognises that young people in particular cannot be successfully coerced into making reparation. The Board's guidance on effective practice, for example, acknowledges that:

> ... *it is important that the young person be given the choice. It is in the public interest ... that every effort is made by youth justice services to achieve the voluntary attendance of those who need to be involved.*
>
> (YJB, undated: 7)

Practitioners have generally found ways of assessing young people's suitability and resisting inappropriate referrals from courts. Sentencers do not normally wish to impose reparation in cases where it might be harmful to victims. The principle of voluntary participation is nevertheless undermined by the Crime and Disorder Act 1998. There was also a widespread fear that the new court orders contained in the 1998 Act would drag more minor offenders into the ambit of the criminal justice system (Monaghan, 2000). It may be that courts, in their concern to provide consistent support, or at least consistent opportunities, to victims, may have sentenced more young people to community penalties. There is certainly some evidence that referral orders have sometimes made disproportionate demands on young people committing minor offences (Crawford and Newburn, 2003).

In much criminal justice policy, there is a tendency to assume that offenders and victims are two completely separate groups. In fact, as we know from practice and research, these are two overlapping groups of people (Williams, 2002; see Chapter 38), and practice with young people who offend may often involve helping them work through their prior experiences of victimisation. In many cases, this is essential before there can be any question of young people empathising with their victims.

Conclusion

Overall, the benefits of the youth justice reforms for victims appear to have outweighed the difficulties encountered. Victims' interests, wishes and needs have come to be taken into account within the youth justice system far more than was previously the case and both sentencers and practitioners have developed greater sensitivity to, and awareness of, victims. There is some cause for concern, however, that this has sometimes been achieved at the expense of young people who offend because of 'net-widening' and 'up-tariffing', and that the involvement of victims in youth justice has been geographically patchy and inconsistent. Where they have been directly involved in restorative interventions, most have found this beneficial, despite the haste with which the changes were implemented and the rushed nature of consultation with victims in some cases.

Not all the new arrangements have been systematically evaluated, however, and rigorous research should precede any further changes. There is potential for further growth and greater standardisation in the provision of services to victims, and for expanding this work into new areas, like YOTs keeping victims informed of progress in the case of relatively minor offences or where the young person was given a custodial sentence; direct restorative work with young people during and after their release from the custodial element of detention and training orders; and the more widespread use of family group conferences to resolve conflicts.

Acknowledgement

I would like to thank Jean Reid of Derbyshire Youth Offending Service, who kindly commented on an earlier version of this chapter.

Further reading

Crawford, A. and Newburn, T. (2003) *Youth Offending and Restorative Justice: Implementing Reform in Youth Justice.* Cullompton: Willan

Williams, B. (2002) Working with the Victims of Young Offenders: What Works? in Dearling, A. and Skinner, A. (Eds.) *Making a Difference: Practice and Planning in Working with Young People in Community Safety and Crime Prevention Programmes.* Lyme Regis: Russell House Publishing

34 Working with Volunteers in the Youth Justice System

Tamara Flanagan

Key points

1. The criminal justice system has a long history of volunteer involvement.

2. It is possible to identify four broad types of volunteering activity within the youth justice system. Volunteers may:
   - contribute directly to the operation of the youth justice process in an official capacity, like youth court magistrates;
   - undertake monitoring functions;
   - work directly with young people as mentors or appropriate adults;
   - in themselves be adjudicated offenders, undertaking voluntary work to benefit the community.

3. Recent years have seen a significant expansion both in the numbers of members of the public who give up their time to work directly with young people who offend and in the involvement of such young people themselves in voluntary activity.

4. The experience of volunteering may be a rewarding and effective way of reintegrating young people who offend into the community.

5. In order to maximise the advantages of voluntary contributions to the youth justice system, proper systems of safeguards and support need to be in place.

Introduction

The youth justice system, like the adult criminal justice system, has a long history of volunteer involvement, but it has expanded considerably in recent years with the gradual retreat by government from responsibility for areas of social welfare, an increased emphasis on civic involvement in the justice system as a whole, and a recognition of the contribution that volunteering can make to developing 'social capital'.

Volunteers take on a broad range of activities, which necessarily involve wide differentials in terms of personal skills, and commitment of time and energy. By the same token, the social benefits and rewards associated with different volunteering functions also vary considerably. It is nonetheless possible to identify at least four general types of voluntary work, which currently make a significant contribution to the youth justice system:

- Activities which are associated with the formal operation of the youth justice process, such as sitting as a magistrate in the youth court or as a community representative on a youth offender panel.

- Activities which involve monitoring a particular aspect of the youth justice system in a 'watchdog' capacity to ensure that its functioning is efficient, fair and accords with the rules and standards expected of it. This form of volunteering is probably best exemplified by lay visitors to police stations and members of Independent Monitoring Boards (formerly known as Boards of Visitors) for young offender institutions.

- Activities undertaken by members of the public to provide a direct service to young people who offend, such as acting as mentors, appropriate adults or 'advocates' to those caught up in the youth justice system.

- Activities undertaken by young people who are 'adjudicated offenders' and, in particular, those serving custodial sentences.

Overall, volunteers make a substantial contribution to the youth justice system, and one, which has taken on a new dimension in the recent period and looks set to continue growing in the coming years.

Voluntary activity associated with the administration of justice

Lay magistrates

There are now more than 30,000 lay magistrates engaged in the criminal justice system throughout England and Wales (see Chapter 13). Magistrates are required to live locally to the area which they serve and must have a reasonable knowledge of the local community. Other personal qualities sought in those volunteering for the role are:

- ability to communicate
- social awareness
- maturity
- sound judgement
- commitment and reliability

Yet there are still concerns over the extent to which lay magistrates can be said to be representative of the community and these are perhaps most pronounced in relation to age, which might be thought to be of particular importance in a youth justice context. While there is a good deal of geographic variation, less than 4% of magistrates nationally are under 40 years of age and almost a third are over 60. In addition, the lay magistracy is disproportionately drawn from those with professional or managerial status and almost certainly financially well off in comparison with the population at large. By contrast, while it is a long-standing complaint that ethnic minorities are under-represented among lay magistrates, the evidence suggests that the ethnic minority composition of this group of volunteers is in fact approaching that of the general population (Morgan and Russell, 2000).

Community members of youth offender panels

The introduction of referral orders, through the Youth Justice and Criminal Evidence Act 1999 was designed to increase significantly the contribution of members of the community to the administration of youth justice. The order involves a referral by the court to a youth offender panel responsible for developing a contract with the young person designed to meet their needs and address the causes of their offending (see Chapter 16). Volunteers are expected to attend panel meetings between 20 and 40 times per year (Biermann and Moulton, 2003).

The most significant aspect of the reform from the current perspective is that two of the three panel members are volunteers, recruited from the local community and trained by the local youth offending team (YOT). The relevant personal qualities are, unsurprisingly, similar to those for magistrates requiring:

- Patience, good judgement and objectivity.
- Commitment and reliability.
- Good listening and communication skills.
- An ability to relate to young people.

Previous convictions are not automatically an obstacle to being accepted as a panel member.

The new order has substantially increased the numbers of volunteers involved in the administration of youth justice. There are upward of 7,000 panel members (Biermann and Moulton, 2003) who between them contribute towards a decision about the disposal in 30% of youth court cases (Youth Justice Board, 2003o). Moreover, the fact that professionals are also represented on the panels, by the YOTs, does not appear to undermine the influence of community members on outcomes. Indeed, research undertaken as part of the national evaluation of referral orders found that 76% of volunteers agreed with the statement that 'community panel members determine the direction of meetings' (Crawford and Newburn, 2003).

It seems clear too that recruitment of community panel members has generated a group of volunteers who are considerably more representative of the community than lay magistrates. In terms of age, for instance, 37% of community panel members are under 40 years of age and employment status largely mirrors that of the general population. Male volunteers are however under-represented (Biermann and Moulton, 2003).

Volunteers as monitors of the youth justice system

Independent custody visitors

In 1986, following a recommendation in the Scarman Report (1981), lay visiting schemes, subsequently re-named independent custody visiting schemes, were established as a mechanism for increasing public confidence in the police in the wake of the Brixton riots. The schemes provide for volunteers who are otherwise unconnected with the criminal justice system to inspect police stations and report on the treatment of detainees and the conditions in which they are held. Home Office guidance issued in 1992, emphasised the importance of establishing schemes in all police service areas and the importance of independent custody visitors providing a check on the way the police carry out their duties in respect of detained young persons (Home Office, 1992a).

Volunteers drawn from the local community visit police stations unannounced to check on the welfare of those in police custody. Research conducted in 1998, found that 80% of police stations in London were visited weekly, though outside of the metropolitan area the frequency of visiting was considerably lower (Home Office, 1998d). Again concerns have been expressed about the extent to which volunteers can be said to represent the community and schemes have drawn attention to the difficulty of attracting visitors below the age of 35.

While independent custody visitors have no specific remit to deal with those who are under the age of 18 years, given the particular vulnerability of young people while they are in police detention, the importance of the function for the youth justice system is clear.

Members of independent monitoring boards for young offender institutions

A similar 'watchdog' function is provided by independent monitoring boards, previously known as Boards of Visitors, whose volunteer members can access the young offender institution to which they are allocated at any time to talk to staff or young people, reporting concerns as required. Each Board is required to submit an annual report to the Home Secretary, which can be influential in directing policy, and contribute directly to the rating allocated to any institution by the prison service.

As a result of the security implications, the process of applying to be a volunteer is a relatively lengthy one and in some cases clearance can take up to six months. Subsequent induction training takes a similar time and members are expected to commit themselves to around two days per month.

The vulnerability of young people in custody is well established (Goldson, 2002d; Nacro, 2003e).

Voluntary activity in this context makes a useful contribution to ensuring that the treatment of such damaged young people is subject to independent scrutiny.

Voluntary services to young people who offend

Appropriate adults

The Police and Criminal Evidence Act 1984 established the role of the appropriate adult to safeguard the rights and welfare of children, young people and other vulnerable suspects while in police detention (see Chapter 11). YOTs are responsible for the provision of a person to act as an appropriate adult where a parent, carer or other family member is not available to attend the police station. In practice however an increasing number of YOTs exercise that responsibility through the establishment of volunteer schemes. This process has been encouraged by the Audit Commission (1996) and, more recently and in a more practical form, by the Youth Justice Board through the provision of funding. As a consequence, the reformed youth justice system has seen a considerable increase in voluntary services provided to young people in a particularly focused and time-limited context.

The role of the appropriate adult is to provide independent support to a young person who may be feeling extremely vulnerable given that they are under arrest and do not have the immediate support of a member of their family. One advantage of the use of volunteers is that they are more likely to be seen as genuinely independent of the police. YOT staff by contrast may be perceived as agents of the youth justice system and accordingly, from the young person's point of view, more closely aligned to the police. However, some commentators have also pointed to the dangers of such a specialist task being undertaken by volunteers. In particular, concerns have been raised about whether volunteers are likely to receive the requisite levels of training and support to carry out the function effectively, and whether they will be able to avoid co-option or intimidation by the police (see Chapter 11).

Mentoring

The major development in recent years in terms of volunteering in the youth justice system is the expansion in mentoring. While volunteer appropriate adults provide a specialist service to young people in particular circumstances, mentors are able to offer a more generic form of support (see Chapter 30).

Mentors have been with us since Homeric times; Mentor was the trusted adult left in charge of Telemachus, the son of Odysseus whilst he was away fighting the Trojan wars. The modern concept comes to us from the Big Brother and Big Sister projects, founded in 1903 in the United States. The use of mentors is now widespread in a range of sectors and their use within the youth justice system has increased substantially as a consequence of the youth justice reforms of the 1990s.

Such mentoring schemes aim to reduce youth crime through the development of relationships of trust between the young person and the volunteer and the positive influence exerted by the latter. They aim also to reduce crime by supporting a young person to comply with requirements of orders and develop a crime free lifestyle. Mentors may be full-time CSV volunteers or part-time community volunteers. The mentoring relationship has proved to be beneficial for young people who may have offended or been excluded from school.

Frequently, YOTs will 'buy in' mentoring expertise from voluntary organisations. One example of such a scheme is BedsMAP (Bedfordshire Mentors and Peers), a community-based mentoring project which works with young people who are: deemed at risk of involvement with the youth justice system; excluded from school; attending a pupil referral unit or whose parents are at risk of prosecution for school attendance problems or are the subject of a parenting order. While the majority of referrals come from the education welfare service, mentors are also provided to work with young people referred by the YOT.

The BedsMAP project has an average of 28 volunteer mentors – 8 part-time and 20 full-time per scheme operating over a 12-month period with 80 young people. Mentors aim to provide support with homework, getting to and from school or involvement in leisure activities. Average length of contact is 3 months but it can involve anything between 12 and 120 meetings (DeMontfort University, 2002).

Where a young person is subject of a court order, they may be offered mentoring support in carrying out activities associated with the programme. The arrangement is however purely voluntary (the young person cannot be breached for failing to meet with their mentor). The role is one of enablement rather than enforcement.

Volunteering by young people including ex-offenders

There also exist universal schemes such as Millennium Volunteers (MV) where the proportion of ex-offenders and those at risk of offending participating in certain areas is relatively high. This has led to a high degree of partnership work with justice agencies. For instance, in one scheme in Essex, an MV volunteer is placed within the police headquarters. In other parts of Essex beat officers actively promote the local MV schemes.

The experience of these young volunteers is noteworthy and reflects the experience of the respondents in Pitts (2001d) three nation study of socially excluded young people. Their recasting as contributors to the community rather then detractors is very powerful; their feeling valued and their experience of taking responsibility as well as the 'gift relationship' of volunteering often results in a refocusing of priorities (CSV, 2003). If this is true for young people in communities it is all the more true for those engaged in voluntary activity whilst in custody or prior to release from custody.

Volunteering in the secure estate

Volunteering is often said to create a sense of citizenship, yet the traditional understanding of citizenship and volunteering becomes problematic when applied to prisoners. Not only are those in custody removed from society, they are stripped of the rights of citizenship, both socially and politically. Volunteering in prisons is seen as a means of promoting and developing prisoners as citizens and promoting at the same time their eventual re-integration into their communities (Farrant and Levinson, 2002).

There are two variants on volunteering for those in the secure estate:

- The volunteer effort undertaken inside the YOI by young prisoners benefiting each other and external communities.
- Pre-release volunteering, which is offered to those in the last 2-3 months of their sentence.

In terms of volunteer effort for the prison community, most of the activity in which young prisoners are involved falls into the category of 'buddying' and 'listener' schemes which exist in 61% (13/22) of young offender institutions (YOIs).

The schemes cover a range of activities including:

- Listener schemes based on Samaritan principles for vulnerable young people.
- Peer support for substance misusers.
- Parenting support which is particularly prevalent in YOIs.
- Support for those with health problems.
- Employment, education and housing support.
- Sport peer support, also widespread in YOIs.

Peer support is one of the clearest examples of volunteering and active citizenship within the secure estate and is the most prevalent form of volunteering available to those in custody. While involvement in peer support is not systematically linked to the chance to gain qualifications or to sentence planning, such activities can now be recognised through young people working towards their Millennium Volunteer Award.

Volunteer effort for external communities involves a range of activities and is available in 58% of YOIs. Activity in workshops involves repairing equipment for charities e.g. wheelchairs and computers and transcribing books into Braille. The Inside Out Trust supports much of this work and whilst some of this activity may be remunerated, the motivation is usually not financial. Other volunteering involves fundraising for charities through a variety of activities including organising raffles.

Young people in custody also support members of the community coming into the institution in 58% of YOIs where children with disabilities are supported to use sports facilities. In some establishments elderly community members may be hosted for activity afternoons, although it is not clear the extent to which this is happening in YOIs.

The activities described above are at the discretion of prison governors. The Youth Justice Board has a target that all young people in secure facilities are engaged in 30 hours a week purposeful activities (Youth Justice Board, 2003c). The kind of voluntary work described here has the potential to contribute to achieving that target.

Volunteering outside the YOI

In 61% of YOIs young people are allowed to volunteer in the community. Those involved will have served most of their sentence and undergone a rigorous risk assessment. They may already have completed off site activities such as Duke of Edinburgh award or Prince's Trust development activities. They will be characterised by not having broken trust in any way and will be perceived as not being a danger to the public. Those who have committed serious sex offences; arson or acts of extreme violence are not eligible. The YOI remains responsible for the behaviour of the young person involved in community activity and any breach of the rules will result in them being withdrawn from the scheme. Day release for this purpose can count towards their hours of purposeful activity or education.

Young people in the last 2-3 months of their sentence who are eligible for release on temporary licence may undertake a full month of volunteering, in a variety of social settings outside of the YOI. This scheme (Pre-release Volunteering) has been funded by the prison service since 1984 and is managed by CSV. It places approximately 70 young people per annum into projects to the benefit of local community groups because the volunteers are available almost full time. The volunteers also benefit because they experience a real opportunity to support professional staff in providing care for those who need help. In addition, the scheme provides an opportunity for valuable work experience.

The success rate for the CSV schemes is impressive with 97% of volunteers successfully completing placements. Those involved in the operation of the schemes consider that this high level of engagement is related both to the value that the young people attach to learning skills and taking responsibility and to the fact that volunteering offers them a chance to form new friendships and to be seen, and see themselves, differently.

While the prison service also has a positive view of these schemes as an effective means of developing skills and contributing to the rehabilitation process, this has unfortunately not been reflected in an increase in such activity proportionate to the rise in the prison population. Despite a 24% rise in the prison population between 1994 and 2000, temporary licences granted for community service fell by 17% in the same period (Farrant and Levinson, 2002).

The future of volunteering in the youth justice system

Volunteers engaged with dispensing justice – those serving as magistrates or sitting on youth offender panels – represent the relationship between government and citizens, embodied in the principle of lay involvement in the criminal justice system. The government would clearly like to expand this relationship: the Home Secretary has for instance outlined proposals to develop 'Community Justice Centres' similar to Red Hook, which the Home Secretary visited in New York, 'where court and community come together to address local problems'. In reality, such a development would require a step-change in the numbers of people willing to engage in such voluntary activity.

Volunteering in this sense is about re-drawing the boundaries between the citizen and the traditional welfare state. Indeed the notion of 'co-production' where welfare, policing and health are founded on equal partnerships between professionals and clients is currently being mooted in some policy areas as a solution for the perceived failure of the welfare state (Boyle, 2004). In this context every citizen is seen as an asset to a community rather than a passive recipient of services.

Where voluntary activity performs a watchdog function, it not only involves members of the community in the operation of the criminal justice system, but also has the potential to increase public confidence in the process. The independence of those involved is obviously key and it is important that they should be representative of the broader community in terms of age, gender and ethnicity.

As the role of volunteers in face to face work with young people in the criminal justice system has expanded, the question of the relationship between voluntary activity and professional delivery has increasingly come to the fore (see Chapter 11). In one sense, volunteers are part of the solution: they are frequently seen by service users as more independent and approachable than paid staff (Joseph Rowntree Foundation, 2004). Volunteering agencies themselves are clear that volunteers should not replace professionals but rather

'lengthen and strengthen' services, adding a dimension that would not otherwise be present. At the same time, clarity of role is crucial and voluntary activity needs to take place within well defined boundaries to avoid the erosion of professional service provision.

The keys to successful volunteering

The single biggest issue in working with volunteers who work with young people in the community in recent years has been Criminal Record Bureau (CRB) clearance. Currently the procedure can take so long – in some instances six to eight months – that it jeopardises the work with young people since volunteers are often no longer available by the time that clearance is obtained. Streamlined procedures for vetting volunteers are thus essential.

Proper training of those engaged in voluntary work with young people is also a prerequisite of success and should cover issues such as equal opportunities, children's rights, child protection, professional boundaries, dealing with difficult behaviours and low self-esteem, as well as more prosaic elements such as claiming expenses and completion of necessary paperwork.

On-going support and a clear management structure are vital if voluntary activity is to be effective and sustainable. Procedures need to be well developed and comprehensive practice guidance provided. At a more personal level, the contribution made by volunteers requires proper recognition, if motivation and interest are to be maintained. Central to the idea of support is reciprocity: those working with volunteers should be aware of the need for voluntary activity to be satisfying and meaningful. Volunteer effort is maximised, and outcomes enhanced, where those engaged identify clear benefits for all parties.

Further reading

Blunkett, D. (2003) *Civil Renewal: A New Agenda*. The CSV Edith Khan Memorial Lecture. London: Home Office

Farrant, F. and Levinson, J. (2002) *Barred Citizens*. London: The Prison Reform Trust

Putnam, R. (2001) *Bowling Alone*. London: Simon and Schuster

Withnot, R. (1995) *Learning to Care; Elementary Kindness in an Age of Indifference*. London: OUP

Part 5   Debates and Controversies in Youth Justice

35 Girls in the Youth Justice System

Loraine Gelsthorpe

Key points

1. Girls have always been treated differently from boys within the youth justice system. But this differentiation was often based on myths, muddles and misconceptions about girls' delinquent behaviour.

2. Research has consistently shown that decisions about girls are often motivated by concerns about their sexuality and their independence as much as concerns about their delinquency.

3. Girls are often seen as a difficult group with which to work but this belief sometimes masks a double standard applied to girls who do not manifest 'gender-appropriate' behaviour.

4. Recent concerns about changes in girls' behaviour, particularly in relation to violence and drug use, have been exaggerated by the media.

5. There is a strong argument for treating girls differently from boys because of what we now know from girls about their real needs. Girls and young women are often neglected in service and programme provision.

Introduction

Children and young people who are in trouble with the law, and how we might best deal with them have long preoccupied politicians and policy makers. One recurring theme which has influenced policy and practice within the criminal justice and care systems, is the relationship between the dichotomous ideologies of 'welfare' and 'justice' (see Chapter 1). Until the changes brought about by the Children Act 1989, the Criminal Justice Act 1991, the Crime and Disorder Act 1998 and the Youth Justice and Criminal Proceedings Act 1999, the criminal justice, legal and related professional local authority care systems were largely characterised by swings between these paradigms, reflecting changes in political philosophies and attitudes to 'children in trouble'. Although attempts have been made to achieve a balance between welfare and justice in the overhaul of the youth justice system in 1998, it is arguable that the basic principles of the two philosophies remain fundamentally irreconcilable. The different and, at times, seemingly unequal treatment of girls and boys within these two paradigms in the criminal justice and care systems makes this a gendered issue. There are a number of difficult issues at play: different perceptions of girls and boys' behaviour and their needs; different

rates of involvement in crime; and different responses on the part of the criminal justice and care systems, for example. But first, it is important to get a sense of the historical background to contemporary concerns.

An historical sketch: early responses to girls and young women

From the 18th century onwards at least, there is evidence of both public and governmental concern about the 'irregularities in the moral behaviour' of girls. There were numerous missions to save the souls of girls (see, Gelsthorpe, 1989) and frequent and vociferous claims that delinquent girls, like their older sisters, were worse than boys. Childcare reformer Mary Carpenter quotes a number of writers on this topic. Mr Thompson, a philanthropist interested in children in industrial schools stated:

> *A poor half-starved outcast girl, trained up in ignorance and filth and sin, is even more painful and a more degrading sight than a boy of the same description. She seems to have fallen or to have been forced, into a state farther below her right place in the world than the boy.*

(cited in Carpenter, 1853: 83)

And Carpenter notes, too, that girls were 'more refractory under imprisonment than boys', a comment which echoes those who wrote about the pains of imprisonment for adult women. Indeed, whilst the youth justice system did not distinguish between girls and boys in terms of sentencing and services in its early development, we can discern different attitudes and perceptions with regard to girls and boys at this time, which have persisted more or less to this day.

Practitioners apparently found it more difficult to retain a hold over the girls and to make an impression on them and a strange dual image of girls persists. Girls were thought to be more vulnerable than boys and to need a lot of care, but at the same time, they were seen as more wicked. Nonetheless, despite these observations and claims that girls were more difficult to 'rescue' than boys, the main aim of the missions and societies to help girls was not straightforwardly to punish them, but to instil good virtues in them, to 'rouse a consciousness in them'. Mary Carpenter, inveterate critic of the penal system adopted for juvenile delinquents, argued all the more strongly that the existing system (whereby many juveniles were imprisoned) was iniquitous when it was used for girls and she argued that the system needed for girls was a 'wise and kind' one (1853: 83).

Twentieth century responses to girls and young women

Shaped by pioneering youth justice developments in Illinois and Australia, and by the increasing domestic use of summary jurisdiction, the modern youth justice system dates from the 1908 Children Act in England and Wales which established new judicial procedures, punishments and reform programmes for children. Children's cases were now to be heard separately from those of adults and, where possible, in a separate courtroom. Persons under the age of 16 were no longer, apart from in exceptional circumstances, to be sent to prison (Gelsthorpe and Morris, 1994). Alongside this development, the 1907 Probation of Offenders Act, introduced probation for children and young persons as well as adults. Those requiring institutional care or correction were to be sent to industrial or reformatory schools. A proportion of those over 16, however, were to be sent to newly

established borstals, set up under the Prevention of Crime Act 1908. Young men and women could be sent to borstals for between one and three years. The first such institution for girls was established in a wing of Aylesbury Convict Prison. Until the 1920s girls in the borstal system shared the penal discipline of the Convict Prison with occupational activities of needlework, laundry work, general housework, cooking and gardening. Further borstal facilities were set up for young women in Holloway, Durham and Exeter and Bullwood Hall was opened in Essex in 1962.

From 1908 onwards, the newly shaped youth justice system brought together abused and neglected children and those who offended into one system. This was a system informed by the twin ideologies of care and protection and control and punishment. The resources for operationalising these ideologies were provided by the criminal justice system, the institutions of the emerging welfare state and the voluntary sector. Indeed, the voluntary sector, which had played such a prominent part in 19th century developments in youth justice continued to play a distinctive role in the regulation of girls (see Zedner, 1991 and Cox, 2003).

Other chapters in this volume describe modern youth justice provision. Suffice to say here that the differentiation in provision for boys and girls persisted throughout the 20th century. One example concerns the Criminal Justice Act 1982. Whilst the Act led to the revitalisation of detention centres for boys with the introduction of a 'short, sharp shock' type of regime, the one such centre for girls was closed. More than this, in the White Paper, *Crime, Justice and Protecting the Public* (Home Office, 1990) which preceded the Criminal Justice Act 1991, the Conservative government suggested that the number of girls under the age of 18 years sentenced to custody by the courts was so small that the abolition of detention in a young officer institution (YOI) for this group might be feasible. Apart from the very few who had committed very serious offences and who could be dealt with by means of Section 53 detention (now sections 90-91 of the Powers of Criminal Courts (Sentencing) Act 2000) (see Chapter 25), it was thought that the 150 or so girls in custody (compared to over 7,000 boys) could be dealt with quite adequately by the 'good, demanding and constructive community programmes for juvenile offenders who need intensive supervision' (Home Office, 1990: 45). In practice, however, the use of custody for girls continued and I return to this below.

To dwell on the differential perceptions of boys and girls behaviour for a moment in children's homes, borstals and approved schools, in many cases girls were thought to need medical treatment and emotional security which would divert their attention from sexual activities. Girls were also thought to appreciate the value of a homely atmosphere (Association of Headmasters, Headmistresses and Matrons of Approved Schools, 1954).

Continuing these themes, Walker (1962), for instance, clearly saw girls as 'less criminally inclined' than boys, as 'vulnerable' and 'at risk' of contamination from the more hardened delinquent boys. And such themes have found echoes in other writings on girls' admission to the youth justice system and approved schools (see Gelsthorpe, 1989 for an overview). When the only existing detention centre for girls was closed, the Home Office Advisory Council on the Penal System (1968) stressed the psychological problems of girls:

> We are sure that the detention centre . . . is not appropriate for girls . . . Girls in trouble are usually unhappy and disturbed, often sexually promiscuous and often rejected by their families. They are usually in great need of help and understanding, however reluctant to accept sympathy and affection they may appear to be. Frequently, they need protection while they are given a chance to sort out their problems.
>
> (Home Office, 1968: 1)

Some of the psychological and behavioural problems of girls are also described in Hoghughi's study of disturbed juvenile delinquents (1978):

> . . . fewer girls seem clinically as impulsive and extroverted with a delinquent self-image, but more are emotionally and socially immature, aggressive, deficient in self-control, stubborn and emotionally unstable.
>
> (1978: 57)

Similar conclusions have been reached elsewhere (Cowie et al., 1968; Richardson, 1969; Goodman et al., 1976). As a result, girls have been seen to be in need of help and protection. Both Ackland's 1982 study of girls in care and Petrie's (1986)

research on girls in residential care describe the importance of the 'social care' model for girls. The causes of admission in each case being predominantly to do with 'status' conditions; being out of control of the parent, being in moral danger, potential or actual sexual abuse, absconding from a place of safety, and so on.

Set in Ireland in the early 1960s, the drama-documentary film *The Magdalene Sisters* (2002, directed by Peter Mullan) captures something of this. The film dramatises the lives of three young women sent to a Magdalene Laundry run by Catholic nuns for 'fallen' young and adult women as a punishment for their 'sins'. Their 'sins' involved mild flirting in one case, being raped by a cousin at a wedding in another, and giving birth to a baby in an unmarried state in the third case. The laundry is akin to the 19th century reformatories for young women (Zedner, 1991).

Common themes in responses to girls and young women

Traditionally theories about delinquency have either virtually ignored girls and their problems or misrepresented them (see Gelsthorpe, 2004 for an overview of theories). Where girls have been given attention, theories based on psychological or sexual dysfunction have dominated (Campbell, 1981; Morris, 1987).

Linked to this is the fact that youth justice system responses to girls and young women have been significantly influenced by broad social expectations of female behaviour. Indeed, their families, teachers, social workers and neighbours have influenced decisions within the system by raising concerns about girls' sexuality and their independence – their 'passionate and wilful' behaviour (Alder, 1998). Feminist research with girls has revealed that the role of the family is particularly important in policing girls' behaviour and sexuality (Cain, 1989).

We might characterise the situation by suggesting that girls' treatment in the youth justice system and related agencies is beset with myths, muddles and misconceptions. Certainly, popular ideas about appropriate female behaviour have confused perceptions of them as 'offenders'. Girls have been viewed as uncontrollable and worse than boys simply because of the high and false expectations of their behaviour in the first place. They have been viewed as more psychiatrically disturbed than boys, but this may reflect the normal discourses of pathology in which women's behaviour is defined (Worrall, 1999). Moreover, double standards have been applied with regard to girls' and boys' sexual behaviour; with girls being subject to scrutiny and social regulation in a way that boys have not been.

As already noted, the history of youth justice has been a history of tension between justice and welfare ideologies. It is precisely because of the muddled perceptions of their behaviour that girls have tended to experience both the advantages and disadvantages of 'welfarism' to a greater extent than boys, on the grounds that they are 'at risk', in 'moral danger' and in 'need of protection'. The advantages here have included diversion from the formal youth justice system, whilst the disadvantages have included sentence up-tariffing (Harris and Webb, 1987). Recent critiques of youth justice (including feminist critiques) have resulted in moves towards a more 'equitable justice' between girls and boys, but as a result of this we have witnessed a greater tendency to categorise girls' behaviour as 'criminal' rather than merely 'problematic' (that is, their behaviour has been 'criminalised' and the resultant net-widening effect has meant that more girls and young women than hitherto are being brought into the criminal justice system (Worrall, 2001).

Contemporary concerns and controversies

Changes in patterns of crime

The late 20th century witnessed something of a panic about girls and crime. They were seen to be committing more crime, becoming more violent and more likely to form or join a 'gang', as well as engaging in illegal drug-taking alongside boys (see Flood-Page et al., 2000, for example). There has been some statistical support for such claims. According to Home Office figures, the ratio of crimes committed by girls rose from 1 in 11 in the late 1950s to 1 in 4 in the late 1990s. During the 1990s, youth crime increased at a faster rate among girls than boys, with notable increases in drug-related and violent crime (Home Office, 2001). The number of arrests of girls for violent offences more than doubled, a rise which was

reported to have increased by 250% in the last quarter of the century (Rutter et al., 1998). However, these percentage increases appear considerably less dramatic when set against the low base-line figures. Moreover, although it appears that girls, as a proportion of juveniles entering court, rose during the 1990s, if cautions, reprimands and warnings are factored into the analysis, the overall percentage of girls involved in the youth justice system is more stable. It could be the case that the rise in convictions is in part explicable by the rate of diversion falling faster for girls than boys. Nevertheless, the increase in girls' arrests has certainly generated panic (see Burman, 2004, for an overview of these changes).

Changing perspectives on girls and young women

Such changes have fuelled concerns about the abandonment of traditional welfare-oriented approaches to offending by girls and its replacement by interventions which criminalise and punish what Anne Worrall (2000) captures in her phrase the 'nasty little madams'. Indeed, strategies to control girls and young women's behaviour which stress their special psychological and social needs are now being rejected in favour of more punitive responses. This tendency is driven in part by concerns about discrimination and a desire to establish a regime of 'just deserts'. As Worrall has noted:

> *In the actuarial language that now dominates criminal justice, a group which has hitherto been assessed as too small and too low-risk to warrant attention is now being re-assessed and re-categorised. No longer 'at risk' and in 'moral danger' from the damaging behaviour of men, increasing numbers of young women are being assigned to the same categories as young men ('violent girls', 'drug-abusing girls', 'girl robbers', 'girl murderers' – 'girl rapists' even) and are being subjected to the same forms of management as young men.*
>
> (2001: 86)

Stories about girl gangs roaming the streets and randomly attacking innocent victims have been a recurring feature of newspaper headlines and magazines in recent years (see, for example, Carroll, 1998; Kirsta, 2000; Mitchell, 2000; Thompson, 2001). Some reports suggest that drunken and wild girls will soon overtake boys in the violence stakes. All this had led to something of a 'moral panic' about girls' behaviour. Contrary to media accounts of girls preying on innocent victims, however, violence between girls occurs within the context of their existing social interactions, most often whilst hanging around with other like-minded young people who are just as likely to be involved in conflict (Burman, 2003). These concerns notwithstanding, young women remain at very low risk when it comes to predicting offending (Kemshall, 2004).

Despite some changes in respect of violent and drug-related offending, gender differences in involvement in crime have remained fairly constant. Set against a background of an overall decrease in the number of recorded offences attributable to children and young people, violent offences represent a growing proportion of the offences for which young females are cautioned or convicted. However, as previously intimated, closer scrutiny of these statistics reveals that these percentage increases represent small increases against a low baseline, and the overall proportion of girls involved in the criminal justice system has remained more stable than is commonly assumed.

Young women inside

In 1997 the Howard League for Penal Reform launched an inquiry into the use of prison custody for girls. The Inquiry focused on the 15-17 year olds who continued to be held in prison custody, despite government proposals in 1991 to abolish it for all but the most serious offenders. In 2002, approximately 500 girls were sentenced to immediate custody, five times the number in 1992 (Home Office, 2003b) and some of these girls were placed in prison alongside young women of 18–20 years; this continues to be of great concern (see also, Wilkinson and Morris, 2000). But beyond concerns about girls in custody (matched by concerns about boys in custody) we need to look at local authority care. There is some suggestion that girls are over-represented in local authority secure children's homes (Worrall, 2001). Analysis of the pathways into such 'care' indicates that girls still tend to come via the welfare route rather more than boys, but the pattern has been changing, and in many ways, girls and boys criss-cross the welfare problems/criminal behav-

iour divide. The Youth Justice Board has aimed to expand provision for girls in this sphere precisely so as to avoid the use of prisons. Few would question the sound motives for the avoidance of prison, but we ought also to question the increased use of local authority accommodation for them, and instead turn our minds to effective community responses.

Challenges for the future

Legislative and policy changes in England and Wales, as in Northern Ireland and increasingly in Scotland, reflect major interest in restorative justice as a way of responding to young people's crime (see Chapter 3). The position of women and girls as victims of violence has been considered in relation to restorative justice (see, for example, Hudson, 1998; Morris and Gelsthorpe, 2001). With few exceptions (see Alder, 2000, for instance) much less attention has been given to girls and young women as offenders in this regard. Girls have often been seen as amenable to more informal elements of social control through the family and social networks (Cain, 1989), so it might be assumed that restorative justice processes, often characterised as informal and integrative, might be an ideal way of dealing with them. Whilst restorative justice, in UK policy at least, often promotes the idea that 'shame' is an integral, and positive, element in the process, for some girls there may be a delicate balance to be found between encouraging contrition and remorse and inducing debilitating feelings of guilt and self-blame which, in the case of vulnerable young women with poor self-esteem, might trigger self-harm. This will militate against the 'empowerment' of these girls, further undermining the emotional resources they will need to survive some of the harsh realities of their lives. Conferencing processes do differ in the degree to which they expect to elicit expressions of contrition alongside the need to establish reparative outcomes, of course, and the implications of gender differences in relation to restorative justice in the UK are worthy of consideration.

In which direction should we go? There are obvious problems in dealing with girls in accordance with the dictates of a 'pure' justice model (see Chapter 9) because they would still be subject to 'double condemnation as offenders and as flouting the values of femininity' (Hudson, 1985:16). As previously indicated, one problem here is that there is an assumption that girls become criminal because of their welfare needs. This then pushes girls up the sentencing tariff more quickly and for more trivial offences than boys in many cases, but it is also true to say that many girls are vulnerable and many have experienced victimisation. Although this is also the case for many boys, girls will often experience this differently (see Chesney-Lind, 1997; Chesney-Lind and Sheldon, 1992; Hedderman, 2004; Worrall, 1999). The real challenge is therefore to find ways of responding to girls' real needs without fuelling stereotypical ideas about female and male behaviour. Girls' *real* needs have often remained invisible. More than this, it is perhaps important to consider how far there are similarities in the needs of girls in trouble. The needs of black and Asian girls, in particular, are often denied or misinterpreted. We should endeavour not only to gauge the impact of the new youth justice reforms on girls and boys, but also to discover how the system currently responds to the needs of girls from minority ethnic groups. A related problem here is that there are currently too few targeted interventions and programmes for girls and young women (Batchelor and Burman, 2004). Girls and young women are generally not a priority for service and programme provision, but effective gender-responsive programmes and interventions, drawing on girls' own thoughts and insights, are necessary to help them deal with the difficult social realities that they experience.

Further reading

Alder, C. and Baines, M. (1996) . . . *And When She Was Bad? Working With Young Women in Youth Justice and Related Areas*. Australia: National Clearinghouse for Youth Studies

Chesney-Lind, M. (1997) *The Female Offender. Girls, Women and Crime*. Thousand Oaks, CA: Sage

Walklate, S. (2001) *Gender, Crime and Criminal Justice*. Cullompton: Willan

36 Race, Crime and Youth Justice

Anita Kalunta-Crumpton

Key points

1. Although information on race and youth justice is very limited, available evidence shows that black young people are over-represented as clients of the youth justice system.

2. The issue of over-representation has given rise to conflicting viewpoints, with some arguing that this is caused by higher offending rates and more serious crimes committed by black young people, while others point to direct and indirect discrimination by agents of the youth justice system.

3. An alternative account suggests that when they enter the youth justice system, the socio-economic and educational disadvantage to which they are particularly prone, predispose black young people to more intrusive and sustained criminal justice intervention.

4. To gain a clearer picture of what is happening to black young people in the youth justice system, it will be necessary to establish a sufficiently sensitive and comprehensive monitoring system.

5. To effect change, anti-discriminatory initiatives would need to address both direct and indirect forms of discriminatory practices.

Introduction

In the past few decades there has been growing concern about the relationship between race, crime and justice (see for example, Bowling and Phillips, 2002) and in particular the disproportionate representation of black people in recorded crime statistics. To date, this disproportion remains controversial and the question of whether or not racial discrimination influences policy and practice in the criminal justice system, particularly as regards black African-Caribbean people, has yet to be satisfactorily resolved. It is surprising that despite this debate, the actual experiences of black youth and young people from other visible minority ethnic groups who get caught up in the system have attracted only limited academic interest. Moreover, despite the fact that the Asian and African-Caribbean populations of the UK are relatively young, with larger numbers concentrated in crime prone age groups as a result, little attention has been paid to age as a factor in the involvement of black and minority ethnic young people in the criminal justice system. Thus, when academics and politicians have talked about 'black youth', it has seldom been clear whether this has concerned only those who fall within the purview

of the youth justice system or, for example, young adults aged between 18 and 25. With a few notable exceptions (see for example, Pitts, 1986; Mhlanga, 1997) studies of race, crime and justice have seldom addressed the relationship between race and age. Furthermore, such discussions are commonly embedded in a more general race and crime narrative which incorporates the adult population as well.

This chapter focuses primarily on black young people eligible for, or involved in, the youth justice system of England and Wales; those aged 10–17 years. However, because of the paucity of data for this age group, it also draws upon research findings concerning those aged up to 25. It also considers the predicament of Asian young people caught up in the justice system.

Black young people, crime and justice: evidence from the research

Although, black young people have been involved with the criminal justice apparatus for decades they have not, until comparatively recently, attracted much criminological attention. In the 1950s and 1960s, when white youngsters were the primary focus of political and media concern about youth crime, the activities and experiences of black youth were treated as a marginal issue. As Hobbs (1997: 811) suggests, where they did appear they tended to be presented:

> . . . *in terms of (their) relationship to the police, and as a social problem, rather than as a socio-cultural entity in their own right; a courtesy afforded to white youth, whose every stylistic nuance was pored over by academics.*

In contrast, Asian youth were neither prominent nor marginalised because they simply never featured (Alexander, 2000).

In the late 1970s, the issue of black involvement in street crime came to the fore, with the media and political commentators linking 'mugging' with the problems of inner city decay in general and 'black youth' in particular (Hall et al., 1978). The mugging panics of the late 1970s spawned a strategy of high profile policing in black localities, of the type that triggered the disturbances in Brixton in 1981. This strategy was prosecuted via the extensive use of police 'stop-and-search' procedures and a sharp rise in the numbers of black defendants attracting prison sentences (Pitts, 1986). The over-representation of black young people in the criminal statistics and in the categories of robbery in particular, dates from this period. In recent years, media and official reports about the involvement of young black males in mobile phone theft (Harrington and Mayhew, 2001) and intra-racial inner city drug-related gun violence (Evans, 2002) have further fuelled concerns about black youth and crime.

The over-representation of black young people in the justice system

In 1975, in the wake of the 'mugging' panics, statistics revealed that black people aged under 25 in the Metropolitan Police District (MPD) had the highest pro-rata arrest rates for all indictable offences, including robbery (Stevens and Willis, 1979). Higher arrest rates were paralleled by higher levels of custody. In 1984/5 a larger proportion of young black people aged 14–20 was sentenced to immediate custody in the MPD than any other ethnic group (Home Office, 1989). Levels of custodial remands for this group were also disproportionately higher (Home Office,

1986). In the 1990s, young black people aged 10 and over have continued to be disproportionately involved at each stage of the youth justice process (Home Office, 1998f; 2000d; 2002e). Furthermore, they appear to enter penal institutions at a younger age than other ethnic groups. As we enter the 21st century, black African-Caribbean children and young people, although they constitute only 2.7% of the 10–17 year old population of England and Wales, represent 6% of all youth court disposals, 11% of all custodial disposals and 20% of the young people given orders for long-term detention (Youth Justice Board, 2003o).

Explaining black over-representation in the justice system: disproportionate involvement in crime

The continuing search for explanations of black over-representation in the criminal statistics and the criminal justice system must inevitably deal with the question of whether black people are disproportionately involved in crime. From a youth justice perspective, it has been argued that since socio-economic disadvantage correlates closely with criminal involvement, the socio-economic marginality of many black people would suggest that they might therefore be more crime-prone as a group. At the same time given that Britain's black population is a relatively young one, contact with the youth justice system will inevitably be higher (Fitzgerald, 1993). However, Solomos (1988) has cautioned against glib generalisation, pointing to the broader processes through which:

> . . . *young blacks were constructed both in policy and popular discourses as caught up in a vicious circle of unemployment, poverty, homelessness, crime and conflict with the police.*

Following the 1980s 'riots' in Brixton and other UK inner city neighbourhoods, both the Scarman Report (1982) and the media suggested that the problem of black youth crime was rooted in the socio-economic deprivation of the black community. As Pilkington (2003) has observed, poor housing, high unemployment rates, educational under-achievement, unskilled and semi-skilled employment, low pay and racism forge the links between race, poverty, marginalisation and crime.

The Bradford riots of 1995, thrust the issue of Asian youth and crime into the political and media spotlight, much as the Brixton riots had a decade or so before. In so doing, it served to undermine the popular belief that Asians are inherently more law-abiding than either black or white people (Alexander, 2000). It also revealed that many Asian families are subject to similar social and economic conditions to those endured by their black counterparts and, as with black youth in the 1980s, commentators have cited these conditions to explain the growing involvement of poor young Bangladeshis in crime and the criminal justice system in socially disadvantaged areas of Asian settlement, of which Tower Hamlets is the example par excellence (Eade and Garbin, 2002).

Indeed, by 1995, 40% of African-Caribbeans and 59% of Pakistanis and Bangladeshis in the UK were located in the poorest fifth of the population compared with 18% of the white population (Power and Tunstall, 1995). In London, by the mid-1990s, up to 70% of residents on the poorest housing estates were from black and ethnic minorities (Power and Tunstall, 1995).

Explaining black over-representation in the justice system: racial discrimination

It is clear that black and Asian people experience much higher levels of poverty than whites and there is a large body of research which points to a close link between poverty and youth crime (Pitts, 2003b). However, the fact that many black and Asian young people occupy a social and economic environment that might predispose them to involvement in crime does not mean that they are not subject to discrimination once they come into contact with the justice system. Moreover, self-report studies tend to suggest that rates of offending for black and white young people are broadly similar (Graham and Bowling, 1995).

There is, for example, a substantial body of evidence to show that black people of all ages are far more likely than other racial groups to be stopped and searched, arrested, prosecuted, remanded in custody pending trial, and sentenced to prison (Stevens and Willis, 1979; Landau, 1981; Pitts, 1988). And so questions are inevitably raised about the contribution of the practices of the

agents of the criminal justice system to this over-representation. Empirical studies have thrown light on what happens to black suspects and defendants at the different stages in the criminal justice process.

Black and Asian young people are far more likely to be stopped on the street by the police than their white counterparts (Smith, 1983; Marlow and Loveday, 2000; Fitzgerald, 2001). This results, in some areas, in disproportionate numbers of black and Asian young people entering police stations. Once there, decisions about further progression through the criminal process must be made.

Landau's pioneering study (1981) of police decision making showed that black juveniles were twice as likely to be immediately charged than their white counterparts and, as a result far less likely to be diverted out of the system to a multi-agency diversion panel. Landau also found that, in general, police decisions were influenced by the arrestee's previous criminal record and offence type. Nonetheless, black first-time arrestees and those arrested for robbery, violence or burglary were far more likely than whites to be charged immediately in the same circumstances (Landau and Nathan, 1983).

Recent studies have produced more mixed findings. A study by the Commission for Racial Equality (1992) showed that numbers of previous convictions and offence type could not account for the higher numbers of young blacks referred for prosecution. Lower cautioning rates for black young people were explained largely by the fact that they are less likely to admit the offence in police interview – a requirement of a caution – than their white counterparts (Fitzgerald, 1993). Research by the West Midlands Joint Data Team (cited in Fitzgerald and Sibbitt, 1997) showed that after accounting for legal criteria such as admission of guilt, cautioning was similar for black and white juveniles but lower for Asian juveniles in most areas of the West Midlands police force.

Phillips and Brown (1998), however, found that black juvenile referrals to multi-agency diversion panels were less common than those for whites and Asians, even taking their lower rates of admissions of guilt into account. It is important to note too that black children and young people who deny offences are subsequently more likely to be acquitted than their white and Asian counterparts. While this might indicate that the police are more willing to initiate prosecutions against young black suspects, Mhlanga (1997) also found that prosecutions of Asian children and young people were higher still.

The replacement of cautioning by reprimands and final warnings by the Crime and Disorder Act 1998 (CDA) places limitations on police discretion at the pre-court stage (see Chapter 12). This might have been expected to reduce the differences in outcome between black, white and Asian young people at the point of arrest. However, data collected by the Youth Justice Board shows that black young people are still more likely to be prosecuted. Thus during 2002/03, 34% of those classified as 'black' or 'black British' entering the youth justice system were given a reprimand or final warning, against 45% for their white counterparts (Youth Justice Board, 2003o).

This initial over-representation of black young people in the court population appears to be amplified as they proceed through the system. Black defendants in the youth court are less likely to be granted bail and more likely to be remanded in custody (Goldson, 2002d; Moore and Peters, 2003), leading Goldson to argue that racism plays a crucial role in remand decisions. When it comes to sentencing, as we have noted above, black young people are four times more likely to be sentenced to custody and over seven times more likely to be subject to long-term detention. A recent study of the experiences of young black males in young offender institutions (Wilson and Moore, 2004) provides a lucid account of the widespread, racially-motivated, verbal and physical abuse, and other discriminatory practices to which African-Caribbean and Asian youngsters are subjected by prison officers.

Youth justice policy and race

The origins of the far-reaching changes in youth justice in England and Wales ushered in by the CDA are complex. However, it is undoubtedly the case that the highly publicised murder of two year old James Bulger by two white 10 year olds in 1993, the 'twocking' and 'ram-raiding' undertaken by white youths on urban housing estates in the north of England, and riots on out-of-town estates, also involving white young people, were

highly influential (Pitts, 2003b). Apart from the uproar caused by the assertion, in 1995, of Sir Paul Condon, the erstwhile Commissioner of the Metropolitan Police, that young black males were responsible for the lion's share of street crime in this country, race did not feature significantly in the debate around youth offending. Nonetheless, black young people continued to be over-represented in the youth justice system during this period, and the available evidence suggests that the imbalance between the involvement of black and white youth at each stage of the criminal justice process probably increased following the introduction of the youth justice reforms (Audit Commission, 2004).

John Pitts' analysis (1986) nicely captures the complex interplay of factors which, in the 1970s and 1980s, served to catapult black young people into penal and childcare institutions. In summary, Pitts argued that:

1. Black young people experienced higher levels of unemployment and homelessness, factors which have an important influence on sentencing and so determine imprisonment rates or receptions into care.
2. Black young people were less likely than whites to receive a supervisory penalty as a result of the concerns of social workers and probation officers about their capacity to 'manage' and undertake effective work with them.
3. For similar reasons, black young people were less likely to be referred to community-based alternatives to custody by probation officers and social workers.

It could be argued that some of the problems identified by Pitts have been addressed in the interim by the development of anti-racist policies and training within the criminal justice system, and the development of 'ethnically sensitive practice'. The Criminal Justice Act 1991 required ethnic monitoring of the criminal justice process and obliged courts to obtain a pre-sentence report (PSR) before imposing a custodial or, higher tariff, community penalty (see Chapter 18) to provide sentencers with information about what interventions are available in the community as alternatives to incarceration. However, as HM Inspectorate of Probation has recently found in the adult criminal justice system, court reports prepared on black defendants are more likely to propose custody, are frequently of a lower quality than those prepared for white defendants and, on occasions, are written in a manner likely to reinforce stereotypical attitudes about race and ethnicity (HMIP, 2000b). There is little reason to suppose that PSRs written on young people are significantly better in these respects.

Moreover, the 1991 Act marked the end of an era in which diversion was a priority of the youth justice system and, very soon, the government set about toughening penalties (see Chapter 1). The 1990s was characterised by a succession of legislative changes which made it easier to incarcerate young people on remand or under sentence (see Chapter 25; Nacro, 2003a). Given their vulnerability to apprehension and prosecution, this change bore particularly heavily upon black young people.

As we have noted above, while straightforward racial discrimination may well influence outcomes in the youth justice system, it is also the case that socio-economic factors, like low income, poor housing, homelessness, lack of educational opportunity and unemployment will shape decisions made by the police, magistrates and other system agents (Taylor, 1982). Thus, because black young people are more likely to be subject to these disadvantages, they have tended to be the subjects of more intrusive or more sustained interventions. However, the fact that black people are disadvantaged by these socio-economic factors has sometimes been utilised to dismiss claims of racial discrimination (see also Kalunta-Crumpton, 1999). Yet, as Roger Hood's acclaimed study revealed:

> *Being unemployed was a factor which correlated significantly with receiving a custodial sentence if the defendant was black but not if he was white or Asian.*
>
> (1992: 86)

Conclusion

The limited amount of contemporary research in the area of race and youth justice makes it difficult to devise strategies to combat injustices. However, strategies developed to monitor the treatment of black people in the justice system in general may well be relevant to improving the treatment of black children and young people in the youth justice system.

The ethnic monitoring system introduced by Section 95 of the Criminal Justice Act 1991 aimed to address discrimination on grounds of race and ethnic origin. Although this represented an important step forward, the strategy had and continues to have problems. Initially, the monitoring system revealed serious gaps in the 'ethnic minority data' held by some justice system agencies, such as the probation service and the Crown Prosecution Service, and this rendered attempts to draw useful conclusions problematic. Secondly, monitoring does not focus upon the practices of system agents, only the outcomes of their interventions and this makes it difficult to identify particular manifestations of discrimination, such as stereotyping. Thirdly, the monitoring system is only able to focus on empirically demonstrable cases of direct discrimination and is unable to identify indirect discrimination, or indeed institutionalised racism, a concept which gained significance in official discourse following the publication of the MacPherson Report in 1999. While some criminal justice bodies, such as the police and the prison service, accepted that MacPherson's definition of institutionalised racism applied to their organisations, those acknowledgements may have been influenced by the fact that MacPherson interpreted this form of racism as *unwitting*, thus stressing unintentional motivations as underlying organisational procedures and practices which disadvantage minority ethnic groups. Some of MacPherson's recommendations, such as race awareness training, may have been put in place in some parts of the criminal justice system but the extent to which indirect discrimination is addressed in practice is yet to be explored in detail. This also means that any effective ethnic monitoring system in youth justice would need to be augmented by qualitative elements which explored the day to day realities of practice.

Most urgently, in the light of the increased incarceration of black and some other ethnic minority young people, there is a pressing need for comprehensive ethnic monitoring of the use made by courts of the more punitive sanctions available to the youth courts, and security and custody in particular.

Further reading

Bowling, B. and Philips, C. (2002) *Racism, Crime and Justice*. Essex: Pearson

Goldson, B. (2002d) *Vulnerable Inside: Children in Secure and Penal Settings*. London: The Children's Society

Marlow, A. and Loveday, B. (2000) *After MacPherson*. Lyme Regis: Russell House Publishing

Pitts, J. (1993) Thereotyping: Anti-Racism, Criminology and Black Young People. in Cook, D. and Hudson, B. (Eds.) *Racism and Criminology*. London: Sage

Wilson, D. and Moore, S. (2004) *'Playing the Game': The Experiences of Young Black Men in Custody*. London: The Children's Society

37 Beyond Formalism: Towards 'Informal' Approaches to Youth Crime and Youth Justice

Barry Goldson

Key points

1. Whether they are characterised by 'welfare', 'justice' or 'punitive' priorities, youth justice systems draw children and young people into *formal* mechanisms of control and regulation.

2. Informalism challenges conventional orthodoxies and is underpinned by a range of radical alternative principles and perspectives.

3. The 'new youth justice' in England and Wales has systematically discarded informal responses to youth crime, favouring instead an expanded and intensified spectrum of formal interventions.

4. In taking the direction that it has, contemporary youth justice policy and practice is intrinsically irrational: it negates a significant body of research findings and practice experience.

5. Informalist perspectives rest upon a robust evidence-base and offer the prospect of more imaginative, humane, responsive, effective and cost-efficient approaches to troubled and troublesome children and young people.

Introduction

Since the early part of the 19th century, policy makers, child welfare agencies, penal reformers and 'experts' from a range of 'professions' and 'disciplines', have been largely preoccupied with developing *formal* mechanisms of intervention and control, designed to hold 'delinquents' and 'young offenders' to account, whilst also protecting them from the full rigours of adult criminal justice processes. It follows that the primary focus of this book is fixed upon such *formal* responses to youth crime and youth justice: the 'apparatus of control', and the 'principles', 'practices' and 'methods' around which statutory interventions are shaped and applied.

This chapter deviates from this dominant tradition. It seeks to move beyond *formalism* to consider *informal* approaches to youth crime and justice. Just as there is no unitary model of 'formal' youth justice however, neither is there a monolithic 'informal' response. Rather, informalism derives from a range of sociological, penological and political perspectives within which conventional youth justice systems are essentially conceived as being ethically problematic, largely counter-

productive (when measured in terms of preventing youth offending at least), extraordinarily costly and often unnecessary.

Defining formalism

Nikolas Rose (1989: 121) has observed that 'childhood is the most intensively governed sector of personal existence'. Moreover, it could be argued, that if children *per se* are so closely governed, those who transgress the law – 'young offenders' – are governed more intensively still. Indeed, maintaining law and order is, and always has been, one of the principal priorities of state agencies and, as we have already noted, such governance is normally executed by way of formal youth justice systems.

Defining 'formalism' is complex however. Certain youth justice systems privilege 'welfare' approaches (rooted in inquisitorial, adaptable, needs-oriented and child-specific imperatives), whilst others emphasise 'justice' responses (derived from adversarial, fixed, proportionate and offence-focused priorities). In some cases formal systems are characterised by explicitly retributive and punitive interventions, whilst many essentially attempt to broker a difficult balance – a hybrid fusion – comprising some combination of welfare, justice and/or punitive dimensions. Furthermore, the extent to which formal youth justice systems favour welfare or justice determinants, or attempt to establish hybrid fusions, is temporally and spatially contingent. In other words policy responses and practice formations not only change over time within the same country (the temporal dimension) (see Chapter 1; Goldson, 2002a), but youth justice systems also vary from one jurisdiction to another (the spatial factor) (see Chapter 3; Goldson, 2004).

Whilst it is important to acknowledge such variation, here we shall take 'formalism' to mean systems that typically:

- Routinely prosecute children and young people.
- Require children and young people to attend tribunals, and/or criminal courts of law, where they are exposed to prescribed rituals and, often, adversarial processes.
- Involve a range of formal 'actors', including any combination of: police officers; prosecutors; defence advocates; court officials; magistrates; judges; social workers; psychologists; psychiatrists; teachers; counsellors and institutional personnel.
- Open official criminal records on children and young people.
- Pass sentences in the form of court orders, conditions and/or statutory interventions with which children and young people are legally obliged to comply, and reserve additional (often more intrusive/punitive) sanctions for those who fail to do so.
- Ultimately retain powers to remove children and young people from their families and communities and to place them in correctional institutions (including children's homes, secure facilities and/or prisons).

Defining informalism

Informalism comprises an amalgam of theoretical perspectives and practical propositions that combine to challenge the legitimacy of formal youth justice systems. The conceptual foundations of informalism emerged in the 1960s and 1970s, alongside a burgeoning scepticism with regard to the practices of closed institutions. As they have developed, informalist approaches have broadened their focus, contending that the range and depth of state intervention should be minimised across the entire justice system. The 'de-structuring impulse' has thus been applied to 'all parts of the machine' (Cohen, 1985: 36).

Central to informalist perspectives is the contention that the formal interventions of youth justice processes essentially stigmatise children and young people by applying criminogenic 'labels'. Such 'labelling' is not evenly applied by state agencies, and working class, and black children and young people, are particularly susceptible. Furthermore, labelling triggers negative 'social reaction' which, in turn, has enduring and spiralling consequences (Becker, 1963). In this way it is argued that formal intervention and labelling 'creates' (or at least consolidates and confirms) criminogenic 'identities' for specific constituencies of disadvantaged children that, once established, tend to produce further offending. This led Edwin Lemert (1967) to conclude that 'social control leads to deviance', and David Matza (1969: 80) to comment on the 'irony' and self-defeating nature of certain professional interventions:

> . . . the very effort to prevent, intervene, arrest and 'cure' persons . . . precipitate or seriously aggravate the tendency society wishes to guard against.

In short, informalism shifts the conceptual emphasis by problematising the formal legal and disciplinary apparatus of youth justice, as distinct from the young person who offends, and the approach is rooted in at least seven intersecting theoretical traditions and practical prescriptions:

- First, *contextualisation* serves to remind us that youth crime is artificially 'amplified', both in terms of gravity and scope. Anxieties about young people and the fear of youth crime is largely a product of 'moral panic', media sensationalism and the demonisation of the young (Scraton, 1997; Cohen, 2002). When compared with 'white collar', organised and corporate crime (the crimes of the powerful), youth offending pales into criminological insignificance. Most youth crime is of a low-level, petty and opportunistic nature and often does not justify formal responses by way of youth justice interventions.

- Second, *normalisation*, an approach that rests upon the recognition that it is not uncommon for children and young people to transgress the law, and the primary difference between those who are conceptualised as 'offenders', and those who are not, is 'understood not as a difference in psychological character but as a consequence of whether or not the young person has become entangled in the criminal justice system' (Pearson, 1994: 1186). The 'normality' of juvenile crime is evidenced in self-report studies that have consistently (over time) indicated that offending is relatively common in adolescence (see for example, Shapland, 1978 and Graham and Bowling, 1995). Formal intervention therefore, serves to confuse 'normality' with pathology, and consequent labelling, stigmatisation and negative social reaction interrupts the 'normal' process of 'growing out of crime' (Rutherford, 1986)

- Third, *decriminalisation* which in policy terms amounts to the claim that generic social policy, as distinct from specific youth justice policy, provides the most appropriate medium for addressing the complex range of inter-related issues within which youth crime is usually located. Closely related to normalisation, this perspective proposes that the scope of criminal law and formal processing should be substantially narrowed, and that *civil* as distinct from *criminal* solutions should be sought. The Dutch criminologist, Louk Hulsman (1986), has even argued that the very notion of 'crime' should be abandoned, and replaced with notions of 'troubles', 'harms', 'conflicts' and/or 'mistakes'.

- Fourth, *diversion* is a strategy for reducing the numbers of children and young people from appearing in court, and thereby avoiding the 'damaging and contaminating consequences . . . of formal intervention' (Muncie, 1999: 291). Diversion by way of cautioning was very widely applied in England and Wales throughout the 1980s and into the 1990s (Goldson, 2000b). Whilst falling short of rejecting penal sanctions in their entirety, cautioning served to secure the exit of children and young people from the court system without penalty, other than a formal record of apprehension.

- Fifth, *radical non-intervention*, a term widely attributed to Edwin Schur (1973), is clearly informed by the consequences of 'labelling' and negative social reaction. In essence it effectively draws on contextualisation, normalisation, decriminalisation and diversion, and it applies such perspectives through the dictum 'leave kids alone wherever possible'. In particular, Schur (1965) argued that 'victimless crimes' should be removed from the corpus of criminal law.

- Sixth, *abolitionism* is in many respects the ultimate expression of informalism. It is a perspective rooted in various critical criminologies that have emerged from Western Europe, Scandinavia and North America, and it presents a competing paradigm to conventional notions of crime and crime control (see in particular, Christie, 1993 and Mathieson, 1990). In relation to youth justice it is normally applied to the abolition of penal custody for children and young people and its replacement by way of community-based 'alternatives'.

- Seventh, *human rights* imperatives and the provisions of international conventions, standards, treaties and rules, serve to provide the authority of the international community to approaches to youth crime and youth justice within which the rights and interests of child 'offenders' are central. Such instruments often comprise *de facto* expressions of informalism (Goldson, 2000b: 47–50).

New youth justice: new formalism

The most recent policy developments in youth justice in England and Wales have served to consolidate formalism, and to substantially extend the reach of the youth justice system. Early intervention in particular, comprises a cornerstone of the new youth justice, and diversionary policies and practices have effectively been abandoned. Sections 65 and 66 of the Crime and Disorder Act 1998 put an end to cautioning and established instead, on a statutory basis, the system of reprimands and final warnings (Goldson, 2000b; Bateman, 2003). Formal intervention by way of 'rehabilitation programmes' attached to final warnings, now applies to children as young as 10, for only their second (usually minor) offence (and in certain cases their first offence). In the event of a third (or possibly even second) transgression, such measures (together with reports relating to the child's standard of compliance with 'rehabilitation') are citable in court. In such circumstances conditional discharges are not normally available to the courts, and children instead face further intervention by way of 'programmes of behaviour' and 'youth offender contracts' attached to the referral order as provided by Part 1 of the Youth Justice and Criminal Evidence Act 1999 (see Chapter 16). Indeed, recently published statistics illustrate that whilst absolute and conditional discharges accounted for 25% of all sentences for indictable offences in 1999, by 2002 this figure had dropped to 9.5% (Home Office, 2003b).

Furthermore, interventions are now being targeted at children and young people below the age of criminal responsibility, who are considered to be 'at risk' of offending, via information sharing and assessment initiatives and so-called Youth Inclusion and Support Programmes (Goldson, 2003). The reach of the formal youth justice system is also being extended to encompass 'anti-social behaviour', and to target children whose presence in public places is 'believed' to be 'likely to cause intimidation, harassment, alarm or distress' (Home Office, 2003f). In this sense young people are being exposed to formal intervention not only on the basis of what they *have done*, but also in respect of what they *might do, who they are*, or who they are *thought to be*.

For an administration ostensibly wedded to evidence-based policy formation (informed by 'what works' principles), such an approach is curious. Indeed, the new emphasis on wider and more intensive intervention at the 'shallow end' of the youth justice process, and expanded and diversified forms of incarceration at the 'deeper end', is fundamentally at odds with research findings and the 'effectiveness' lessons drawn from previous practice experience (Goldson, 2000b; 2002c).

Re-stating the case for informalism

Informalism appeals to rights-based perspectives which oppose the criminalisation of (usually disadvantaged) children and young people. Moreover, its supporting foundations are also underpinned by research evidence and practice experience that confirm their efficacy. Before we consider the guiding principles of informal practices, and the evidence that substantiates them, it is worth emphasising two key points by way of clarification.

First, advocating informalism should not be taken to imply either that nothing should be done in relation to youth crime, or that children and young people who transgress the law should be left to fend for themselves without the care, guidance, support and supervision that they may need. Indeed, youth crime is predominantly situated within the poorest, most disadvantaged and distressed communities. Identifiable victims of youth crime are frequently also victims of social injustice. So too are the majority of young 'offenders', who are normally further damaged by their 'offending', either directly or indirectly. The central argument however, is that at the policy level the solutions to such complex problems, conflicts and harms, are to be found in the broad corpus of *social and economic policy* rather than the narrower confines of *youth justice policy*. Criminalisation, and formal exposure to youth justice systems, is more likely to compound the very problems it aims to prevent.

Second, informalism must seek to *replace*, as distinct from *co-exist with*, formal youth justice interventions. If diversionary and informalist initiatives simply become an adjunct to the youth justice system, rather than a direct alternative to it, then they will merely serve to draw more children and young people within its reach ('net-widening'), intensify the *level* of intervention ('net-strengthening'), and ultimately serve to provide new *forms* of intervention ('different nets') (Austin and Krisberg, 1981; Cohen, 1985). Equally, informal initiatives must be available to *all* 'young offenders', rather than being limited to those who are deemed to be most compliant. Otherwise 'bifurcated' responses are created, whereby the 'undeserving' are routinely exposed to formal criminalisation (and often custodial detention), whilst the 'alternatives' are reserved for a select constituency of 'deserving' children and young people. This can hardly be termed 'justice'.

Informal practices might rest upon the following applied principles therefore:

- State policy should comprehensively address the social and economic conditions that are known to give rise to conflict, harm, social distress and 'crime', particularly poverty and inequality.
- The 'normal' institutions of society – including families, schools and other forms of educational/training provision, 'communities', youth ser-

vices, health provision, leisure and recreational services, youth labour markets -should be required, and adequately resourced, to provide the widest range of opportunities for *all* children and young people.

- Children and young people should be routinely diverted away from formal youth justice interventions, and such systems should be replaced by informal and imaginative configurations providing support, guidance, advice, opportunities, holistic care and welfare.
- Interventions which are known to aggravate the very problems that they seek to reduce (perhaps most notably child imprisonment) should be abolished.
- In the minority of cases where *only* formal intervention is deemed appropriate, it should be provided outside the youth justice system, its intensity and duration should be limited to what is absolutely necessary, and its rationale should be explicit, evidenced-based, and likely to provide positive outcomes for the 'young offender' and any injured party.
- All forms of intervention should be consistent with the provisions of the Human Rights Act 1998 together with the full range of international standards, treaties, conventions and rules that have been formally adopted by the UK government (including the United Nations Convention on the Rights of the Child).
- Systematic efforts should be made to increase public knowledge, tolerance and understanding of 'youth crime'.

On first reading, such principles may seem little more than naive ideals, but they are actually grounded in robust research evidence and substantial practice experience. Bateman and Pitts (see Chapter 39) provide a more detailed overview of such evidence, but for the purposes here it is worth noting that *diversionary strategies* are: extraordinarily cost effective (Muncie, 1999); yield positive results in terms of comparatively low re-conviction rates (Hughes, 1998; Bell et al., 1999; Goldson, 2000b; Bateman, 2003; Smith, 2003); and normally satisfy victims (Dignan, 1992). It is also noteworthy that many European countries can demonstrate the effectiveness of diversion and informalism (Buckland and Stevens, 2001). Perhaps more significantly, the study led by James Howell from the US Department of Justice

– probably one of the most ambitious and comprehensive research analyses of youth crime prevention programmes in the world – concluded that many of the most promising approaches were intrinsically informalist. In other words some of the best 'results' emanated from initiatives that: were located *outside* of the formal criminal justice system (decriminalisation, diversion); built on children's and young people's strengths as distinct from emphasising their 'deficits' (normalisation); and adopted a social-structural approach to understanding and responding to troubled and troublesome children and young people, rather than drawing on individualised, criminogenic and/or medico-psychological perspectives (contextualisation) (Howell, et al., 1995).

Conclusion

In 1995 (United Nations, 1995), and again in 2002 (United Nations, 2002), the United Nations Committee on the Rights of the Child raised a range of concerns about youth justice policy and practice in England and Wales. The concerns essentially originate in the criminalising interventions to which children and young people are exposed at such a young age, and they are ultimately expressed via extraordinarily high rates of custodial detention. Such penological phenomena are the inevitable consequence of increasingly formalised responses to youth crime and youth justice. The same responses are generally ineffective and costly. Only by re-engaging with informal alternatives will policy makers be able to:

- address the concerns of the UN Committee;
- tackle the troubles of troublesome children;
- attend to the needs of 'victims';
- and deliver a rights-informed, effective and efficient approach to youth crime and youth justice befitting a civilised nation.

Further reading

Bell, A., Hodgson, M. and Pragnell, S. (1999) Diverting Children and Young People from Crime and the Criminal Justice System. in Goldson, B. (Ed.) *Youth Justice: Contemporary Policy and Practice*. Aldershot: Ashgate

Cohen, S. (1985) *Visions of Social Control*. Cambridge: Polity Press

Goldson, B. (2000b) Wither Diversion? Interventionism and the New Youth Justice. in Goldson, B. (Ed.) *The New Youth Justice*. Lyme Regis: Russell House Publishing

Hulsman, L. (1986) Critical Criminology and the Concept of Crime. in Bianchi, H. and van Swaaningen, R. (Eds.) *Abolitionism: Towards a Non-repressive Approach to Crime*. Amsterdam: Free University Press

Rutherford, A. (1986) *Growing Out of Crime*. Harmondsworth: Penguin

38 The Criminal Victimisation of Children and Young People

John Pitts

Key points

1. Children and young people are more vulnerable to criminal victimisation than adults.

2. They are particularly vulnerable to violent victimisation.

3. This vulnerability is heightened if they are poor or socially disadvantaged.

4. There appears to be a link between criminal victimisation and offending although it is not clear whether this is a result of victims and offenders sharing similar personal characteristics or living in the same high risk neighbourhoods.

5. Interventions to reduce youth victimisation may also reduce involvement in youth offending.

The prevalence of child and youth victimisation

In most media stories about young people and crime, the young person is the perpetrator not the victim. Yet all available research points to the fact that, in Britain, children and young people are more likely to be the victims of crime than any other age group. Moreover, if they are socially disadvantaged they have a heightened vulnerability to criminal victimisation and if they commit offences the risk is higher still.

A Victim Support study carried out in 2003 found that one in four children and young people aged 12-16 had been criminally victimised in the preceding year (cited in Nacro, 2003l). On the one occasion that the British Crime Survey included questions about child and youth victimisation, in 1992, the results showed that two thirds had been victimised in the preceding 6–8 months, of whom one third had been assaulted. A Crime Stoppers survey of 1,064 boys and girls aged 10–15, conducted in 2002, indicated that 45% did not tell their parents about their victimisation and that 51% did not tell the police. This survey also showed that 7% of respondents had been victimised five times or more in the preceding year (Nacro, 2003l). A survey of 11–15 year olds conducted in Glasgow concluded that, on average, children and young people in Scotland were four times more likely to be victimised than adults (Scottish Office, 1995).

Taking the findings of recent child and youth victimisation surveys together, Nacro (2003l) constructed the following table which shows the probability of child and adult victimisation.

	Average adult victimisation rate	Average child/youth victimisation rate
Theft	5%	30%
Assault	7%	10%
Property vandalised	5%	15%

Children's disproportionate susceptibility to violent victimisation is also revealed in a recent Crime Concern survey in Camberwell and Gospel Oak, in London, which found that over 20% of children and young people had been 'mugged' in the preceding year (Nacro, 2003l). This is 25 times the adult rate as recorded by the British Crime Survey. A contemporaneous US national survey indicated that those aged 12–19 are three times more likely to be the victims of assault, rape and robbery than adults. If young people are socially disadvantaged, however, their susceptibility to violent crime is likely to be much higher.

Victimisation and social disadvantage

It is not just age which heightens people's susceptibility to criminal victimisation; neighbourhood and social status are also key factors. As Tim Hope (2003) has argued:

> It is no exaggeration to say that we are now two nations as far as crime victimisation is concerned. Half the country suffers more than four fifths of the total amount of household property crime, while the other half makes do with the remaining 15 percent.
>
> (p.15)

This polarisation of risk has its origins in the seismic social and economic shifts which occurred in the UK in the 1980s and 1990s. The 1992 British Crime Survey (BCS), showed that between 1982 and 1992 not only had criminal victimisation risen at an unprecedented rate, there had also been significant changes in its nature and distribution as well (Hope, 1995a). The survey divides neighbourhoods into 10 categories on the basis of the intensity of the criminal victimisation of their residents. It revealed that by 1992, the chances of a resident in the lowest crime neighbourhood ever being assaulted had fallen to a point where it was barely measurable. Residents in the highest crime neighbourhoods, by contrast, now risked being assaulted twice a year. This polarisation of risk is made clearer when we recognise that by 1992, residents in the highest crime neighbourhoods experienced twice the rate of property crime and four times the rate of personal crime than those in the next worst category. These findings point to a significant redistribution of victimisation towards the poorest and most vulnerable over the intervening 10 years.

A major factor in this redistribution of crime and victimisation was the introduction of market mechanisms into the management of public sector housing by the Thatcher administration, via the 'Right to Buy' schemes, which diminished the amount of available housing, and 'Tenant Incentive' schemes which shifted more affluent tenants into the private sector (Page, 1993; Hope, 1994). Between 1970 and 1990, owner occupation in the UK rose from 55.3% of households to 67.6%. This 'secession of the successful' meant that, increasingly, it was the least 'successful' who were entering 'social housing'. As the 1980s progressed, relatively prosperous, middle-aged, higher income families left social housing, to be replaced by poorer, younger, often lone parent, families (Page, 1993).

Meanwhile, reductions in income support for the payment of the mortgage interest of unem-

ployed homeowners, and the house price slump of the early 1990s, which forced many separating couples to hand back their keys to the building societies, meant that 44,000 families moved from owner occupation into social housing. Between 1984 and 1994 annual residential mobility in social housing increased from 4 to 7% of households. Whereas in the 1980s and 1990s, 40% of heads of households in social housing were aged 65 or over, 75% of newly formed households entering social housing were headed by someone aged between 16 and 29. A high proportion of these new residents were unemployed, not least because they included a heavy concentration of lone parents.

In its report, *Bringing Britain Together*, the Social Exclusion Unit (1998) identified 1,370 housing estates in Britain which it characterised as 'poor neighbourhoods' which have 'poverty, unemployment, and poor health in common, and crime usually comes high on any list of residents' concerns'.

The estates which experienced the greatest changes saw increasing concentrations of children, teenagers, young single adults and young single parent families. Old social ties, constructed of kinship, friendship or familiarity withered away to be replaced by transience, isolation and mutual suspicion. Neighbours no longer watched out for one another's property or their shared amenities. Nor did they approach strangers, rowdy adolescents or naughty children, for fear of reprisals. In their study of one such estate, Tim Hope and Janet Foster (1992) discovered a five fold increase in burglaries over a three year period. Between 1981 and 1991 in Britain, those people most vulnerable to criminal victimisation, and those most likely to victimise them, were progressively thrown together on the poorest housing estates in Britain. By 1997, 25% of the children and young people under 16 in the UK were living in these neighbourhoods (Burroughs, 1998). As Chapter 36 of this volume indicates, the African-Caribbean and Asian populations of the UK are very young, and by the mid-1990s, up to 70% of the residents on the poorest housing estates were from these and other ethnic minorities (Power and Tunstall, 1997), and this is a major reason why their levels of victimisation are far higher than for whites (Lea and Young, 1984; Hope and Foster, 1992; Sampson and Phillips, 1995; Pitts and Smith, 1995).

This would suggest that any attempt to reduce child and youth victimisation in such neighbourhoods must therefore include strategies which aim to reconnect these destabilised neighbourhoods with the economic mainstream (Pitts, 2003b).

Youth and child victimisation and offending

Following the death of Maria Colwell at the hands of her parents in 1974, cases of suspected and proven child abuse are now entered on Child Protection Registers. On the basis of this data, the NSPCC Research Unit estimated, in 1986, that 2.29 per 1,000 children were abused or neglected each year in England and Wales (Creighton, 1987). The researchers also discovered that the average age at which a child was physically abused was six years nine months while the average age at which children were sexually abused was 10 years 2 months. When a local authority receives information that a child is likely to suffer, or has suffered, abuse or neglect, section 47 of the Children Act 1989 requires it to investigate. Around 160,000 section 47 investigations take place each year in England and Wales and initial suspicions are substantiated in about 135,000 of these. However, this could be an underestimate, because physical injury is far more likely to come to light as a result of a visit by a social worker than sexual or emotional abuse, which is more difficult to identify and prove.

Whether, and how, abuse, neglect or exposure to domestic violence leads a child to subsequent involvement in crime or violence is a contentious issue. While it is evident that most children who are abused or neglected do not go on to become perpetrators, studies of perpetrators reveal a high correlation with prior victimisation (Widom, 1992; Lewis et al., 1989). US studies cite physical abuse rates of between 13% and 40% for young people involved in youth justice systems, while estimated sexual abuse rates vary between 19% and 82%, depending on the definition being used (Finkelhor et al., 1994). There is also some evidence that children witnessing abuse and domestic violence are more likely to become perpetrators of violent and property offences (Hotaling et al., 1989). A study by Kate Jones and John Pitts (2001) found a close correlation between early childhood victimisation, in the forms of abuse and neglect, and

subsequent involvement in the youth justice system. Between 40% and 65% of young people, placed under the supervision of a London YOT in any one year had previously been on the child protection register as a result of chronic neglect or violent or sexual abuse.

The Edinburgh Study of Youth Transitions and Crime is a longitudinal investigation of 4,300 children who started secondary school in 1998. Early results suggest that being a victim of crime at the age of 12 appears to be a powerful indicator that a child will be offending at age 15. This could be, as some academics have suggested, that victims and perpetrators often share a similar lifestyle and personality traits, indicating that both groups may be 'impulsive risk takers' (McAra, 2003). However, as we note above, studies which have focused upon the impact of neighbourhood factors on child and youth crime and victimisation suggest that in low socio-economic status neighbourhoods, children and young people with low, or no, familial or personal 'risk factors', such as impulsiveness or a propensity to take risks, may be significantly more prone to both crime and criminal victimisation because of the risks present within high crime neighbourhoods, where much child and youth victimisation occurs (Sampson and Laub, 1993; Hagan, 1993; Wikstrom and Loeber, 1997).

Acutely disadvantaged young people, crime and victimisation

The study by Kate Jones and John Pitts (2001), cited above, revealed that children on the child protection register who subsequently fell foul of the criminal justice system tended to come from families with a multiplicity of difficulties, including parental drink and drug abuse and serious parental mental health problems. Around 40% of this group had had ten or more residential or foster placements between the ages of one and 15. The incidents which triggered initial registration were frequently followed by placement in a children's home or a foster placement. There was a very high incidence of placement breakdown; followed by unsuccessful short-term placement back at home; followed by placement in a new residential setting or foster home. These young people frequently experienced bullying and victimisation in both the care system and in school. However, after the

point of initial registration, the focus of profes
sional intervention tended to shift towards problems of offending, school attendance and conduct,
rather than the abuse and neglect they had
suffered at the hands of their parents, and its
effects, or their subsequent victimisation in school
and in the care system.

Colin Pritchard and Alan Butler (2000), in their
study of the prevalence of criminal victimisation,
murder and suicide amongst 814 former 'looked
after' children between the ages of 11–15, found
a murder rate 33 times the national average for
boys and 43 times the national average for girls.
The sexual assault rates for 'looked after' boys and
girls were 2.5 and 5 times the national average
respectively. These young people were particularly
prone to violent assault and their assailants were
often other family members or step fathers and
co-habitees in particular. As many US commentators have argued, to break the link between acute
social disadvantage, crime and victimisation, mod
ern societies require well resourced, pro-active
child protection services capable of following
young people through the transition to adulthood
if necessary (Currie, 1985). This was an issue
raised by the *Joint Inspectors Report on Safeguarding
Children* which pointed to the fact that YOTs
often give insufficient attention to the welfare or
child protection needs of the children and young
people they supervise because of the excessive
emphasis they place upon their offending. This
point is also made by Patricia Gray in Chapter 21.
Such considerations have led to provisions in the
Children Bill, before parliament at the time of
writing, requiring that YOTs should be amongst
the agencies which monitor the welfare of and
safeguard children and young people from victimisation and abuse.

Victimisation in schools

The 'neighbourhood effect' that leads to
heightened child and youth victimisation in low
socio-economic status areas, discussed above, is
replicated in the classrooms of the schools which
serve these neighbourhoods. In a study of an
inner London school undertaken in the late 1990s
(Porteous, 1998b), the transience of the housing
estates which fed the school was reflected in a
50% turnover in the school roll between years 7
and 11. Because the nature of the changes in the

neighbourhood had been to replace more prosperous residents with less prosperous ones, by 1997
over 50% of school students qualified for free
school meals, the key indicator of social deprivation.

Because poverty and transience generate educational disadvantage in children, and erode the
capacity of adults to offer consistent parenting,
schools in these neighbourhoods must absorb a
higher proportion of children with special educational and behavioural needs. Thus, 43% of the
students attending the London school had been
assessed as having *special educational needs*, twice the
borough average. As a result, behaviour in the
playground and the corridors deteriorated. The
impact of the resultant atmosphere could be
measured in increased truancy and lateness
amongst students who were previously seen to
pose no attendance problems.

A further consequence of rapid student turnover is that schools carry a large number of
vacancies. In the current economic climate, in
which local education authorities are striving to
reduce surplus capacity, these schools are under
constant pressure to absorb students who wish to
transfer in from other schools in the borough. In
the London school, 64% of year 10 and 40% of
year 11 students had previously attended another
secondary school. However, beyond the destabilis-
ing effect of this steady influx of transferring
students, is the fact that many of them brought
additional academic and behavioural problems
which, in some cases, had caused them to be
excluded from other schools. This process was
exacerbated significantly by the introduction of
market mechanisms and league tables into state
education in the 1980s and 1990s (Pitts, 2003b).

One consequence of the destabilisation of
schools has been an increase in the numbers of
serious fights, particularly inter-racial fights. These
disputes, which may have started in the school or
in the neighbourhood, would quickly attract older
adolescents and young adults from the surrounding area who, having nothing better to do, would
get 'stuck in'. This violence contributed significantly to the risks faced by school students who
were not directly involved in the original fight. In
the London school, between September 1996 and
April 1997, 41% of year 11 students were assaulted, with 30% of these assaults occurring in the
vicinity of the school or on the way home from

school, in the hour or so following the end of the school day. 80% of the perpetrators were male, and 48% were either strangers or students from another school. 24% of respondents reported being threatened or assaulted with a weapon. In a similar study undertaken in a similar neighbourhood in another part of London (Pitts and Smith, 1995), over 30% of victimised students identified their assailant as being older than them and, in some cases, as an adult. It is, of course, ironic that schools in destabilised neighbourhoods, confronting formidable social problems, are nonetheless required to import further problems of disruption, crime and violence from other neighbourhoods.

However, as Michael Rutter et al. (1978) have shown, levels of victimisation in particular schools are not simply determined by the nature of the area served by the school. They suggest that the structure and ethos of schools can have a significant impact upon attendance, attainment, behaviour in class, student involvement in crime and levels of student victimisation. Similarly, Olweus (1989) suggests that structure, culture and patterns of communication have a significant impact on the conduct of students. Recent UK initiatives which have aimed to increase participation by students, enhance their study skills, increase teachers' inter-personal competence and cultivate pride in the school have led to significant decreases in both levels of student victimisation and 'self-report delinquency' (Graham, 1988; Pitts and Smith, 1995). The early findings from the evaluation of restorative justice in schools also suggests that training teaching staff in mediation techniques can reduce absenteeism due to bullying and increase perceptions that school is a safe environment (Bitel, 2004).

In high crime neighbourhoods, behaviour in and out of school is closely linked. Effective intervention in the school to improve communication between staff and students, clarify expectations, rewards and sanctions and offer training and support to staff and students can have a marked effect upon child and youth victimisation (Graham, 1988).

Victimisation on public transport

One of the key findings from the study into student victimisation conducted by Pitts and Smith (1995) was that many children and young

people were particularly vulnerable to victimisation when travelling to and from school on public transport. Children and young people are major users of public transport. School journeys account for a quarter of all children's travel and 20% of journeys to school are made by bus or coach (Association of Transport Coordinating Officers, 1997).

Anti-social behaviour by young people on buses and, especially, school services has been identified by transport providers as a national problem.

However, young people are as much victims as perpetrators of crime and anti-social behaviour on public transport. Moreover they are victimised by both adults and other young people and the majority of incidents go unreported.

Consultations with children and young people in Merseyside (Crime Concern, 1995) suggest that they have far more contact with, or involvement in, criminal incidents than adult passengers. The incidents that young people see and experience on public transport include having their personal belongings stolen and being bullied or threatened by older children, especially when they are alone, and inter-school 'rivalry', which can sometimes result in bullying and theft. The Merseyside consultation also revealed that girls and young women are more likely than adults to be molested by men on the upper decks of buses and that both school girls and school boys are disproportionately likely to be the victims of adults exposing themselves on buses or at bus stops.

Waiting for buses was regarded as a problem by many young women and girls, especially when they were waiting in unfamiliar areas or at stops which were dark and isolated. Some younger children of both sexes admitted to feeling scared waiting for buses in the dark. Children and young people said that the presence of staff made them feel safer. Using train stations after dark was also a concern for young people and lack of visible staff tended to make them feel unsafe.

Responding to child and youth victimisation

It appears that many young people who become involved in crime have themselves been the victims of crime. This is particularly so in the case of violence. David Porteous (1998) found a high level of overlap between perpetrators and victims of inter-racial youth violence, while a recent study in South London revealed that young people who had been mugged would sometimes 'mug' somebody else in order to re-establish their status in the neighbourhood and regain lost respect (Sanders, 2003). Studies of bullying suggest a close relationship between behaviour in and out of school and that if in-school behaviour changes, out of school behaviour will as well (Graham, 1988; Olweus, 1989). Moreover, a large body of research links early childhood victimisation to subsequent involvement in the youth justice system.

These findings would seem to point to a range of child protection and community safety initiatives in families, neighbourhoods and schools which focus upon the heightened vulnerability to victimisation of children and adolescents. But the logic of the evidence base does not always inform practice.

A recent NSPCC survey of crime and disorder partnerships (2001) found that 40% '. . . prioritise working towards the increased safety of children and young people'. However, in practice, this was often a reference to strategies which aimed first and foremost to combat youth crime rather than youth victimisation. Less than half the partnerships acknowledged the need for enhanced child protection services or victim support. The report recommends that partnerships should consult young people, prioritise their needs, address their vulnerability, particularly in relation to domestic violence, consider the particular needs and vulnerabilities of children and young people when developing community safety strategies and be prepared to mediate between them and adults (Nacro, 2003l). If such strategies were adopted, it appears likely that the consequent fall in the rate of child and youth victimisation might well be followed by a fall in youth crime.

Further reading

Graham, J. (1988) *Schools, Disruptive Behaviour and Delinquency*. Research Study 96. London: Home Office

Hope, T. and Foster, J. (1992) Conflicting Forces: Changing Dynamics of Crime and Community on a Problem Estate, *British Journal of Criminology* 32:92

Jones, K. and Pitts, J. (2001) *Early Childhood Child Protection Registration and Subsequent Involvement with a Youth Justice Team/Youth Offending Team in a London Borough*. Luton: Vauxhall Centre for the Study of Crime, University of Luton

Nacro (2003l) *Youth Victimisation: A Literature Review*. Community Safety Practice Briefing, London: Nacro

Porteous, D. (1998b) Young People's Experience of Crime and Violence: Findings from a Survey of School Pupils: in Marlow, A. and Pitts, J. (Eds.) *Planning Safer Communities*. Lyme Regis: Russell House Publishing

39 Conclusion: What the Evidence Tells Us

Tim Bateman and John Pitts

Evidence, policy and public opinion

One of the defining features of contemporary youth justice is its emphasis upon 'evidence'. Nowadays, as we are frequently reminded, policy must be 'evidence-led' and practice, 'evidence-based'. The current emphasis on 'evidence' is part and parcel of what Mair (2000) describes as the politics of 'good governance', which became influential in the 1990s. Good governance is rooted in the idea that what matters to modern electorates is the technical and managerial competence of governments rather than their ideological commitments. This new 'post-political' politics aims to sideline party political horse-trading by establishing a direct relationship with the electorate, making policy commitments based on scientific analyses of what ordinary people really want, and 'delivering' 'hard outcomes' with maximum economy, efficiency and effectiveness (Mair, 2000).

This ostensibly rational endeavour is not without its difficulties because the various constituencies which comprise New Labour's centre-left electoral constituency often disagree with one another about what the government should be trying to achieve. This confronts government with a dilemma; who should they listen to?

A great deal of effort, both before and after the 1997 general election, has gone into courting, winning, and trying to retain the support of ex-Tory 'floaters'. This is because New Labour psephologists believe that this small and potentially volatile group of voters hold the key to New Labour's electoral fortunes (Kettle, 2004). This supposition has had an important impact upon the ways in which government garners public opinion; as John Humphrys (2000), has observed:

> *The political technicians and strategists are now adept at identifying the relatively small number of people who can swing an election and put their clients in power, and they are the people they will listen to most*

carefully. All of Gould's focus groups consisted only of people who had voted Tory in 1992 and had become 'floaters'. So no one else gets a look in.

If the policy choices on offer are fashioned with an eye to ensnaring the ephemeral loyalties of this rightward-leaning constituency, it should not surprise us if those choices resonate with the ideological proclivities of traditional conservatism.

So while it is true that contemporary youth justice policy and practice are informed by 'evidence', the evidence is not the starting point of the policy making process. Nor, for that matter, are political principles, for in the post-political politics of the 'third way', 'what counts' has tended to be 'what works' for the 'floaters'. Thus, it is only after the political parameters of policy have been extrapolated from the deliberations of the focus groups and opinion polls that the evidence is assembled (Pitts, 2003b). Not surprisingly, some evidence like that which points to the deleterious effects of penal confinement upon the criminal careers and life-chances of disadvantaged children and young people, for example, is found to be inadmissible (Goldson, 2001).

Our criticism, here, is not of the evidence base of contemporary youth justice *per se*, but rather that this evidence is, perhaps inevitably, selected, first and foremost, on the basis of its fit with psephologically-derived policy goals rather than its explanatory power or practical efficacy. Policy cannot therefore be said to be genuinely 'evidence-led'. If it were, that evidence would inform both the assumptions underlying policy and the goals fashioned in the light of those assumptions; not just the techniques developed to facilitate policy implementation.

From 'nothing!' to 'what?'

New Labour's commitment to 'evidence' marks a departure from the mixture of good intentions, habit, political vindictiveness, pragmatism and inertia which informed the development of youth justice in the UK for best part of the 20th century (Pitts, 2003b). This was partly due to a tradition of 'common sense' policy making in the UK but also to the paucity of research in this area. Not so in the USA where, from the 1950s, youth justice research and evaluation became a sizeable industry. This research was highly influential until the 1970s, but thenceforth, under presidents Reagan, Bush I, Clinton and Bush II, 'evidence-led' policy was eclipsed by a strategy of 'penal populism' in which policy tended to echo the visceral sentiments of the 'moral majority' rather than the deliberations of disinterested social scientists (Krisberg and Austin, 1993). Nonetheless, when New Labour ushered in a new evidential era in youth justice, it was to North America that they turned because this was where most of the research had been conducted. The difficulty was that the abundance of evidence did not appear to point unequivocally towards any particular rehabilitative intervention.

In an attempt to assemble evidence of the effectiveness of rehabilitation, in the mid-1970s, Martinson (1974) undertook an analysis of what he deemed to be the 231 best evaluated rehabilitative interventions. But he was soon drawn to the conclusion that:

> . . . these data, involving over two hundred studies and hundreds of thousands of individuals as they do, are the best available and give us little reason to hope that we have in fact found a sure way of reducing recidivism through rehabilitation. This is not to say that we have found no instances of success or partial success; It is only to say that these instances have been isolated, producing no clear pattern to indicate the efficacy of any particular method.

This sombre assessment was underscored by subsequent studies which produced similarly uneven results. It was on the basis of this evidence that, in the mid-1970s, criminologists reluctantly announced the 'decline of the rehabilitative ideal' (Preston, 1980). Those with a less delicate touch simply stated that 'nothing works'. Over the next decade or so, a broad consensus emerged in government, the academy and the 'helping professions' to support this view. Whereas the political right read Martinson's work as a vindication of retributive justice, on the left and in the liberal centre the new common sense held that the best

we could hope for was to minimise the negative impact of prosecution, imprisonment and social work intervention on the lives of those involved in the criminal justice system (Currie, 1986).

This response from the criminological community was surprising since, as Pawson and Tilley (1997) have pointed out, Martinson had laid down an 'impossibly stringent criterion for success' which, by bundling programmes together into broad treatment categories, inevitably produced mixed results.

However, the backlash against the 'nothing works' orthodoxy, when it came, had little to do with subsequent scientific advances and a great deal to do with the changing politics of crime and justice. By the late 1980s, a rising crime rate and growing concern about violent youth crime were placing mounting pressure on the Conservative government, the Home Office and, via them, academic criminology, to come up with something that did 'work'. Stanley Cohen has observed that much criminology operates on a 'Midas-in-reverse' principle, i.e. if it's gold, criminologists tend to touch it. And soon canny criminologists were returning to the data upon which the belief that 'nothing works' had been based and, not altogether surprisingly, discovering that it now told a somewhat different story:

> . . . the outcome research of the early 1970s was capable of being interpreted in other ways than 'Nothing works' . . . This has recently led some writers . . . who worked at the Home Office Research Unit in the 1970s to argue that the pessimistic conclusions drawn from this research were not necessarily justified.
>
> (Blagg and Smith, 1989: 86)

In this they are no doubt correct since the 'nothing works' doctrine based on meta-analysis of reconviction rates, failed to pinpoint those individuals, projects and institutions whose endeavours did, in fact, 'work', or to explain why they did. While such localised data do not undermine the thesis that, in the majority of cases, rehabilitative methods cannot be shown to have been instrumental in reducing crime rates, it does suggest that sometimes, with some people, in some circumstances, for some reason, some things do 'work' (Pitts, 2003b).

However, this rehabilitation of rehabilitation was palpably political in intent. As Christopher

Nutall, described by *The Independent* as the 'hard-headed' director of research and statistics at the Home Office (Pitts, 2003b), told a meeting of chief probation officers in 1992:

> *'Nothing works' should be killed; not just because it's not right but because it has had a terrible effect. Let's not talk about it any more. Let's talk about what does work.*

The consistency of inconsistency

'Nothing works' was dead; long live 'what works'! Ironically, however, the methodological problems afflicting Martinson's evidence were more or less the same as those afflicting the evidence deployed by the 'what works' generation that followed him (Pawson and Tilley, 1997). The problem was that the studies they cited consistently revealed inconsistent outcomes for the same kinds of interventions in the same kinds of settings with the same kinds of people. Confronted with such inconsistencies researchers often pointed the finger at 'implementation failure', suggesting that while the theory was fine, the practice, and by implication the practitioners, had made a 'pig's ear' of it. However, the problem appears to have been more fundamental than this, having its origins in the researchers' understanding of the nature of the human sciences and their beliefs about human nature.

Epistemological problems: the nature of social science

The vision of science which informs mainstream US evaluative research in youth justice is rooted in a belief that to attain scientific validity, it must replicate the protocols, methods and, indeed, the language of the natural sciences. Thus the talk is of 'experimentation', 'control groups', 'impulse control', 'treatment' and 'dosage'. The method, however, is simplicity itself. It is known as quasi-experimental method.

Ostensibly similar research subjects, either matched or randomly selected, are allocated to an 'experimental' group and to a 'control' group. The experimental group undertakes the treatment and the control group does not. The factors which the 'treatment' is designed to change are measured before and after the 'treatment', the treated and

Figure 39.1: Quasi-experimental method

	Pre-test	Treatment	Post-test
Experimental group	01	×	02
Control group	01	×	02

(Derived from Pawson and Tilley, 1997)

untreated groups are then compared with one another. The underlying assumption here is that, because the experimental and control groups are more or less identical, any post-test differences between the two will be attributable to the treatment. This method is sometimes referred to as 'black box' research because, while it endeavours to tell us whether a particular mode of treatment 'works', or not, it is unable to tell us why. In short, it lacks any theory of change. As Nick Tilley (2001) has observed:

> *Programs do not work unconditionally and useful answers to evaluation questions entail penetrating the contexts for the activation of varying causal mechanisms to produce changed patterns of behaviour. We take evaluation to require a theory to explain or predict how changes introduced by an intervention alter the balance of causal mechanisms at work and lead to change in behaviour.*

Although it is now well established within the social scientific community that different methodologies are required if one is to capture the meanings which motivate the actions of human beings, this view has made little headway in mainstream evaluative research.

Ontological problems: the nature of human nature

At the heart of quasi-experimental method is an unacknowledged assumption that if the correct treatment dosage can be applied to the research subject, cognitive-behavioural change, or whatever, will somehow follow. This presumes that the subject of these rehabilitative interventions is merely reactive and adaptive. Yet, as David Matza has argued, human reflexivity, rather than mere reactivity, is the defining feature of human nature and so:

The existence of subjects is not quite exhausted by the arduous natural processes of reactivity and adaptation . . . mere reactivity or adaptation should not be confused with the distinctively human condition. They are better seen as an alienation or exhaustion of that condition. A subject actively addresses or encounters his circumstance: accordingly, his distinctive capacity is to reshape, strive toward creating, and actually transcend circumstance. Such a distinctively human project is not always feasible, but the capacity always exists.

(Matza, 1969· 2–93)

Thus, Pawson and Tilley (1997) argue that a critical component in behavioural change is the motivation and predisposition of offenders. In opposition to the implicit assumption within cognitive behavioural interventions, for example, that programmes work *on* individuals, they argue that programmes must work *through* individuals. They write (p.38):

Social programs involve a continual round of interactions and opportunities and decisions. Regardless of whether they are born of inspiration or ignorance, the subject's choice at each of these junctures will frame the extent and nature of change. What we are describing here is not just the moment when the subject signs up to enter a program but the entire learning process. The act of volunteering merely marks a moment in a whole evolving pattern of choice. Potential subjects will consider a program (or not), cooperate closely (or not), stay the course (or not), learn lessons (or not), apply the lessons (or not). Each one of these decisions will be internally complex and take its meaning according to the chooser's circumstances.

This being the case, they argue, it is unsurprising that results based upon experiments with matched cohorts of research subjects are consistently inconsistent. By quantifying the aggregated behaviours of the experimental and control groups, we never learn about the motivation, mood or personal circumstances of particular research subjects, which have shaped their responses to treatment. Indeed, one of the ironies is that within experimental groups which register no positive change, there may well be people for whom the treatment has been a life-changing experience, but this gets lost in the statistical 'shuffle', because the method is only able to deal with aggregated, rather than individual effects. Pawson and Tilley's solution to this problem is to develop a different sort of evaluative strategy, 'realistic evaluation', in which human reflexivity and the personal, social, cultural and economic context in which the key life decisions of 'research subjects' are made, rather than being edited out of the equation by arcane methodological devices, become a key element within it (Pawson and Tilley, 1997). It would seem to follow from this that instead of asking 'what works?' we probably need to ask:

What kind of interventions have what kind of impact upon what kinds of people under what kinds of circumstances and why?

As John Pitts (1992) has argued:

The answer to the question 'What is the most effective method?' is the same as the answer to the question 'What is the most effective tool?' and it is, 'It depends.' Working out what it depends on is what distinguishes the professional role from that of the technician. Effective rehabilitative ventures are reflexive rather than directive; they respond to situations as they unfold. Their language is an innovative dialogue not a prescriptive monologue. For these reasons effective interventions can seldom be categorized, cloned and transplanted. To do so may be helpful to researchers, administrators and politicians, because it tidies up a messy and idiosyncratic world but, unfortunately, successful interventions do not seem to travel well.

Quasi-experimentation has of course attracted criticism. Beyond the widely accepted reservation that the methods of the natural sciences are largely inappropriate for the study of human action, already noted, quasi-experimentation continues to 'bang the drum' for scientific protocols and statistical methods, long since abandoned by most natural scientists and statisticians in favour of more sensitive and flexible tools. This would appear to raise important questions about whether, and to what extent, it is possible to tell 'what works' on the basis of such hit and miss methods. Nonetheless, in both the UK and the USA, quasi-experimental method remains the gold standard against which interventions with young people who offend are measured.

Promises, promises

As we have noted, the measures incorporated into New Labour's youth justice strategy were what David Farrington (1996) has described as 'those which research points to as the most thorough and best designed programmes showing the most promising results'. But, as he points out there have been few well designed studies in the UK, resulting in 'an unavoidable emphasis on innovative work in the United States.' Here, he is referring particularly to the Maryland review of crime prevention studies undertaken by the National Institute of Justice (NIJ), a division of the US Department of Justice, in response to a mandate from the US Attorney-General and the US Congress in 1996. The Maryland review provides much of the foundations for the claims of the 'What Works' movement in the UK. The NIJ distinguishes programmes which are 'promising' from those that 'work': the former refer to interventions for which 'the level of certainty from available evidence is too low to support generalisable conclusions, but for which there is some empirical basis for predicting that further research could support such conclusions' (Sherman et al., 1998). Programmes identified as working are those which 'we are reasonably certain prevent crime or reduce risk factors for crime in the kinds of social contexts in which they have been evaluated and for which findings can be generalised to similar settings in other places and times'. This statement raises important questions about whether, or to what extent, the UK might qualify as an analogous social context, a difficulty which the authors of the Maryland review fully recognise:

> *The weakest aspect of this classification . . . is that there is no standard means of establishing external validity: exactly what variations in programme content and setting might affect the generalisability of findings from evaluations.*

This causes Tilley (2001) to observe that:

> *If 'what works' depends on a conducive context, and it is accepted that failure using the same measure might occur in a non-conducive context, it then follows that a trial that has failed may have been undertaken in one of these non-conducive settings [and so] no number of failures could show that the measure could never be successful.*

Pawson and Tilley (1997) note that this takes us no further forward and so basing policy on such unsafe foundations constitutes a hazardous enterprise.

The problem of recidivism as a measure of success

Beyond these methodological problems is the question of the adequacy of the measure used to demonstrate the impact of programmes. This is, almost invariably, recidivism. Yet recidivism is by no means as robust a measure as it might appear. *Re-arrest rates* may tell us little about actual patterns of re-offending since the proportion of crime solved by the police is so low (see Chapter 2). In the 1990s, under pressure from governmentally imposed performance indicators, police arrest rates rose sharply but the proportion of convictions of those arrested fell almost as precipitously as arrest rates had risen (Hallam, 2000). *Reconviction* data, the preferred measure for most studies, suffer from much the same problem: inevitably they understate significantly the extent of re-offending. As a result, we know a great deal less than is often assumed about the impact of rehabilitative programmes.

Putting 'what works' to work in the UK youth justice system

These complexities do not appear to have troubled contemporary UK youth justice policy makers and administrators unduly. The commitment to effective practice, in itself highly desirable, has frequently been accompanied by an unwarranted certainty about 'what works', allowing little space for debate. Thus, Charles Pollard, when acting chair of the Youth Justice Board (YJB), felt able to tell a conference audience in 2003 that the Board 'knows what works in preventing offending . . . we must ensure that all forces deliver our successful programmes' (Young People Now, 2003). 'Delivery' has been facilitated by encouraging standardised interventions, reflected in performance targets, to be implemented without deviation, in order, it is said, to avoid the problems of 'implementation failure' discussed above. However, given the equivocal evidence on which the model is founded, some critics have argued that the ascendancy of this approach to dealing with young people in trouble owes more to the fact that it facilitates the micro-management of the youth justice system than its likely impact upon re-offending (see for example, Pitts, 2001a).

To advance the 'what works' project, the YJB has published a series of 'simple manuals' entitled *Key Elements of Effective Practice* (KEEPs) on a range of topics, each of which identifies 16 'key indicators of quality' for practitioners and managers. The KEEPs are intended to describe the main features of effective youth justice services and practices; as such they are brief manuals following a single format. Each is, however, underpinned by a 'source document' containing references to the relevant supporting research evidence. The Board's quality assurance system for YOTs is built around these key indicators of quality and its learning development strategy aims to ensure that practitioners are familiar with them. The conception of effective practice embodied in this approach is one of process: individual needs are identified through standardised assessment; interventions are designed to address assessed needs; monitoring and evaluation ensure that interventions are delivered in accordance with the plan and adherence to it is presented as a necessary and sufficient condition for preventing offending.

The difficulty, of course, is that while the process itself is internally coherent and (from a practitioner's point of view) readily understandable, it nonetheless rests upon questionable assumptions. To the extent that the assessment procedures are based on the 'risk factor paradigm', for instance, the process relies on an account of the origins of offending based upon a combination of correlation and speculation (see Chapter 19). What constitutes effective intervention does not spring unbidden from the standardised assessment, however well conducted. Indeed, the link between the two is the largely unstated assumption that offending behaviour is associated with individual deficiencies, which should, therefore, be the focus of intervention. Nor are these complexities necessarily articulated in the source documents which purports to provide the 'evidence base'. Indeed, all too often they appear to be restating what they claim to be evidencing.

The final warning source document, for instance, provides some evidence that a graduated response to escalating youth offending is likely to be effective but simply takes it as given that 80%

of young people who receive a final warning, echoing the YJB's performance target, will benefit from a YOT intervention (Youth Justice Board, undated d). Nor is there any acknowledgement of research evidence pointing to the potentially criminogenic effects of pre-emptive criminal justice interventions (see Chapter 12). Similarly, while there may be good grounds for reducing unnecessary delay in terms of preventing offending, the source document on the swift administration of justice fails to provide an evidential rationale for doing so. It relies instead on an assertion that meeting the government's pledge that 'persistent young offenders' should be processed within 71 days, is an 'important objective' for the criminal justice system and that 'timeliness remains an important indicator of efficiency' (Youth Justice Board, undated e). This conflation of science, policy and administration to produce what C. Wright Mills (1959) called 'bureaucratic social science' is exemplified in session 6 of the Board's Professional Certificate in Effective Practice (Youth Justice) that deals with the *History of the youth justice system and the role of YOTs*. The session consists of three slides in which there is this one historical allusion:

> *YOTs were established in 2000. Before that time, youth justice teams largely comprised staff from a social services or probation background.*
>
> (Youth Justice Board, 2003a)

This oversimplified understanding of the history of youth justice, which manages to ignore welfarism, corporatism and progressive minimalism without missing a beat (see Chapter 1), has parallels with the partial reading of criminological research which informs much of what stands for the 'evidence base' of evidence led practice. These remarkable omissions are justified on the grounds that such abbreviated accounts of the world render it more comprehensible to YOT workers who must act in it, while on the other hand it facilitates consistency of practice.

This selective reading of the evidence base has, in the past, sometimes found its corollary in a selective presentation by the YJB and the Home Office of the results of its rehabilitative endeavours. Burnett and Appleton (2004b), in their perceptive assault upon the YJB's history of 'news management', point to the ways in which the evidence derived from the YOTs has often been presented selectively and, on occasions, simply misrepresented, to paint a far more optimistic picture than is warranted. Aidan Wilcox (2003), in his measured assessment of the fate of his own evaluations comes to a similar conclusion, suggesting that the motivation behind this misrepresentation may well be the need, on the part of the YJB, to attract continued political support from the Home Office and funding from the Treasury. However, whatever else this is, evidence-led policy and evidence-based practice it is not.

Indeed, the emphasis on 'responsibilisation' of young people (see Chapter 1), lying at the heart of the youth justice reforms has been constructed within a punitive discourse, reflecting a determination to appear tough on crime, which tends at many points to subvert evidence-led policy making. Thus, one of the practical consequences of reform has been to reinforce trends likely to increase youth offending rather than reduce it. At the front end of the system, diversion from court has declined rapidly leading to higher rates of prosecution for younger children whose offending is less serious (see Chapters 2 and 12). Further down the line, the growth in overtly punitive interventions has paved the way for what one commentator has described as a custodial bonanza (Pitts, 2004; see Chapter 25). Neither development, according to available research evidence, is conducive to preventing offending.

What the evidence really says

As we note in Chapter 2, *Criminal Statistics* indicate that youth crime is falling, a trend which predates, by some years, the implementation of the youth justice reforms. The YJB's self-report studies, meanwhile, suggest that offending by young people is broadly stable (MORI, 2003). In any event, the extent to which changes in overall levels of youth crime are attributable to the reforms of the youth justice system by the CDA is debatable. Fewer than one in twenty of the offences committed by young people results in an official response (see Chapter 2) and it is unlikely, therefore, that intervention with those young people who are processed by the youth justice system – no matter what is done with, to, or for them – will make much of an impact on overall rates of youth offending.

Pre-court preventive intervention

Preventive intervention, and pre-emptive intervention, with children below the age of criminal responsibility and those considered to be 'at risk' of offending, is an attempt to address the problem that the youth justice system has no contact with the bulk of young people who break the law. This approach has drawn criticism from commentators who point to evidence that interventions delivered by criminal justice agencies may be counter-productive. The argument is that the identities of younger children, inducted into the criminal justice system at such an impressionable age, may be recast as deviant. The consequent stigma may disrupt and weaken their relationships with family, peers, neighbourhood and school; they will be thrust into closer association with similarly 'labelled' children and young people, and this might in turn project them into a 'criminal justice system career'. Just such an argument is developed by Barry Goldson in this volume (see Chapter 37). The YJB counters that because mainstream service providers have simply failed to deliver 'broad-brush' preventive services, it is better that the youth justice system provides them (see Chapter 32). Evidence of the effectiveness of such intervention is mixed.

The most recent of the Board's excursions into pre-emptive intervention, Youth Inclusion and Support Panels (YISPs) which target 8–13 year olds deemed to be at risk of future offending, has yet to generate any outcome data. There is however evidence from the national evaluation of the first phase of the Youth Inclusion Programme (YIP) which was launched in 2000. YIPs target the 50 13–16 year olds deemed by local agencies to be those most 'at risk' in project neighbourhoods, and encourages the participation of a wider group of 'at risk' young people. The evaluation report indicates that the YIP initiative met only one of its three objectives. There was a fall in exclusions from school amongst YIP participants, albeit below the target level, but truancy had risen. Overall levels of crime within the project areas had increased, by 11.4% over a two-year period, although taking into account changes in police recording practice, the authors conclude that the 'true' increase was somewhat lower, at just under 6%. Whether area crime rates offer a useful measure of the impact of an intervention with a relatively small number of young people living in a high crime area is of course debatable. Arrest rates for the core group is likely to be a more robust measure of effectiveness and these fell substantially (Morgan Harris Burrows, 2003). However, as the report acknowledges, the majority of the young people attending YIPs were very low level 'offenders', a large majority of whom had never previously been arrested or arrested on only one occasion. A high rate of desistance can accordingly be expected in any event. During 2001, for example, 83% of young people receiving a formal reprimand did not come to police attention again in the following 12 months (Jennings, 2003). It is therefore hard to gauge precisely what effect the YIP has had upon the offending of those involved with it.

Cognitive-behavioural intervention

The 'what works' movement, as we note above, sets considerable store by the effectiveness of programmes with a cognitive-behavioural element. Between 1999 and 2002, the Youth Justice Board established a development fund, £3.9m of which was allocated to 23 cognitive-behavioural projects. Of these 15 were classified by the national evaluators as working with 'persistent offenders'.

An early problem encountered by these projects was that referrals were less than a third of those anticipated in the initial bids. Completion rates were also relatively low at 47%. Re-offending, by contrast, appeared to be high with 71% of completers re-offending within 12 months. It is however unclear what these figures mean in terms of effectiveness: the national evaluators appointed by the YJB have argued that the 'methodological shortcomings' of the reconviction study prevented them from assessing the independent effectiveness of the projects in reducing offending behaviour (Feilzer et al., 2004).

If one turns to other recent findings for similar programmes, albeit with adults in a prison setting, the outcomes there do not appear to bode especially well either. While research published in 2002, showed promising results in terms of significantly lower reconviction rates for prisoners attending cognitive skills courses than for the control groups (up to 14%) (Friendship et al., 2002), two subsequent evaluations revealed that this 'treatment effect' had not been sustained

(Falshaw et al., 2003; Cann et al., 2003). The most recent of these, based on the largest sample which includes a cohort of 'young offenders', reported no significant differences in re-offending rates between participants and non-participants (Cann et al., 2003). These findings may not be directly relevant to the development of effective community-based programmes for children and young people. They do however suggest that caution should be exercised in claiming, as some scientists, professionals, administrators and politicians have, that such interventions simply 'work'.

Restorative justice

A second major plank underpinning the youth justice reforms of 1998 has been restorative justice (RJ). The approach, as Guy Masters argues in this volume, has achieved promising results in other jurisdictions (see Chapter 28). Similarly, the UK referral order, intended to be largely a restorative measure, has been well received by young people, victims, parents and professionals (Crawford and Newburn, 2003), although concerns remain that, in some instances, it is being imposed on young people whose offending is very trivial (see Chapter 16; Audit Commission, 2004). Yet there is little evidence so far that restorative justice initiatives in the UK have had a significant impact upon re-offending rates.

The national evaluation of 46 YJB funded restorative justice projects pointed to an over-reliance on 'community reparation' and a correspondingly low level of victim involvement, a feature shared to some extent with the referral order (Wilcox and Hoyle, 2004). In terms of preventing offending, the authors conclude that it was not possible to ascertain whether restorative justice interventions 'worked'. The overall reconviction rate for the RJ sample was slightly, but not significantly, higher than a comparator sample provided by the Home Office. Moreover, it appears that reconviction rates for different types of intervention were not related to the degree to which they were restorative. So while interventions which involved direct meetings between the victim and the young person generated the lowest rates of reconviction, re-offending following work on victim awareness, the least restorative of the categories employed in the study, was also relatively low (Wilcox and Hoyle, 2004).

Mentoring, education, training, employment and substance misuse

Research into the impact of the YJB's mentoring, drugs and alcohol and education, training and employment projects have been equally inconclusive (Tarling et al., 2004; Hammersley et al., 2004; Hurry and Moriarty, 2004). In each case, the absence of good comparative data was cited as the principal reason for being unable to make any firm assessment of the intervention's impact on re-offending

One-to-one supervision

While referral to a variety of correctional or restorative programmes, according to assessed need, is currently the favoured practice model, in most cases individual supervision of the young person by their YOT worker still represents the consistent thread running through a young person's involvement with the YOT. However, although the youth justice landscape has changed almost beyond recognition in recent years, for young people subject to community penalties, the average level of contact with the YOT, at 1.1 hours a week, has barely risen since 1996, despite a huge increase in available resources (Audit Commission, 2004). Thus far, there has been no systematic evaluation of this form of supervision by YOT staff, but a recent study which followed 199 adult offenders, aged 17–35, who were the subjects of probation (now community rehabilitation) orders over a four year period is of some relevance (Farrall, 2002). The study relies on the careful use of self-reported offending, and to a certain degree therefore avoids some of the problems associated with more formal measures of re-offending discussed above. Farrall calculates that only 0.3% of a probationer's life is spent in contact with a probation officer (PO) and that this encounter tends to take the form of the PO talking to the probationer. This, he argues, may be one of the reasons why probation appears to have little impact on offending, but since many, if not most, of the factors research points to as being associated with persistence in, or desistence from, crime are beyond the control of the supervising officer, we should not expect too much from this encounter.

The study shows that POs and probationers tend to identify different barriers to desistance, with POs identifying problems of motivation and attitude and probationers seeing income, employment and family life as crucial. Staying out of trouble, or reduced offending, where it occurred, appeared to have been a product of changes in the social circumstances of probationers which they, rather than their POs, had often engineered. Probationers were able to predict fairly accurately whether they would stop offending or not, and those who were confident about reducing their offending generally did so. Such confidence appeared to be related either to having fewer 'obstacles to desistance' or being better motivated to overcome these obstacles.

Farrall believes that probation supervision can contribute to desistance from crime but suggests that POs may need to content themselves with more modest gains than outright desistance; steps along the path to eventual desistance, like improving motivation to go straight, gradually changing attitudes to family and partners, the development of more realistic employment goals, or reductions in the frequency and seriousness of offending, which can, he believes, be painstakingly achieved over time.

He also points to the centrality of practical advice which, he argues, can help to build the 'human capital' that gives individuals the skills to tackle obstacles. Above all, practical assistance designed to increase opportunities for employment, income generation or to enhance family life, can make a real if modest difference. He concludes, however, that if probation supervision continues to be measured in terms of simple desistance, the causes of which POs are often powerless to influence, probation is being set-up to fail.

The overall rate of re-offending

In the light of the findings of the evaluations discussed here, one might conclude that the prospects for significant changes in re-offending amongst children and young people involved with the youth justice system are not especially good. However, as we have noted, the problem with these evaluations is that they attempt to measure the effects of particular forms of intervention rather than the impact of intervention overall. This would suggest that re-offending rates for those in contact with the reformed youth justice system per se, rather than particular programmes, would be a more accurate indicator of impact.

Understandably perhaps, the government and the YJB has been fairly up-beat about reconviction data for its new, post-1998, non-custodial penalties, evaluations of which appear to show a 22.5% reduction in re-offending against predicted outcomes for 2001, compared with 1997 (Jennings, 2003). The Board has claimed that this research allows them to have confidence in the evidence base for their published guidance (Youth Justice Board, 2003e).

In fact, contrary to what has often been claimed for this study, what it actually shows is not a 22.5% reduction in the *rate of re-offending,* but a fall from the baseline 'adjusted predicted rate' of 7.7%. The 22.5% is the reduction in the *predicted number of further offences.* No doubt, the amended figure would still appear to represent a significant achievement. However, as the Audit Commission has pointed out, the reductions in re-offending are far from uniform, with most of them following pre-court and lower tariff interventions (Audit Commission, 2004). Indeed, the more substantial community penalties register a slight increase in re-offending, which the Commission attributes to the relatively low levels of contact time associated with such disposals.

Other improvements in re-offending rates are similarly ambiguous. *Final warnings,* for example, appear to outperform the *caution,* which they replaced in 1998, by almost 7%. This finding tends to be explained in terms of the efficacy of the YOT assessment and intervention which usually accompanies the final warning (see Chapter 12). However, such an explanation does not account for the fact that the results for *reprimands,* the measure which precedes the final warning and does not usually generate any form of intervention, are better still. Nor can earlier or more effective intervention explain the impressive reduction in offending recorded by lower tariff court disposals, such as conditional discharges and fines. The most probable explanation for the improvements in the effectiveness of disposals which were left unchanged by the 1998 reforms, is the progressive abandonment of informal responses to minor offenders. Large numbers of children and young people, who would previously have been dealt with informally, have become 'adjudicated offenders' with a criminal record.

Thus, young people currently subject to reprimands are likely to have a less serious offending history than their pre-1998 counterparts who were the subjects of a caution. Further research is needed, but it is clear that the findings routinely presented to demonstrate the increased efficacy of the reformed youth justice system, lend themselves to a very different interpretation.

Towards a post-autistic evaluative and rehabilitative ethic

Autism is a condition marked by 'withdrawal from the world of reality and severely limited responsiveness to other persons' (OED). This, we would argue, serves as a useful description of the dominant modes of evaluation and rehabilitation discussed in this chapter.

The reality is that everything 'works' with somebody, somewhere, in that, for reasons we barely understand, it just happens to be the right thing at the right time. It is also true, of course, that most things don't 'work' with most people most of the time, and this is why, in the past, we have placed such a heavy emphasis upon the professionalisation of the criminal justice workforce, in order to produce workers who could make these difficult, 'horses-for-courses'-type judgements.

Maybe it's time to 'come clean'. We know that youth crime is normal, in the sense that most children and young people are bound to break the law at some time; as are most adults of course. Moreover, we have only the most approximate understanding of the origins of more persistent and serious youth offending, but suspect that they are both diverse and complex. What is clear however is that those factors which appear to be most closely associated with persistent and serious youth crime, like disadvantaged neighbourhood of residence, poverty, early childhood abuse and rejection, illiteracy and so on are also those which are least amenable to intervention by agents of the youth justice system. Indeed, there is plenty of evidence that, sometimes, such interventions can make a bad situation even worse (Becker, 1963; Lemert, 1970; Sampson and Laub, 1997).

We also know that, from time-to-time, new 'claim-makers' will emerge to market the latest of rehabilitative panaceas to governments who understand little of the complexity of the problem but, being anxious to find a solution, will buy what's on offer. Then, earlier orthodoxies will be rejected, as the claims of the new grow bolder. But we know too that these newer forms of intervention will in due course fail to fulfil their early promise. This is just about where we are currently with the panaceas of the late 1990s.

The challenge for youth justice is to resist the temptation to embrace the next simplistic, 'one-size-fits-all', evidence-based concoction, just because it is instantly comprehensible and fits snugly with the prevailing political orthodoxy. Richard Titmus (1968) once observed that 'the denial of complexity is the essence of tyranny'. The doctrinaire tyranny of the 'what works' movement is wasting the creativity of youth justice professionals as it places at risk much of the genuinely good practice undertaken by them (Burnett and Appleton 2004b and see Chapter 21). An alternative approach would see professionals, in dialogue with a far broader range of practitioners, theorists and researchers, striving to create new, innovative, rehabilitative interventions which were equal in their sophistication to the complexity and diversity of the problems faced by the children and young people with whom they work. The challenge for those who would research or evaluate these interventions is similar. Forsaking the spurious certainties of quasi-experimental method, they would embark upon a process of collaborative theory-building in an attempt to develop the far richer body of knowledge necessary to support such an endeavour. Such a human-sized enterprise may not have the political cache of a 'what works' crusade, but it might just work better.

References

Ackerman, J.R. (1986) Applying Electronic Surveillance Systems to Probation and House Arrest in New York State. *Journal of Probation and Parole.* 17: 5–9

Ackland, J. (1982) *Girls in Care: A Case Study of Residential Treatment.* Aldershot: Gower

Aitchison, A. and Hodgkinson, J. (2003) Patterns of Crime in England and Wales. in Simmons, J. and Dodd, T. (Eds.) *Crime in England and Wales 2002/2003.* Statistical Bulletin 07/03. London: Home Office

Alder, C. (1998) Passionate and Wilful Girls. *Women and Criminal Justice.* 9: 81–101

Alder, C. (2000) Young Women Offenders and the Challenge for Restorative Justice. in Strang, H. and Braithwaite, J. (Eds.) *Restorative Justice. Philosophy to Practice.* Aldershot: Ashgate

Alder, C. and Baines, B. (1996) *... And When She was Bad? Working with Young Women in Youth Justice and Related Areas.* Hobart: National Clearing House for Youth Studies

Alexander, C. (2000) *The Asian Gang.* Oxford: Berg

Allen, C., Crow, I. and Cavadino, M. (2000) *Evaluation of the Youth Court Demonstration Project.* Research Study 214. London: Home Office

Anderson, S., Kinsey, R., Loader, I. and Smith, C (1994) *Cautionary Tales: Young People, Crime and Policing in Edinburgh.* Aldershot: Avebury

Andrews, D. (1995) Criminal Conduct and Effective Treatment. in McGuire, J. *What Works: Reducing Offending.* Chichester: Wiley

Andrews, D.A., Keissling, J.J., Russell, R.J. and Grant, B.A. (1979) *Volunteers and the One-to-one Supervision of Adult Probationers.* Ontario: Ministry of Correctional Services

Armstrong, C., Hill, M. and Secker, J. (1998) *Listening to Children.* London: Mental Health Foundation

Ashford, M. and Chard, A. (2000) *Defending Young People in the Criminal Justice System.* 2nd edn. London: Legal Action Group

Ashworth, A. (1997) Sentencing. in Maguire, M., Morgan, R. and Reiner, R. *The Oxford Handbook of Criminology.* 2nd edn. Oxford: Clarendon Press

Assay, T.P. and Lambert, M.J. (1999) The Empirical Case for The Common Factors in Therapy: Quantitative Findings. in Hubble, M.H. et al. (Eds.) *The Heart and Soul of Change: What Works in Therapy.* Washington DC: American Psychological Association

Association for Youth Justice (1993) *Memorandum to Home Affairs Committee*

Association of Chief Officers of Probation (1989) *How do You Plead?* London: ACOP

Association of Chief Police Officers/Youth Justice Board (2002) *Final Warning Scheme: Guidance for Police and Youth Offending Teams.* London: Home Office

Association of Chief Police Officers/Youth Justice Board (2003) *A Guide to Anti-Social Behaviour Orders and Anti-Social Behaviour Contracts.* London: Home Office

Association of Headmasters, Headmistresses and Matrons of Approved Schools (1954) *Girls in Approved Schools.* Monograph No. 6 Supplement to *Approved Schools Gazette.* No. 48 Apr.

Association of Transport Coordinating Officers (1997) *Annual Report 1997.* London: ATCO

Audit Commission (1996) *Misspent Youth: Young People and Crime.* London: Audit Commission

Audit Commission (1998) *Misspent Youth '98: The Challenge for Youth Justice.* London: Audit Commission

Audit Commission (2004) *Youth Justice 2004: A Review of the Reformed Youth Justice System.* London: Audit Commission

Audit Scotland (2002) *Dealing With Offending by Young People.* Edinburgh: Auditor General Accounts Commission

Austin, J. and Krisberg, B. (1981) Wider, Stronger and Different Nets: The Dialectics of Criminal Justice Reform. *Journal of Research in Crime and Delinquency.* 18: 1, 165–96

Aye Maung, N. and Hammond, N. (2000) *Risk of Re-Offending and Needs Assessments:* The User's Perspective. Research Study 216. London: Home Office

Bailey, R. and Williams, B. (2000) *Inter-Agency Partnerships in Youth Justice: Implementing The Crime and Disorder Act 1998.* Sheffield: University of Sheffield Joint Unit for Social Service Research

Baker, K., Jones, S., Appleton, C. and Roberts, C. (2002) *Assessment, Planning, Interventions and Supervision.* London: Youth Justice Board

Baker, K., Jones, S., Roberts, C. and Merrington, S. (2003) *The Evaluation of the Validity and Reliability of the Youth Justice Board's Assessment for Young Offenders: Findings From the First Two Years of the Use of ASSET.* London: Centre for Criminological Research, University of Oxford and Youth Justice Board

Ball, C. (2000) The Youth Justice and Criminal Evidence Act 1999, Part 1. *Criminal Law Review.* 211–22

Ball, C., McCormack, K. and Stone, N. (2002) *Young Offenders: Law, Policy and Practice.* 2nd edn. London: Sweet and Maxwell

Bandalli, S. (2000) Children, Responsibility and the New Youth Justice. in Goldson, B. (Ed.) *The New Youth Justice.* Lyme Regis: Russell House Publishing

Barry, M. (2000) The Mentor/Monitor Debate in Criminal Justice. *British Journal of Social Work.* 30: 575–95

Batchelor, S. and Burman, M. (2004) Working With Girls and Young Women. in McIvor, G. (Ed.) *Women Who Offend.* London: Jessica Kingsley

Bateman, T. (2003) Living With Final Warnings: Making the Best of a Bad Job? *Youth Justice.* 2: 3, 131–40

Bateman, T. and Stanley, C. (2002) *Patterns of Sentencing: Differential Sentencing Across England and Wales.* London: Youth Justice Board

Beck, U. (1992) *Risk Society: Towards A New Modernity.* London: Sage

Becker, H. (1963) *Outsiders: Studies in the Sociology of Deviance.* New York: Free Press

Bell, A., Hodgson, M. and Pragnell, S. (1999) Diverting Children and Young People From Crime and the Criminal Justice System. in Goldson, B. (Ed.) *Youth Justice: Contemporary Policy and Practice.* Aldershot: Ashgate

Bell, M. (2002) Promoting Children's Rights Through the Use of Relationship. *Child and Family Social Work.* 7: 1–11

Bellson, W.A. (1977) *Juvenile Theft: The Causal Factors.* London: Harper Row

Benioff, S. (1997) *A Second Chance.* Swindon: Crime Concern

Berry, B. and Matthews, R. (1989) Electronic Monitoring and House Arrest: Making the Right Connections. in Matthews, R. (Ed.) *Privatising Criminal Justice.* London: Sage

Bhui, H. S. (1999) Race, Racism and Risk Assessment: Linking Theory to Practice With Black Mentally Disordered Offenders. *Probation Journal.* 46: 3, 171–81

Biermann, F. and Moulton, A. (2003) *Youth Offender Panel Volunteers in England and Wales December 2002.* Online Report 34/03: Home Office

Bitel, M. (2004) *Preliminary Findings From the Evaluation of Restorative Justice in Schools.* London: Youth Justice Board

Blackwell, G. (1990) In on the Act. *Community Care.* 813: 13–5

Blagg, H. and Smith, D. (1989) *Crime and Social Policy.* London: Longman

Blunkett, D. (2003) *Civil Renewal: A New Agenda.* The CSV Edith Khan Memorial Lecture. London: Home Office

Bottoms, A.E. (2001) Compliance and Community Penalties. in Bottoms, A.E. Gelsthorpe, L. and Rex, S.A. (Eds.) *Community Penalties: Change and Challenges.* Cullompton: Willan

Bowlby, J. (1953) *Child Care and the Growth of Love.* Harmondsworth: Penguin

Box, L. (2001) Supporting Black and Minority Ethnic Teenagers and Their Parents. in Coleman, J. and Roker, D. (Eds.) *Supporting Parents of Teenagers.* London: Jessica Kingsley

Boyle, D. (2004) Is This How to End Public Service Failure? *New Statesman.* 23rd Feb.

Braithwaite, J. (1989) *Crime, Shame and Reintegration.* Cambridge: Cambridge University Press

Brown, D. (1989) *Detention at the Police Station Under the Police and Criminal Evidence Act 1984.* Research Study 104. London: Home Office

Brown, D. (1997) *PACE Ten Years on: A Review of the Research.* Research Study 155. London: Home Office

Brown, D., Ellis, T. and Larcombe, K. (1992) *Changing the Code: Police Detention Under the Revised PACE Codes of Practice.* Research Study 129. London: Home Office

Bucke, T. and Brown, D. (1997) *In Police Custody: Police Powers and Suspects' Rights Under the Revised PACE Codes of Practice.* Research Study 174. London: Home Office

Buckland, G. and Stevens, A. (2001) *Review of Effective Practice With Young Offenders in Mainland*

Europe. Canterbury: University of Kent European Institute of Social Services

Burman, M. (2003) Girls Behaving Violently. *Criminal Justice Matters.* 53: 20–1

Burman, M. (2004) Breaking the Mould. Patterns of Female Offending. in McIvor, G. (Ed.) *Women Who Offend.* London: Jessica Kingsley

Burnett, R. (2000) Understanding Criminal Careers Through a Series of In-Depth Interviews. *Offender Programs Report.* 4: 1, 1–16

Burnett, R. (2003) *One-to-one Ways of Promoting Desistance.* Unpublished Paper Presented to the Probation Studies Unit Colloquium, Oxford

Burnett, R. and Appleton, C. (2004a) Joined-up Services to Tackle Youth Crime: A Case-Study in England. *British Journal of Criminology.* 44: 1, 34–54

Burnett, R. and Appleton, C. (2004b) *Joined-up Youth Justice: Tackling Youth Crime in Partnership.* Lyme Regis: Russell House Publishing

Burnham, T. (2003) *Work With Juveniles. Electronic Monitoring in Europe* (Conference Report) Utrecht: CEP

Burroughs, D. (1998) *Contemporary Patterns of Residential Mobility in Social Housing in England.* York: University of York

Butler-Sloss, Dame (2003) A Deeply Troubling Inconsistency in Society's Attitude to Children. *Youth Justice Board News.* 18: Jul.

Butt, J. and Box, L. (1998) *Family Centred: A Study of the Use of Family Centres by Black Families.* London: Race Equality Unit

Bylington, D. (1997) Applying Relational Theory to Addiction Treatment. in Straussner, S. and Zelvin, E. (Eds.) *Gender and Addictions.* Northvale, NJ; Aronson

CAFCASS (2003) *Third Report Children and Family Court Advisory and Support Service,* HC 614–1, Session 2002–3. London: CAFCASS

Cain, M. (Ed.) (1989) *Growing up Good. Policing the Behaviour of Girls in Europe.* London: Sage

Campbell, A. (1981) *Girl Delinquents.* Oxford: Basil Blackwell

Cann, J., Falshaw, L., Nugent, F. and Friendship, C. (2003) *Understanding What Works: Accredited Cognitive Skills Programmes for Adult Men and Young Offenders.* London: Home Office

Carpenter, M. (1853) *Juvenile Delinquents: Social Evils, Their Causes and Their Cure.* London: Cash

Carroll, R. (1998) Gangs Put Boot Into Old Ideas of Femininity. *The Guardian.* 22 Jul.

Carter, P. (2003) *Managing Offenders, Reducing Crime.* London: Cabinet Office

Castle, C. (2000) *For Every Child: the Rights of the Child in Words and Pictures.* London: Red Fox Books in Association With Unicef

Catalano, R.F., Arthur, M.W., Hawkins, J.D., Berglund, L. and Olson, J.J. (1998) Comprehensive Community and School Based Interventions to Prevent Behaviour. in Loeber, R. and Farrington, D.P. (Eds.) (1998) *Serious and Violent Juvenile Offenders: Risk Factors and Successful Interventions.* London: Sage

Cavadino, P. and Gibson, B. (1993) *Bail: The Law, Best Practice and the Debate.* Winchester: Waterside Press

Chapman, S. and Savage, P. (1999) The New Politics in Law and Order: Labour, Crime and Justice. in Powell, M. (Ed.) *New Labour, New Welfare State: The Third Way in British Social Policy.* Bristol: The Policy Press

Chapman, T. (1995) Creating a Culture of Change: A Case Study of a Car Crime Project in Belfast. in Maguire, J. (Ed.) *What Works: Reducing Offending.* Chichester: Wiley

Chapman, T. and Hough, M. (1998) *Evidence Based Practice: A Guide to Effective Practice.* London: Home Office

Chesney-Lind, M. (1997) *What About Girls? Hidden Victims of Congressional Juvenile Crime Control.* Policy Report. Washington, DC: Justice Policy Institute

Chesney-Lind, M. and Sheldon, R.G. (1992) *Girls Delinquency and Juvenile Justice.* Pacific Grove, CA: Brooks Cole

Children's Legal Centre (No Date) *At the Police Station: The Role of The Appropriate Adult.* Colchester

Children's Rights Alliance for England (2003) *Review of UK Government Action on 2002: Concluding Observations of the UN Committee on the Rights of the Child.* London: Children's Rights Alliance for England

Childtrauma Academy (Undated) *About Child trauma Academy* at www.Childtrauma.Org/Aboutcta/CT_Academy.Asp#Anchor-Progra-41264

Christian, L. (1983) *Policing by Coercion.* London: GLC Police Committee Support Unit

Christie, N. (1993) *Crime Control as Industry.* London: Routledge

Coates, R. and Gehm, J. (1989) An Empirical Assessment. in Wright, M. and Galaway, B.

(Eds.) *Mediation and Criminal Justice*. London: Sage

Cohen, S. (1985) *Visions of Social Control*. Cambridge: Polity Press

Cohen, S. (2002) *Folk Devils and Moral Panics*. 3rd edn. London: Routledge

Coleman, J. and Schofield, J. (2003) *Key Data on Adolescence*. Brighton: Trust for the Study of Adolescence

Commission for Racial Equality (1992) *Cautions and Prosecutions*. London: CRE

Community Care (2002) News in Brief. *Community Care*. 5–11 Dec.

Corbett, R. and Petersillia, J. (1994) 'Intensive Rehabilitation Supervision: The Next Generation of Community Corrections?', in *Federal Probation* 58, 72–8

Cowie, J., Cowie, V. and Slater, E. (1968) *Delinquency in Girls*. London: Heinemann

Cox, P. (2003) *Gender, Justice and Welfare. Bad Girls, 1900–1950*. Basingstoke: Palgrave Macmillan

Crawford, A. (1994) The Partnership Approach: Corporatism at The Local Level? *Social and Legal Studies*. 3: 497–519

Crawford, A. (2001) Joined-up But Fragmented: Contradiction, Ambiguity and Ambivalence at the Heart of New Labour's 'Third Way'. in Matthews, R. and Pitts, J. (Eds.) *Crime, Disorder and Community Safety: A New Agenda?* London: Routledge

Crawford, A. and Newburn, T. (2002) Recent Developments in Restorative Justice for Young People in England and Wales: Community Participation and Representation. *British Journal of Criminology*. 42: 476–95

Crawford, A. and Newburn, T. (2003) *Youth Offending and Restorative Justice: Implementing Reform in Youth Justice*. Cullompton: Willan

Creighton, S. (1987) *Annual Update of Statistics: NSPCC*. London: NSPCC

Crime Concern (1995) *Public Transport in Merseyside, Children and Young People: Their Experiences and Perceptions of Travelling in Merseyside*. London: Crime Concern

Crimestoppers (2002) Youth Survey 2002. London: Crimestoppers

Crimmens, D. (2004) *Having Their Say: Young People, Rights and Participation*. Lyme Regis: Russell House Publishing

Crimmens, D. and Storr, F. (1998) *The Hull Compact Mentoring Programme: An Evaluation*.

Humberside Education Business Partnership and Hull Compact Ltd

Crimmens, D., Factor, F., Jeffs, T., Pitts, J., Pugh, C., Spence, J. and Turner, P. (2004) *Reaching Socially Excluded Young People*. Leicester: Joseph Rowntree Foundation/NYA

CSV (2003) *Internal Report to Bedfordshire YOT on Millenium Volunteers*. CSV

Currie, E. (1985) *Confronting Crime: An American Challenge*. New York: Pantheon

Dalston Youth Project (1996/97) *Project Information*

Davis, G. (1992) *Making Amends: Mediation and Reparation in Criminal Justice*. London: Routledge

De Montfort University (2002) *Evaluation of The Bedsmap Project*. De Montfort University

De Winter, M. and Noom, M. (2003) Someone Who Treats You as an Ordinary Human Being. *British Journal of Social Work*. 33: 325–37

Delaney, M. and Milne, C. (2002) *Mentoring for Young Offenders: Results From an Evaluation of a Pilot Programme*. Paper Presented at the Crime Prevention Conference, Sydney, 12–3 Sep.

Department for Education and Skills (2003a) *Children Accommodated in Secure Units, Year Ending 31 March 2003: England and Wales*. SFR 21/2003. London: DfES

Department for Education and Skills (2003b) *Every Child Matters*. London: DfES

Department for Education and Skills (2003c) *Permanent Exclusions From Schools and Exclusion Appeals, England 2001/2002 (Provisional)*. SFR 16/2003. London: DfES

Department for Education and Skills (Undated) *Behaviour and Education Support Teams at* www.Dfes.Gov.Uk/Best/ DfES

Department of Health (1999) *Working Together to Safeguard Children*. London: Department of Health

Dersley, I. (2000) *Acceptable or Unacceptable? Local Probation Service Policy on Non-Compliance and Enforcement*. Dissertation Submitted for BA (Hons). Birmingham: University of Birmingham

DHSS (1985) *PACE: Implications for Children and Young Persons*. LAC (85)18 London: DHSS

Dignan, J. (1992) Repairing the Damage: Can Reparation Work in the Service of Diversion? *British Journal of Criminology*. 32: 453–72

Dignan, J. (2000) *Youth Justice Pilots Evaluation: Interim Report on Reparative Work and Youth Offending Teams*. London: Home Office

Dignan, J. (2002) Reparation Orders. in Williams, B. (Ed.) *Reparation and Victim-Focused Social Work*. London: Jessica Kingsley

Ditchfield, J. and Catan, L. (1992) *Juveniles Sentenced to Serious Offences: A Comparison of Regimes in Young Offender Institutions and Local, Authority Community Homes*. London: Home Office

Dixon, D. (1990) Juvenile Suspects and the Police and Criminal Evidence Act. in Freestone, D. (Ed.) *Children and the Law: Essays in Honour of Professor H K Bevan*. Hull: Hull University Press

Dixon, D., Bottomley, K., Coleman, C., Gill, M. and Wall, D. (1990) Safeguarding the Rights of Suspects in Police Custody. *Policing and Society*. 1: 115–50

Dodgson, K. and Mortimer, E. (2000) *Home Detention Curfew: The First Year of Operation*. Research Findings 110. London: Home Office

Donovan, T. (2004) The Cheaper Option for Young Offenders. *Young People Now*. 4–10 Feb.

Downes, D. and Rock, P. (1998) *Understanding Deviance: A Guide to the Sociology of Crime and Rule Breaking*. Oxford: Oxford University Press

DPP V Blake (1989) W.L.R 432

Drakeford, M. and Williamson, H. (1997) Social Work and Youth Homelessness. in Shaw, I. and Clapham, D. (Eds.) *Social Work and Housing*. London: Jessica Kingsley

Drakeford, M., Haines. K., Cotton. B. and Octigan, M. (2001) *Pre-Trial Services and the Future of Probation*. Cardiff: University of Wales Press

Driscoll, J. (1986) Juveniles and The Criminal Law: The Police and Criminal Evidence Act 1984, Parts 1 and 2. *Journal of Social Welfare Law*. 8: 32–41 and 65–76

Eade, J. and Garbin, D (2002) Changing Narratives of Violence, Struggle and Resistance: Bangladeshis and The Competition for Resources in the Global City. *Oxford Development Studies*. 30: 2

Eadie, T. and Canton, R. (2002) Practising in a Context of Ambivalence: The Challenge for Youth Justice Workers. *Youth Justice*. 2: 1, 14–26

Eadie, T. and Willis, A. (1989) National Standards for Discipline and Breach Proceedings in Community Service: an Exercise in Penal Rhetoric? *Criminal Law Review*. Jun. 412–9

Earle, R. and Newburn, T. (2002) Creative Tension? Young Offenders, Restorative Justice and the Introduction of Referral Orders. *Youth Justice*. 1: 3

ECOTEC Research Consulting Ltd (2002) *Education, Training and Employment*. London: Youth Justice Board

Elliott, A., Lindfield, S. and Cusick, J. (2002) *Parents' Views*. Brighton: Trust for the Study of Adolescence

Ellis, T. (2000) Enforcement Policy and Practice: Evidence-Based or Rhetoric-Based? *Criminal Justice Matters*. 39: 6–7

Ellis, T., Hedderman, C. and Mortimer, E. (1996) *Enforcing Community Penalties*. Research Study No. 158. London: Home Office

Essex County Council (2002) *Essex Family Group Conference: Young People Who Offend Project. Executive Summary*. Braintree: Essex County Council

European Mentoring Centre (1999) *What is Mentoring?* (Web-Site No Longer Accessible)

Evans, D. (2002) Drug Crime: What's the Colour of Money. *Fed Express, Special Report*. Jun.

Evans, R. (1993) *The Conduct of Police Interviews With Juveniles*. RCCJ Research Study 8. London: HMSO

Evans, R. and Rawsthorne, S. (1997) Appropriate Behaviour. *Community Care*. 1181 30–1

Falshaw, L., Friendship, C., Travers, R. and Nugent, F. (2003) *Searching for 'What Works': an Evaluation of Cognitive Skills Programmes*. Findings 206. London: Home Office

Farrall, S. (2002) *Rethinking What Works With Offenders, Probation, Social Context and Desistance From Crime*. Cullompton: Willan

Farrall, S. and Bowling, B. (1999) Structuration, Human Development and Desistance From Crime. *British Journal of Criminology*. 39: 2, 253–68

Farrant, F. and Levinson, J. (2002) *Barred Citizens*. London: Prison Reform Trust

Farrington, D. (1996) *Understanding and Preventing Youth Crime*. York: Joseph Rowntree Foundation

Farrington, D. (2000) Explaining and Preventing Crime: The Globalisation of Knowledge. *Criminology*. 38: 1, 1–24

Farrington, D. (2002) Understanding and Preventing Youth Crime. in Muncie, J., Hughes, G. and Mclaughlin, E. (Eds.) (2002) *Youth Justice: Critical Readings*. London: Sage

Farrington, D. and West, D. (1993) Criminal, Penal and Life Histories of Chronic Offenders: Risk and Protective Factors and Early Identification. *Criminal Behaviour and Mental Health*. 3

Fathers Direct (Undated) In Partnership With Working With Men, NFPI and Newpin, *Father Facts*, www.Fathersdirect.Com/Fatherfacts

Faulkner, D. (2001) *Crime, State and Citizen: A Field Full of Folk.* Winchester: Waterside Press

Feeley, M. and Simon, J. (1992) The New Penology: Notes on The Emerging Strategy of Corrections and Its Implementation. *Criminology.* 30: 4, 452–74

Feeley, M. and Simon, J. (1994) Actuarial Justice: The Emerging New Criminal Law. in Nelken, D. (Ed.) (1994) *The Futures of Criminology.* London: Sage

Feilzer, M. with Appleton, C., Roberts, C. and Hoyle, C. (2004) *The National Evaluation of the Youth Justice Board's Cognitive Behaviour Projects.* London: Youth Justice Board

Finkelhor, D. and Dziuba-Leatherman, J. (1994) Victimisation of Children. *American Psychologist.* 49: 173–83

Fionda, J. (2001) Youth and Justice. in Fionda, J. (Ed.) *Legal Concepts of Childhood.* Oxford: Hart Publishing

Fisher, H. (1977) *Report of an Inquiry by the Hon. Sir Henry Fisher Into the Circumstances Leading to the Trial of Three Persons Arising out of the Death of Maxwell Confait and the Fire at 27 Doggett Rd, London SE6.* London: HMSO

Fitzgerald, M. (1993) *Ethnic Minorities in the Criminal Justice System.* Research Study 20. London: Home Office

Fitzgerald, M. (2001) Ethnic Minorities and Community Safety. in Matthews, R. and Pitts, J. (Eds.) *Crime Disorder and Community Safety.* London: Routledge

Fitzgerald, M. and Sibbitt, R. (1997) *Ethnic Monitoring in Police Forces: A Beginning.* Research Study 173. London: Home Office

Flood-Page, C. Campbell, S., Harrington, V. and Miller, J. (2000) *Youth Crime: Findings From the 1998/99 Youth Lifestyles Survey.* Research Study 209. London: Home Office

Forrester, D., Frenz, S., O' Connell, M. and Pease, K. (1990) *The Kirkholt Burglary Prevention Project. Phase II.* London: Home Office

Friendship, C., Blud, L., Erikson, M. and Towers, R. (2002) An *Evaluation of Cognitive-Behavioural Treatment for Prisoners.* Findings 161. London: Home Office

Fry, E. (1993) On *Remand: Foster Care and the Youth Justice Service.* London: Fostering Networks

Fry, E. (2002) *Support Care and Youth Offending: Model of Best Practice.* London: Fostering Network

Furniss, J. (2000) *Enforcement. HMIP Annual Report 1999/2000.* London: HMIP

Garland, D. (1985) *Punishment and Welfare: A History of Penal Strategies.* Aldershot: Gower

Garland, D. (1997) Probation and the Reconfiguration of Crime Control. in Burnett, R. (Ed.) *The Probation Service: Responding to Change* Oxford: University of Oxford Centre for Criminological Research

Garland, D. (2001) *The Culture of Control.* Oxford: Oxford University Press

Gelsthorpe, L. (1989) *Sexism and the Female Offender.* Aldershot: Gower

Gelsthorpe, L. (2001) Accountability: Difference and Diversity in the Delivery of Community Penalties. in Bottoms, A.E., Gelsthorpe, L. and Rex, S.A. (Eds.) *Community Penalties: Change and Challenges.* Cullompton: Willan

Gelsthorpe, L. (2002) Recent Changes in Youth Justice Policy in England and Wales. in Weijers, I. and Duff, A. (Eds.) *Punishing Juveniles: Principle and Critique.* Oxford: Hart Publishing

Gelsthorpe, L. (2004) Female Offending: A Theoretical Overview. in McIvor, G. (Ed.) *Women Who Offend.* London: Jessica Kingsley

Gelsthorpe, L. and Morris, A. (1994) Youth Justice 1945–1992. in Maguire, M., Morgan, R. and Reiner, R. (Eds.) *The Oxford Handbook of Criminology.* Oxford: Oxford University Press

Gendreau, P., Goggin, C. and Fulton, B. (2000) Intensive Supervision in Probation and Parole Settings. in Hollin C. (Ed.) *Handbook of Offender Assessment and Treatment.* Chichester: Wiley

Ghate, D. and Ramella, M. (2002) *Positive Parenting: The National Evaluation of the Youth Justice Board's Parenting Programme.* London: Policy Research Bureau and Youth Justice Board

Giddens, A. (1991) *Modernity and Self Identity. Self and Society in the Late Modern Age.* Cambridge: Polity Press

Giddens, A. and Pierson, C. (1998) *Conversations With Anthony Giddens: Making Sense of Modernity.* Cambridge: Polity Press

Gifford, Lord (1989) *Broadwater Farm Revisited.* London: Karia Press

Gladwell, M. (2000) *The Tipping Point.* Little: Brown and Co

Goldson, B. (2000b) Wither Diversion? Interventionism and The New Youth Justice. in Goldson, B. (Ed.) *The New Youth Justice.* Lyme Regis: Russell House Publishing

Goldson, B. (2001) A Rational Youth Justice?

Some Critical Reflections on the Research, Policy and Practice Relation. *Probation Journal.* 48: 2

Goldson, B. (2002a) Children, Crime and the State. in Goldson, B., Lavalatte, M. and Mckechnie, J. (Eds.) *Children, Welfare and The State.* London: Sage

Goldson, B. (2002b) New Labour, Social Justice and Children: Political Calculation and The Deserving-Undeserving Schism. *British Journal of Social Work.* 32

Goldson, B. (2002c) New Punitiveness: The Politics of Child Incarceration. in Muncie, J., Hughes, G. and Mclaughlin, E. (Eds.) *Youth Justice: Critical Readings.* London: Sage

Goldson, B. (2002d) *Vulnerable Inside: Children in Secure and Penal Settings.* London: The Children's Society

Goldson, B. (2003) Social Support Not Social Stigma. *Safer Society.* 18: 17–8

Goldson, B. (2004) Differential Justice? A Critical Introduction to Youth Justice Policy in UK Jurisdictions. in Mcghee, J., Mellon, M. and Whyte, B. (Eds.) *Meeting Needs Addressing Deeds: Working With Young People Who Offend.* London: NCH

Goldson, B. (Ed.) (2000a) *The New Youth Justice.* Lyme Regis: Russell House Publishing

Goldson, B. and Jamieson, J. (2002) Community Bail or Penal Remand? A Critical Analysis of Recent Policy Developments in Relation to Unconvicted and Unsentenced Juveniles. *British Journal of Community Justice.* 1: 2, 63–76

Goldson, B. and Peters, E. (2000) *Tough Justice: Responding to Children in Trouble.* London: The Children's Society

Goodman, N., Maloney, E. and Davies, J. (1976) *Borstal Girls Eight Years After Release: Further Studies of Female Offenders.* Research Study No. 33. London: HMSO

Gouldner, A. (1971) *The Coming Crisis in Western Sociology.* London: Heinemann Educational

Graham, J. (1988) *Schools, Disruptive Behaviour and Delinquency.* Research Study No. 96. London: Home Office

Graham, J. and Bowling, B. (1995) *Young People and Crime.* Research Study 145. London: Home Office

Gray, P., Moseley, J. and Browning, S. (2003) An *Evaluation of The Plymouth Restorative Justice Programme.* Plymouth: University of Plymouth

Greenwood, P.W., Rydell, P., Abrahamse, A., Caulkins, J., Model, K.E. and Kelin, S.P. (1994) *Three Strikes and You're Out: Estimated Benefits and Costs of California's New Mandatory Sentencing Laws.* Santa Monica, CA: RAND

Gudjohnnson, G. (1992) *The Psychology of Interrogations, Confessions and Testimony.* Chichester: Wiley

Hagan, J. (1993) The Social Embeddedness of Crime and Unemployment. *Criminology.* 31: 455–91

Hagell, A. and Hazel, N. (2001) Macro and Micro Patterns in the Development of Secure Custodial Institutions for Serious and Persistent Young Offenders in England and Wales *Youth Justice.* 1: 1, 3–16

Hagell, A. and Newburn, T. (1994) *Persistent Young Offenders.* London: Policy Studies Institute

Hagell, A., Hazel, N. and Shaw, K. (2000) *Evaluation of Medway Secure Training Centre.* London: Home Office

Haines, K. (1998) Some Principled Objections to a Restorative Justice Approach to Working With Juvenile Offenders. in Walgrave, L. (Ed.) *Restorative Justice for Juveniles.* Leuven University Press

Haines, K. and Drakeford, M. (1998) *Young People and Youth Justice.* Basingstoke: Macmillan

Hale, S. (2002) Professor MacMurray and Mr Blair: The Strange Case of The Communitarian Guru That Never Was. *Political Quarterly.* 73: 2, 191–7

Hall, S. et al. (1978) *Policing the Crisis: Mugging, the State and Law and Order.* London: Macmillan

Hall, S. (1980) *Drifting Into a Law and Order Society.* London: Cobden Trust

Hallam, S. (2000) Effective and Efficient Policing: Some Problems With The Culture of Performance. in Marlow, A. and Loveday, B. (Eds.) *After Macpherson: Policing After the Stephen Lawrence Inquiry.* Lyme Regis: Russell House Publishing

Hallett, C., Murray, C. with Jamieson, J. and Veitch, B. (1998) *The Evaluation of Children's Hearings in Scotland, Volume 1: Deciding in Children's Best Interest.* Edinburgh: The Scottish Office Central Research Unit

Hammersley, R., Reid, M., Oliver, A., Genova, A., Raynor, P., Minkes, J. and Morgan, M. (2004) *The National Evaluation of the Youth Justice Board's Drug and Alcohol Projects.* London: Youth Justice Board

Hancock, S. (2000) Practical Implications of The Crime and Disorder Act for Youth Offending

Teams: A Youth Offending Team's Perspective. in Pickford, J. (Ed.) *Youth Justice: Theory and Practice.* London: Cavendish Publishing

Hansard (Lords) (1998) Lord Mostyn, Vol 586: Col 654

Harper, R. and Hardy, S. (2000) An Evaluation of Motivational Interviewing as a Method of Intervention With Clients in a Probation Setting. *British Journal of Social Work.* 30: 393–400

Harrington, V. and Mayhew, P. (2001) *Mobile Phone Theft.* Research Study 235. London: Home Office

Harris, R. and Webb, D. (1987) *Welfare, Power and Youth Justice.* London: Tavistock

Hazel, N., Hagell, A., Liddle, M., Archer, D., Grimshaw, R. and King, J. (2002) *Detention and Training: Assessment of The Detention and Training Order and its Impact on the Secure Estate Across England and Wales.* London: Youth Justice Board

Hedderman, C. (1999) *The ACOP Enforcement Audit: Stage One.* London: ACOP (Available at http://www.Sbu.Ac.Uk/Cpru)

Hedderman, C. (2003) Enforcing Supervision and Encouraging Compliance. in Hong Chui, W. and Nellis, M. (Eds) *Moving Probation Forward: Evidence, Arguments and Practice.* Harlow: Pearson Longman

Hedderman, C. (2004) The Criminogenic Needs of Women Offenders. in McIvor, G. (Ed.) *Women Who Offend.* London: Jessica Kingsley

Hedderman, C. and Hearnden, I. (2000) *Improving Enforcement: The Second ACOP Audit.* London: ACOP (Available at http://www.Sbu.Ac.Uk/Cpru)

Hill, M. (1999) What's the Problem? Who Can Help? *Journal of Social Work Practice.* 13: 2, 135–45

Hine, J. and Celnick, A. (2001) *A One Year Reconviction Study of Final Warnings.* Sheffield: University of Sheffield

HM Inspectorate of Constabulary, Ofsted, HM Crown Prosecution Inspection Service, HM Magistrates' Court Service Inspectorate, HM Inspectorate of Prisons, HM Inspectorate of Probation, Social Services Inspectorate (2003) *Streets Ahead: A Joint Thematic Inspection of the Street Crime Initiative.* London: Home Office

HM Inspectorate of Prisons (1997) *Young Prisoners: A Thematic Review by HM Chief Inspector of Prisons for England and Wales.* London: Home Office

HM Inspectorate of Prisons (2000) *Unjust Deserts: A Thematic Review by HM Chief Inspector of Prisons for The Treatment and Conditions for Unsentenced Prisoners in England and Wales.* London: Home Office

HM Inspectorate of Prisons (2002) *Inspections of Young Offender Institutions 2000–2001.* London: Home Office

HM Inspectorate of Probation (2000a) *Making National Standards Work: A Study by HMIP of Enforcement Practice in Community Penalties.* London: Home Office

HM Inspectorate of Probation (2000b) *Towards Racial Equality: A Thematic Review.* London: HMIP

HMSO (1995) *Child Protection: Messages From Research.* London: HMSO

Hobbs, D. (1997) Criminal Collaboration: Youth Gangs, Subcultures, Professional Criminals and Organised Crime. in Maguire, M., Morgan, R. and Reiner, R. (Eds.) *The Oxford Handbook of Criminology.* Oxford: Clarendon Press

Hochschild, A. (1983) *The Managed Heart: Commercialisation of Human Feeling.* University of California Press

Hochschild, A. (2001) Global Care Chains and Emotional Surplus Value. in Hutton, W. and Giddens, A. (Eds.) *On the Edge.* London: Verso

Hodgkin, R. (2002) *Rethinking Child Imprisonment.* London: The Children's Rights Alliance for England

Hodgson, J. (1997) Vulnerable Suspects and the Appropriate Adult. *Criminal Law Review.* 785–95

Hoghughi, M. (1978) *Troubled and Troublesome: Coping With Severely Disordered Children.* London: Burnett

Holdaway, S., Davidson, N., Dignan, J., Hammersley, R., Hine, J. and Marsh, P. (2001) *New Strategies to Address Youth Offending: The National Evaluation of the Pilot Youth Offending Teams.* London: Home Office

Holt, P. (2000) *Case Management: Context for Supervision.* Leicester: De Montfort University

Home Affairs Committee (1993) *Juvenile Offenders.* London: HMSO

Home Office (1922) *Criminal Statistics.* London: HMSO

Home Office (1985) *The Cautioning of Offenders.* Circular 14/85. London: Home Office

Home Office (1986) *The Ethnic Origins of Prisoners: The Prison Population on 30 June 1985 and Persons*

Received, July 1984–March 1985. Statistical Bulletin 22/84. London: Home Office

Home Office (1988a) *Punishment, Custody and the Community*. London: HMSO

Home Office (1988b) *Sentencing Practice in the Crown Court*. Research Study 103. London: Home Office

Home Office (1989) *The Ethnic Group of Those Proceeded Against or Sentenced by the Courts in the Metropolitan Police District in 1984 and 1985*. Statistical Bulletin 6/89. London: Home Office

Home Office (1990) *Crime, Justice and Protecting the Public*. London: HMSO

Home Office (1991a) *Criminal Justice Act 1991. Custodial Sentences and the Sentencing Framework*. London: Home Office

Home Office (1991b) *Police and Criminal Evidence Act: Codes of Practice*. London: Home Office

Home Office (1992a) *Lay Visitors to Police Stations: Revised Guidance*. Circular 4/92. London: Home Office

Home Office (1992b) *National Standards for the Supervision of Offenders in the Community*. London: Home Office

Home Office (1994) *The Cautioning of Offenders*. Circular 18/94. London: Home Office

Home Office (1995a) *National Standards for the Supervision of Offenders in the Community*. London: Home Office

Home Office (1995b) *Report of the Appropriate Adult Review Group*. London: Home Office

Home Office (1997a) *New National and Local Focus on Youth Crime*. London: Home Office

Home Office (1997b) *No More Excuses: A New Approach to Tackling Youth Crime in England and Wales*. London: The Stationery Office

Home Office (1997c) *Tackling Delays in The Youth Justice System: A Consultation Paper*. London: Home Office

Home Office (1998a) *Final Warning Schemes: Guidance on the Crime and Disorder Act 1998*. London: Home Office

Home Office (1998b) *Guidance on Statutory Crime and Disorder Partnerships: Crime and Disorder Act 1998*. London: Home Office

Home Office (1998c) *Inter-Departmental Circular on Establishing Youth Offending Teams*. London: Home Office

Home Office (1998d) *Lay Visiting to Police Stations*. Research Study 188. London: Home Office

Home Office (1998e) *Prison Statistics England and Wales 1997*. London: The Stationery Office

Home Office (1998f) *Statistics on Race and the Criminal Justice System*. London: Home Office

Home Office (1998g) *Youth Justice: The Statutory Principal Aim of Preventing Offending by Children and Young People*. London: Home Office

Home Office (2000a) *Human Rights Act. Core Guidance for Public Authorities: A New Era of Rights and Responsibilities*. London: Home Office

Home Office (2000b) *Implementation of Referral Orders: Draft Guidance for Youth Offending Teams*. London: Home Office

Home Office (2000c) *National Standards for the Supervision of Offenders in the Community*. London: Home Office

Home Office (2000d) *Statistics on Race and the Criminal Justice System* London: Home Office

Home Office (2000e) *The Crime and Disorder Act Guidance Document: The Action Plan Order*. London: Home Office

Home Office (2001) *New Strategies to Address Youth Offending: The National Evaluation of the Pilot Youth Offending Teams*. London: Home Office

Home Office (2002a) *Beating Bureaucracy: Blueprint to Put Bobbies Back on The Beat. Policing Bureaucracy Task Force Sir David O'Dowd*. www.Policereform.Gov.Uk

Home Office (2002b) *Justice for All*. White Paper. London: Home Office

Home Office (2002c) *Narrowing the Justice Gap*. www.Cjsonline.Org/Njg

Home Office (2002d) *National Standards for the Supervision of Offenders in the Community 2000; Revised 2002*. London: Home Office

Home Office (2002e) *Race and the Criminal Justice System*. London: Home Office

Home Office (2002f) *Statistics on Women and the Criminal Justice System*. London: Home Office

Home Office (2003a) *Criminal Justice Act 2003: Changes Affecting PACE*. Circular 60/03. London: Home Office

Home Office (2003b) *Criminal Statistics England and Wales 2002*. London: The Stationery Office

Home Office (2003c) *Important Changes to Referral Orders From 18 August 2003. Supplementary Guidance for Courts, Youth Offending Teams and Youth Offender Panels*. London: Home Office

Home Office (2003d) *Police and Criminal Evidence Act 1984 (S60(1)(A) and S66(1): Codes of Practice A–E Revised Edition*. London: The Stationery Office

Home Office (2003e) *Prison Statistics for England and Wales 2002*. London: The Stationery Office

Home Office (2003f) *Respect and Responsibility: Taking a Stand Against Anti-Social Behaviour.* London: The Stationery Office

Home Office (2003g) *Restorative Justice: The Government's Strategy.* London: Home Office

Home Office (2003h) *Youth Justice: The Next Steps.* London: Home Office

Home Office (2003i) *Youth Offender Panel Volunteers in England and Wales.* On-Line Report 34/03. Home Office

Home Office (2003j) *Every Child Matters: The Next Steps.* London: Home Office

Home Office (2004a) *Guidance on Parenting Orders and Contracts.* London: Home Office

Home Office (2004b) *Youth Justice: The Next Steps. Summary of Responses and Government Proposals.* London: Home Office

Home Office (Undated) *Guidance for Appropriate Adults.* London: Home Office

Home Office Advisory Council on the Penal System (1968) *Detention of Girls in a Detention Centre.* Interim Report

Home Office and Lord Chancellor's Department (1998) *Opening up Youth Court Proceedings.* London: Home Office

Home Office/Youth Justice Board (2001) *Referral Orders and Youth Offender Panels: Guidance for Courts, Youth Offending Teams and Youth Offender Panels.* London: Home Office

Home Office/Youth Justice Board (2002) *Final Warning Scheme. Guidance for The Police and Youth Offending Teams.* London: Home Office/Youth Justice Board

Home Office/Youth Justice Board/Department for Constitutional Affairs (2004) *Guidance on Parenting Orders and Contracts.* London: Home Office

Hood, R. (1992) *Race and Sentencing.* Oxford: Clarendon

Hook and Hobbs Consulting (2000) *Research Into Effective Practice With Young People in Secure Facilities.* London: Youth Justice Board

Hope, T. (1995a) Building a Safer Society: Strategic Approaches to Crime Prevention. in Tonry, M. and Farringdon, D.P. (Eds.) *Crime and Justice, 19.* Chicago: University of Chicago Press

Hope, T. (1995b) Inequality and the Future of Community Crime Prevention. Labs, S.P. (Ed.) *Crime Prevention at a Crossroads.* Cincinnati: Anderson Publishing

Hope, T. (2003) The Crime Drop in Britain. *Community Safety Journal.* 2: 4

Hope, T. and Foster, J. (1992) Conflicting Forces: Changing Dynamics of Crime and Community on a Problem Estate. *British Journal of Criminology.* 32: 92

Hopley, K. (2002) National Standards: Defining the Service. in Ward, D., Scott, J. and Lacey, M. *Probation Working for Justice.* Oxford: Oxford University Press

Hotaling, G., Straus, M. and Lincoln, A. (1989) Witnessing Family Violence. in Ohlin, L. and Tonry, M. (Eds.) *Family Violence.* Chicago: Chicago University Press

Hough, M. and Jacobson, J. (2004) Getting to Grips With Anti Social Behaviour. *Communities, Social Exclusion and Crime.* London: The Smith Institute

Howard League for Penal Reform (1996) *The Howard League Troubleshooter Project Lessons for Policy and Practice on 15 Year Olds in Prison.* London: Howard League for Penal Reform

Howard League for Penal Reform (1997) *Lost Inside: The Imprisonment of Teenage Girls.* London: The Howard League Home Office/Youth Justice Board

Howell, J., Krisberg, B., Hawkins, D. and Wilson, J. (Eds.) (1995) *Serious Violent and Chronic Juvenile Offenders: A Sourcebook.* London: Sage

Hoyle, C., Young, R. and Hill, R. (2002) *Proceed With Caution: an Evaluation of the Thames Valley Police Initiative in Restorative Cautioning.* York: York Publishing Services

Hucklesby, A. and Goodwin, T. (2002) *Pre-Trial Accommodation for Young People: Report to The Youth Justice Board.* (Unpublished)

Hudson, A. (1989) Troublesome Girls: Towards Alternative Definitions and Policies. in Cain, M. (Ed.) *Growing Up Good.* London: Sage

Hudson, B. (1985) Sugar and Spice and All Things Nice. *Community Care.* 4 Apr. 14–7

Hudson, B. (1998) Restorative Justice: The Challenge of Sexual and Racial Violence. *Journal of Law and Society.* 25: 237–56

Hughes, G. (1998) *Understanding Crime Prevention: Social Control, Risk and Late Modernity.* Buckingham: Open University Press

Hughes, G. and Muncie, J. (2002) Models of Youth Governance: Political Rationalities, Criminalisation and Resistance. in Muncie, J., Hughes, G. and Mclaughlin, E. (Eds.) (2002) *Youth Justice: Critical Readings.* London: Sage

Hughes, G., Mclaughlin, E. and Muncie, J. (Eds.) (2002) *Crime Prevention and Community Safety: New Directions*. London: Sage

Hulsman, L. (1986) Critical Criminology and the Concept of Crime. in Bianchi, H. and Van Swaaningen, R. (Eds.) *Abolitionism: Towards a Non-Repressive Approach to Crime*. Amsterdam: Free University Press

Humphrys, J. (2000) *Devil's Advocate*. London: Arrow

Hurry, J. and Moriarty, V. (2004) *The National Evaluation of the Youth Justice Board's Education, Training and Employment Projects*. London: Youth Justice Board

Inner London Youth Justice Service (1995) *Statement of Principles and Practice Standards*. London: Nacro

Irving, B.I. and McKenzie, I. (1989) *Police Interrogation: The Effects of the Police and Criminal Evidence Act 1984*. London: Police Foundation

Jamieson, J., McIvor, G. and Murray, C. (1999) *Understanding Offending Among Young Offenders*. Edinburgh: Scottish Executive

Jennings, D. (2003) *One Year Juvenile Reconviction Rates: First Quarter of 2001 Cohort. On Line Report 18/3*. London: Home Office

Joint Chief Inspectors (2002) *Safeguarding Children: A Joint Chief Inspectors' Report on Arrangements to Safeguard Children*. London: Department of Health

Joint Committee on Human Rights (2003) *The United Nations Convention on The Rights of The Child, Tenth Report of Session 2002/3*. London: The Stationery Office

Jones, D. (2000) Letter. *Guardian Society*. 20 Dec.

Jones, D. (2001a) It's Only a Caution: or How an Appropriate Adult Can Make a Difference. *The Criminal Lawyer*. 109, Jan. 6

Jones, D. (2001b) Misjudged Youth: A Critique of the Audit Commission's Reports Into Youth Justice. *British Journal of Criminology*. 41: 2, 362–80

Jones, D. (2002) Questioning New Labour's Youth Justice Strategy: A Review Article. *Youth Justice*. 1: 3, Feb. 14–26

Jones, H. (1987) Practice Without Precedent. *Community Care*. 668: 22–3

Jones, K. and Pitts, J. (2001) *Early Childhood Child Protection Registration and Subsequent Involvement With a Youth Justice Team/Youth Offending Team in a London Borough*. Luton: Vauxhall Centre for The Study of Crime, University of Luton

Jones, P.W., Harris, J.F. and Grubstein, L. (2000) *Identifying Chronic Juvenile Offenders*. Paper Presented to The British Criminological Conference, Leicester

Joseph Rowntree Foundation (2004) *Mentoring for Vulnerable Young People*. York: Joseph Rowntree Foundation

Judicial Studies Board (2001) *The Youth Court Bench Book*. London: Judicial Studies Board

JUSTICE (2000) *Restoring Youth Justice*. London: JUSTICE

Kalunta-Crumpton, A. (1999) *Race and Drug Trials*. Aldershot: Ashgate

Kantor, D. and Lehr, W. (1975) *In the Family*. San Francisco: Jossey Bass

Kay, N. and Quao, S. (1987) To be or Not to be an Appropriate Adult. *Community Care*. 668: 20–2

Kearney, B. (2000) *Children's Hearings and the Sheriff Court*. 2nd edn. Edinburgh: Butterworth

Kemp, V., Sorsby, A., Liddle, M. and Merrington, S. (2002) *Assessing Responses to Youth Offending in Northamptonshire*. Research Briefing 2. London: Nacro

Kempf-Leonard, K. and Peterson, E. (2002) Expanding Realms of the New Penology: The Advent of Actuarial Justice for Juveniles. in Muncie, J., Hughes, G. and Mclaughlin, E. (Eds.) *Youth Justice: Critical Readings*. London: Sage

Kemshall, H. (1996) *Reviewing Risk. A Review of Research on the Assessment and Management of Risk and Dangerousness: Implications for Policy and Practice in the Probation Service*. London: Home Office

Kemshall, H. (1998) Defensible Decisions for Risk: or 'It's the Docrs Wot Get the Blame'. *Probation Journal*. 45: 2, 67–72

Kemshall, H. (2002a) Effective Practice in Probation: an Example of 'Advanced Liberal' Responsibilisation? *Howard Journal*. 41: 1, 41–58

Kemshall, H. (2002b) *Risk, Social Policy and Welfare*. Buckingham: Open University Press

Kemshall, H. (2004) Risk, Dangerousness and Female Offenders. in McIvor, G. (Ed.) *Women Who Offend*. London: Jessica Kingsley

Kershaw, C., Budd, T., Kinshott, G., Mattinson, J., Mayhew, P. and Myhill, A. (2000) *The 2000 British Crime Survey*. London: Home Office

Kettle, M. (2004) Our Future in the Hands of the Selfish and Pampered. *The Guardian*. 04 May 20

Kirsta, A. (2000) In the Next Ten Seconds the Woman Walking Past is Going to Either . . . A.

Catch a Bus, B. Meet a Friend, C. Violently Attack You and Steal Your Credit Cards. *Nova*, Jul.

Krisberg, B. and Austin, J. (1993) *Reinventing Juvenile Justice*. London: Sage

Kumpfer, K.L. and Alvarado, R. (1998) *Effective Family Strengthening Interventions*. Juvenile Justice Bulletin Nov. Washington DC: US Department of Justice

Laming, Lord (2003) *The Victoria Climbié Inquiry*. London: Home Office

Landau, S. (1981) Juveniles and The Police. *British Journal of Criminology*. 21/2

Landau, S. and Nathan, G. (1983) Selecting Delinquents for Cautioning in the London Metropolitan Area. *British Journal of Criminology*. 28/2

Law Society (1993) *Memorandum to Home Affairs Committee*. 133–40

Lea, J. and Young, J. (1984) *What is to be Done About Law and Order*. Harmondsworth: Penguin

Lemert, E. (1967) *Human Deviance, Social Problems and Social Control*. Englewood Cliffs, NJ: Prentice Hall

Lemert, E. (1970) *Social Action and Legal Challenge: Revolution Within the Juvenile Court*. Chicago: Aldine

Levy, A. (2001) Children in Court. in Fionda, J. (Ed.) *Legal Concepts of Childhood*. Oxford: Hart Publishing

Lewis, D., Mallouh, C. and Webb, V. (1989) Child Abuse, Delinquency and Violent Criminality. in Cicchetti, D. and Carlson, V. (Eds.) *Child Maltreatment*. Cambridge: Cambridge University Press

Liddle, M. and Gelsthorpe, L. (1994) *Crime Prevention and Inter-Agency Co-Operation*. Crime Prevention Unit Paper 53. London: Home Office

Liddle, M. and Solanki, A. (2000) *Missed Opportunities: Key Findings From an Analysis of the Backgrounds and Life Experiences of a Sample of Persistent Young Offenders in Redbridge*. Nacro

Liddle, M. and Solanki, A. (2002) *Persistent Young Offenders*. London: Nacro

Liebling, A. (1996) *Suicide and Suicide Attempts Amongst Young Prisoners: The UK Experience*. London: Routledge

Liebmann, M. and Masters, G. (2000) Victim-Offender Mediation in the UK. in Peterson, T. (Ed.) *Victim-Offender Mediation in Europe*. Leuven: Leuven University Press

Liebrich, K. (2000) *The Guardian, Society*. 13 Dec. 71–2

Lindsay, T. and Chapman, T. (2001) Youth Justice in Northern Ireland. in Roche, J. and Vernon, S. (Eds.) *Youth Justice: Topic 10 K201 Working With Young People*. Milton Keynes: The Open University

Lipscombe, J. (2003a) *Another Side of Life; Foster Care for Young People on Remand*. Ph.D. Thesis. Bristol: University of Bristol

Lipscombe, J. (2003b) Another Side of Life; Foster Care for Young People on Remand. *Youth Justice*. 3: 1

Lipsey, M.W. (1995) What Do We Learn From 400 Research Studies on the Effectiveness of Treatment With Juvenile Delinquents? in Mcguire, J. (Ed.) *What Works: Reducing Reoffending. Guidelines From Research and Practice*. Chichester: Wiley

Little, M., Kogan, J., Bullock, R. and Van Der Laan, P. (2004) ISSP: an Experiment in Multi Systemic Responses to Persistent Young Offenders Known to Children's Services. *British Journal of Criminology*

Littlechild, B. (1995) Reassessing the Role of the Appropriate Adult. *Criminal Law Review*. Jul. 540–5

Littlechild, B. (1996) *The Police and Criminal Evidence Act 1984: The Role of The Appropriate Adult*. Birmingham: BASW

Littlechild, B. (1998) An End to 'Inappropriate Adults'? *Childright*. Mar. 144, 8–9

Littlechild, B. (Ed.) (2001) *Appropriate Adults and Appropriate Adult Schemes: Service User, Provider and Police Perspectives*. Birmingham: Venture Press

Lobley, D. and Smith, D. (2000) *Evaluation of Restriction of Liberty Orders*. Edinburgh: Scottish Executive Central Research Unit

Lobley, D., Smith, D. and Stern, C. (2001) *Freagarrach: an Evaluation of a Project for Persistent Juvenile Offenders*. The Scottish Executive Central Research Unit

Lockyer, A. and Stone, F. (Eds.) (1998) *Juvenile Justice in Scotland: Twenty Five Years of the Welfare Approach*. Edinburgh: Tandt Clark

Longford, Lord (1964) *Crime: A Challenge to Us All*. Report of a Labour Party Study Group. London: Labour Party

Lord Chief Justice (2000) *Trial of Children and Young Persons in the Crown Court: Practice Direction*. London: Lord Chancellor's Department

Losel, F. (1993) The Effectiveness of Treatment in Institutional and Community Settings. *Criminal Behaviour and Mental Health*. 3: 416–37

Lowe, W. (2004) *Average Time From Arrest to Sentence for Persistent Young Offenders: February 2004*. Statistical Bulletin. London: Department for Constitutional Affairs

Lowe, W. and Gray, J. (2003) *Average Time From Arrest to Sentence for Persistent Young Offenders: July–September 2003*. London: Department for Constitutional Affairs

Lupton, D. (1999) *Risk*. London: Routledge

Magistrates' Association (1995) *Discretion to Dispense With a Pre-Sentence Report and the New National Standard*. London: Magistrates' Association

Mainprize, S. (1995) Social, Psychological and Familial Aspects. in Schulz, D. (Ed.) *Electronic Monitoring and Corrections*. British Columbia: Simon Fraser University

Mair, P. (2000) Partyless Democracy. *New Left Review*. 2. Mar/Jun.

Marshall, T. (1999) *Restorative Justice: an Overview*. London: Home Office

Marshall, T. and Merry, S. (1990) *Crime and Accountability*. London: Home Office

Martinson, R. (1974) 'What Works?' Questions and Answers About Prison Reform. *The Public Interest*. 35

Maruna, S. (2001) *Making Good*. Washington, DC: American Psychological Association

Masters, G. (2002a) Family Group Conferencing: A Victim Perspective. in Williams, B. (Ed.) *Reparation and Victim-Focused Social Work*. London: Jessica Kingsley

Masters, G. (2002b) In or Out? Some Critical Reflections Upon the Potential for Involving Victims of Youth Crime in Restorative Processes in England and Wales. *British Journal of Community Justice*. 1: 99–110

Masters, G. (2003) *Restorative Justice and Referral Orders*. Unpublished Paper Delivered to The National Referral Order Conference, 12 Sep., Leicester

Mathieson, T. (1990) *Prison on Trial*. London: Sage

Matthews, R. (2003) Enforcing Respect and Reducing Responsibility: A Response to the White Paper on Anti-Social Behaviour. *Community Safety Journal*. 2: 4

Matthews, R. and Pitts, J. (Eds.) (2001) *Crime, Disorder and Community Safety*. London: Routledge

Mattinson, J. and Mirrlees-Black, C. (2000) *Attitudes to Crime and Criminal Justice: Findings From the 1998 British Crime Survey*. Research Study 200. London: Home Office

Matza, D. (1969) *Becoming Deviant*. Engelwood Cliffs, NJ: Prentice-Hall

Maxwell, G. and Morris, A. (1993) *Family, Victims and Culture: Youth Justice in New Zealand*. Wellington: Social Policy Agency and Institute of Criminology, Victoria University

Maxwell, G. and Morris, A. (1996) Research on Family Group Conferences With Young Offenders in New Zealand. in Hudson, J., Morris, A., Maxwell, G. and Galaway, B. (Eds.) *Family Group Conferences: Perspectives on Policy and Practice*. New York: Willow Tree Press

Maxwell, G. and Morris, A. (1998) *Understanding Re-Offending*. Wellington: Institute of Criminology, Victoria University

May, C. (1999) *Explaining Reconviction Following A Community Sentence: The Role of Social Factors*. London: Home Office

Mayhew, P. (2003) Detection of Crime. in Simmons, J. and Dodd, T. (Eds.) *Crime in England and Wales 2002/2003*. Statistical Bulletin 07/03 London: Home Office

McAra, Dr. L. (2003) Cited in Hunter, M., Out of the Shadows, Zero2Nineteen. *Community Care*

McBarnet, D. (1978) The Fisher Report on The Confait Case; Four Issues. *Modern Law Review*. 41: 455–63

McBarnet, D. (1981) The Royal Commission and the Judges Rules. *British Journal of Law and Society*. 8: 109–17

McCold, P. (2000) Towards a Mid-Range Theory of Restorative Criminal Justice: A Reply to the Maximalist Model. *Contemporary Justice Review*. 3: 4, 357–414

McCold, P. (2001) Primary Restorative Justice Practices. in Morris, A. and Maxwell, G. (Eds.) *Restorative Justice for Juveniles*. Oxford: Hart

McGuire, J. (2000) an *Introduction to Theory and Research: Cognitive-Behavioural Approaches*. HM Inspectorate of Probation Report. London: Home Office

McGuire, J. (Ed.) (1995) *What Works: Reducing Offending*. Chichester: Wiley

McGuire, J. and Priestley, P. (1995) Reviewing 'What Works', Past, Present and Future. in Mcguire, J. *What Works: Reducing Offending*. Chichester: Wiley

McGuire, J., Kinderman, P. and Hughes, C. (2002) *Offending Behaviour Programmes.* London: Department of Clinical Psychology, University of Liverpool and Youth Justice Board

McIvor, G. and Barry, M. (1998) *Social Work and Criminal Justice: Volume 6 – Probation.* Edinburgh: The Stationery Office

McLaughlin, E. and Muncie, J. (2000) The Criminal Justice System: New Labour's New Partnerships. in Clarke, J., Gewirtz, S. and McLaughlin, E. (Eds.) *New Managerialism, New Welfare?* London: Sage

McNeill, F. (2001) Developing Effectiveness: Frontline Perspectives. *Social Work Education.* 20: 6, 671–88

McNeill, F. (2003) Desistance-Focused Probation Practice. in Chui, W.H. and Nellis, M. (Eds.) *Moving Probation Forward.* Harlow: Pearson Education

McNeill, F. and Batchelor, S. (2004) *Persistent Offending by Young People.* London: NAPO

McRoberts, C., Burlingame, G.M. and Hoag, M.J. (1998) Comparative Efficacy of Individual and Group Psychotherapy: A Meta-Analytical Perspective. *Group Dynamics.* 2: 2, 101–17

Merrington, S. (1998) *A Guide to Setting up and Evaluating Programmes for Young Offenders.* London: ISTD

Merrington, S., Baker, K. and Wilkinson, B. (2003) Using Risk and Need Assessment Tools in Probation and Youth Justice. *VISTA.* 8: 1, 31–8

Mhlanga, B. (1997) *The Colour of English Justice.* Aldershot: Avebury

Miller, W.R. and Rollnick, S. (Eds.) (2002) *Motivational Interviewing.* 2nd edn. New York: Guilford Press

Mills, C.W. (1959) *The Sociological Imagination.* Harmondsworth: Penguin

Mitchell, V. (2000) What Turned this Innocent Young Schoolgirl Into a Murderer? *The Daily Mail.* 10 Mar.

Moffat, H. and Shaw, M. (2000) Reforming the Prison, Rethinking Our Ideals. in Moffat, H. and Shaw, M. (Eds.) *An Ideal Prison?* Halifax, Canada: Fernwood Publishing

Monaghan, G. (2000) The Courts and the New Youth Justice. in Goldson, B. (Ed.) *The New Youth Justice.* Lyme Regis: Russell House Publishing

Monaghan, G., Hibbert, P. and Moore, S. (2003) *Children in Trouble: Time for Change.* London: Barnardo's

Moore, G. and Whyte, B. (1998) *Social Work and Criminal Law in Scotland.* Edinburgh: Mercat Press

Moore, R., Gray, E., Roberts, C. and Taylor, E. (2004) *ISSP: the initial report.* London: Youth justice Board

Moore, S. (2000) Child Incarceration and the New Youth Justice. in Goldson, B. (Ed.) *The New Youth Justice.* Lyme Regis: Russell House Publishing

Moore, S. and Peters, E. (2003) A Beacon of Hope: Children and Young People on Remand. London: The Children's Society

Moore, S. and Smith, R. (2001) *The Pre-Trial Guide: Working With Young People From Arrest to Trial.* London: The Children's Society

Morgan Harris Burrows (2003) *Evaluation of The Youth Inclusion Programme.* London: Youth Justice Board

Morgan, R. (2003) Thinking About the Demand for Probation Services. *Probation Journal.* 50: 1, Mar.

Morgan, R. and Russell, N. (2000) *The Judiciary in The Magistrates' Courts.* RDS Occasional Paper No 66. London: Home Office

MORI (2003) *Youth Survey 2003.* London: Youth Justice Board

Morris, A. (1987) *Women, Crime and Criminal Justice.* Oxford: Basil Blackwell

Morris, A. (2002) Critiquing the Critics: A Brief Response to Critics of Restorative Justice. *British Journal of Criminology.* 42: 3, 596–615

Morris, A. and Gelsthorpe, L. (2001) Revisioning Men's Violence Against Female Partners. *The Howard Journal.* 39: 4, 412–28

Morris, A., Maxwell, G. and Robertson, J. (1993) Giving Victims a Voice: A New Zealand Experiment. *Howard Journal of Criminal Justice.* 32: 4, 304–21

Mullender, A. and Ward, D. (1991) *Self-Directed Groupwork: Users Take Action for Empowerment.* London: Whiting and Birch

Muncie, J. (1999) *Youth and Crime: A Critical Introduction.* London: Sage

Muncie, J. (2000) Pragmatic Realism? Search for Criminology in the New Youth Justice. in Goldson, B. (Ed.) *The New Youth Justice.* Lyme Regis: Russell House Publishing

Muncie, J. (2001) A New Deal for Youth? Early Intervention and Correctionalism. in Hughes, G., Mclaughlin, E. and Muncie, J. (Eds.) *Crime*

Prevention and Community Safety: New Directions. London: Sage

Muncie, J. (2002) Policy Transfers and 'What Works': Some Reflections on Comparative Youth Justice. *Youth Justice.* 3: 1

Nacro (1996) *The Code of Practice for Juvenile Remand Proceedings.* London: Nacro

Nacro (1997) *A New 3Rs for Young Offenders.* London: Nacro

Nacro (2000a) *Proportionality in the Youth Justice System.* Youth Crime Briefing. London: Nacro

Nacro (2000b) *The Detention and Training Order.* Youth Crime Briefing. London: Nacro

Nacro (2001a) *A Brief Outline of the Youth Justice System in England and Wales as at December 2001.* Youth Crime Briefing. London: Nacro

Nacro (2001b) *Girls in the Youth Justice System.* Youth Crime Briefing. London: Nacro

Nacro (2001c) *Public Opinion and Youth Justice.* Youth Crime Briefing. London: Nacro

Nacro (2002a) *Children Who Commit Grave Crimes.* London: Nacro

Nacro (2002b) *Children's Rights – Recommendations for Youth Justice.* Youth Crime Briefing. London: Nacro

Nacro (2003a) *A Failure of Justice: Reducing Child Imprisonment.* London: Nacro

Nacro (2003b) *Acting as an Appropriate Adult: A Good Practice Guide.* London: Nacro

Nacro (2003c) *Anti-Social Behaviour Orders and Associated Measures (Part 1).* Youth Crime Briefing. London: Nacro

Nacro (2003d) *Bail as It Affects Young People in Court.* Youth Crime Briefing. London: Nacro

Nacro (2003e) *Counting the Cost: Reducing Child Imprisonment.* London: Nacro

Nacro (2003f) *Detention and Training Order Early Release: The Revised Guidance and Use of Electronic Monitoring.* Youth Crime Briefing. London: Nacro

Nacro (2003g) *Pre-Sentence Reports for Young People: A Good Practice Guide.* 2nd edn. London: Nacro

Nacro (2003h) *Remands to Local Authority Accommodation.* Youth Crime Briefing. London: Nacro

Nacro (2003i) *Reviewing Remands in Custodial Establishments.* Youth Crime Briefing. London: Nacro

Nacro (2003j) *Some Facts About Young People Who Offend: 2001.* London: Nacro

Nacro (2003k) *The Sentencing Framework for Children and Young People.* Youth Crime Briefing. London: Nacro

Nacro (2003l) *Youth Victimisation: A Literature Review.* Community Safety Practice Briefing. London: Nacro

Nacro (2004a) *Anti Social Behaviour Orders and Associated Measures (Part 2).* Youth Crime Briefing. London: Nacro

Nacro (2004b) *New Legislation: Impact on Sentencing.* Youth Crime Briefing. London: Nacro

Nacro (2004c) *Some Facts About Young People Who Offend – 2002.* Youth Crime Briefing. London: Nacro

NAPO News (2000) *Practice Guidance on the Enforcement of Orders and Licences.* Issue 121. London: NAPO

NAPO News (2003) *Enforcement Uplift.* Issue 151. London: NAPO

National Assembly for Wales (2000) *Extending Entitlement: Supporting Young People in Wales.* Cardiff: National Assembly for Wales

National Association for Youth Justice (1996) *Policy and Practice Guidelines for Youth Justice.* Leicester

National Audit Office (2004) *Youth Offending: The Delivery of Community and Custodial Sentences.* London: The Stationery Office

National Family Parenting Institute (2002) *National Mapping of Family Services in England and Wales.* London: NFPI

Newburn, T. (1995) *Crime and Criminal Justice Policy.* London: Longman

Newburn, T. (2002a) The Contemporary Politics of Youth Crime Prevention, in Muncie, J., Hughes, G. and Mclaughlin, E. *Youth Justice: Critical Readings in History, Theory and Policy.* London: Sage

Newburn, T. (2002b) Young People, Crime and Youth Justice. in Maguire, M., Morgan, R. and Reiner, R. (Eds.) *The Oxford Handbook of Criminology.* Oxford: Oxford University Press

Newburn, T., Crawford, A., Earle, R., Goldie, S., Hale, C., Masters, G., Netten, A., Saunders, R., Hallam, A., Sharpe, K. and Uglow, S. (2002c) *The Introduction of Referral Orders Into the Youth Justice System: Final Report.* London: Home Office

Newburn, T., Crawford, A., Earle, R., Goldie, S., Hale, C., Masters, G., Netten, A., Saunders, R., Sharpe, K., Uglow, S. and Campbell, A. (2001) *The Introduction of Referral Orders Into the Youth Justice System: 2nd Interim Report.* London: Home Office

Norrie, K. (1997) *Children's Hearings in Scotland.* Edinburgh: W. Green/Sweet and Maxwell

North Tyneside and Nexus (1997) *Young People and Metro – Audit Consultation*. Newcastle: North Tyneside and Nexus

Ogden, J. (1992) Murder Report Leads to Guidance Call. *Social Work Today*. 23: 39, 3

Ohen, S. (1980) *Folk Devils and Moral Panics*. London: Martin Robinson

Olweus, D. (1989) Bully/Victim Problems Amongst School Children; Basic Facts and the Effects of a School-Based Intervention Programme. in Robin, K. and Pepler, D. (Eds.) *The Development and Treatment of Childhood Aggression*. Hillsdale NJ: Enbaum

PA Consulting Group (2003) *The Content of Short DTOs Compared With ISSP*. Youth Justice Board

Page, D. (1993) *Building for Communities: A Study of New Housing Association Estates*. York: Joseph Rowntree Foundation

Palmer, C. (1996) The Appropriate Adult. *Legal Action*. May, 6–7

Palmer, C. and Hart, M. (1996) *A PACE in the Right Direction?* Sheffield: University of Sheffield

Parsloe, P. (1978) *Juvenile Justice in Britain and the United States*. London: Routledge and Kegan Paul

Paterson, L. (2000) Civil Society and Democratic Renewal. in Baron, S., Field, J. and Schuller, T. (Eds.) *Social Capital: Critical Perspectives*. Oxford: Oxford University Press

Pawson, R. and Tilley, N. (1997) *Realistic Evaluation*. London: Sage

Peachy, D. (1989) The Kitchener Experiment. in Wright, M. and Galaway, B. (Eds.) *Mediation and Criminal Justice*. London: Sage

Pearse, J. (2001) The Problems Associated With Implementing the Appropriate Adult Safeguard. in Littlechild, B. (Ed.) *Appropriate Adults and Appropriate Adult Schemes: Service User, Provider and Police Perspectives*

Pearse, J. and Gudjohnnson, G. (1996) How Appropriate Are Appropriate Adults. *Journal of Forensic Psychiatry*. 7, 570–80

Pearson, G. (1975) *The Deviant Imagination*. London: Macmillan

Pearson, G. (1983) *Hooligan: A History of Respectable Fears*. London: Macmillan

Pearson, G. (1994) Youth, Crime and Society. in Maguire, M., Morgan, R. and Reiner, R. (Eds.) *The Oxford Handbook of Criminology*. Oxford: Clarendon Press

Penal Affairs Consortium (1997) *The Crime (Sentences) Bill*. London: PAC

Petrie, C. (1986) *The Nowhere Girls*. Aldershot: Gower

Pettifer, E.W. (1992) *Punishments of Former Days*. Winchester: Waterside Press

Phillips (1981) *The Royal Commission on Criminal Procedure: Report*. Cm 8092. London: HMSO

Phillips, C. and Brown, D. (1998) *Entry Into the Criminal Justice System: A Survey of Police Arrests and Their Outcomes*. Research Study 185. London: Home Office

Pierpoint, H. (2000) How Appropriate Are Volunteers as 'Appropriate Adults' for Young Suspects: The 'Appropriate Adult' System and Human Rights. *Journal of Social Welfare and Family Law*. 22 383–400

Pilkington, A. (2003) *Racial Disadvantage and Ethnic Diversity in Britain*. Hampshire: Palgrave

Pitcher, J., Bateman, T., Johnston, V. and Cadman, S. (2004) *The Provision of Health, Education and Substance Misuse Workers in Youth Offending Teams and The Health/Education Needs of Young People Supervised by Youth Offending Teams*. London: Youth Justice Board

Pitts, J. (1986) Black Young People and Juvenile Crime: Some Unanswered Questions. in Matthews, R. and Young, J. (Eds.) *Confronting Crime*. London: Sage

Pitts, J. (1988) *The Politics of Juvenile Crime*. London: Sage

Pitts, J. (1992) The End of an Era. *The Howard Journal of Criminal Justice*. 31: 2, 133–49

Pitts, J. (1999) *Working With Young Offenders*. 2nd edn. Basingstoke: Macmillan

Pitts, J. (2000) Review of Mentoring Research. *Research Matters*. Apr.–Oct.

Pitts, J. (2001a) Korrectional Karaoke: New Labour and the Zombification of Youth Justice. *Youth Justice*. 1: 2, 3–16

Pitts, J. (2001b) The New Correctionalism: Young People, Youth Justice and New Labour. in Matthews, R. and Pitts, J. (Eds.) *Crime, Disorder and Community Safety*. London: Routledge

Pitts, J. (2001c) *The New Politics of Youth Crime: Discipline or Solidarity?* Basingstoke: Palgrave

Pitts, J. (2001d) Young People Talking About Social Inclusion: A Three Nation Study. *Social Work in Europe*. 8: 1

Pitts, J. (2003a) Changing Youth Justice. *Youth Justice*. 3: 1

Pitts, J. (2003b) *The New Politics of Youth Crime: Discipline or Solidarity*. 2nd edn, Lyme Regis: Russell House Publishing

Pitts, J. (2004) What Do We Want? The SHAPE Campaign and the Reform of Youth Justice. *Youth Justice*. 3: 3

Pitts, J. and Smith, P. (1995) *Preventing School Bullying*. London: Home Office

Porteous, D. (1997) *Befriender Mentoring in Camden: A Feasibility Study*. Luton: University of Luton

Porteous, D. (1998a) *Evaluation of the CSV on Line Mentoring Scheme*. London: Community Service Volunteers

Porteous, D. (1998b) Young People's Experience of Crime and Violence: Findings From a Survey of School Pupils. in Marlow, A. and Pitts, J. (Eds.) *Planning Safer Communities*. Lyme Regis: Russell House Publishing

Porteous, D. (2002) *Haringey Personal Trainers Project, Final Evaluation Report*. Luton: University of Luton

Power, A. and Tunstall, T. (1995) *Swimming Against The Tide: Polarisation or Progress*. York: Joseph Rowntree Foundation

Pratt, J. (1989) Corporatism: the Third Model of Juvenile Justice. *British Journal of Criminology*. 29: 3, 236–54

Preston, R.H. (1980) Social Theology and Penal Theory and Practice: The Collapse of The Rehabilitative Ideal and The Search for an Alternative. in Bottoms, A.E. and Preston, R.H. (Eds.) *The Coming Penal Crisis*. Edinburgh: Scotland Academic Press

Price, C. and Kaplan, J. (1997) *The Confait Confessions*. London: Marion Boyars

Prime, J., White, S., Liriano, S. and Patel, K. (2001) *Criminal Careers of Those Born Between 1953 and 1978*. Statistical Bulletin 4/01. London: Home Office

Prins, H. (1999) *Will They do it Again? Risk Assessment and Management in Criminal Justice and Psychiatry*. London: Routledge

Pritchard, C. and Butler, A. (2000) A Follow-Up Study of Victims of Crime, Murder and Suicide Found in English Cohorts of Former 'Excluded-From-School' or 'In-Care' ('Looked After Children') Adolescents. *Int.J. Adolesc. Med. Health*. 12: 4, 275–94

Probation Circular 24/00 (2000) *Guidance on Enforcement of Orders Under National Standards 2000*.

Quill, D. and Wynne, J. (1993) *Victim and Offender Mediation Handbook*. London: Save The Children

Raynor, P. (1998) Attitudes, Social Problems and Reconvictions in the 'STOP' Probation Experiment. *The Howard Journal of Criminal Justice*. 37: 1, 1–15

Raynor, P. (2001) Community Penalties and Social Integration: 'Community' as Solution and as Problem. in Bottoms, A., Gelsthorpe, L. and Rex, S. (Eds.) *Community Penalties: Changes and Challenges*. Devon: Willan

Reiner, R. (2000) *The Politics of the Police*. Oxford: Oxford University Press

Restorative Justice Family Group Conference Project (2002) *Research Outcomes and Lessons Learned*. Essex

Rex, S. (1999) Desistance From Offending. *The Howard Journal of Criminal Justice*. 38: 4, 366–83

Richardson, H. (1969) *Adolescent Girls in Approved Schools*. London: Routledge and Kegan Paul

Robertson, G., Pearson, R. and Gibb, R. (1996) Police Interviewing and the Use of Appropriate Adults. *Journal of Forensic Psychiatry*. 7: 297–309

Robinson, G. (2001) Power, Knowledge and 'What Works' in Probation. *The Howard Journal of Criminal Justice*. 40: 3, 235–54

Robinson, G. (2003) Risk and Risk Assessment. in Hong Chui, W. and Nellis, M. (Eds.) (2003) *Moving Probation Forward: Evidence, Arguments and Practice*. Harlow: Pearson

Roche, D. (2003) *Accountability in Restorative Justice*. Oxford: Oxford University Press

Roker, D. and Coleman, J. (1998) Parenting Teenagers Programmes: A UK Perspective. *Children and Society*. 12: 359–72

Rose, N. (1989) *Governing the Soul*. London: Routledge

Royal Commission on Criminal Justice (1993) *Report*. Cm. 2263, London: HMSO

Rutherford, A. (1986) *Growing Out of Crime*. Harmondsworth: Penguin

Rutherford, A. (2002) Youth Justice and Social Inclusion. *Youth Justice*. 2: 2

Rutter, M. and Giller, H. (1983) *Juvenile Delinquency: Trends and Perspectives*. Harmondsworth: Penguin

Rutter, M., Giller, H. and Hagell, A. (1998) *Antisocial Behaviour by Young People*. Cambridge: Cambridge University Press

Rutter, M., Maughan, B., Mortimore, P., Ouston, J. and Smith, A. (1978) *Fifteen Thousand Hours*. London: Open Books

Salisbury, H. (2003) Trends in Crime. in Simmons, J. and Dodd, T. (Eds.) *Crime in England and Wales 2002/2003*. Statistical Bulletin 07/03. London: Home Office

Sampson, A. and Phillips, C. (1995) *Reducing Repeat Racial Victimisation on an East London Estate.* Crime Detection and Prevention Series, Paper 67. London: Home Office

Sampson, R. and Laub, J. (1993) *Crime in the Making: Pathways and Turning Points.* Harvard: Harvard University Press

Sampson, R. and Laub, J. (1997) A Life-Course Theory of Cumulative Disadvantage and the Stability of Delinquency. in Thornberry, P. (Ed.) *Developmental Theories of Crime and Delinquency: Advances in Criminological Theory (Volume 7).* New Brunswick, NJ: Transaction Publishers

Sampson, R., Raudenbush, S. and Earls, F. (1997) Neighbourhoods and Violent Crime: A Multi-Level Study of Collective Efficacy. *Science.* 277: 918–23

Sanders, W. (2003) *Our Manor: Youth Crime and Youth Culture in the Inner City.* Unpublished PhD Thesis. London: Goldsmiths College

Scarman, Lord (1981) *The Scarman Report: The Brixton Disorders 10–12 April 1981.* Harmondsworth: Penguin

Schoon, I. J. and Brymer, H. (2003) Risk and Resilance in the Life Course: Implications for Interventions and Social Policies. *Journal of Youth Studies*

Schur, E. (1965) *Crime Without Victims.* Englewood Cliffs, NJ: Prentice-Hall

Schur, E. (1973) *Radical Non Intervention.* Engelwood Cliffs, NJ: Prentice-Hall

Schwartz, W. (1961) The Social Worker in the Group. in *New Perspectives on Services to Groups: Theory, Organisation and Practice.* New York: National Association of Social Workers

Scottish Executive (2002) *Statistical Bulletin: Criminal Proceedings in Scottish Courts, 2001.* Edinburgh: Scottish Executive

Scottish Office (1995) *The Scottish Crime Survey 1995.* Edinburgh: The Scottish Office

Scraton, P. (Ed.) (1997) *'Childhood' in 'Crisis'?* London: UCL Press

Scull, A. (1977) *Decarceration.* New Jersey: Spectrum Books

SED (1966) *Social Work in the Community.* Edinburgh: HMSO

Shapland, J. (1978) Self-Reported Delinquency in Boys Aged 11 to 14. *British Journal of Criminology.* 18: 3

Sherman, L., Gottfredson, D., Mackenzie, J., Reuter, P. and Bushway, S. (1998) *Preventing Crime: What Works, What Doesn't, What's Promising.* Washington DC: US Department of Justice

Shulman, L. (1979) *The Skills of Helping Individuals and Groups.* Illinois: Peacock

Shulman, L. (1991) *Interactional Social Work Practice.* Itasca, Illinois: F.E. Peacock

Silverman, E. (1999) *NYPD Battles Crime.* Boston: Northeastern University Press

Simon, J. (2000) From the Big House to the Warehouse: Re-Thinking Prisons and State Government in The 20th Century. *Punishment and Society.* 2: 2, 213–34

Skinner, A. and Fleming, J. (1999) *Quality Framework for Mentoring With Socially Excluded Young People.* Manchester: National Mentoring Network

Smith, C. (1996) *Developing Parenting Programmes.* London: National Children's Bureau

Smith, D. (1983) *Police and People in London.* London: Policy Studies Institute

Smith, D. (2000a) Corporatism and the New Youth Justice. in Goldson, B. (Ed.) *The New Youth Justice.* Lyme Regis: Russell House Publishing

Smith, D. (2000b) The Logic of Practice in the Probation Service Today. *Vista.* 5: 3, 210–8

Smith, R. (2003) *Youth Justice: Ideas, Policy, Practice.* Cullompton: Willan

Social Exclusion Unit (1998) *Bringing Britain Together.* London: The Stationery Office

Social Exclusion Unit (2000) *National Strategy for Neighbourhood Renewal: Report of Policy Action Team 12: Young People.* London: The Stationery Office

SOHD (1964) *Report of the Committee on Children and Young Persons.* (Kilbrandon Committee) Edinburgh: HMSO

Solomos, J. (1988) *Black Youth, Racism and the State.* Cambridge: Cambridge University Press

St James Roberts, I. and Samlal Singh, C. (1999) *Using Mentors to Change Problem Behaviour in Primary School Children.* Research Findings 95. London: Home Office

Stevens, M. (2002) *Custody for Children: The Impact of PSRs.* Presentation to Working in the Youth Justice System Conference. Nacro and the London Association for Youth Justice, December 2002

Stevens, P. and Willis, C. (1979) *Race, Crime and Arrests.* Research Study 58. London: HMSO

Stewart, G. and Tutt, N. (1987) *Children in Custody.* Aldershot: Avebury

Stokes, E. (2000) Abolishing the Presumption of Doli Incapax: Reflections on the Death of a Doctrine. in Pickford, J. (Ed.) *Youth Justice: Theory and Practice.* London: Cavendish

Stone, N. (2003) Legal Commentary: Warnings, Reprimands and Informed Consent. *Youth Justice.* 3: 2

Stone's Justices' Manual (2003) Vol. 1, Part V, Youth Courts

Strang, H. (2000) *Victim Participation in a Restorative Justice Process: The Canberra Reintegrative Shaming Experiments.* PhD Thesis. Centre for Restorative Justice, Australian National University

Strathan, R. and Tallant, C. (1997) Improving Judgement and Appreciating Biases Within the Risk Assessment Process. in Kemshall, H. and Pritchard, J. (Eds.) *Good Practice in Risk Assessment and Risk Management 2: Protection, Rights and Responsibilities.* London: Jessica Kingsley

Streatfeild, G. (1961) Report of the Interdepartmental Committee on The Business of The Criminal Courts. London: HMSO

Svensson, K. (2003) Social Work in the Criminal Justice System. *Journal of Scandanavian Studies in Criminology and Crime Prevention.* 4: 1, 84–100

Swain, D. (1995) Family Group Conferences in Child Care and Protection and in Youth Justice in Aotearoa/New Zealand. *International Journal of Law and The Family.* 9, 155–207

Tapsfield, R. (2003) Family Group Conferences: Family-Led Decision Making. *ChildRIGHT.* 195: 16

Tarling, R., Burrows, J. and Clarke, A. (2001) *Dalston Youth Project Part II (11–14), an Evaluation.* Research Study 232. London: Home Office

Tarling, R., Davison, T. and Clarke, A. (2004) *The National Evaluation of the Youth Justice Board's Mentoring Projects.* London: Youth Justice Board

Taylor, I., Walton, P. and Young, J. (1973) *The New Criminology.* London: Routledge

Taylor, P. (1993) *The Texts of Paulo Freire.* Oxford: Oxford University Press

Taylor, W. (1982) Black Youth, White Man's Justice. *Youth and Society.* Nov.

The Howard League V Secretary of State, Home Department and Department of Health, EWHC 2497, November 2002

Thomas, S. and Goldman, M. (2001) *A Guide to the National Standards for Bail Supervision and Support Schemes.* London: Nacro Cymru and The Youth Justice Board

Thomas, S. and Hucklesby, A. (2002) *Remand Management.* London: Youth Justice Board

Thomas, T. (1988) The Police and Criminal Evidence Act 1984: The Social Work Role. *The Howard Journal.* 27: 256–65

Thompson, T. (2001) Girls Lead the Pack in New Gangland Violence. *The Observer.* 15 Apr.

Thorpe, D., Smith, D., Green, C. and Paley, J. (1980) *Out of Care.* London: Allen and Unwin

Tilley, N. (2001) Evaluation and Evidence-Led Crime Reduction Policy and Practice. in Matthews, R. and Pitts, J. (Eds.) *Crime, Disorder and Community Safety.* London: Routledge

Titmus, R. (1963) The Social Division of Welfare. in Titmus, R. (Ed.) *Essays on the Welfare State.* London: Allen and Unwin

Titmus, R. (1968) *Commitment to Welfare.* London: George, Allen and Unwin

Tombs, S. (2002) Beyond the Usual Suspects: Crime, Criminology and the Powerful. *Safer Society.* 15

Trailblazers (2002) *Project Information.* www.Trail-Blazers.Org.Uk

Trotter, C. (1996) The Impact of Different Supervision Practices in Community Corrections *Australian and New Zealand Journal of Criminology.* 28: 2, 29–46

Trotter, C. (1999) *Working With Involuntary Clients.* London: Sage

Tuckman, B.W. (1965) Developmental Sequence in Small Groups. *Psychological Bulletin.* 63: 384–99

Umbreit, M. and Roberts, A. (1996) *Mediation of Criminal Conflict in England and Wales, an Assessment of Services in Coventry and Leeds.* University of Minnesota: Center for Restorative Justice and Mediation

Unicef (1995) *The Convention on the Rights of the Child.* London: Unicef

United Nations (1985) *United Nations Standard Minimum Rules for the Administration of Juvenile Justice.* New York: United Nations

United Nations (1989) *The United Nations Convention on the Rights of the Child.* New York: United Nations

United Nations (1990) *Guidelines for the Prevention of Juvenile Delinquency (The Riyadh Guidelines).* Geneva: United Nations

United Nations (1995) *Concluding Observations of the Committee on the Rights of the Child: United Kingdom of Great Britain and Northern Ireland.* Committee on the Rights of the Child. Geneva: United Nations

United Nations (2000) *UN International Crime Victimization Survey*. Geneva: United Nations Interregional Crime and Justice Research Institute. (http://www.Unicri.It/Icvs/)

United Nations (2002) *Concluding Observations of the Committee on the Rights of the Child: United Kingdom of Great Britain and Northern Ireland*. Committee on the Rights of the Child. Geneva: United Nations

Vanstone, M. (2000) Cognitive-Behavioural Work With Offenders in the UK. *Howard Journal of Criminal Justice*. 39: 2, 171–83

Vennard, J. and Hedderman, C. (1998) Effective Interventions With Offenders. in Goldblatt, P. and Lewis, C. (Eds.) *Reducing Offending: an Assessment of Research Evidence on Ways of Dealing With Offending Behaviour*. London: Home Office

Walker, A. (1962) Special Problems of Delinquents and Maladjusted Girls. *Howard Journal of Penology and Crime Prevention*. xi: 26–36

Walker, M. and Hill, M. (2002) *Fostering and Secure Care: an Evaluation of the Community Alternative Placement Scheme (CAPS)*. Interchange 72. Edinburgh: Scottish Executive

Warner, Lord (2003) Youth Justice: 'Do What Works'. *Criminal Justice Matters*. 52, 30–1

Waterhouse, L., Mcghee, J., Loucks, N., Whyte, B. and Kay, H. (2000) *The Evaluation of Children's Hearings in Scotland, Volume 3: Children in Focus*. Edinburgh: The Scottish Executive Central Research Unit

Waters, I., Moore, R., Roberts, C., Merrington, S. and Gray, E. (2003) *Interim National Findings of the ISSP Evaluation*. Oxford: University of Oxford

Wheatcroft, G. (2003) Hammered by the Scots. *The Guardian*. 23 Jun.

White, C. (2002) Re-Assessing the Social Worker's Role as an Appropriate Adult. *Journal of Social Welfare and Family Law*. 24: 355–73

Whitehead, E. (2003) *Enforcement in Probation Practice: A Worker's Perspective*. De Montfort University: Community and Criminal Justice Monograph 5

Whitfield, D. (2001) *The Magic Bracelet: Technology and Offender Supervision*. Winchester: Waterside Press

Widom, C. (1992) *The Cycle of Violence*. US Department of Justice, National Institute of Justice

Wikstrom, T. and Loeber, R. (1997) Individual Risk Factors, Neighbourhood SES and Juvenile Offending. in Tonry, M. (Ed.) *The Handbook of Crime and Punishment*. New York: Oxford University Press

Wilcox, A. (2002) *Final Reconviction Study of Restorative Justice Projects for the Youth Justice Board*. Oxford: Centre for Criminological Research, University of Oxford

Wilcox, A. (2003) Evidence-Based Youth Justice? Some Valuable Lessons From an Evaluation for the Youth Justice Board. *Youth Justice*. 3: 1, 19–33

Wilcox, A. and Hoyle, C. (2002) *Final Report for the Youth Justice Board on the National Evaluation of Restorative Justice Projects*. Oxford: Centre for Criminological Research, University of Oxford

Wilcox, A. with Hoyle, C. (2004) *The National Evaluation of the Youth Justice Board's Restorative Justice Projects*. London: Youth Justice Board

Wilkins, L. (1964) *Social Deviance*. London: Tavistock

Wilkinson, C. and Morris, A. (2000) Victims or Villains: Challenging the Use of Custody for Girls Who Offend. *Prison Service Journal*. 132: 48–52

Williams, B. (1995) Introduction. in Williams, B. (Ed.) *Probation Values*. Birmingham: Venture Press

Williams, B. (2000) Victims of Crime and The New Youth Justice. in Goldson, B. (Ed.) (2000) *The New Youth Justice*. Lyme Regis: Russell House Publishing

Williams, B. (2001) Reparation Orders for Young Offenders: Coerced Apologies? *Relational Justice Bulletin*. 9, 8

Williams, J. (2000a) The Inappropriate Adult. *Journal of Social Welfare and Family Law*. 22: 43–57

Williams, J. (2000b) The Crime and Disorder Act 1998: Conflicting Roles for the Appropriate Adult. *Criminal Law Review*. Nov. 911–20

Wilson, D. and Moore, S. (2004) *Playing the Game: The Experiences of Young Black Men in Custody*. London: The Children's Society

Wilson, J.Q. (1975) *Thinking About Crime*. New York: Vintage

Wilson, J.Q. and Kelling, G. (1982) Broken Windows: The Police and Neighbourhood Safety. *Atlantic Monthly*. Mar. 29–38

Wonnacot, C. (1999) The Counterfeit Contract: Reform, Pretence and Muddled Principles in the New Referral Order. *Child and Family Law Quarterly.* 11: 3

Worrall, A. (1999) Troubled or Troublesome? Justice for Girls and Young Women. in Goldson, B. (Ed.) *Youth Justice: Contemporary Policy and Practice.* Aldershot: Ashgate

Worrall, A. (2000) Governing Bad Girls: Changing Constructions of Female Juvenile Delinquency. in Bridgeman, J. and Monk, D. (Eds.) *Feminist Perspectives on Child Law.* London: Cavendish Publishing

Worrall, A. (2001) Girls at Risk? Reflections on Changing Attitudes to Young Women's Offending. *Probation Journal.* 48: 2, 86–92

Yolam, I.D. (1995) *The Theory and Practice of Group Psychotherapy.* New York: Basic Books

Young People Now (2003) News In Brief. 8–14 October 2003

Youth Justice Board (1998) *Juvenile Secure Estate. Preliminary Advice From the Youth Justice Board for England and Wales to the Home Secretary.* London: Youth Justice Board

Youth Justice Board (1999) *Mentoring Guidance Notes.* London: Youth Justice Board

Youth Justice Board (2000a) Detention and Training Order: A Better Sentence for Young Offenders. *Youth Justice Board News.* Issue 4, Jun.

Youth Justice Board (2000b) *Factors Associated with Differential Rates of Youth Custodial Sentencing.* London: Youth Justice Board

Youth Justice Board (2000c) *Juvenile Secure Estate Placement Strategy From April 2000.* London: Youth Justice Board

Youth Justice Board (2000d) *National Standards for Youth Justice.* London: Youth Justice Board

Youth Justice Board (2001a) *Grants to Assist in the Development of Volunteer Appropriate Adult Schemes. Letter to YOT Managers,* 6.6.01

Youth Justice Board (2001b) *Risk and Protective Factors Associated With Youth Crime and Effective Interventions to Prevent it.* London: Youth Justice Board

Youth Justice Board (2002a) *Asset: Intervention Plan: Guidance.* London: Youth Justice Board

Youth Justice Board (2002b) *Building on Success: Youth Justice Board Review 2001/2002.* London: Youth Justice Board

Youth Justice Board (2002c) *Key Elements of Effective Practice: Assessment, Planning Interventions and Supervision.* London: Youth Justice Board

Youth Justice Board (2002d) *Key Elements of Effective Practice: Parenting.* London: Youth Justice Board

Youth Justice Board (2002e) *Letter From Ruth Allan to ISSP Managers of 24th April 2002: ISSP Eligibility Criteria.* London: Youth Justice Board

Youth Justice Board (2003a) £1.5m Extra Funding for Parenting Programmes. *Youth Justice Board News.* 20, Dec.

Youth Justice Board (2003b) Children in Custody: Dramatic Fall in Numbers. *Youth Justice Board News.* 19, Sep.

Youth Justice Board (2003c) *Corporate and Business Plan: 2003/4 to 2005/6.* London: Youth Justice Board

Youth Justice Board (2003d) *Counting Rules: April–June 2004.* www.Youth-Justice-Board.Gov.Uk

Youth Justice Board (2003e) *Gaining Ground in the Community.* Youth Justice Board Annual Review, 2002/2003. London: Youth Justice Board

Youth Justice Board (2003f) Improvements to the Juvenile Secure Estate. *Youth Justice Board News.* 19, Sep.

Youth Justice Board (2003g) *Key Elements of Effective Practice: Final Warning Interventions.* London: Youth Justice Board

Youth Justice Board (2003h) *Key Elements of Effective Practice: Intensive Supervision and Surveillance Programmes.* London: Youth Justice Board

Youth Justice Board (2003i) *Professional Certificate in Effective Practice (Youth Justice): Effective Practice Tutor Pack.* London: ECOTEC

Youth Justice Board (2003j) *Referral Orders: A Summary of Research Into the Issues Raised.* London: Youth Justice Board

Youth Justice Board (2003k) Referral Orders' First Birthday. *Youth Justice Board News.* 17, Apr.

Youth Justice Board (2003l) *Restorative Justice: A Reader for the Professional Certificate in Effective Practice.* London: Youth Justice Board

Youth Justice Board (2003m) *Secure Facilities Monthly Monitoring Report to 30 November 2003.* London: Youth Justice Board

Youth Justice Board (2003n) *Youth Inclusion and Support Panels.* Press Release, Mar. London: Youth Justice Board

Youth Justice Board (2003o) *Youth Justice Annual Statistics 2002/03.* London: Youth Justice Board

Youth Justice Board (2003p) *Youth Survey 2003: Research Conducted for the Youth Justice Board by MORI, January–March 2003.* London: Youth Justice Board

Youth Justice Board (2003q) *Speaking Out: The Views of Young People, Parents and Victims About* the *Youth Justice System and Interventions to Reduce Offending*. London: Youth Justice Board

Youth Justice Board (2004a) *Families to Get Involved in Preventing Crime*. Press Release, 4 Feb.

Youth Justice Board (2004b) *National Audit Office Report on Youth Justice*. Letter to YOT Managers From Mark Perfect, 3 February 2004

Youth Justice Board (2004c) *National Standards for Youth Justice*. London: Youth Justice Board

Youth Justice Board (2004d) *Youth Justice Board Cuts Places in Young Offender Institutions*. Press Release 21 Jan.

Youth Justice Board (Undated a) *Key Elements of Effective Practice: Restorative Justice,* Available Online at http://www.Youth-Justice-Board.Gov. Uk

Youth Justice Board (Undated b) *Key Elements of Effective Practice: Mentoring*. London: Youth Justice Board

Youth Justice Board (Undated c) *Safer Schools Partnerships* at www.Youth-Justice-Board.Gov. Uk/Youthjusticeboard/Prevention/SSP

Youth Justice Board (Undated d) *Source Document: Final Warning Interventions*. London: Youth Justice Board

Youth Justice Board (Undated e) *Source Document: Swift Administration of Justice*. London: Youth Justice Board

Zedner, L. (1991) *Women, Crime and Custody in Victorian England*. Oxford: Clarendon

Index